The Revolutionary Legacy of Rosa Luxemburg

Marie Frederiksen

Wellred Books
London

The Revolutionary Legacy of Rosa Luxemburg
Marie Frederiksen

Wellred Books, March 2022

UK distribution: Wellred Books, wellred-books.com
152-160 Kemp House, City Road
London
EC1V 2NX
books@wellredbooks.net

USA distribution: Marxist Books, marxistbooks.com
WR Books
250 44th Street #208
Brooklyn
New York
NY 11232
sales@marxistbooks.com

DK distribution: Forlaget Marx, forlagetmarx.dk
Degnestavnen 19, st. tv.
2400 København NV
forlag@forlagetmarx.dk

Cover design by Jesse Murray-Dean

Layout by Wellred Books

ISBN: 978 1 913 026 05 9

Printed in Great Britain by Bell and Bain Ltd, Glasgow

Contents

Preface

The intentions of this book are explicitly political. Whilst the author *is* a historian, the goal of writing this book was never to produce an academic assessment of Rosa Luxemburg's life. Rather, it is an examination of Rosa Luxemburg's revolutionary legacy as expressed through her own writings and actions. Its purpose is to arm a new generation with the treasure trove of ideas and revolutionary theory that her life and works encompass. These are ideas that can help us understand the world so that we can change it for the better.

The biographical facts about Rosa Luxemburg in this book are primarily drawn from two sources: Paul Frölich's *Rosa Luxemburg: Ideas in Action* and J. P. Nettl's *Rosa Luxemburg.*

Paul Frölich was a leading member of the Spartacus League and the German Communist Party. While Rosa Luxemburg was alive, Frölich belonged to the ultra-left wing of the party. Expelled from the Communist Party in 1928, he was subsequently involved in a series of political groups. His biography of Rosa Luxemburg was written in the late 1930s from exile in France, where he had fled after Hitler's seizure of power in Germany. The book contains first-hand accounts of Luxemburg, particularly in the final period of her life. Nevertheless, the biography is somewhat superficial with regard to political conclusions and is characterised by a few inaccuracies.

J. P. Nettl was professor of political science and sociology at the University of Pennsylvania. In 1966, he published a two-volume biography of Rosa Luxemburg. Nettl's biography is well researched and is more reliable with regard to dates, names and other facts than Frölich's. Where there have been discrepancies between the two, I have referred to Nettl. I have used the 1969 single-volume edition with a preface by Hannah Arendt. Nettl's biography contains a wealth of information about Luxemburg's life and writings, and Nettl remains, as far as I know, one of the few people to have undertaken a thorough study of her writings in Polish. His research provides us with new and valuable insight into her ideas and activities in the Polish and Russian movements. Nettl, however, was not a revolutionary. He is therefore incapable of really understanding Luxemburg politically. This is evident for instance when he describes her move to Germany as a step towards furthering her "career". Luxemburg was not in the least concerned with any such "careers". She moved to Germany because she believed that was where she could do the most to further the world socialist revolution. Furthermore, Nettl is an anti-Leninist and this leads to him to draw politically questionable, and often completely incorrect conclusions, when discussing the debates between Luxemburg and Lenin. He argues for instance that Luxemburg was opposed to the "dictatorship of the proletariat", a claim directly contradicted by her own writings.

I have attempted throughout this book to allow Rosa Luxemburg's revolutionary ideas to speak for themselves. I have therefore decided to include many quotes of hers, several of which are quite lengthy. This may make this book a more challenging read, but it will hopefully allow Luxemburg's ideas to reach the reader in her own words.

To grasp Luxemburg's ideas, one must consider them in their context and in their process of development. She revised her opinion on multiple occasions as events unfolded, so a number of quotes are followed by long explanations.

Furthermore, although this is a book about Rosa Luxemburg, the reader will notice that Lenin plays a fairly prominent role. When Luxemburg is falsely portrayed as anti-Bolshevik and even as non-revolutionary, it is most often her polemics against Lenin that are used to justify this. In order to counter the misrepresentation of these polemics, it has been necessary to dive into them and present both points of view. I have attempted to do this as objectively as possible.

However, no biography is ever truly 'neutral'. This is doubly true in the case of a biography concerning a revolutionary individual like Rosa Luxemburg. I do not claim to be non-partisan. Quite the contrary, I wish to make no secret of the fact that I stand on the same side of the barricades as Rosa Luxemburg. This does not exclude an objective reproduction of her life, her actions, and the times she lived in. In fact it could be argued that it compels us to be *more* objective. Rosa Luxemburg cared not for "uncritical admiration and eager imitation", but instead insisted upon a critical evaluation of all ideas and movements. In this spirit, the present book is not an uncritical tribute to the 'icon' of Rosa Luxemburg. Rather, it is an attempt to portray both her strengths and weaknesses. Whether or not I have succeeded in this attempt, I leave for the reader to decide.

* * *

A special thanks to Hamid Alizadeh and Jonas Foldager for their comments and edits.

Marie Frederiksen,
Copenhagen,
December 2018

Introduction:
Reclaiming the Revolutionary
Legacy of Rosa Luxemburg

Rosa Luxemburg was born in 1871. Coincidentally, this was the same year that the workers of Paris rose up and established the Paris Commune: the first ever attempt by the working class to seize power. The euphoria that inaugurated the Commune was short-lived. After a couple of months, the Parisian Revolution was beaten down by the ruling class in a counter-revolutionary inferno of bullets and blood. In *la semaine sanglante* ("the bloody week") that followed its crushing, 30,000 workers were murdered.

Almost fifty years later, in 1919, Rosa Luxemburg herself was murdered by the German counter-revolution as it crushed the German workers' uprising. Her life coincided with the awakening of the working class in Europe and was inseparable from the class struggle. She was no mere spectator to the world historical events with which her lifetime coincided: the First World War, the Russian Revolution of 1917 and the German Revolution of 1918. In fact, she was an active participant in an attempt to change the course of human history. In her own words, Rosa Luxemburg saw that humanity was faced with the choice between barbarism or socialism. She threw herself into the struggle to ensure that it was the latter that triumphed and fought to the end for the world socialist revolution.

Today, Rosa Luxemburg is one of the most iconic figures on the left. The crisis of capitalism since 2008 has radicalised layers of society, and particularly the youth, among whom there has been a revival of interest in revolutionary ideas and personalities. Rosa Luxemburg stands out as a woman who not only dared to stand up to the entire political establishment, but in the end made the ultimate sacrifice in the struggle for socialism. The growing interest in Rosa Luxemburg and her ideas is a sign that something is happening beneath the surface of society. More and more people are seeking to draw the lessons of history. This is extremely positive.

But Rosa Luxemburg is not simply an icon. Following her death, few other figures on the left have been surrounded by as much controversy. By every means of manipulation and distortion, a picture has been formed over time that is the antithesis of the revolutionary class fighter that she actually was. She is represented as a woman, a feminist, an advocate of a more 'soft' and spontaneous socialism opposed to the October Revolution and Lenin.

Many of those who worship Rosa Luxemburg as an icon today are not aware of her history. As such, they are not aware of what she really stood for. If one attempts to find out more about Luxemburg's life and ideas, one is often confronted with this twisted and distorted image of her. The purpose of this book is to correct this; to draw a truer and fairer picture of Rosa Luxemburg and her ideas. It was not written to idealise but to bring out the *true* Rosa Luxemburg: the revolutionary fighter, who possessed a profound faith in the will and ability of the working class to transform society.

It is a lamentable paradox that the authority of Rosa Luxemburg is used today to justify reformism, political softness, and anti-revolutionary ideas. If we read Rosa Luxemburg's writings, there is no doubt that she was a revolutionary from the beginning to the bitter end. Everything she did and wrote was permeated by the fight for socialist revolution, a fight that cost Luxemburg her life.

It is characteristic of her life that before she reached the age of twenty, she was forced to flee from Poland to Switzerland to avoid arrest on account of her revolutionary activities. When she later moved to Germany to become active in the enormous German Social Democratic Party (SPD), she boldly threw herself into the pivotal debate that was raging at the time. In response to the attempts of the reformist Eduard Bernstein to revise the ideas of Marx, Rosa Luxemburg presented the party with a brilliant defence of revolutionary Marxism.

To this day, the arguments of reformists bear a striking resemblance to Bernstein's. As such, Rosa Luxemburg's critique retains its relevance to the debates currently taking place within the left. Over 120 years since it was first published, the pamphlet *Reform or Revolution?*, Luxemburg's polemic against

Bernstein, is just as relevant as when it was first written. Already in her day, Luxemburg had warned that if the social-democratic movement abandoned the goal of socialist revolution, it would forfeit the right to exist. From a revolutionary lever for the overthrow of capitalism, it would be converted into a mere supporting pillar of capitalism. The history of social democracy has vindicated Rosa Luxemburg's position.

But *Reform or Revolution?* ought to be seen as much more than a mere prediction of the fate that would befall social democratic parties. It should also stand as a warning to that 'new' left which seeks to convert Rosa Luxemburg into an icon. Luxemburg would have had little time for this 'new' left, which has discarded theory, and which in reality has discarded any belief in socialist revolution altogether:

> What appears to characterise this practice [reformism] above all? A certain hostility to 'theory'. This is quite natural, for our 'theory', that is, the principles of scientific socialism, impose clearly marked limitations to practical activity – insofar as it concerns the aims of this activity, the means used in attaining these aims, and the method employed in this activity. It is quite natural for people who run after immediate 'practical' results to want to free themselves from such limitations and to render their practice independent of our 'theory'.[1]

Rosa Luxemburg fought against the dissemination of reformism into the workers' movement until the very end of her life. In every struggle, she was to be found on the same side of the barricade: with the revolution. Her belief that the working class would move to change society was absolutely unwavering.

Distortions

Attempts to distort the real picture of Rosa Luxemburg have various origins. The ruling class, who are naturally concerned with preserving the *status quo* and securing their power and privileges, attempt to paint a picture of Luxemburg as 'bloody' Rosa. They are only interested in scaring workers from rebelling by equating revolution to blood and violence. In reality, it has been the ruling class that has spilled torrents of blood in defence of their system throughout history. It was the ruling class that brutally suppressed the German Revolution and murdered Rosa Luxemburg, along with so many other revolutionaries. However, we also find a distorted image of Rosa Luxemburg on the left.

---

1   R. Luxemburg, *Reform or Revolution?*, *The Essential Rosa Luxemburg*, p. 101.

In the first years following the October Revolution, when Lenin and Trotsky were still leading the young workers' state, Rosa Luxemburg's legacy was highly prized. She was recognised and celebrated as the revolutionary that she was. In 1922 Lenin even criticised the German Communist Party (KPD) for having thus far failed to publish her collected works. Luxemburg's legacy in the communist movement, however, was inseparably linked to the fate of the Russian Revolution. The October Revolution had occurred in a backward country. Lenin and Trotsky's perspective had *always* been to spread the revolution to the developed capitalist nations, and above all to Germany, as the only guarantee for the survival of the revolution in Russia and its development towards socialism. This was a perspective that Rosa Luxemburg fully shared and did her utmost to fulfil. Unfortunately, the German Revolution was defeated, and the young Soviet power remained isolated. This laid the foundation for the degeneration of the revolution and the seizure of power by a usurping bureaucracy led by Stalin. To consolidate his power, Stalin had to exterminate the Leninist, proletarian wing, not only of the Russian Communist Party, but of the entire international communist movement. Stalin stopped at nothing. The Left Opposition was physically exterminated, and workers' democracy was abolished. The revolutionary tradition was suppressed.

Like Trotsky, and others who uncompromisingly struggled for a revolutionary programme, the ideas of Rosa Luxemburg soon found themselves in the crosshairs of Stalin and his henchmen. The Stalinist bureaucracy was terrified that the ideas of Luxemburg might inspire young communists to question their policy. Her memory, therefore, had to be smeared. This fact alone bears witness to the enormous role that she had played and indeed continued to play following her death.

Already in 1923, the basis was laid for the smear campaign which was to follow later on, when the then leader of the German Communist Party, Ruth Fischer, described Luxemburg's influence on the German labour movement as "syphilitic". Later on in 1931, after degeneration of the Soviet Union, Stalin embarked on a full-blown smear campaign, with an article titled 'Some Questions Concerning the History of Bolshevism', in which he placed Luxemburg in the reformist, anti-Leninist camp. As he so often did, Stalin achieved this little manoeuvre by shamelessly twisting historical facts. The Stalinists pointed to Luxemburg's polemics against Lenin and used them to fabricate the myth of 'Luxemburgism': a distinct, reformist, anti-Leninist theory, in which the spontaneous movement of the masses was elevated to an all-important position, in opposition to organisation and the party. She was blamed by the Stalinists for all of the defeats and mistakes of the German Revolution; mistakes which in fact to a large degree were due to the advice and instructions the German Communist Party received from the leading layer of the Communist International, which was compose of individuals who gradually drifted into Stalin's inner circle.

It was up to Leon Trotsky, who had led the Russian Revolution together with Lenin in 1917, and who, following Lenin's death in 1924, had fought against the Stalinist bureaucracy, to defend Rosa Luxemburg against Stalinist smears:

> Yes, Stalin has sufficient cause to hate Rosa Luxemburg. But all the more imperious therefore becomes our duty to shield Rosa's memory from Stalin's calumny that has been caught by the hired functionaries of both hemispheres, and to pass on this truly beautiful, heroic, and tragic image to the young generations of the proletariat in all its grandeur and inspirational force.[2]

As Stalin consolidated his position, the anti-Stalinist left developed a renewed interest in Luxemburg, on account of the bile that the Stalinists directed towards her. But in the struggle against Stalin, there was a tendency to go too far in the opposite extreme. Namely, this anti-Stalinist left effectively accepted the invention of 'Luxemburgism' and argued not only for the rejection of Stalin's legacy, but that of Lenin as well. They mistook Stalin's distorted image of Luxemburg for the original and began defending it. This mythical Rosa Luxemburg, who supposedly advocated 'spontaneity' in opposition to organisation – an anti-revolutionary position – was defended by this left as essentially something positive. Trotsky criticised this ultra-left tendency to "make use only of the weak sides and the inadequacies which were by no means decisive in Rosa". He pointed out that these so-called lefts "generalise and exaggerate the weaknesses to the utmost and build up a thoroughly absurd system on that basis."[3] This is how things stood when Rosa Luxemburg's ideas were once more brought to the fore during the revolutionary wave that swept the world in the late 1960s. Rosa Luxemburg was held aloft as an icon for the new, anti-authoritarian, anti-Stalinist left, the so-called 'New Left'. But in actual fact, they were merely repeating the same Stalinist lie: that of the 'soft' Luxemburg, who simply focused on the spontaneity of the

---

2 L. Trotsky, 'Hands off Rosa Luxemburg!', *Writings of Leon Trotsky: 1932*, p. 142.

3 L. Trotsky, 'Luxemburg and the Fourth International', *Writings of Leon Trotsky: 1935-36*, p. 29.

masses – the antithesis of Lenin. For instance, in the early 1960s, Bertram D. Wolfe published a collection of Rosa Luxemburg's writings titled *Leninism or Marxism?*

Wolfe was a former communist who had left the communist movement and instead made an academic career for himself. In his book, we find Luxemburg's article, 'Organisational Questions of the Russian Social Democracy', under the new title that Wolfe had chosen for it: 'Leninism or Marxism?' In the original article from 1904, Luxemburg expressed criticisms of Lenin's view of the revolutionary organisation. This served as an opportunity to paint Rosa Luxemburg as the 'democratic', 'anti-authoritarian' and 'humane' socialist, as opposed to Lenin's centralist and 'authoritarian' disposition. But what Wolfe fails to mention is that, after the first Russian Revolution of 1905, Rosa Luxemburg explicitly stated that her critique of Lenin belonged in the past. Here are her own words about Lenin and the Bolsheviks, written after the October Revolution of 1917:

> The Bolsheviks have shown that they are capable of everything that a genuine revolutionary party can contribute within the limits of historical possibilities.
>
> [...] In this, Lenin and Trotsky and their friends were the *first*, those who went ahead as an example to the proletariat of the world [...]
>
> This is the essential and enduring in Bolshevik policy. In this sense theirs is the immortal historical service of having marched at the head of the international proletariat [...][4]

All those who paint a distorted image of Rosa Luxemburg have one thing in common: they use quotations taken out of context so that they can use Luxemburg's authority to support their own views. In this book I will attempt to contextualise and allow Rosa Luxemburg to speak for herself to a far greater extent by using a number of long quotations. The image of Luxemburg that this approach produces is very different from that of the soft anti-Leninists. It is an image of a fierce revolutionary.

The Woman

A full assessment of Rosa Luxemburg's ideas and legacy can only be made by reading her own words. There remains a large quantity of Luxemburg's writings that are yet to be translated, not only from Polish to English, but also from German to English. As mentioned, the German Communist Party made little effort to publish Luxemburg's collected works, and with the

---

4 R. Luxemburg, 'The Russian Revolution', *Rosa Luxemburg Speaks*, p. 395.

degeneration of the Soviet Union, this project came to a complete halt. Only much later, in the 1960s and 70s, with the renewed interest in Luxemburg, did translation and publication of her works recommence, though there is still a long way to go.[5]

Among Luxemburg's writings that *have* been translated and published are her letters. Shortly after Luxemburg's death, her letters from prison to Karl Liebknecht's wife, Sophie,[6] were published. A couple of years later, Luise Kautsky, the wife of Karl Kautsky and a close friend of Luxemburg, published her own correspondence with Luxemburg. The intention of publishing this entire correspondence was to disprove the ruling class's public portrayal of Rosa Luxemburg as 'bloody Rosa': a cold, cynical fanatic of violence; an image crafted to justify her murder. The intention, by bringing these letters to light, had been to show that she also had an emotional and empathetic side. The letters did indeed change public opinion. However, the picture they presented was also quite one-sided; the revolutionary Rosa Luxemburg had vanished.

A number of Rosa Luxemburg's letters to Leo Jogiches, with whom she essentially lived as a partner for fifteen years, were also translated from Polish and published by Elzebieta Ettinger under the title *Comrade and Lover* in 1979. Ettinger details in the preface how she, naturally enough, had to select which of the roughly 1,000 letters in the Luxemburg–Jogiches correspondence she wished to translate. According to her, there were three possibilities: correspondence relating to Luxemburg's involvement in the Second International; her involvement in the German and Polish Social Democratic Parties; or her personal relationship with Jogiches:

> While the first two would have provided students of the European, and especially the Polish, Russian, and German movements, with a wealth of material, they would have left Luxemburg as she is at present – faceless.
>
> The third choice would reveal a woman, hitherto unknown, whose sex did not diminish her political stature and whose politics did not interfere with her private life. It would also expose the fragility of the concept that a woman cannot, without giving up love, realise her talent.[7]

A translator of course has the right to translate anything they wish. But Ettinger is not the only one to highlight Rosa Luxemburg 'the woman',

---

5 The publishing house Verso Books have started a project to translate and publish her writings, which is much needed.

6 Sophie Liebknecht – often referred to as Sonja.

7 E. Ettinger, *Comrade and Lover: Rosa Luxemburg's Letters to Leo Jogiches*, pp. viii-ix.

rather than Rosa Luxemburg the revolutionary. Luxemburg was also a private individual. Did she really wish to have her highly personal letters to her lover published? This focus on the personal completely overshadows the fact that Luxemburg was first and foremost a revolutionary. Yes, she was a woman, she was Jewish, she was a Pole. But above all, she saw herself as a part of the international struggle of the working class for socialism; a struggle that cuts across all of these divisions.

In a letter to Mathilde Wurm, written on 28 December 1916, when Luxemburg was imprisoned, she writes on the subject of being human:

> As far as I am concerned I was never soft but in recent months I have become as hard as polished steel and I will not make the slightest concessions in future, either politically or in my personal friendships. [...] To be human is the main thing, and that means to be strong and clear and *of good cheer* in spite and because of everything, for tears are the preoccupation of weakness. To be human means throwing one's life 'on the scales of destiny' if need be, to be joyful for every fine day and every beautiful cloud – oh, I can't write you any recipes how to be human, I only know how to *be* human [...] The world is so beautiful in spite of the misery and would be even more beautiful if there were no half-wits and cowards in it.[8]

Besides mentioning Jogiches, who was of importance to Rosa Luxemburg's political life, I have chosen not to go into her personal relations. The story of Rosa Luxemburg has to be written as if we were writing about any other great revolutionary: as the story of ideas and works, without becoming absorbed in personal feelings or an individual's love life.

In recent years it has become fashionable to call Rosa Luxemburg a socialist feminist. The increasing focus on the women's question today is a sign that we are entering a revolutionary period. More and more people are beginning to question the *status quo* and rise up in opposition to inequality and oppression. This is an extremely positive development. Rosa Luxemburg fully supported equality between women and men, and the emancipation of women as integral to the emancipation of humankind. But she never called herself a feminist. To do so now is to impose conceptions drawn from the present onto the past in a way that distorts her actual position.

First of all, Luxemburg wrote very little about the women's question. This was not because she thought it unimportant, but because she was busy with other things. Upon her arrival in Germany, the leadership of the SPD attempted to file away this young and rebellious woman, whose presence

---

8   Quoted in J. P. Nettl, *Rosa Luxemburg*, p. 662.

was so inconvenient to them, by proposing that she become active in the women's movement of the SPD. Luxemburg refused outright. Instead, she threw herself into all the great theoretical debates raging in the party. She was also fiercely opposed to the bourgeois and the petty-bourgeois women's movement. For her, the only way to secure the emancipation of women was through the struggle of the working class for a socialist revolution. In this struggle, bourgeois women would not be on the side of working-class women. She described the bourgeois women of the suffrage movement as "lambs":

> Most of those bourgeois women who act like lionesses in the struggle against "male prerogatives" would trot like docile lambs in the camp of conservative and clerical reaction if they had suffrage. Indeed, they would certainly be a good deal more reactionary than the male part of their class.[9]

Rosa Luxemburg is clearly an inspiration to many, both women and men, all over the world. This is because she played a prominent role in the international working-class movement – despite the barriers she faced on account of her sex. But that should not cause us to demean her ideas and works by describing them as inspirational simply *because* she was a woman. She is an inspiration because she was consistently revolutionary to the bitter end. Lenin described her as one of the "outstanding representatives of the revolutionary proletariat and of unfalsified Marxism".[10] It is for this that she ought to be remembered: her revolutionary legacy.

If one wishes to change the world, one has to understand it. This requires us to learn from those who came before us. But before we can learn from the experiences of Rosa Luxemburg, we must uncover her true legacy, removing the mountain of distortions, misrepresentations, and smears that have been piled upon it. This is the purpose of this book: to recover the true, revolutionary legacy of Rosa Luxemburg.

---

9 R. Luxemburg, 'Women's Suffrage and Class Struggle', *Selected Political Writings of Rosa Luxemburg*, p. 219.

10 V. I. Lenin, 'A Contribution to the History of the Question of the Dictatorship', *Collected Works* (Henceforth referred to as *LCW*), Vol. 31, p. 342.

1. Becoming a Revolutionary

Rosa Luxemburg was born on 5 March 1871 in the town of Zamość in the south-east of Poland, which at that time was under the domination of the Russian Empire. She grew up in a petty-bourgeois Jewish family, but religion was not observed in family life. There was, however, a focus on education and culture. Only a few years after she was born, the family moved to Warsaw and, at the age of thirteen, she was accepted into a gymnasium. Gymnasiums then were almost exclusively places of education for Russian children. It was extremely difficult for Poles to be accepted, and doubly so for Jews. All teaching was conducted in Russian, and students were forbidden from speaking to one another in Polish.

In her final years at the gymnasium, Rosa Luxemburg began her political involvement with the *Proletariat* group, and after completing her finals in 1887 she began familiarising herself with the works of Karl Marx and Friedrich Engels. However, the Russian secret police were always vigilant in suppressing the work of left-wing political groups. Any revolutionary activity had to be conducted in secrecy. After two years of agitation amongst the students of Warsaw, Luxemburg was confronted with the threat of arrest, and so, in 1889, she escaped abroad, smuggled under the hay of a peasant's wagon.

She found herself in Zürich, Switzerland, a gathering place for many exiled revolutionaries. There, Luxemburg began her university studies whilst continuing her political work. At the time, Switzerland was *the* most important centre for revolutionary Russian Marxism. It was here that the precursor of the Russian Social Democratic Labour Party, the Emancipation of Labour group, was headquartered. Leading this group was Georgi Plekhanov,[1] known to many as 'the father of Russian Marxism', having been the first to bring Marxism to Russia. But the milieu of small circles in which the *émigrés* moved was characterised by the intertwining of the personal and the political. Plekhanov had a hard time working with anybody, something Lenin and Trotsky would later learn for themselves, and he and Luxemburg quickly developed a life-long, personal enmity.

It was also while in Zürich that Luxemburg met Leo Jogiches.[2] From the age of sixteen, Jogiches had been active in revolutionary politics in Vilna, where he was born. Coming from a wealthy family, he brought a considerable sum of money to Switzerland for the purpose of publishing classic Marxist texts. He offered to work with Plekhanov, but the latter refused, thus commencing a relationship of enduring mutual antipathy between Jogiches and Luxemburg on the one side, and Plekhanov on the other. Jogiches and Luxemburg became lovers in a relationship which lasted for many years and, as Jogiches was not a skilled speaker or writer, Luxemburg became the public face of their partnership. However, Jogiches was Luxemburg's most important political sparring partner, and she discussed most of her ideas and articles with him prior to publication. Jogiches' main skill was as an organiser. He became one of the ringleaders of the Polish Social Democratic Party and later he would be involved in the secret work of building the Spartacus League in Germany during the First World War.

The SDKPiL

The *Proletariat* group, in which Luxemburg first became politically active, was destroyed by police repression. However, in 1892, a congress was called to bring all of the exiled Polish socialists together. This congress produced the united Polish Socialist Party (PPS), which unified all the Polish socialist *émigré* groups and some organisations which operated within Poland. Luxemburg and Jogiches joined the party.

---

1 Georgi Valentinovich Plekhanov (1856-1918) – laid the foundations of the Russian Social-Democratic Labour Party. Followed the Mensheviks after the split in the Russian Social-Democratic Labour Party and eventually became a social-chauvinist during the First World War.

2 Leo Jogiches was also known as Leo Tyszko or Tyshka. Most revolutionaries in tsarist Russia used pseudonyms. I have chosen to follow Nettl and use their real names, unless the pseudonym is better known, as in the case of Lenin and Trotsky, for instance. Rosa Luxemburg primarily used her own name.

However, Poland was a divided nation, occupied by Germany, Austria, and Russia. The new party failed to overcome these territorial divisions and so the PPS only ever operated in Russian-occupied territory, with separate parties in German and Austrian occupied Poland.

In collaboration with a small group of young students, Luxemburg and Jogiches began the publication of a newspaper, *Sprawa Robotnicza* (*The Workers' Cause*). Whilst Luxemburg was a guiding force for the paper, and had been its editor since 1894, it did not receive any support from the leadership of the PPS, which was in fact hostile towards it. This wariness was an anticipation of a split that would develop in the Polish movement between the PPS leadership and those who supported the line of *Sprawa Robotnicza*, headed by Luxemburg. The former placed a heavy emphasis on the struggle for independence from Russia, whilst the latter called for collaboration with the Russian working class against the common oppressor, opposing the demand for Polish independence.

The first edition of *Sprawa Robotnicza* was published shortly before the congress of the Second (Socialist) International in August 1893. The Second International was the international organisation that unified the social-democratic parties of different countries. However, the question of which Russian organisation had the right to be represented at its congresses was always a source of confusion, as there was a host of small illegal groups. Nonetheless, a group that had established a newspaper had a certain right to representation. This was precisely what the Sprawa Robotnicza group demanded. Rosa Luxemburg wrote a minority report for the congress on the development of the Social Democratic Party in Russian-occupied Poland on behalf of *Sprawa Robotnicza*, in opposition to the official report given by the PPS leadership.

For this reason, the leadership of the PPS was against Luxemburg's participation in the congress. Their delegation contested her mandate, forcing the congress to pass judgement on whether she ought to be able to participate as a delegate. The PPS leadership made their arguments purely on organisational grounds, claiming that *Sprawa Robotnicza* and Rosa Luxemburg were completely unknown to the International. Rosa Luxemburg, who had to single-handedly defend her mandate before the whole congress, instead posed the question politically, using this opportunity to present her group's critique of the PPS's politics to the congress delegates.

The Belgian socialist leader Vandervelde described the situation in the following manner:

Rosa, twenty-three years old at the time, was quite unknown outside one or two Socialist groups in Germany and Poland […] but her opponents had their hands full to hold their ground against her […] She rose from among the delegates at the back and stood on a chair to make herself better heard. Small and looking very frail in a summer dress, which managed very effectively to conceal her physical defects, she advocated her cause with such magnetism and such appealing words that she won the majority of the Congress at once and they raised their hands in favour of the acceptance of her mandate.[3]

Vandervelde's recollection of events were perhaps carried away by the impact of Rosa Luxemburg's intervention – her mandate was in fact rejected in the end and she was forced to leave the congress. But his description speaks about the impression she must have made. She might have failed to get recognition for her mandate, but she succeeded in presenting her case and gave a political response to the attacks against her group. When the Second International held its subsequent congress, in 1896, Luxemburg was present as the delegate of a small but recognised political tendency in the Polish socialist movement. After the experience at the world congress, the *Sprawa Robotnicza* group decided to break with the PPS and, in March 1894, it formed the Social Democracy of the Kingdom of Poland (SDKP), which in 1898 fused with the Lithuanian party to form the Social Democracy of the Kingdom of Poland and Lithuania (SDKPiL). At the core of the party were Luxemburg and Jogiches, as well as Marchlewski (Karski) and Warszawski (Warski). According to the party's own statutes, it was constructed on strongly centralised lines, much like those upon which the Bolshevik Party would later be built. Yet, in practice, the party was highly informal and held no congresses in the six years that followed its formation. The same year that the SDKPiL formed, however, Rosa Luxemburg moved to Germany to become active in the German Social Democratic Party (SPD).

---

3   Quoted in J. P. Nettl, *Rosa Luxemburg*, p. 73.

2. Reform or Revolution

In 1897, Rosa Luxemburg received a doctorate degree in law and graduated from university. Her thesis was titled 'The Industrial Development of Poland'. Following a marriage of convenience to secure herself a residence permit in Germany, in May 1898 she moved to Berlin. She immediately began her work in the SPD, which was the largest party in the Second International. It possessed an enormous authority on a world scale and was hailed by many, including Lenin, as a model. Luxemburg had barely set foot on German soil when she flung herself into the theoretical struggles then raging inside the party. One of the first of these was the struggle against the attempt to revise the SPD's Marxist foundations.

The History of Revisionism

The Second International was made up of parties whose programmes were based on revolutionary Marxist ideas. The SPD – the party of Karl Marx's country of origin and whose leadership was in direct contact with Friedrich Engels – was widely recognised as a party that defended the Marxist doctrine. On the surface of things, everything looked fine. In the various party programmes, resolutions, speeches, and articles, the German leaders spoke of class struggle, internationalism, and socialism. But Marx and Engels had already criticised the leaders of the SPD for their lack of theoretical sharpness and their opportunism. The founders of scientific socialism had identified in the SPD leaders a tendency to sacrifice their principles for short-sighted, 'practical' victories. Since its foundation, Marx and Engels had therefore engaged in internal criticism of the party leadership's policies. After many years of the SPD leadership trying to hush up this criticism, Friedrich Engels finally decided to publish a selection of their criticisms in the famous 1891 text, *Critique of the Gotha Program*. But despite all of this, it seemed to most people that the party was fundamentally healthy and headed in the right direction.

The industrialisation of Germany in the latter half of the nineteenth century had enlarged the working class enormously, drawing in new, fresh layers. When Germany was hit by an economic crisis in the 1870s, the SPD grew immensely. In an attempt to curb this growth, the German chancellor, Bismarck, introduced the Anti-Socialist Laws of 1878, which banned all social-democratic activity outside the Reichstag and the Landtage (regional assemblies) of the federal states. But even under the Anti-Socialist Laws, the party grew. By 1890 the SPD emerged from semi-legality with about 100,000 to 150,000 members and triple the number of voters it previously had. The party won about 20 per cent of the votes cast in the elections that followed its legalisation.

Thereafter, the party continued to grow steadily in both membership and votes. In 1903, the party received more than 30 per cent of the votes.[1] By 1906, the party had 384,327 members; and by 1912, its membership ballooned to 907,112.[2]

However, the period of semi-legality had left its mark. Part of the SPD leadership, and particularly the intellectuals of the party, used the threat of being banned as an excuse to water down the revolutionary, socialist essence of the party's programme.

The SPD was formed in a period where capitalism across Europe was experiencing a vigorous economic upswing. During the crisis of 1873-1882 the economy had grown by a mere 3 per cent over the whole decade. Conversely, between 1887-1896, the economy grew by 36 per cent. This served to sow illusions in capitalism. Some reforms were carried out and, for a layer of the working class, living conditions improved. All of this served to soften class contradictions, which in turn conditioned the psychology of the leading layer of the SPD. They began to believe that capitalism had in fact solved its internal contradictions. These were the social and economic prerequisites for the emergence of a reformist tendency in the SPD, and indeed the rest of the Second International.

With the party's growth in membership and votes, its apparatus expanded enormously. In 1914, the party published ninety daily newspapers and had

---

1   C. E. Schorske, *German Social Democracy: 1905-1917: The Development of the Great Schism*, p. 7.

2   Ibid., p. 267.

roughly 3,500 employees working for the party and the party press, as well as about 3,000 employees working for the trade unions and other associated organisations.[3] Every apparatus has its conservative side. In order for an organisation to function, a certain routine is required. Meetings have to be organised; money has to be collected; newspapers have to be sold; budgets have to be worked out; alongside a thousand and one other day-to-day tasks. Completion of these routine tasks is indispensable. But they can also end up overshadowing the political tasks of the organisation. That is to say, routinism can set in.

The growth of the working-class movement in Germany and several other European countries in these years created an entirely new layer of party and trade union employees. The lives and social circles, and with it the political outlook of this layer, bit by bit became further and further divorced from those they were supposed to represent: the working class. This apparatus began to reflect the pressures of capitalist society that surrounded it, and thus a bureaucracy crystallised.

On the national level, the SPD was excluded from participating in government at this time. But on the federal level, especially in southern Germany, the party came under huge pressure from the ruling class to participate in budget negotiations and in the government. This pressure increasingly had its effect on the local party leaders. The trade union leaders also bowed to this pressure from the employers and the state to focus on the day-to-day work of negotiating within the framework of the system and to shelve its 'utopian' socialist politics. To the SPD's trade union leaders, talk of 'socialism' and 'revolution' was seen as simply a source of unnecessary chaos and unrest, which detracted from what, in their view, was the more important routine side of the work. This layer, which became relatively wealthy and which had illusions in capitalism's success, formed the social base of revisionism.[4]

It was Eduard Bernstein[5] who gave this pressure its theoretical expression within the party when he opened what came to be known as the 'revisionism'

---

3   A. Woods and N. Albin Svensson, 'Rosa Luxemburg – Reform or Revolution', *In Defence of Marxism* [website].

4   Revisionism and reformism were used more or less synonymously at this time. Revisionism presented the need of a revision of Marxism in order to change it from a revolutionary theory and practice to a reformist one. Therefore, these two words will also be used more or less as synonyms here.

5   Eduard Bernstein (1850-1932) – leading member of the SPD. A member of the German Parliament (the Reichstag) for the party between 1902-1918.

debate. Bernstein was one of the party's leaders and held great authority. This was not least because he had been appointed as one the literary executors of Engels' posthumous works, which had been left in the care of the International after his death in 1895.

Bernstein believed that Marxism required revision on a number of points. He laid out his ideas in an article titled 'Problems of Socialism', published in the party's theoretical journal, *Die Neue Zeit*, in 1897-8, and in his book, *The Preconditions of Socialism and the Tasks of Social Democracy*.[6] Bernstein himself believed that he was simply describing the world as it was, and that the facts showed that some of Marxism's basic postulates needed revising, not least of which was its insistence on the necessity of socialist revolution. In other words, Marxism needed 'updating'.

According to Bernstein, capitalism's internal contradictions – through adaptations like credit, the stock market, cartels, and trusts, would tend to become softened – and capitalism would cease to tend towards crisis. The middle class would grow, and with the rise of this buffer, class contradictions would also soften. According to Bernstein, the growth of capitalism had no limits, and whilst economic crises might still come to pass, there was no necessity for them to become increasingly acute. Capitalism could be regulated and controlled. This, he contended, was the task of Social Democracy.

As for the working class, Bernstein argued that they were only interested in bettering their *immediate* living conditions, and as such the "movement was everything, the goal nothing". The socialist revolution was not something the Social Democratic Party should concern itself with. The party and the unions should instead focus on the practical, daily struggle for reforms. Through their implementation, socialism would be introduced gradually.

Despite the fact that his articles were a direct attack on the party's Marxist foundations, at first, the party leadership allowed Bernstein's ideas to go completely unchallenged. None of the leaders of the party commented on this revisionism. Neither, initially, did the editor of *Die Neue Zeit* itself, Karl Kautsky.[7] This was despite the fact that Kautsky, who had been given the moniker 'the pope of Marxism', was regarded as one of the leading theoreticians of the SPD and the defender of the party's Marxist doctrine. Instead of criticising Bernstein's revisionism, Kautsky described his articles as

6   *Die Voraussetzungen des Sozialismus und die Aufgaben der Sozialdemokratie.*

7   Karl Kautsky (1854-1938) – worked together with Friedrich Engels in London in the 1880's and then moved to Germany, where he became the leading theoretician of the SPD. Editor of *Die Neue Zeit* from 1883 to 1917.

"extremely attractive". Parvus[8] was one of the first to raise criticism of these ideas, causing Bernstein to interrupt his series of articles to respond to the critique. Meanwhile, Kautsky accompanied Bernstein's article in *Die Neue Zeit* with an editorial note explaining that he had received "a number of polemical comments on Bernstein's articles which we have to turn down for publication because they are based on a mistaken conception of Bernstein's intentions".[9]

But pressure on Kautsky was building up. The leading Russian Marxist, Plekhanov, wrote an article titled 'What Should We Thank Him For?' in which he not only attacked Bernstein but also criticised Kautsky for his failure to respond. Plekhanov wrote to Kautsky:

> You say your readers have no interest in philosophy... then you must force them to take an interest... If you want me to write against Bernstein you must give me full freedom of speech. Bernstein must be destroyed and I will gladly undertake this task if you let me.[10]

The answer from the SPD leadership was vague and evasive. Above all, they wished to avoid jeopardising the 'unity' of the party with what they saw as merely an abstract, theoretical discussion. The official newspaper of the party, *Vorwärts*, also welcomed Bernstein's writings, although they claimed they could lead to "misunderstandings". But as the debate developed even Kautsky, the party's chairman August Bebel,[11] and other party leaders, could see that Bernstein had gone too far. And yet their attitude remained evasive, as they hoped that the issue would resolve itself.

Rosa Luxemburg, on the other hand, threw herself into the debate with a number of articles that comprehensively responded to Bernstein, and which were collected in the book, *Reform or Revolution?* In it she explained that what was at stake were not harmless, minor revisions but that, if accepted by the party, they would amount to a complete break with Marxism. Luxemburg showed that even though Bernstein dressed his writing in Marxist terminology, the content was, at its very core, in direct opposition to Marxism: "On this

---

8 Parvus (1867-1924) – a pseudonym of Alexander Helphand, he was a Russian-German social democrat. After the defeat of the Russian Revolution of 1905 he fled to Germany, where he settled.

9 Quoted in J. P. Nettl, *Rosa Luxemburg*, p. 146.

10 Quoted ibid., p. 202.

11 August Bebel (1840-1913) – one of the founders of the SPD and its chairman from 1892 to 1913.

account," she wrote, "we must, unconcerned by its outer forms, pick out the sheathed kernel of Bernstein's theory".[12]

In *Reform or Revolution?*, Rosa Luxemburg pierces Bernstein's arguments one by one and launches a fierce attack against his "doing away" with the necessity of the socialist revolution. To Rosa Luxemburg, it was clear that what was at stake in the revisionism debate was nothing less than the *raison d'etre* of the Social Democratic Party, its very right to exist:

> But since the final goal of socialism constitutes the only decisive factor distinguishing the social democratic movement from bourgeois democracy and from bourgeois radicalism, the only factor transforming the entire labour movement from a vain effort to repair the capitalist order into a class struggle against this order, for the suppression of this order – the question, "Reform or revolution?" as it is posed by Bernstein, equals for the social democracy equal to the question: "To be or not to be?" In the controversy with Bernstein and his followers, everybody in the party ought to understand clearly it is not a question of this or that method of struggle, or the use of this or that set of tactics, but of the very existence of the social democratic movement.[13]

To Rosa Luxemburg, the polemic was no mere academic exercise. Theory was a direct guide to action, and the foundation of the party's tactics and strategies.

Bernstein's book was of tremendous significance for the German and international labour movement, as it was the first attempt to give a theoretical basis for opportunist currents that had become widespread in social democracy.

> What appears to characterise this practice [reformism] above all? A certain hostility to 'theory'. This is quite natural, for our 'theory', that is, the principles of scientific socialism, impose clearly marked limitations to practical activity – insofar as it concerns the aims of this activity, the means used in attaining these aims, and the method employed in this activity. It is quite natural for people who run after immediate 'practical' results to want to free themselves from such limitations and to render their practice independent of our 'theory'.[14]

The same attitude to theory as a guide to revolutionary action can be found in the writings of Lenin and his attacks on Bernstein's Russian counterparts, known as the 'Economists':

---

12 R. Luxemburg, *Reform or Revolution?*, *The Essential Rosa Luxemburg*, p. 42.

13 Ibid., p. 101.

14 Ibid.

Without revolutionary theory there can be no revolutionary movement. This idea cannot be insisted upon too strongly at a time when the fashionable preaching of opportunism goes hand in hand with an infatuation for the narrowest forms of practical activity.[15]

Capitalist Adaptation

At the time that Bernstein was writing his articles, capitalism was experiencing an upswing that lasted for twenty years. From this, he and others concluded that the cyclical crises could be overcome. Marx had said, after all, that crises would return about once every ten years, but now the period of boom had been somewhat longer. But Luxemburg had no time for this empiricism, and Bernstein's hopes that capitalism had resolved its contradictions were dashed shortly after. In the year 1900, capitalism was once again hit by crisis, and then again in 1907.

Marx explained that the crises of capitalism are crises of overproduction. In this, they are quite unlike anything that had hit earlier modes of production. In pre-capitalist societies, crises occurred as a result of scarcity, such as when harvests failed or as a result of the dislocation of war. But the crises of capitalism are different. Here, crises occur because there is 'too much'. Of course, there is no excess with respect to social needs; but rather, with respect to what the market can actually profitably absorb. These crises of overproduction occur fundamentally because the working class produces more value than it is paid in wages. The value that the working class creates beyond the value that covers its wages, Marx termed surplus value. This surplus value is the source of profit, which is appropriated by the capitalists who own the means of production (factories, machines, land etc.). As workers are paid less than the value they create, as consumers, they are unable to buy back all of the commodities that they produce. This is the fundamental reason for recurring crises of overproduction.

The only reason there isn't a constant crisis of overproduction is that the capitalists must reinvest the majority of their profits in new means of production if they wish to remain competitive on the free market. This process is what Marx termed the accumulation of capital. The creation of new means of production provides jobs for workers, who receive wages and thus continue to consume in an upward spiral. But instead of abolishing the contradiction between the production of the working class and its purchasing power as consumers, it simply reproduces this contradiction on a higher level. New means of production and an expanded production capacity must result

---

15 V. I. Lenin, *What is to Be Done?*, p. 26.

in even *more* commodities being produced, which, in the end, also have to be sold on a market that remains constricted.

This is where credit enters the picture. It serves as a means of artificially expanding the market. With credit, workers can purchase more with borrowed money, and the capitalists can make larger and more frequent investments. Credit affects the market in manifold ways, but its most important role, besides speeding up the turnover of capital, is to temporarily expand the market beyond the limits it would otherwise meet. Thus, for a time, it can counteract the tendency for production to outstrip demand.

Bernstein believed that this way of understanding the dynamics of capitalism was outdated and that, through a number of "adaptations" such as modern credit institutions, capitalism had solved its internal contradictions. Luxemburg ruthlessly criticised Bernstein's logic. According to Luxemburg, credit was not a "means of adapting" that averts crises, but rather a means of *delaying* crises. The expansion of credit moreover means that crises tend to be far bigger when they do hit. This is because, far from removing the obstacle of overproduction, it allows it to operate for much longer:

> But credit strikes from two sides. After having (as a factor of the process of production) provoked overproduction, credit (as a factor of exchange) destroys, during the crisis, the very productive forces it itself created.[16]

In the same considered manner, Luxemburg also addressed another of capitalism's "adaptations" as hailed by Bernstein: the rise of cartels and trusts. It was, she explained, a matter that had yet to be sufficiently investigated. Lenin later thoroughly explored this very question in his book *Imperialism: The Highest Stage of Capitalism*. But despite the fact that a thorough analysis of the rise of monopolies remained to be undertaken when Luxemburg wrote *Reform or Revolution?*, she was able to answer Bernstein's argument that they would be able to solve the anarchy of capitalism, and thus its crises, firmly in the negative. According to Luxemburg, for this to happen, cartels and trusts were to become the predominant form of production. But this was itself impossible. First of all, since cartels and trusts make extraordinarily high rates of profit in one industry, this naturally has to be offset by an opposing tendency in other sectors. Secondly, this association of capitalists would only last until a crisis hit. When the crisis comes, the cartels and trusts would "burst like soap bubbles and give way to aggravated competition."[17]

---

16 R. Luxemburg, *Reform or Revolution?*, *Essential Rosa Luxemburg*, p. 48.
17 Ibid., p. 51.

For this reason, cartels and trusts, according to Luxemburg, were not a way to counteract crises. On the contrary, they increased the anarchy of capitalism and sharpened its inner contradictions.

Luxemburg showed that Bernstein's "means of adaptation" were unable to do away with the fact that production existed on a capitalist foundation. On the contrary, Luxemburg explained that they would only increase the inner contradictions of capitalism, the contradiction between socialised production and private acquisition. Under capitalism, the means of production are privately owned by the capitalists, and production occurs for a market, over which the capitalists compete for the purpose of creating profits. But production takes place on an ever-increasing scale, involving more and more workers in a widening division of labour. In the words of Marx, production has been socialised under capitalism.

Luxemburg argued that credit (and the stock market) *increasingly* socialise the character of production by combining smaller capitals into larger ones, without changing the fact that the means of production remain in private hands. Credit therefore simply serves to accentuate the contradictions of the capitalist economy between large-scale, socialised production, and private ownership of the means of production. The only way to ensure that socialised production actually benefits the great majority of people would be to abolish private ownership of the means of production. That is to say: a socialist revolution is necessary. What Bernstein saw as "means of adaptation", Luxemburg saw as the opposite. Far from having rendered socialist revolution obsolete, for Rosa Luxemburg they had, on the contrary, made it an even greater necessity.

Bernstein's way of thinking is not uniquely his own. His reasoning has been reproduced by thousands of left reformists that came after him. For Bernstein, the question of socialism was not a question of production but one of distribution. The struggle was not one of classes, arising from the mode of production itself and the question of who owns the means of production. Bernstein failed to recognise that this is the key question that must be asked if a serious change is to be brought about in the sphere of distribution.

Among other things, Bernstein proposed the establishment of cooperatives as a means of ameliorating inequality. Luxemburg plainly showed why this was utopian. She called the cooperatives "a hybrid form in the midst of capitalism."[18] All production under capitalism is subject to competition. This means that workers in cooperatives are forced to act as their own employers.

---

18 Ibid., p. 80.

They cannot simply choose to avoid the market. According to Luxemburg, there could only be one result:

> Labour is intensified. The workday is lengthened or shortened, according to the situation of the market. And, depending on the requirements of the market, labour is either employed or thrown back into the street. In other words, use is made of all methods that enable an enterprise to stand up against its competitors in the market. The workers forming a cooperative in the field of production are thus faced with the contradictory necessity of governing themselves with the utmost absolutism. They are obliged to take toward themselves the role of capitalist entrepreneur [...][19]

Luxemburg's conclusion was unequivocal: either the cooperatives would become capitalist enterprises; or else they would end up dissolving. No islands of socialism can exist in a sea of capitalism – all production is subjugated to the market's ruthless law of competition.

The Inevitable Collapse of Capitalism?

In her arguments against Bernstein on the question of whether the regulation of capitalism can be used to evade crises, Rosa Luxemburg was as sharp as a razor. However, as is often the case in polemics, she ended up bending the stick a bit too far in the other direction. Her main criticism of Bernstein was that he, with his "means of adaptation", denied that capitalism would collapse:

> And to this he replies: "With the growing development of society a complete and almost general collapse of the present system of production becomes more and more improbable, because capitalist development increases on the one hand the capacity of adaptation and, on the other – that is, at the same time – the differentiation of industry."[20]

Luxemburg further developed the idea of a final collapse of capitalism or, to use her own words, a "the period of the final crises of capitalism",[21] in her book, *The Accumulation of Capital*, which we will deal with in chapter five. Her argument was that, if one abandons the idea of a final collapse of capitalism, one must also surrender the idea of the objective necessity of socialism:

---

19 Ibid., pp. 80-1.

20 R. Luxemburg, *Reform or Revolution?, Rosa Luxemburg Speaks*, p. 40.

21 R. Luxemburg, *Sozialreform oder Revolution*, p. 16, our translation.

> According to scientific socialism, the historic necessity of the socialist revolution manifests itself above all in the growing anarchy of capitalism, which drives the system into an impasse. But if one admits with Bernstein that capitalist development does not move in the direction of its own ruin, then socialism ceases to be objectively necessary.[22]

It is hard to guess exactly what Rosa Luxemburg meant by the phrase "general collapse". Her prediction that the choice before humanity was one of "socialism or barbarism" was certainly correct. If capitalism is allowed to exist for a sufficiently long time, it will threaten civilisation itself with destruction. Two World Wars, which claimed the lives of some 60 million people, came dangerously close to realising this perspective. Viewed from our own time, we can again see how human civilisation might meet its end, either in the form of nuclear war or of man-made environmental destruction.

However, Luxemburg writes of the collapse of capitalism more specifically as the direct product of its inner economic contradictions, which in the end she claims must bring about a final crisis and a final economic collapse. In a word, this approach is fatalistic. Nevertheless, the practical conclusions that she drew contained no trace of passivity. As regards both theory and practice, she insisted on the necessary role of the working class, and of a party armed with revolutionary tactics and strategy, as an essential factor in the *conscious* and *organised* overthrow of the capitalist system. This makes up precisely the subject matter of the remaining parts of *Reform or Revolution?* For Rosa Luxemburg, socialism was not something that spontaneously springs from the collapse of capitalism. This does then leave ambiguity over exactly what was meant by the collapse of capitalism.

With this argument of a "final crisis of capitalism", Rosa Luxemburg unnecessarily shot herself in the foot. It was not for nothing that Marx never spoke of this, nor of the system collapsing of its own accord. The history of capitalism has shown that it can continue until it is consciously overthrown by the working class. Crises serve to destroy 'excess' production and means of production, and thus pave the way for a new upturn. Capitalism can overcome its crises, but only at an enormous cost for the working class and the poorest people on the planet. We saw this in the Second World War, the 'solution' to the worldwide economic depression of the 1930s.

Where Luxemburg was right however – and this is essential in the discussion of *Reform or Revolution?* – was in pointing out that socialism is not *simply* a

---

22 Ibid., p. 40.

question of morality, but an objective necessity. As capitalism expands, its internal contradictions increase. As such, capitalism itself becomes an ever-larger barrier to the development of the productive forces. The gravity of each new crisis therefore tends to multiply, increasingly expressing itself as a systemic crisis.

Whether one accepts the theory of collapse or not, Luxemburg showed in her polemic with Bernstein that it is impossible to 'regulate' capitalism's crises out of existence, and thus that socialist revolution is a necessity. To Bernstein, the necessity of socialism was not something that originated from the inner material contradictions of capitalism, but rather an abstract idealistic 'principle'. To him, the question of whether socialism was a necessity was a moral question.

Rosa Luxemburg, on the other hand, defended historical materialism. She understood that capitalism was simply one stage of historical development, and that its internal contradictions would become increasingly evident as it became more of a barrier to the development of society. Socialism for Luxemburg was – as it was for Marx before her – an *objective* necessity, and the germ of socialism had already developed under capitalism in the form of large-scale production. Once private ownership of the means of production is done away with, and these tremendous productive forces are brought under a democratic plan, production on the scale created by capitalism would allow society to eliminate scarcity, classes and inequality.

The Role of the Trade Unions

According to Bernstein, the growing role of the trade unions was capitalism's final means of adaptation. The Bernsteinian, gradualist road to socialism was to occur by means of the regulation of capitalism by "trade unions, social reforms, and [...] the political democratisation of the state".[23] Rosa Luxemburg firmly opposed this argument.

Marx explained that labour power is a commodity which, under capitalism, is sold on the market like any other commodity. The value of labour power is determined by the socially necessary cost of its production and reproduction, i.e., of the commodities needed to support the workers and their family including housing, food, clothes, education, the raising of the next generation, etc. How much value this amounts to is determined by historical and social factors, one of which is the strength of the trade union movement. But wages (the price of labour power) fluctuate around

---

23 Ibid., p. 56.

this value according to the law of supply and demand. For example, when unemployment is high, the capitalists have more leverage, which allows them to push wages to below their value.

Luxemburg pointed out that, in his articles, Bernstein himself described the most important function of the trade unions as, "providing the workers with a means of realising the capitalist law of wages, that is to say, the sale of their labour power at current market prices."[24] In other words, the trade unions can help "realise the law of wages" by making sure wages stay around the value of labour power also in times of crisis. But, Rosa Luxemburg explained, the trade unions had no influence on the overall economic configuration and changed nothing fundamental about the relationship between the owners of capital on the one hand, and wage labourers on the other. Thus, the trade unions were unable to overthrow the law of wages.

> Under the most favourable circumstances, the best they can do is to impose on capitalist exploitation the 'normal' limit of the moment. They have not, however, the power to suppress exploitation itself, not even gradually.[25]

In the end, they fight within the framework of the capitalist economy and cannot change this.

Furthermore, Luxemburg pointed out that trade unions, with their narrow focus on labour struggles, often end up resisting technological developments. This is despite the fact that improved technology, objectively speaking, is in the interest of the workers, when we consider the end goal of a socialist society. The trade unions however are forced to fight the consequences of the introduction of technology under capitalism, such as layoffs or increased workload. The task of Social Democracy was, according to Rosa Luxemburg, to emphasise the interests of the whole of the working class. As Marx and Engels wrote in the *Communist Manifesto*:

> The Communists […] point out and bring to the front the common interests of the entire proletariat, independently of all nationality. […] In the various stages of development which the struggle of the working class against the bourgeoisie has to pass through, they always and everywhere represent the interests of the movement as a whole.[26]

---

24 Ibid., p. 56.

25 Ibid.

26 K. Marx and F. Engels, *The Communist Manifesto*, *The Classics of Marxism: Volume One*, p. 15.

Luxemburg concluded that the task of the unions was limited to regulating capitalist exploitation, but that they themselves could not abolish it. Luxemburg described the work of the unions as a "Sisyphean labour", with reference to Sisyphus, who, according to Greek mythology, was doomed to roll a rock up a mountaintop, after which it would always roll down again. Despite the fact that she emphasised the necessity of this "Sisyphean labour", as it secured the wages and living conditions of the workers, she won the eternal enmity of the trade union leadership due to this particular choice of words, and due to her more general critique of their opportunistic practices.

It was in the trade union wing of the SPD in particular that revisionism predominated. The labour leaders did not partake in the theoretical debates, but it was these people above all others who, in practice, were the torchbearers of the revisionist tendency. Rosa Luxemburg subjected this practice to a powerful critique: to her, it was obvious that the practical labour policies of the party had to be subordinated to its political line and goal. It was in the party that the long-term goal of the movement rested: the emancipation of the working class through a socialist revolution. All practical activity had to be subordinated to efforts for the realisation of this goal.

Rosa Luxemburg's view was that it was as clear as day that the practice of the trade unions could not be separated from the political struggle of the party. It was also clear to her that the labour leaders of the SPD did not necessarily care for the long-term goal of their membership. To her, there was nothing 'socialist' whatsoever about extending the regulation of capitalism:

> What functions today as 'social control' – labour legislation, the control of industrial organisations through share holding, etc. – has absolutely nothing to do with his 'supreme ownership'. Far from being, as Schmidt believes, a reduction of capitalist ownership, his 'social control', is, on the contrary, a protection of such ownership. Or, expressed from the economic viewpoint, it is not a threat to capitalist exploitation, but simply the regulation of exploitation. When Bernstein asks if there is more or less of socialism in a labour protective law, we can assure him that, in the best of labour protective laws, there is no more 'socialism' than in a municipal ordinance regulating the cleaning of streets or the lighting of street lamps.[27]

The question, Rosa Luxemburg claimed, was not so much *what* the trade unions should do: they should fight for social reforms. The importance lay in the *way* in which it was done. The revisionists believed that the struggle for

27 R. Luxemburg, *Reform or Revolution?*, *The Essential Rosa Luxemburg*, p. 61.

immediate material results gradually limited the power of capital, and thus made the seizure of power by the workers redundant. For Rosa Luxemburg, on the contrary, the struggle for reforms should form a preparatory school for the proletariat's seizure of power, as they realise, through the struggle, the impossibility of fundamentally changing society through reforms.

Reform and/or Revolution?

From the title of her book "Reform *or* Revolution" a misunderstanding has arisen that Rosa Luxemburg saw the struggle for reforms and the struggle for revolution as opposites: that revolutionaries, according to her, had to reject the struggle for reforms. Nothing could be further from the truth.

To Rosa Luxemburg, the struggle for reforms and the struggle for revolution were inseparable. But there was also a clear hierarchy: the former was subordinate to the latter. According to her, it was Bernstein who artificially portrayed the struggle for reforms and the struggle for revolution as opposites. Luxemburg, on the contrary, argued that the daily, practical struggle of the Social Democracy for reforms – i.e., for improvements for workers within the framework of the existing society – was the only way the proletarian class struggle could lead to its final goal: the socialist revolution. According to Luxemburg, these two had to be connected. The struggle for reforms was the means, while the socialist transformation of society was the end.

Bernstein presented the relationship between revolution and reform as a question of the speed of development. According to him, it was unnecessary to conquer political power – society would be changed one law at a time and thus gradually shifted in a socialist direction.

Luxemburg, on the contrary, argued that the socialist revolution was not simply an unimportant, abstract goal lying far in the future with only the struggles of daily life for reforms achieving concrete results. Quite the opposite. She argued that if we were to abandon the goal of socialist revolution, it would have a very concrete effect. The movement would end up on a very different road, one that led *away* from socialism. Legislative changes fortify that which exists, while the conquest of power overturns it:

> From the first appearance of class societies having the class struggle as the essential content of their history, the conquest of political power has been the aim of all rising classes. Here is the starting point and end of every historic period. This can be seen in the long struggle of the Latin peasantry against the financiers and nobility of ancient Rome, in the struggle of the medieval nobility against the

bishops, and in the struggle of the artisans against the nobles in the cities of the Middle Ages. In modern times, we see it in the struggle of the bourgeoisie against feudalism.

Legislative reform and revolution are not different methods of historic development that can be picked out at the pleasure from the counter of history, just as one chooses hot or cold sausages. Legislative reform and revolution are different *factors* in the development of class society. They condition and complement each other, and are at the same time reciprocally exclusive, as are the north and south poles, the bourgeoisie and proletariat.

Every legal constitution is the *product* of a revolution. In the history of classes, revolution is the act of political creation, while legislation is the political expression of the life of a society that has already come into being. Work for reform does not contain its own force, independent from revolution. During every historic period, work for reforms is carried on only in the direction given to it by the impetus of the last revolution and continues as long as the impulsion of the last revolution continues to make itself felt. Or, to put it more concretely, in each historic period work for reforms is carried on only in the framework of the social form created by the last revolution. Here is the kernel of the problem.

It is contrary to history to represent work for reforms as a long-drawn-out revolution and revolution as a condensed series of reforms. A social transformation and a legislative reform do not differ according to their duration but according to their content. The secret of historic change through the utilisation of political power resides precisely in the transformation of simple quantitative modification into a new quality, or to speak more concretely, in the passage of an historic period from one given form of society to another.

That is why people who pronounce themselves in favour of the method of legislative reform *in place and in contradistinction* to the conquest of political power and social revolution do not really choose a more tranquil, calmer and, slower road to the *same* goal, but a *different* goal. Instead of taking a stand for the establishment of a new society they take a stand for surface modifications of the old society. If we follow the political conceptions of revisionism, we arrive at the same conclusion that is reached when we follow the economic theories of revisionism. Our program becomes not the realisation of *socialism*, but the reform of *capitalism*; not the suppression of the system of wage labour, but the diminution of exploitation, that is, the suppression of the abuses of capitalism instead of suppression of capitalism itself.[28]

---

28 Ibid., pp. 89-90.

The struggle for democratic demands and reforms, such as the right to vote, an eight-hour working day, and the like, has thus always been essential for Marxists, but not in and of itself, as Luxemburg explained. Through such demands, the workers can be mobilised to fight. In the course of the struggle, the working class becomes increasingly conscious of the class divisions in society, of the character of the class struggle, and of its own strength. The limitations of capitalist society are brought into sharp relief, and the necessity of a socialist revolution impresses itself on the minds of workers. Where freer, more democratic conditions are won, their existence makes clear that the workers' problems cannot be solved through this or that democratic reform. Rather, the system itself is further underlined as the real problem. The struggle for reforms is thus nothing in and of itself, but rather has to be integrated into the struggle for a socialist revolution.

The Debate

Rosa Luxemburg's entry into the debate against Bernstein piled pressure onto the leaders of the SPD. Leading individuals such as Karl Kautsky and August Bebel could no longer continue evading the debate. They too began criticising Bernstein. Their objections were not aimed at his ideas, however, but rather against the fact that the very debate itself threatened party unity.

The party leadership had hoped they could bury the problem. They attempted to suppress the discussion and were especially deaf to calls to move against the revisionists. Only under enormous pressure did they issue a response to Bernstein and even then, it remained worded in the vaguest terms. Kautsky had waited for more than one-and-a-half years before he answered Bernstein. He in no way shared Rosa Luxemburg's view that this was a debate about principles and even the very right of the Social Democracy to exist. In a personal letter sent to Bernstein in advance of his official response, Kautsky wrote:

> It seems to me that what divides us is not opinions and conclusions, but the tone with which we espouse them.[29]

When the debate was finally brought up at a party congress in 1898, Kautsky had soothing words:

> Social Democracy will do everything possible to carry out democratic and economic reforms and to organise the proletariat. And Bernstein has a completely false idea of the party. He believes that we are contemplating a clash with armed

---

29 Quoted in R. Sewell, *Germany 1918-1933: Socialism or Barbarism*, p. 31.

authority, and that development will not be so rapid as many suppose. This is a question of *temperament*, not of viewpoints.[30]

The vague approach of the SPD leaders was in sharp contrast to that of Luxemburg. Her approach to revisionism was a declaration of war. She, and others of the left wing, demanded that the revisionists be expelled from the party – a demand they gave up after the congress in 1899, when the party leaders finally accepted the theoretical critique of revisionism without going as far as exclusion.

To Rosa Luxemburg, the party was a tool, not a debating society open to perpetual discussion and the 'right to critique':

> As in every political party freedom to criticise our way of life must have a definite limit. That which is the very basis of our existence, the class struggle, cannot be the subject of 'free criticism'. We cannot commit suicide in the name of freedom to criticise. Opportunism, as Bebel has said, breaks our backbone, nothing less.[31]

The ideas of Bernstein were voted down at a series of congresses. But Luxemburg's intention, in raising the discussion, was not simply to 'win' the majority at the party congress. She intended first and foremost to educate the SPD membership; to raise their political level:

> As long as theoretical knowledge remains the privilege of a handful of 'academicians' in the party, the latter will face the danger of going astray. Only when the great mass of workers take the keen and dependable weapons of scientific socialism in their own hands will all the petty-bourgeois inclinations, all the opportunistic currents, come to naught. The movement will then find itself on sure and firm ground. "Quantity will do it."[32]

Although the ideas of Bernstein were voted down at the congress, reformist ideas had gained increasing ground at the top of the SPD, and were expressed in the practical activity of the party. Indeed, Bernstein himself was not arguing for a change in the party's practice, but simply that the party should "dare to show itself for what it was: a democratic-socialist party of reform".[33]

Ignaz Auer, party secretary of the SPD, expressed the thinking of many of the leaders and functionaries when he wrote personally to Bernstein: "My

---

30 Quoted ibid., p. 33 (emphasis by Sewell).

31 Quoted in J. P. Nettl, *Rosa Luxemburg*, p. 235.

32 R. Luxemburg, *Reform or Revolution?, Essential Rosa Luxemburg*, p. 43.

33 R. Luxemburg, *Sozialreform oder Revolution*, p. 63, our translation.

dear Ede, one does not formally make a decision to do the things you suggest, one doesn't *say* such things, one simply *does* them."[34]

In the Footsteps of Marx and Engels

With her political struggle against Bernstein, Rosa Luxemburg was picking up where Marx and Engels had left off. As mentioned, two decades earlier they had criticised the reformism in the SPD that was just then beginning to show itself. They saw numerous signs of an adaptation to capitalism and an excessive focus on the parliamentary struggle. When the Socialist Laws were annulled, a cherished argument of the party leadership was the need to make sure the Laws were not reintroduced and the party was once more made illegal.

The excuse of the possible reintroduction of the Socialist Laws was used against Friedrich Engels, who had written the introduction to Karl Marx's *The Class Struggles in France*. The secretary of the executive committee of the SPD, Richard Fischer, asked Engels to water down the introduction, arguing that some of its formulations could be used by the government to reintroduce restrictions against the party. Engels acquiesced, omitting certain passages, mainly about the armed struggle of the working class. But he wasn't wholly happy with the result. He wrote to Fischer:

> I have taken as much account as possible of your grave objections although I cannot for the life of me see what is objectionable about, say, half of the instances you cite. For I cannot after all assume that you intend to subscribe heart and soul to absolute legality, legality under any circumstances, legality even *vis-à-vis* laws infringed by the promulgators, in short, to the policy of turning the left cheek to him, who has struck you on the right. True, the *Vorwärts* sometimes expends almost as much energy on repudiating revolution as once it did – and may soon do again – on advocating the same. I cannot regard that a criterion.

> My view is that you have nothing to gain by advocating complete abstention from force. Nobody would believe you, *nor* would *any* party in any country go as far as to forfeit the right to resist illegality by force of arms.[35]

Without informing Engels, *Vorwärts* published only selected parts of the introduction, which caused Engels to protest his portrayal as a "peace-loving advocate for adherence to law no matter what". He demanded that *Vorwärts* publish the complete text. Engels died that same year, and *Vorwärts* never

34 Quoted in J. P. Nettl, *Rosa Luxemburg*, p. 156.

35 Quoted in R. Sewell, *Germany 1918-1933: Socialism or Barbarism*, p. 26.

did publish the full text. Instead, they presented the amputated edition as Engels' testament and as a condemnation of any form of violence – and thus also of any kind of revolution. Instead, Engels was depicted as glorifying adherence to the law. The party tops consciously concealed Engels' protest from the party membership and used the watered-down version to further their own ends. Only in 1924 was it rediscovered and published in its original wording.

Despite the fact that the complete manuscript only saw the light of day five years after her death, and she therefore could know nothing of Engels' protests, Luxemburg instinctively refused to accept that the watered-down version was representative of Engels' views. In her speech to the founding congress of the German Communist Party in 1918, she hypothesised that Engels might have written the preface under pressure from the Reichstag fraction of the party, and that he would have protested vehemently at how it had been used. This 'parliamentarism-only' tactic would lead to betrayal on 4 August 1914 when the SPD voted in favour of war credits in the Reichstag:

> Engels died the same year, and had therefore no chance to see the practical results of this application of his theory.
>
> I am certain that those who know the works of Marx and Engels, those who are familiar with the living, genuine revolutionary spirit that inspired all their teachings and their writings, will be convinced that Engels would have been the first to protest against the debauch of parliamentarism-only, against the corruption and degradation of the labour movement which was characteristic of Germany before 4 August. 4 August did not come like thunder out of a clear sky; what happened on 4 August was the logical outcome of all that we had been doing day after day for many years.[36]

Revisionism in Practice

The enormous growth of the SPD led to a large expansion of the party apparatus, which was sucked into countless daily issues and questions without being subjected to party control. In city councils, trade union offices, and so on, there were hundreds, if not thousands, of party functionaries who had never been educated in or even thought about Marxist ideas. The livelihoods of this layer increasingly depended upon the growth of the party itself, and upon conditions that guaranteed there wasn't too much unrest or too fierce a

36 R. Luxemburg, 'Our Program and the Political Situation', *Selected Political Writings of Rosa Luxemburg*, p. 384.

class struggle that might disrupt their daily work. To these people, the party
and their positions in the movement became a goal in itself. They didn't
defend revisionism in theory. They simply practised it on a daily basis.

This practical revisionism was on open display among the elected political
representatives of the SPD – both in the national Reichstag, and on a federal
and local level. The orthodox social-democratic method of parliamentary
work, which Luxemburg defended, was to use parliamentary seats to
politically educate the masses and to take no responsibility for legislation
in the bourgeois parliament. But, as discussed, there was pressure on local
social-democratic representatives, which the latter transmitted into the party,
especially in the south of Germany, to partake in negotiations and vote for
local budgets, etc. This was against everything that the SPD had earlier stood
for. Luxemburg fought this trend tooth and nail, despite the attempts of the
southern German social democrats to remain aloof from the revisionism
debate, claiming that special conditions justified their conduct in southern
Germany.

Revisionism wasn't simply a German phenomenon. It also manifested itself
internationally. As early as 1899, the French socialist, Alexandre Millerand,
had taken up a post in Waldeck-Rousseau's[37] radical ministry. His step was
welcomed by the leader of the French Socialist Party, Jean Jaurès. Millerand
was made Minister of Trade in the very same government where General
Gallifet served as minister of war. Gallifet was notorious for slaughtering
30,000 Communards when he crushed the Paris Commune of 1871. This was
the first time that a socialist had participated in a bourgeois government, and
it created shockwaves that provoked discussion throughout the International.

The events following the Dreyfus Affair provided the excuse for taking
up a government ministry. It was claimed that the republic was under
attack, and that socialists had to defend it through their participation in the
government. Dreyfus was a French Jewish officer who was the victim of a
miscarriage of justice and condemned for espionage. When the fact that he
was falsely accused and condemned was uncovered, it blew up into a huge
scandal. Waldeck-Rousseau led the government that would acquit Dreyfus
for "defending the republic", and which had sought to ward off the explosive
situation that erupted following the Affair. The situation was so explosive that
Lenin even believed that it had the potential to spark a revolutionary situation.
According to Jaurès and the reformists of the International, it was no longer
the bourgeoisie alone, but the bourgeoisie and the proletariat together, who

---

37 Pierre Waldeck-Rousseau (1846-1904) – French Republican politician.

ought to hold political power. They thus argued that Millerand's entry into government was actually a step on the road to socialism. The revolutionary wing of the International, on the contrary, explained that the French socialists were only drawn into government to provide a cover for its reactionary politics, as evidenced by their acquittal of the masterminds of the Dreyfus Affair, their imperialist intervention in China and their support for the Russian Tsar.

This was precisely how events unfolded. As soon as the socialists had played their role and rendered assistance to the government, they were cast aside. The only thing the socialists got from their time in government was to discredit themselves in the eyes of the working class. A few years later, even Jaurès became disillusioned with this class collaboration, and so he broke with Millerand, as well as Briand and Vivani, who had also entered government. In the end, the latter three were expelled from the Socialist Party.

The revolutionary wing of the International denounced the entry of socialists into bourgeois governments. Lenin described it as the practical expression of Bernsteinism:

> If Bernstein's theoretical criticism and political yearnings were still unclear to anyone, the French took the trouble strikingly to demonstrate the 'new method'… Millerand has furnished an excellent example of practical Bernsteinism…[38]

Luxemburg was among the harshest critics of this 'ministerial-socialism'. She believed that the entry of the French socialists into government gave the latter a cover for its imperialist policies whilst reducing the French Socialist Party to a toothless opposition. A key plank of the argument for participating in government was the need to pry away practical results – reforms – from the government. But, as Luxemburg said, there are reforms and there are reforms. The *way* in which reforms are obtained is an essential question. Only those won through class struggle have a socialist character. Far from guiding the country towards socialism, participation in government turned the socialists into advocates of the bourgeois:

> The character of a bourgeois government isn't determined by the personal character of its members, but by its organic function in bourgeois society. The government of the modern state is essentially an organisation of class domination, the regular functioning of which is one of the conditions of existence of the class state. With the entry of a socialist into the government, and class domination continuing to exist, the bourgeois government doesn't transform itself into a

---

38 V. I. Lenin, *What is to Be Done?*, p. 9.

socialist government, but a socialist transforms himself into a bourgeois minister. The social reforms that a minister who is a friend of the workers can realise have nothing, in themselves, of socialism; they are socialist only insofar as they are obtained through class struggle. But coming from a minister, social reforms can't have the character of the proletarian class, but solely the character of the bourgeois class, for the minister, by the post he occupies, attaches himself to that class by all the functions of a bourgeois, militarist government. While in parliament, or on the municipal council, we obtain useful reforms by combating the bourgeois government, while occupying a ministerial post we arrive at the same reforms by supporting the bourgeois state. The entry of a socialist into a bourgeois government is not, as it is thought, a partial conquest of the bourgeois state by the socialists, but a partial conquest of the socialist party by the bourgeois state.[39]

In these lines, Luxemburg describes the entry of socialists into a bourgeois government. The bourgeois state – and thus the bourgeois government, which she refers to – has the defence of the interests of the capitalist class and the maintenance of bourgeois society at its core. The bourgeoisie brought Millerand in as a minister for the purpose of incorporating socialists into government so that they would assist in helping maintain capitalism and, in particular, in keeping the struggle of the working class in check.

In Luxemburg's opinion, for socialists to accept to join a bourgeois government was a completely incorrect strategy. Instead, she argued, socialists ought to present a clear opposition in parliament and use their platform to educate the working class as to the class character of the bourgeois state:

The circumstance which divides socialist politics from bourgeois politics is that the socialists are opponents of the entire existing order and must function in a bourgeois parliament fundamentally as an opposition. The most important aim of socialist activity in a parliament, the education of the working class, is achieved by a systematic criticism of the ruling party and its politics. The socialists are too far removed from the bourgeois order to be able to achieve practical and thorough-going reforms of a progressive character. Therefore, principled opposition to the ruling party becomes, for every minority party and above all for the socialists, the only feasible method with which to achieve practical results.[40]

---

39 R. Luxemburg, 'The Dreyfus Affair and the Millerand Case', *Marxist Internet Archive* [website].

40 R. Luxemburg, 'The Socialist Crisis in France', Part 3, *Marxist Internet Archive* [website].

The Millerand incident proved that revisionism was no mere German phenomenon. The same process of political degeneration was under way in the other parties of the Second International. Opportunism was an international phenomenon. But the extent of that opportunism was not fully revealed until the outbreak of war in August 1914.

Luxemburg's Work in the SPD

Luxemburg's work in the party was not limited to her polemic against Bernstein. Before even arriving in Germany, she threw herself into the political work. One of the first tasks she undertook for the party was a campaign in the German-occupied part of Poland. Following tremendous successes in this highly industrialised region amongst some of the most oppressed layers of the German working class, she began to receive invitations to speak and to write regularly for several party magazines. During the Reichstag election in 1903, Luxemburg led a very successful campaign in German-occupied Poland, helping the party secure eighty-one seats.

However, she had a hard time finding her place in the party's official structures. For a short while she was the editor of the *Sächsische Arbeiterzeitung* in Dresden, but quickly withdrew. She then began regularly writing for the *Leipziger Volkszeitung*, of which she was made the editor for a short while. Besides these activities, she often wrote for the main newspaper of the party, *Vorwärts*, as well as its theoretical magazine, *Die Neue Zeit*.

Despite the fact that she could not find her own place in the party structures, she had personal contact with most of the leading members. She was, practically speaking, the neighbour of Karl Kautsky, and developed a close friendship with him and his wife Luise. She also met regularly with the party leader, August Bebel, among others, despite the fact that the party leadership would often complain of her "uncompromising tone" and revolutionary temper. Luxemburg had her own reservations about the party leadership in turn. One day in 1907, when she and Clara Zetkin were out for a morning walk, they lost track of time and managed to wander into a military rifle exercise, thereby arriving late for lunch with Bebel at Kautsky's home. Amongst the amusement at the story, the guests began speculating about what Bebel would have had to write in their epitaph if they had been killed. With Bebel becoming "tangled in superlatives", Luxemburg commented that he could "simply write 'Here lie the last two men of German Social Democracy'".[41]

---

41 P. Frölich, *Rosa Luxemburg*, p. 163.

Luxemburg's work soon drew the attention of the German state. When she returned to Germany following the world congress of the International in 1904, she was immediately condemned to three months imprisonment for insulting the German Emperor Wilhelm II.[42]

The German state had good reason to fear Rosa Luxemburg. From the day she arrived in Germany, she had placed herself on the revolutionary left wing, where she remained until her death. Although it wasn't so clear at the time, we can see already from the revisionism debate how she and her former friend Karl Kautsky, who later placed himself in the centre of the party, had very different stances. Kautsky, along with the party leadership, attempted to smooth over disagreements. Rosa Luxemburg meanwhile, without fear of swimming against the stream, threw herself directly into the struggle, clearly outlining the disagreements in order to bring the greatest possible theoretical clarity to the party. She was convinced that the workers' movement above all required a revolutionary Marxist foundation, and she threw everything into securing this. She was thus following in the footsteps of Marx and Engels. Her behaviour in the revisionism debate clearly showed who the real Rosa Luxemburg was. She would later show that same fighting spirit in her revolutionary practice.

If one has read *Reform or Revolution?*, one cannot, without arguing in bad faith, portray Rosa Luxemburg as a proponent of reformism, as we hear today from parts of the 'soft' left. To Rosa Luxemburg, the struggle for reforms was a means in the struggle for a socialist revolution. If the party gave up on the revolution it would, in reality, make itself redundant, reducing itself to a pillar of support for bourgeois society. This gloomy perspective was confirmed by history, not least on 4 August 1914, when the party leadership betrayed all its internationalist and revolutionary principles and threw its weight behind the German bourgeoisie in the First World War.

---

42 Ibid., p. 75

3. The Russian Organisational Question

In 1903 the Russian Social Democratic Labour Party held a congress. It was the first real congress of the party, where the party set out to define its role and character. It was here that the signs of a split made their first appearance – if somewhat unclearly – between the 'hard' Bolshevik and 'soft' Menshevik factions of the party. In this question too, Luxemburg was not one for sitting on the sidelines.

Rosa Luxemburg and the SDKPiL were strongly opposed to any form of nationalism and, as such, they were opposed to Polish independence from Germany, Austria, and Russia. As social democrats of the Russian-controlled part of Poland, they therefore believed, in principle, that they should form part of the Russian Social Democratic Labour Party. At the SDKPiL congress of July 1903, the party resolved to begin negotiations concerning merging with the Russian party. They therefore elected two delegates, Warszawski and Hanecki, who were sent to participate in the Russian congress in order to determine whether they ought to join.

When Luxemburg moved to Germany, she ceased being active in the Polish party, though after Jogiches arrived in Berlin in 1900, she recommenced her activity, albeit unofficially. As such, Luxemburg didn't directly participate in the merger negotiations with the Russians. Despite believing that a joint party was correct in principle, it doesn't seem as though she was especially bent on the idea that the relatively well-established Polish party ought to subject itself to the Russian party, which was only now taking steps towards becoming a united party. Furthermore, as has been explained, a fairly hostile personal relationship existed between herself and Plekhanov. She did not oppose a fusion but did give rather detailed instructions to the Polish delegates at the congress.

The driving force behind the congress of the Russian party in 1903 was the group centred around the newspaper *Iskra*, the editorial board of which was made up of Lenin and Plekhanov, among others. The *Iskraists* were fighting for a union of the many isolated social-democratic groups in Russia into one unified party, and for the liquidation of Economism – the Russian variant of Bernstein's revisionist tendency. In the beginning, it seemed there was agreement between the Russians and the Poles on all the essential political questions. Luxemburg could only have agreed with the *Iskraists'* political critique of the Russian advocates of Bernsteinism. According to Nettl,[1] the Polish party made no comments on Lenin's *What is to Be Done?*, which formed the political foundation of the congress for the *Iskraists*.

The congress then achieved its goal of creating a unified party to a large extent. However, internal disagreements between the *Iskraists* started to appear. These were the beginnings of the split between the Mensheviks and the Bolsheviks. Later, the Stalinists would present the formation of the Bolshevik Party as being akin to the rising of a phoenix out of the ashes, with the Russian party congress of 1903 being given almost mythical status. However, things were not as simple as the Stalinists made out, as we shall see.

The split at the congress also led to a confrontation between Rosa Luxemburg and Lenin, who she subjected to a scathing critique. This has later been used to 'prove' the anti-Leninism and anti-Bolshevism of Luxemburg, but here too things were not quite so simple. Before we take a closer look at her critique, however, we have to examine the question that led to the Polish delegation leaving the congress in 1903, before the split between the Mensheviks and the Bolsheviks took place.

The National Question

The national question formed a fundamental point of disagreement between Russian and Polish social democrats. During the congress, the Polish delegates became aware of an article that Lenin had written a short while earlier for *Iskra*, outlining the Russian Marxists' position on the national question. In his

---

1   J. P. Nettl – professor of political science and sociology at University of Pennsylvania. Wrote a very thorough (and academic) biography of Rosa Luxemburg, published in 1962.

article, Lenin stressed the need for the Russian party to support the oppressed nations' "right to self-determination". Lenin argued that, in general, social democrats must advocate that the people of the oppressed nations be allowed to decide for themselves whether they wished to form an independent nation or not.

Lenin's article said nothing new. The essential ideas it contained were part of the draft programme of the Russian Social Democratic Labour Party, which the Poles had been familiar with for a long time and had made objections to. But the article specified that, for the Russians, the slogan of "the right of nations to self-determination" was no mere empty phrase. Rather, it was an important part of their programme, both theoretically and tactically. The article was not intended as a provocation against the Poles, and Lenin went to great lengths to explain that it was not to be understood as support for Polish nationalism or for the nationalist-oriented PPS.

Luxemburg and Jogiches reacted swiftly and instructed the Polish delegates to make it clear to the Russians that negotiations were now hanging by a thread. In Luxemburg's detailed instructions, she demanded, among other things, that the paragraph containing the formulation on the rights of nations to self-determination be changed, or else the Poles would be forced to break off their plans for affiliation to the Russian party. When the Russian party congress refused to submit to these demands, the Polish delegation withdrew. The rest of the congress, which was moved from Brussels to London because of the interference of the Belgian police, took place without the Polish delegation.

On many questions, Rosa Luxemburg appears to have changed her opinion as revolutionary events drew nearer. However, her views on the national question do not fall under this category. This question formed a real point of political disagreement between Lenin and Luxemburg. For both of these great revolutionaries, it stood at the very heart of what they were fighting for. When Luxemburg and the group around her broke with the PPS to form the SDKPiL, it was over the question of Polish independence. The PPS had supported the demand for Polish independence while the SDKPiL had rejected it.[2]

---

2   Luxemburg did not only disagree with the PPS on this question, but with more or less all leading figures of the Second International. On behalf of the Polish comrades, she put forward a motion for a resolution at the world congress of 1896, which sought to make the International reject any and all demands of Polish independence. Both Plekhanov and Kautsky wrote a response, criticising her position. The Polish

Rosa Luxemburg quite bluntly decried the demand of Polish independence as "a utopian mirage, a delusion of the workers to detract them from their class struggle".[3] She fought tooth and nail against Polish nationalism from what was fundamentally a position of uncompromising internationalism. However, her position led her to lump together and reject *all* struggles against national oppression as, in essence, reactionary nationalism. First putting forward her ideas on the question in the early 1890s, she further developed them in a number of articles on the national question and the question of autonomy between 1908 and 1909.[4]

Lenin too settled his position on the question early on, further developing it over years without fundamentally changing its essence. In 1914, Lenin wrote a lengthy article titled 'The Right of Nations to Self-Determination'. Despite the fact that he penned the piece five years after Luxemburg had written her own articles, it was principally formulated as a response to her writings. Lenin was provoked into writing the article after a number of opportunists within the Bolshevik Party attacked paragraph nine of the party's constitution, which committed the party to the defence of the right of nations to self-determination. But according to Lenin, "none of the opportunists named [...] has offered a single argument of his own; they all merely repeat what Rosa Luxemburg said in her lengthy Polish article of 1908-09: 'The National Question and Autonomy'."[5] That it was *her* arguments Lenin picked out to criticise despite a five-year delay speaks volumes about the authority Luxemburg enjoyed in the movement.

Rosa Luxemburg's position on the question can be summed up as follows: the goal of socialism is to abolish all forms of oppression, including

---

resolution was rejected, as was the position of the PPS for an independent Poland. Eventually, a resolution which did not concretely speak of Poland, but recognised the right of nations to self-determination, was adopted. It was a resolution that was directly opposed to Luxemburg's position, which viewed all struggles for national self-determination as reactionary by definition.

3 Quoted in J. P. Nettl, *Rosa Luxemburg*, p. 76.

4 The starting point of the articles from 1908 and 1909 was a critique of paragraph nine in the programme of the Bolsheviks, about the right of nations to self-determination. Very uncharacteristic of Luxemburg – who often criticised the leaders of the SPD when they did not follow congress resolutions – she brushed aside the Bolsheviks, stating that they simply repeated the decision made by the congress, but that it was not intended such as they wrote it.

5 V. I. Lenin, 'The Right of Nations to Self-Determination', *LCW*, Vol. 20, p. 395.

the oppression of one nation by another. Without abolishing all forms of oppression, there can be no socialism. But that does not mean that Marxists should struggle for national autonomy. Above all, in the era of imperialism, the autonomy of one nation would go against the grain of the historical tendency of capitalism towards larger and larger economic units. According to Luxemburg, this is a historically progressive tendency. Thus, there could be nothing progressive about Marxists supporting the right of nations to self-determination, as it would simply mean the fragmentation rather than the unification of larger economic units. At any rate, small oppressed nations can never be free of the economic and political domination of the imperialist nations, and therefore to speak of autonomy amounts to pulling the wool over people's eyes. Not only would the demand for national self-determination be misused by the national bourgeoisie of the oppressed nation, but it would also be used by the great powers of imperialism in the furtherance of their own interests. In Rosa Luxemburg's opinion, the call for the right of nations to self-determination was, therefore, a bogus, reactionary and petty-bourgeois demand:

> […] the hope of realising this "right" on the basis of the existing setup is a utopia; it is in direct contradiction to the tendency of capitalist development on which Social Democracy has based its existence. A general attempt to divide all existing states into national units and to re-tailor them on the model of national states and statelets is a completely hopeless and, historically speaking, reactionary undertaking.[6]

According to Luxemburg, in the oppressed nations it was only the national bourgeoisie who had any interest in presenting the demand for national self-determination. Even then, the national bourgeoisie had no serious intention of fighting to achieve real autonomy but, rather, they only put forward such demands to further their own narrow interests. As such, the demand for national self-determination, she believed, could only express a reactionary nationalism. The proletariat, on the contrary, has no interest in the right to self-determination. Under capitalism, the demand constitutes a petty-bourgeois utopia. Under socialism, it would be rendered wholly unnecessary, as socialism would remove all national borders – at least of an economic kind – and secondary linguistic and cultural questions could be solved with little fuss.

---

6 R. Luxemburg, *The National Question*, 'Chapter 1. The Right of Nations to Self-Determination', *Marxist Internet Archive* [website].

Strategically speaking, she believed that it was extremely dangerous for the international workers' movement to raise such a demand. To do so, she believed, would merely strengthen nationalist movements, which must inevitably come under the domination of the national bourgeoisie. The strengthening of such movements would only create or exacerbate existing divisions within the working class along national lines. What was actually needed was, on the contrary, a unified struggle against the ruling class of all nations.[7]

Lenin completely agreed with Rosa Luxemburg and the SDKPiL insofar as they argued it was necessary to fight against Polish and indeed all forms of nationalism. He also agreed that larger economic units were progressive, and that the goal of Marxists was to do away with the nation-state and borders. But, in Lenin's view, this was far from exhausting the question. Many nations were suffering under the most brutal national oppression. For the masses of these countries, the struggle against such domination could form the starting point for a struggle against *all* forms of oppression. It thus contained within it a revolutionary potential. According to Lenin, it was therefore the task of revolutionaries to connect with this struggle. By doing this, Marxists could explain how liberation from national oppression in and of itself cannot solve the problems that the masses face. Rather, it would also be necessary to take the fight to the national bourgeoisie. That is, it would be necessary to turn the struggle of the working class against national oppression into a generalised struggle against class oppression. If Marxists simply *rejected* the struggle against national oppression, they would leave the door open for the bourgeoisie. The latter would then channel the struggle towards the furtherance of their own class interests, thus giving the struggle for national independence a reactionary character.

Luxemburg's disagreement with Lenin was certainly coloured by her own personal background, given that she was born in an oppressed nation: Poland. The oppression of Poland by the Russian Tsar meant that the Polish Marxists came under a great deal of pressure from petty-bourgeois Polish nationalism. As a true internationalist, Luxemburg fought mercilessly against every manifestation of this nationalism that penetrated the Polish working class. Lenin on the other hand came from Russia, which was an oppressor nation, and as such he fought consistently against any sign of Great Russian chauvinism infiltrating the Russian workers' movement.

---

7   The above summary is based on Mary-Alice Waters' excellent introduction to *Rosa Luxemburg Speaks*.

Whilst Luxemburg considered the question from a Polish point of view, Lenin regarded it with a broader perspective. According to him, the paragraph on the right of nations to self-determination in the programme of the Russian Social Democratic Labour Party did not exclude Luxemburg and the Polish Marxists, as future members of the Russian party, from concretely opposing Polish independence. Lenin actually supported the struggle of Luxemburg and the Polish comrades against every instance of Polish nationalism. But the right to self-determination took on a completely different significance in Russia, as Lenin explained:

> The question of the "right to self-determination" is of course not so important to the Polish Social-Democrats as it is to the Russian. It is quite understandable that in their zeal (sometimes a little excessive, perhaps) to combat the nationalistically blinded petty bourgeoisie of Poland, the Polish Social-Democrats should overdo things. No Russian Marxist has ever thought of blaming the Polish Social-Democrats for being opposed to the secession of Poland. These Social-Democrats err only when, like Rosa Luxemburg, they try to deny the necessity of including the recognition of the right to self-determination in the programme of the *Russian* Marxists.[8]

The Tsarist Russian Empire was made up of a great number of oppressed national minorities, which were violently subjugated by the chauvinist Great Russian regime. Lenin, like Luxemburg, knew that secession would not, in and of itself, solve the problems of the working class of any given nationality. Being exploited and oppressed by a Polish rather than a Russian capitalist would make no difference to the worker. Nonetheless, Lenin argued that it was essential for Marxists in Russia, as the oppressor nation, to demonstrate to the oppressed minorities that the Russian Marxists really did wish to bring about a complete end to Great Russian oppression and chauvinism. Emphasising the right to self-determination was imperative in order that the Russian party might clearly demonstrate to the workers of the oppressed nationalities that the Great Russian workers had no interest in maintaining their oppression. Lenin's goal was the same as Luxemburg's: to overcome the national divisions which split the world working class. But Lenin believed that real unity could not be forced onto the oppressed national minorities. Actual unity would arrive only on the basis of a voluntary association.

After the seizure of power in 1917, the Bolsheviks showed that they were quite serious about this point in their programme. By leaving the choice up to

8   V. I. Lenin, 'The Right of Nations to Self-Determination', *LCW*, Vol. 20, p. 430.

the workers of the oppressed nations themselves as to their future affiliation – which included the right to secession should they choose it – the Bolsheviks showed that they had no interest in perpetuating national oppression. It was with this policy that they won over the populations of the oppressed nations and a voluntary association of Soviet Republics became possible. Incidentally, this policy was completely abandoned upon Stalin's rise to power.

In short, Lenin's disagreement with Rosa Luxemburg was not concerned with the struggle being waged by herself and her Polish party comrades against Polish nationalism and the Polish bourgeoisie. Rather, his criticism was that from this she went too far, drawing out a generalised, principled rejection of the right of nations to self-determination in all instances. Rosa Luxemburg's categorical approach meant that, in her struggle against the Polish bourgeoisie, she inadvertently and indirectly ended up supporting the Great Russian nationalism of the Russian ruling class:

> We have seen that the following argument is one of Rosa Luxemburg's 'trump cards' in her struggle against the programme of the Marxists in Russia: recognition of the right to self-determination is tantamount to supporting the bourgeois nationalism of the oppressed nations. On the other hand, she says, if we take this right to mean no more than combating all violence against other nations, there is no need for a special clause in the programme, for Social-Democrats are, in general, opposed to all national oppression and inequality.

> The first argument, as Kautsky irrefutably proved nearly twenty years ago, is a case of blaming other people for one's own nationalism; in her fear of the nationalism of the bourgeoisie of oppressed nations, Rosa Luxemburg is *actually* playing into the hands of the Black-Hundred[9] nationalism of the Great Russians![10]

And:

> If, in our political agitation, we fail to advance and advocate the slogan of the *right* to secession, we shall play into the hands, not only of the bourgeoisie, but also of the feudal landlords and the absolutism of the *oppressor* nation.[11]

However, according to Lenin, defending the right of nations to self-determination by no means implied that Marxists ought to positively support

9   The Black-Hundred was a fascist group in Russia which, amongst other things, carried out pogroms against Jewish people and the left, and was unofficially supported by the Russian Tsar.
10 Ibid., pp. 414-5.
11 Ibid., p. 412.

every concrete demand for national self-determination, or every national movement at all times, irrespective of context, as Luxemburg claimed. Rather, Lenin understood this as essentially a *negative* right. In order to explain his position, Lenin compared the question of self-determination to divorce: just because Marxists support the *right* to divorce, this by no means implies that Marxists must demand that every married couple ought to divorce. In a similar manner, this or that concrete demand for self-determination had to be answered by a concrete analysis. What is the character of this particular movement for national self-determination? What are the relations between the classes within such a national group? And so on, and so forth. But, at all times, for Lenin the question always had to be subordinated to the class struggle. This meant that the proletariat must never, regardless of the character of the national movement, allow itself to be led by the national bourgeoisie and that it must always have an independent class position. In other words, only the proletariat could put a real stop to national oppression:

> *Insofar as* the bourgeoisie of the oppressed nation fights the oppressor, we are always, in every case, and more strongly than anyone else, *in favour* [of the struggle], for we are the staunchest and the most consistent enemies of oppression. But insofar as the bourgeoisie of the oppressed nation stands for *its own* bourgeois nationalism, we stand against [it]. We fight against the privileges and violence of the oppressor nation, and do not in any way condone strivings for privileges on the part of the oppressed nation.[12]

Lenin also criticised Luxemburg's view that self-determination could not be achieved under capitalism. Lenin highlighted the example of Norway, which achieved independence from Sweden following a referendum in 1905. The ruling class in Sweden opposed Norwegian independence, but the threat of strike action from the Swedish workers left the ruling class with no choice but to reluctantly accept the decision of the Norwegians to secede.

Lenin argued that Marxists must support the right to self-determination just as they must support other democratic demands. Lenin used the same argument that Luxemburg herself had used in *Reform or Revolution?* – namely, that it is through the struggle for democratic demands that the working class will become conscious of the limitations of bourgeois democracy. In response to Luxemburg's argument that the demand of the right of the nations to self-determination would be used by the bourgeoisie, Lenin responded that

---

12 Ibid., pp. 411-2.

all democratic demands could be used in a similar manner to deceive and distract the workers.

However, Lenin and Luxemburg were firmly in agreement on one point: that in the revolutionary party, there should exist no divisions along national lines. So it was somewhat paradoxical that in the beginning it was precisely differences over the national question that kept the Polish party outside the unified Russian party. Lenin and Luxemburg agreed that the task of Marxists is to do away with national division, and that the working class has no country, just as Marx and Engels themselves explained in *The Communist Manifesto*. Their disagreement was over how this unity could be achieved. But to both, the party was the highest organisation of the working class and therefore must represent the highest ideas, including the purest internationalism. From this, it followed that the party could not allow any room for expressions of nationalism or of any other prejudice. The vanguard of the working class must foster the greatest possible unity in the party, such that its members are knitted together as closely as possible by a voluntary class discipline across nationality.

This agreement on party unity was expressed during the party congress of 1903, in which the Poles supported the position of Lenin and the *Iskraists* on the need for a single, unified party, which was incompatible with the existence of separate groups for separate communities, each claiming the exclusive right to speak on that community's behalf. This question particularly concerned the Bund, an organisation which represented the Jewish social democrats. The Bundists demanded, as a condition of their fusion with the Russian social democrats, the exclusive right to speak on behalf of Jewish workers in the Russian Social Democratic Labour Party. *Iskra*, on the contrary, demanded that the Bund dissolve itself and become an integrated part of the party, and in this they were supported by the Poles. The Poles, however, were not ready to allow the same principles to be applied to their own party. In a speech which Luxemburg probably had a hand in writing, the two Polish delegates put forward two conditions for fusion: Firstly, that the SDKPiL become the exclusive representative of the Polish social democrats in the Russian party (a condition intended to keep the PPS outside of the party), and secondly that the SDKPiL be allowed to keep its organisational structures intact. Whether the Russians and Poles would have been able to reach an agreement on this question, we will never know. Their disagreement over the paragraph concerning the right of nations to self-determination meant that the Poles left the congress before fusion negotiations progressed that far.

The walk-out by the Polish delegates subsequently caused a certain amount of internal unrest in the Polish party. The leadership never gave the members an official report from the congress and there was discontent over the fact that Luxemburg and Jogiches had primarily conducted the negotiations themselves through informal channels, without the rest of the party necessarily being in agreement with their perspective on the question, ending finally with the breaking off of negotiations. Incidentally, this dispute led Cezaryna Wojnarowska, the Polish representative in the International Bureau, which was the leadership of the Second International, to withdraw from her role, with Rosa Luxemburg replacing her.

The Split Between Bolsheviks and Mensheviks

Later on in the 1903 congress, after the Polish delegation had departed, a number of disagreements arose in the *Iskra* group, which subsequently sparked a fierce debate not only in Russia, but in the entire International. Luxemburg threw herself into this debate on the side of the Mensheviks, and in 1904 wrote a scathing critique of *What is to Be Done?* and *One Step Forward, Two Steps Back* – the two principal books in which Lenin had laid out his view concerning the construction of a revolutionary organisation in Russia. His two books were written shortly before and shortly after the 1903 congress, respectively.

Luxemburg put forward her critique in an article titled 'Organisational Questions of the Russian Social Democracy', to which Lenin wrote a response. This polemic has since become the centrepiece of all efforts to portray Rosa Luxemburg as the democratic anti-centralist in contradistinction to Lenin, the ultra-centralist, whose ideas led directly to the dictatorship of Stalin. The anti-Leninist Bertram D. Wolfe later even re-christened Luxemburg's article, 'Leninism or Marxism?', precisely to further emphasise this presentation of the polemic. But the commonplace conceptions of both Luxemburg's and Lenin's positions on the question of organisation are wrong.

Luxemburg's developed view on questions of organisation cannot be separated from her piece on the mass strike, which she wrote in the year that followed the Russian Revolution of 1905. The revolution cast the polemic between these two Marxists in a completely different light, and clarified most of their disagreements. It will be dealt with in the next chapter. But before we come onto these events, we first must kill off the myths that directly concern the 1904 polemic between Luxemburg and Lenin.

The Background to the Split of 1903

Before we delve into Luxemburg's critique, it is first of all necessary to give something of an introduction to the split that emerged in the RSDLP during the now-fabled party congress of 1903.

The founding congress of the RSDLP was actually held in 1898, but almost immediately, the eight participants in this meeting were arrested. As such, the attempt to form a unified organisation remained largely unrealised. The party continued to consist of what were essentially unconnected groups spread out across Russia and in the exterior. One of the groups that worked most tirelessly for the holding of a proper party congress was gathered around the newspaper *Iskra* (*The Spark*), of which Plekhanov was the editor. As the first person to introduce Marxist ideas into the Russian movement, Plekhanov enjoyed an enormous authority among Russia's revolutionaries. Alongside Plekhanov, the editorial board consisted of Lenin and Martov – who later became the leaders of the Bolshevik and the Menshevik factions respectively – as well as Axelrod, Vera Zasulich and Potresov.

The congress of 1903 was larger than that of 1898 and drew in representatives from a variety of groups, serving to lay the groundwork for a real, unified Russian Social Democratic Labour Party. The *Iskra* group had argued that it was imperative that the dispersed social democratic groups unite into a centralised political party. Before the congress, Lenin expounded his view on this in the book *What is to Be Done?* Here he outlined what the *Iskraists* saw as the most important struggle: the struggle against Economism, the Russian variant of Bernstein's tendency, which Luxemburg had fought valiantly in Germany.

The Economists believed that it was the task of revolutionaries to raise the economic demands of the workers to the exclusion of engaging in political and theoretical struggle. By extension, they aimed to build the party on the model of a loose and trade union-like organisation. While the Economists spoke of an organisation of the working class, in practice they showed a condescending attitude towards the workers. According to them, workers either could not understand or were unconcerned about questions of theory. Lenin replied that, on the contrary, workers were interested not only in daily economic questions, but in understanding the world more broadly, and as such there existed a demand for theory. Indeed, Lenin explained that, without revolutionary theory there could be no revolutionary movement at all. Luxemburg had used the same arguments in her struggle against Bernstein.

The following formulation by Lenin from *What is to Be Done?* has long been the cause of dispute:

> The history of all countries shows that the working class, exclusively by its own effort, is able to develop only trade union consciousness, i.e., the conviction that it is necessary to combine in unions, fight the employers, and strive to compel the government to pass necessary labour legislation, etc. The theory of socialism, however, grew out of the philosophic, historical, and economic theories elaborated by educated representatives of the propertied classes, by intellectuals. By their social status the founders of modern scientific socialism, Marx and Engels, themselves belonged to the bourgeois intelligentsia.[13]

Based on this exaggeration, the assertion has been made that Lenin simply viewed the workers as cattle who could only be educated by a revolutionary elite. At the 1903 congress, Lenin himself admitted that he had gone too far in this passage: "We all now know that the 'economists' have gone to one extreme. To straighten matters out somebody had to pull in the other direction – and that is what I have done."[14] History has indeed shown that the working class can achieve socialist consciousness through struggle, beginning with the Chartist movement in Britain in the 1840s. But the purpose of what Lenin called his "simplified sharpness" was obvious. He wanted to hammer home the point that the task of Marxists is not to pander to the lowest common denominator, as per the Economists' misguided conception of the workers as uninterested in anything other than economic struggle and "tangible results" – i.e., reforms – in the here and now. Rather, he emphasised that Marxists have the task of *raising* the consciousness of the working class; of elevating their outlook above daily life and immediate problems. Incidentally, the workers themselves are quite aware of their daily problems. The Marxists instead must connect these daily questions to the broader political questions, and the question of the struggle against the overall system itself. That is to say, Marxists must play the role of the vanguard of the workers' struggle, not of a mere appendage to it.

The *Iskraists* also clashed with the Economists over questions of organisation. The Social Democratic circles were more or less isolated and, as such, were in need of a unifying direction and perspective. In the opinion of Lenin and the other *Iskraists*, centralisation and a central party organ were necessary

---

13 V. I. Lenin, *What is to Be Done?*, p. 33.

14 V. I. Lenin, 'Speech on the Party Programme', Second Congress of the RSDLP, 17 (30) July – 10 (23) August 1903, *LCW*, Vol. 6, p. 491.

to give a political perspective that transcended the narrow, local view that dominated in the small circles spread across Russia. Under the Tsarist regime, the average Social-Democratic small circle would generally only survive for six months. It would then find itself crushed by the secret police, after which the circle would have to be built afresh by new, inexperienced forces. This led, naturally enough, to the circles suffering chronic "dilettantism", as Lenin called it. On the contrary, he explained, the revolutionary organisation had to primarily consist of professional revolutionaries, schooled in conspiratorial work. This was by no means incompatible with simultaneously attempting to build a broader labour organisation among the workers. Nonetheless, for Lenin, building a revolutionary party of professional revolutionaries had to be a prerequisite.

In the period preceding the congress, there was agreement among the *Iskraists* over Lenin's core ideas in the struggle against Economism. This consensus encompassed individual members of *Iskra* including Martov and Plekhanov, who, following the split between Bolsheviks and Mensheviks, ended up on the opposite side of the division to Lenin.

During the congress, however, disagreements started to appear internally among the *Iskraists*. The first of these arose over the formulation of the first paragraph of the party statutes dealing with who could be a member. Lenin's proposed formulation was as follows:

> A member of the Russian Social-Democratic Labour Party is one who accepts its programme and who supports the Party both financially and by personal *participation in one of the Party organisations.*[15]

Martov proposed an alternative that defined a member of the party as one who accepts its programme and who supports the Party both financially and by personal "*work under the control and direction of one of the Party organisations*".[16] The difference was virtually unnoticeable. The small difference lay in the fact that Lenin proposed that only those who actively participated in the work of the party under the direction of the party leadership could be viewed as members, whilst Martov's proposal was somewhat more ill-defined. For instance, under Martov's definition of membership, a professor who was not prepared to work directly under the control of the party but who viewed himself as a social democrat might still be considered a member. Martov's proposal won in the end but, in Lenin's opinion, this was not a catastrophe.

---

15 V. I. Lenin, 'Account of the Second Congress of the RSDLP', *LCW*, Vol. 7, p. 27.
16 Ibid., p. 27.

The split between the two tendencies really became well defined upon the election of a new editorial board for *Iskra*. The old board had agreed to reduce the number of members from six to three: Plekhanov, Martov, and Lenin. Potresov, Zasulich, and Axelrod had played an important role in the difficult years when Marxist ideas were engaged in a tough struggle swimming against the stream. But they no longer played a role in developing the organisation and in writing for the newspaper. They had a hard time adjusting to the new tasks and in adapting themselves to the professionalism that was now required. Furthermore, a reduction in the size of the editorial board from six to three would make its work easier and would eliminate the possibility of a tied vote on the body. Despite the fact that the proposal of the new editorial board had been agreed upon beforehand, the question suddenly created outrage at the congress, as some delegates expressed a mood of pity for the three 'rejected' editors. Nonetheless, Lenin's proposal gained the majority – and henceforth his faction came to be known as the '*Bolsheviki*', meaning majority, whilst the opposing faction came to be known as the '*Mensheviki*', meaning minority.

Martov was able to win the majority for his formulation of the conditions of membership, while Lenin could win the majority for his proposal of the composition of the editorial board, because several delegates left the congress in the meantime, dissatisfied with the decisions that had been made. Among others, these included the Economists and representatives of the Jewish Bund. These tendencies accused all *Iskraists* – that is *both* Bolsheviks and Mensheviks – of wanting to introduce ultra-centralism, "organised distrust", "martial law" etc., into the party. In a word, they accused both factions of everything that Lenin would later be accused of by the Mensheviks and by Rosa Luxemburg.

After the congress, the split escalated. The Mensheviks refused to accept their position as a minority, and whipped up hostility towards Lenin and the Bolsheviks, throwing around all kinds of accusations. They also sought support from their international contacts. Lenin, for example, was accused by Karl Kautsky of excluding the three members from the editorial committee. The claim was an absurd one. The three were not excluded by Lenin. He didn't have the power to exclude anyone from the editorial board, even if he had wished to do so. Rather, they were simply not re-elected by the congress. The minority, the Mensheviks, refused to take the posts they had been elected to on the editorial board and on the central committee following the congress, despite the fact that twelve out of the fourteen local committees in Russia condemned their undemocratic behaviour. But the Mensheviks, despite being a minority, continued to sabotage the decisions of the congress and hurl accusations at the majority. They claimed that the latter wanted to introduce blind obedience, strangle all initiative, etc. Plekhanov, who had initially sided with Lenin, finally succumbed to the pressure and went over to the Mensheviks. In the end, Lenin withdrew from the editorial board of *Iskra* and as such the minority ended up taking over the central organ of the party and the rest of the leading institutions, despite having been in the minority at the congress.

At the time, the significance of the split was unclear to most. It even came as a shock to Lenin himself, although he very soon began to grasp what lay behind it. In his response to Rosa Luxemburg's criticism in 1904, he wrote:

> Anyone who does not wilfully close his eyes to what happened at our Congress is bound to see that our new division into minority and majority is only a variant of the old division into a proletarian-revolutionary and an intellectual-opportunist wing of our Party.[17]

Despite making this point, Lenin continued to make it clear that he definitely did not view the differences as being of such a principled character that they must necessarily lead to a split:

> I would willingly respond to this appeal [i.e., for an agreement with the 'Mensheviks'] for I by no means consider our differences so vital as to be a matter of life or death to the Party. We shall certainly not perish because of an unfortunate clause in the Rules![18]

The political disagreements behind the split did, however, begin to become more clear. It became increasingly obvious that the Mensheviks formed a 'soft' wing of the party that did not believe the working class had an independent role to play in a future revolution in Russia. The role of the working class, they believed, was limited to supporting the liberal bourgeoisie and of hoping the latter would bring about a parliamentary republic. The Bolsheviks, known as the 'hard' wing of the party, instead focused on the independent, revolutionary role of the working class. All of this, however, only became clear along the way. Indeed, before the final parting of the ways

---

17 V. I. Lenin, '*One Step Forward, Two Steps Back* – Reply by Lenin to Rosa Luxemburg', *LCW*, Vol. 7, p. 482.

18 V. I. Lenin, 'Second Speech in the Discussion on the Party Rules', Second Congress of the RSDLP, 17 (30) July – 10 (23) August 1903, *LCW*, Vol. 6, p. 501.

between the two factions in the split of 1912, the Bolsheviks and Mensheviks even achieved a brief reunification after the revolution of 1905. After the February Revolution of 1917, however, it became abundantly clear that the Mensheviks were moderate socialists who were not prepared to go further than the bourgeois revolution. During the Russian Civil War, they ended up on the side of the counter-revolutionary White Army, engaged in an armed struggle against the Soviet power. But, naturally, none of this could have been foreseen in 1903.

Luxemburg's Criticism of Lenin

After the congress of 1903, both the Mensheviks and the Bolsheviks attempted to win the International to their side. In this, the German SPD was a decisive factor. The Mensheviks, among whom could be found most of the 'old' leaders of the party, had made numerous acquaintances across the whole European labour movement through their many years of exile. As such, it was they who emerged with the most support in the international movement. Indeed, the Mensheviks managed to win over most of the prominent leaders of the German SPD, among whom could be counted Karl Kautsky and Rosa Luxemburg. Incidentally, it was on the basis of the requests of, and relying upon information from the Mensheviks, that Luxemburg wrote 'Organisational Questions of Russian Social Democracy'. The article was written as a response to Lenin's book *One Step Forward, Two Steps Back*, in which he evaluated the congress and subsequent split. Luxemburg's article was published both in *Iskra*, which had fallen under the control of the Mensheviks after the congress, and in the German theoretical magazine, *Die Neue Zeit*.

Luxemburg opened her article by reviewing the tasks faced by the Russian social democrats: principally, the task of transitioning from small, divided, local organisations to a unified, centralised organisation:

> The problem on which Russian Social Democracy has laboured for several years is how to effect a transition from the type of divided, totally independent circles and local clubs – which corresponds to the preparatory, mostly propagandistic phase of the movement – to an organisation such as is necessary for a unified political action of the masses in the entire state. Division and total autonomy, the self-rule of the local organisations, were the dominant characteristics of the old type of organisation. Inasmuch as the old organisational model has become unbearable and politically out of date, it is natural that the motto of the new phase of the great organisational work should be: centralism.

The accentuation of the idea of centralism was the theme of the three-year campaign of the *Iskra* in preparation for the last Party Congress, which was, in fact, the constituent assembly of the Party. The same idea is dominant among the entire young guard of Social Democracy in Russia.[19]

We can see then that Luxemburg did not argue against the necessity of centralism – a view that has so often been attributed to her. She explained that centralism was part of the very character of Social Democracy. What she criticised Lenin for was what she referred to as "*ultra-centralism*" and "Blanquism",[20] in which the revolutionaries are separated from the masses in a small conspiratorial group:

> The book [Lenin's *One Step Forward, Two Steps Back*] is the systematic presentation of the ultra-centralist viewpoint in the Russian party. The conception expressed here in a rigorous and exhaustive manner is that of a relentless centralism. The life-principle of this centralism is, on the one hand, the sharp accentuation of the distinction of the organised troops of explicit and active revolutionaries from the unorganised, though revolutionary, milieu which surrounds them; on the other hand, it is the strict discipline and the direct, decisive, and determining intervention of the central committee in all activities of the local organisations of the party. It is sufficient to remark that, for example, according to this conception the central committee has the power to organise all partial committees of the party.[21]

Furthermore, Luxemburg accused Lenin of elevating the idea of uniting a strong, organised centralism with a social democratic mass movement to the level of a "specific revolutionary-Marxist principle".[22]

Lenin's Response

At this time, Lenin was still little-known outside of Russian revolutionary circles. He wrote a response to Luxemburg's critique, but Kautsky refused to publish it. In the German party, it was primarily the Menshevik leaders who

19 R. Luxemburg, 'Organisational Questions of Russian Social Democracy', *Selected Political Writings of Rosa Luxemburg*, pp. 285-6.

20 Blanquism refers to the ideas put forward by Louis Auguste Blanqui (1805-1881) who argued that the socialist revolution had to be carried via a coup by a small conspiratorial group rather than through the political mass movement of the workers.

21 Ibid., p. 286.

22 Ibid., p. 287.

were known, and, furthermore, there was an opinion among the leadership that the Russian disagreements were unlikely to be of any interest to German social democrats.

Kautsky told Lyadov, who had been sent to put the position of the Bolsheviks:

> Look, we do not *know* your Lenin. He is an unknown quantity for us, but we do know Plekhanov and Axelrod very well. It is only thanks to them that we have been able to obtain any light on the situation in Russia. We simply cannot accept your contention that Plekhanov and Axelrod have turned into opportunists all of a sudden.[23]

Furthermore, *Vorwärts* explained their refusal to print Lenin's article, arguing that they "could not spare much space for the movement abroad, especially the Russian, which is still so young and can give so little to the German movement".[24]

The leaders of the German movement looked down on the split in the Russian party – they did not understand it, or else did not care about the questions that were at play. To them, the Russians were simply splitters who put party unity at risk and whose disagreements wasted time that could be put to better use. Thus, one could already see the germ of a narrow national view among the German social-democratic leaders, which would find its full expression in the support rendered by the SPD to the German bourgeoisie during the First World War in 1914.

According to Lenin, Rosa Luxemburg had dealt with the organisational question entirely in the abstract, and she had failed to respond to his concrete analysis of the congress, as outlined in *One Step Forward, Two Steps Back*. Rather, she had accepted the arguments of the Mensheviks as good coin, and had ended up reinforcing the same straw men that they had erected.

In order to illustrate Luxemburg's abstract approach, Lenin highlighted the 'evidence' Luxemburg had laid out as part of her allegation of Lenin's ultra-centralism, disproving it bit by bit. For instance, Luxemburg used as evidence a formulation which did not in fact belong to Lenin, but which was actually a creation of the Mensheviks, namely that he had argued for the right of the central committee to "organise all of the party's sub-committees". This formulation did not exist in Lenin's draft statutes. It was a formulation introduced into the statutes by the statutes commission of the congress,

---

23 Quoted in J. P. Nettl, *Rosa Luxemburg*, p. 284.
24 Quoted in A. Woods, *Bolshevism: The Road to Revolution*, p. 161.

in which the Mensheviks held a majority. In a similar fashion, the rest of Luxemburg's 'evidence' of Lenin's 'ultra-centralism' turned out to be equally false.

But Lenin's main line of argument against Luxemburg's article was that she had falsely believed he was defending one organisational principle against another. This, Lenin explained, was simply untrue; he was simply trying to ensure that the decisions made by the congress of 1903 were actually upheld.

> Comrade Luxemburg says, for example, that my book [*One Step Forward, Two Steps Back*] is a clear and detailed expression of the point of view of "intransigent centralism". Comrade Luxemburg thus supposes that I defend one system of organisation against another. But actually that is not so. From the first to the last page of my book, I defend the elementary principles of any conceivable system of party organisation. My book is not concerned with the difference between one system of organisation and another, but with how any system is to be maintained, criticised, and rectified in a manner consistent with the party idea.[25]

And furthermore:

> Comrade Rosa Luxemburg says that there are no two opinions among the Russian Social-Democrats as to the need for a united party, and that the whole controversy is over the degree of centralisation. Actually that is not so. If Comrade Luxemburg had taken the trouble to acquaint herself with the resolutions of the many local Party committees that constitute the majority, she would readily have seen (which incidentally is also clear from my book) that our controversy has principally been over whether the Central Committee and Central Organ should represent the trend of the majority of the Party Congress, or whether they should not. About this "ultra-centralist" and "purely Blanquist" demand the worthy comrade says not a word, she prefers to declaim against mechanical subordination of the part to the whole, against slavish submission, blind obedience, and other such bogeys. I am very grateful to Comrade Luxemburg for explaining the profound idea that slavish submission is very harmful to the Party, but I should like to know: does the comrade consider it normal for supposed party central institutions to be dominated by the minority of the Party Congress? – can she imagine such a thing? – has she ever seen it in any party?[26]

---

25 V. I. Lenin, '*One Step Forward, Two Steps Back* – Reply by Lenin to Rosa Luxemburg', *LCW*, Vol. 7, p. 474.

26 Ibid., pp. 475-6.

Politically, *What is to Be Done?* was an attack on the opportunism of the Economists. At its core, *What is to Be Done?* and *One Step Forward, Two Steps Back* did not express eternal organisational principles applicable to the party for once and for all time. Rather, these books addressed the concrete task of the moment: how can a centralised, nationwide party organisation, operating under illegality and the constant threat of the tsarist secret police, be established?

Lenin's view of the organisation was based on democratic centralism: that there must be free debate inside the party, but that once the majority has made a decision, every member must pull together to enact that decision. Once enacted, however, each of the party's actions could be once more submitted for democratic evaluation. Beyond this general position, Lenin believed that a revolutionary organisation had to be extremely adaptable to the given conditions it faced.

It was precisely the conditions faced by the Marxists in Russia in 1903 that gave the *Iskraists* reason for insisting on the necessity of conspiratorial methods, and on certain restrictions on internal democracy compared to what was possible for parties operating in those countries enjoying greater democratic freedoms and less persecution. Lenin's flexible views on organisational questions were later demonstrated in practice. In the midst of the revolutionary movement of 1905, just two years after arguing for the application of stringent criteria for party membership, Lenin now argued for opening the doors of the party to the revolutionary masses. But this was at a time when membership to such an organisation carried extreme danger with it, ensuring that careerists and opportunists would keep a safe distance from the party. In 1912, when the Mensheviks and the Bolsheviks had definitively divided into two separate parties and the Bolshevik Party was a mass force, Lenin once more argued that the party must open the doors wide to all workers who considered themselves as Bolsheviks. Such a formulation went much further even than Martov's formulation of 1903. This by no means meant that Lenin had come round to the view that Martov had in fact been correct in 1903. In 1903, the organisational task of the day was to lay the foundations of the party. This meant that it was paramount to centralise and professionalise the work of the party, especially with regard to conspiratorial methods, and to begin by building cadres, i.e., Marxists educated in the ideas and methods of Marxism.

Lenin later became concerned that *What is to Be Done?* could be misinterpreted and misused. In 1921, he wrote the following lines in response to a proposal to translate *What is to Be Done?* for the guidance of the Communist Parties springing up outside Russia:

> That is not desirable; the translation must at least be issued with good commentaries, which would have to be written by a Russian comrade very well acquainted with the history of the Communist Party of Russia, in order to avoid false application.[27]

In the preface to a collection of texts about the history of the party from the period 1895-1905, he described *What is to Be Done?* as a "controversial correction of the Economistic distortions", which it would be "incorrect to view […] in any other way". In this preface, he gives the real context to the book and the entire internal party struggle of 1903:

> The basic mistake made by those who now criticise *What Is To Be Done?* is to treat the pamphlet apart from its connection with the concrete historical situation of a definite, and now long past, period in the development of our Party.
>
> […] Unfortunately, many of those who judge our Party are outsiders, who do not know the subject, who do not realise that *today* the idea of an organisation of professional revolutionaries has *already* scored a complete victory. That victory would have been impossible if this idea had not been pushed to the *forefront* at the time, if we had not 'exaggerated' so as to drive it home to people who were trying to prevent it from being realised.[28]

The Stalinists, on the other hand, would later distort the organisational ideas developed in *What is to Be Done?* and *One Step Forward, Two Steps Back*, elevating them to the level of principles that are true regardless of time and place. The ideas developed by Lenin were part of a polemic in a relatively small organisation, aimed at combating tendencies towards the dissolution of the party into a simple trade union organisation. All the while, this small party had to operate under illegal conditions, and for this reason it was forced to put a limit on internal information, to appoint leaders from above, etc. To apply these methods to a large mass organisation in a completely different context would be fatal to the internal life of that organisation. By such means, the Stalinists have distorted Lenin's ideas on the question of organisation beyond all recognition in order to justify their own undemocratic organisations.

It was for such purposes that the Stalinists would later attempt to make use of this debate between Luxemburg and Lenin. However, whilst her criticisms

---

27 Quoted in P. Le Blanc, *Lenin and the Revolutionary Party*, p. 57.
28 V. I. Lenin, 'Preface to the Collection *Twelve Years*', *LCW*, Vol. 13, pp. 101-2.

and formulations miss the target in the case of Lenin and the Bolsheviks circa 1903, they sound remarkably exact as a description of the *bureaucratic* centralism after Stalin's seizure of power in the late 1920s. For example, Luxemburg says that:

> [...] errors made by a truly revolutionary labour movement are historically infinitely more fruitful and more valuable than even the infallibility of the best of all possible 'central committees'.[29]

Blind obedience, the "infallible central committee" which cannot be refuted, and members reduced to the position of obedient automata carrying out the commands of the leadership was characteristic of the atmosphere inside the stalinised communist parties.

But we have yet to address an important question: why did Luxemburg take such a sharp approach in her polemic against Lenin? In reality, her criticism was not so much aimed at the Bolsheviks, but rather at the bureaucratic tendencies inside the SPD.

The German SPD

Luxemburg's sharp critique of Lenin can only be understood by looking at the context in which it was written. By the time Luxemburg wrote it, she had been an active member of the German SPD for some years. In the SPD, as discussed, a process of bureaucratisation had set in among its full-time apparatus. A job in the party was far from a question of putting one's life on the line. In fact, it offered rather good career opportunities and prestige. The party apparatus increasingly represented a conservative bloc which acted as a brake on the initiative and movement of the masses. Luxemburg observed this process at close quarters and identified it much earlier than, say, Lenin, who was far away and not in a position to intimately observe the internal life and debate of the party. On the contrary, Lenin regarded the SPD as a model all the way up until 1914.

In the introduction to her article about the split in Russia, Luxemburg explained that her piece was in fact intended for a German audience, and that on several occasions she dealt with the problems of the German party rather than of the Russian. She described the conservative role played by the social-democratic leadership, which focused on parliamentary tactics to the exclusion of all else. Thus, Luxemburg was actually polemicising to a

---

29 R. Luxemburg, 'Organisational Questions of the Russian Social Democracy', *Selected Political Writings of Rosa Luxemburg*, p. 306.

far greater degree against the bureaucratic centralism which existed in the German SPD than against the ideas of Lenin:

> But what do we see in the previous developments of the Russian movement? Its most important and most fruitful tactical developments during the last decade have not been "invented" by several leaders of the movement, and even less by any directional organisations. In each case, they were the spontaneous product of the movement in action. This was the case in the first stage of the veritable proletarian movement in Russia, which began with the rudimentary outbreak of the giant strike in Petersburg in 1896, an event which inaugurated the economic mass action of the Russian proletariat. The same is true of the second phase, that of political street demonstrations, which began in a wholly spontaneous manner with the student agitation in Petersburg in March 1901. The next significant tactical turn was the mass strike in Rostov-on-Don, which opened new horizons. "By itself", with its street agitation, great outdoor meetings, and public speeches – all improvised ad hoc – this strike was such that the boldest Social Democratic daredevil would not have dared to imagine it only a few years before.

> In all these cases, in the beginning was "the act". The initiative and conscious direction of the Social Democratic organisations played an extremely limited role. This was not, however, the fault of the insufficient preparation of these specific organisations for their roles (though this may, to a certain degree, have entered into the picture), and it was certainly not that of the absence of an all-powerful central committee, as Lenin's plan presents it. On the contrary, such a central committee would more than likely have only had the effect of increasing the indecisiveness of the individual committees of the party, and have brought forth a division between the turbulent masses and the temporising Social Democracy.

> The same phenomenon – the limited role of the conscious initiative of the party direction in the formation of tactics – can be seen in Germany and in all other countries. In general, the tactical policy of Social Democracy, in its main lines, is not "invented"; it is the product of a progressive series of great creative acts in the often rudimentary experiments of the class struggle. Here too, the unconscious comes before the conscious, the logic of the objective historical process before the subjective logic of its bearers. The role of the Social Democratic leadership is, therefore, of an essentially conservative character. On the basis of these new experiences, it attempts to develop the newly won terrain of struggle to its most extreme consequences. But this attempt reverses itself and becomes a bulwark against further great innovations on a wider scale. The present tactics of German Social Democracy, for example, are universally admired for their remarkable

multiformity, suppleness, and reliability. But this only signifies that in its daily struggle our party has adapted itself wonderfully, in the smallest detail, to the parliamentary system, that it knows how to exploit the entire field of struggle offered by parliamentarism, and to do this in accord with its principles. At the same time, however, this specific tactical form so thoroughly covers the further horizons that, to a great degree, the inclination to eternalise, to consider the parliamentary tactic as purely and simply the tactic of Social Democracy makes itself felt.[30]

It is in the light cast by the context in Germany that one must consider her warning against Lenin's proposal for centralisation, which in the SPD would only serve to strengthen the conservative party bureaucracy:

> However, to grant to the party leadership such absolute powers of a negative character as Lenin does is to artificially strengthen to a dangerous extent the conservatism inherent in the essence of that institution. If the Social Democratic tactics are not created by a central committee but by the whole party – or, better still, by the whole movement – then it is obviously necessary that the individual party organisations have the elbow-room which alone makes possible the utilisation of the means presented by the given situation to strengthen the struggle, as well as to develop the revolutionary initiative. The ultra-centralism which Lenin demands seems to us, however, not at all positive and creative, but essentially sterile and domineering. Lenin's concern is essentially the control of the activity of the party and not its fruition, the narrowing and not the development, the harassment and not the unification of the movement.[31]

What Luxemburg warned would happen in the Bolshevik Party was exactly what happened in the German SPD: the conservatism of the leading layer gained the upper hand over the movement of the masses. That was demonstrated in the wake of the movement in 1905 and to an even greater degree during the German Revolution of 1918-1919, which we will return to later. The masses were not able to simply 'correct' the opportunist tendency in the SPD. Rather, it was the leaders of the SPD who managed to divert the mass movement and betray the revolution.

Nettl, who was certainly no fan of Lenin, wrote of the debate between Lenin and Luxemburg that there was no fundamental disagreement between the two, but that one had to bear in mind that Lenin and Luxemburg came from different starting points:

---

30 Ibid., pp. 292-4.
31 Ibid., pp. 294-5.

But the debate should not be seen – though it usually is – as a collision between two fundamentally irreconcilable concepts of organisation, or even revolution. First, Rosa Luxemburg's knowledge of Russian conditions was in fact more limited than might appear; her competence was substantial only by comparison with other people in Germany. [...] She was arguing from the German experience to the Russian. [...] Moreover, as we have noted, her own attitudes in the Polish party hardly bore out such demands for more 'democracy'; instead of controlling local organisations, she simply ignored them altogether.[32]

Luxemburg had emphasised the spontaneous movement of the masses as a counterweight to the conservative bureaucracy of the SPD. This bureaucracy enjoyed an enormous and almost all-encompassing apparatus, which conducted legal work within parliament and had politically drifted far from revolutionary politics. Reacting against this bureaucracy in disgust, Luxemburg ended up going to the opposite extreme.

Lenin emphasised the necessity of building a centralised – and above all a fiercely revolutionary – organisation where no such organisation as yet existed. Where it ought to be, there existed only an array of small groups, which were regularly broken up by the secret police on account of their amateurism. The difference between Luxemburg and Lenin was fundamentally a difference of approach. Lenin considered the question of organisation *concretely*: how was the organisation to be built; what were its tasks here and now, in Russia in 1903?

On the contrary, Rosa Luxemburg dealt with the question of organisation in an *abstract* manner: she agreed that an organisation was necessary, yet she did not deal concretely with how such a thing ought to be built. In Poland, it was Jogiches and other comrades who undertook the organisational side of the work, taking care of the myriad of daily tasks connected to building an organisation. In Germany, meanwhile, a strong organisation already existed.

The wisdom of hindsight is a marvellous thing. History has shown that Lenin managed to build the Bolshevik Party, which was the determining factor in leading the victorious Russian Revolution of 1917. Fatally, Luxemburg did not manage to build an organisation capable of leading the German workers to victory.

But what is easy to see in hindsight was not so clear in the midst of events. In 1903 and subsequent years, Lenin stood out as more or less the only political leader in the international labour movement who understood the

---

32 J. P. Nettl, *Rosa Luxemburg*, pp. 287-8.

necessity of building a revolutionary cadre organisation. That is to say, he alone understood the necessity of building an organisational core on the solid foundations of Marxist theory, composed of cadres firmly educated in Marxist theory and schooled in the class struggle. Once the masses began to move, such a core could constitute the spine of a future mass party.

Lenin himself saw the German SPD as his model. For him, the Bolshevik Party was merely the German party adapted to Russian conditions. Very few people supported him. Indeed, Trotsky, who ended up standing side by side with Lenin at the forefront of the Russian Revolution in 1917, held the same position as Luxemburg back in 1903. Trotsky later described how he had simply been 'lucky' in Russia, as Lenin had already built the Bolshevik Party. Luxemburg in Germany was not blessed with such luck.

Despite the fact that, fundamentally, Luxemburg was incorrect in her critique of Lenin and the Bolsheviks, in the course of the 1905 Revolution in Russia it became apparent that some of the dangers she pointed to are undeniably implicit in a centralised and professional party apparatus. We will deal with this question in the coming chapter.

In short, it is quite true that there were disagreements between Luxemburg and Lenin on the question of organisation. However, their disagreement was not a question of whether one favours a revolutionary organisation, or the necessity or otherwise of such an organisation being centralised, much less a question of whether one was for or against revolution in general. On these questions they were in wholehearted agreement. For both Luxemburg and Lenin, the essential question was: how do we most efficiently achieve the socialist revolution? The meaning of Luxemburg's critique certainly was not, as anti-Leninists have distorted it to suggest, that the organisation Lenin was building would lead to dictatorship. Rather, she was concerned that Lenin's organisation would not be able to fulfil its goal – the goal of leading the revolution. As Paul le Blanc writes:

> The essence of Luxemburg's 1904 critique, however, is the opposite of that put forward by latter-day anti-Leninists. She is *not* saying that the kind of party Lenin is building will establish a bureaucratic dictatorship once it makes a revolution. She is saying that such a party is in danger of degenerating into a sect that is *incapable of leading a revolution.*[33]

Shortly after the congress of 1903 and the polemic between Lenin and Luxemburg, the first Russian Revolution of 1905 erupted. Leaders and

---

33 P. Le Blanc, *Lenin and the Revolutionary Party*, p. 78.

organisations were put to the test in practice. Rosa Luxemburg threw herself fully into the revolution, joining Lenin on the same side of the barricade. The revolution turned her view of the Bolsheviks and the Mensheviks on its head. In her article 'Blanquism and Social Democracy', written in June 1906 in response to Plekhanov's attack against the Bolsheviks, she described how the revolution had pushed the disagreements of 1903-4 into a distant past:

> We would dispute comrade Plekhanov's reproach to the Russian comrades of the current 'majority' [the Bolsheviks] that they have committed Blanquist errors during the revolution. It is possible that there were hints of them in the organisational draft that comrade Lenin drew up in 1902 [*What is to Be Done?*], but that belongs to the past – a distant past, since today life is proceeding at a dizzying speed. These errors have been corrected by life itself and there is no danger they might recur. And we should not be afraid of the ghost of Blanquism, for it cannot be resuscitated at this time.[34]

The congress of 1903 had not led to a unified party in Russia. Rather, it had ended with a split in the *Iskra* group between Bolsheviks and Mensheviks, while the Poles had maintained their own independent party. The congress had revealed certain fundamental disagreements and had brought about a division that, with time, would prove to contain historical significance. Luxemburg sided with the Mensheviks against Lenin during the first debate because she viewed the disagreement in the Russian party through the lens of the situation prevailing in the German SPD. But shortly thereafter, everything was turned on its head. The 1905 Russian Revolution drew out the essence of the schism that lurked behind the polemics of the different wings of the party. This clarification led to a regroupment among social democrats and, thereafter, Luxemburg and Lenin ending up in the same revolutionary camp: in opposition to the Mensheviks.

34 R. Luxemburg, 'Blanquism and Social Democracy', *Marxist Internet Archive* [website].

4. Mass Strike and Spontaneity

22 January 1905[1] has gone down in history as Bloody Sunday – the day that the first shots of the 1905 Russian Revolution were fired. That fateful day set in motion a revolutionary movement that culminated, eleven months later, in a mass armed uprising against the Tsar, led by the revolutionaries. All of the processes, parties and trends that would play a part in the Russian Revolution of 1917 were already present in 1905, if only in embryo. Lenin would later describe the mighty events of 1905 as the "dress rehearsal" for the October Revolution itself. It was a revolutionary movement that tested all programmes, all parties, and all leaders. And it showed that, for all their disagreements on the question of organisation, on the crucial questions of the revolution, Luxemburg and Lenin were on the same side.

Rosa Luxemburg enthusiastically welcomed the arrival of the revolution. On 8 February she hailed the fact that, while it would not be easy, and while the struggle would be long and not without setbacks, nevertheless, the revolution had arrived:

---

1   Russia at that time followed the Julian calendar, which at that time was thirteen days behind the Gregorian calendar used by most of the capitalist world. Unless noted otherwise, I will be using the Russian dates when dealing with events in Russia, since it was that calendar that ended up being used for naming the revolutionary events (for example, the February Revolution of 1917 started on 8 March and the October Revolution started on 7 November following the Gregorian calendar). The new Soviet power changed to the Gregorian calendar in February 1918.

[A]ll lovers of civilisation and freedom, that is, the international working class, can rejoice from the bottom of their hearts. The cause of freedom has now been won in Russia; the cause of international reaction has now, on 22 January, on the streets of Petersburg, had its bloody Jena.[2] For on this day the Russian proletariat burst on the political stage as a class for the first time; for the first time the only power which historically is qualified and able to cast Tsarism into the dustbin and to raise the banner of civilisation in Russia and everywhere has appeared on the scene of action.[3]

Luxemburg analysed the situation as it progressed, both as a participant through the Polish party, SDKPiL, and in order to digest and transfer the Russian experience to Germany for the benefit of members of the SPD.

While the leaders of the SPD had narrow, national horizons, Rosa Luxemburg was an internationalist not only in words but also in deeds. To her, the Russian Revolution was of fundamental importance to the world political situation:

The connection of political and social life among all capitalist states is today so intense that the effects of the Russian revolution will be enormous throughout the whole so-called civilised world – much greater than the effect of any bourgeois revolution in history.[4]

Simultaneously with the 1905 Revolution in Russia, a large strike wave swept across Germany. The German workers watched the developing revolution in Russia with sympathy. The leadership of the SPD thus found itself pushed significantly to the left in the debate that unfolded over the so-called 'mass strike'. But it was also in the wake of these events that the beginnings of a split started to emerge between Rosa Luxemburg and the revolutionaries of the German party on the one hand, and the reformist leadership of the SPD on the other. For Luxemburg, the first Russian Revolution formed an important element in her understanding of a revolutionary mass movement. It only served to strengthen her belief in the necessity of the revolutionary overthrow of the old social system.

The 1905 Revolution

In her piece 'The Mass Strike, the Political Party and the Trade Unions', Rosa Luxemburg described the revolution and the process that led to it in detail.

---

2 Rosa Luxemburg is likely referring here to the battle of Jena and Auerstadt (German towns) in 1806 where the Prussian army was defeated by Napoleon and the French army.

3 R. Luxemburg, 'The Revolution in Russia (1905)', *Marxist Internet Archive* [website].

4 Quoted in J. P. Nettl, *Rosa Luxemburg*, p. 296.

The 1905 Russian Revolution did not materialise out of thin air. Rather, it developed following a period of years in which strikes had broken out among various layers of workers. In the same period, flames of discontent among broad layers of the population were fanned by Russia's war with Japan.

Luxemburg described how strikes broke out over seemingly minor questions but that, dialectically, these became "the straw that broke the camel's back".

The strike movement intensified, culminating in a procession of workers, women and children to present a petition to the Russian tsar on 22 January 1905. In front of the Winter Palace they read aloud their appeal. They pleaded with the Tsar to alleviate their need and misery:

> Sire, our strength is at an end! The limit of our patience has been reached: the terrible moment has come for us when it is better to die than to continue suffering intolerable torment.[5]

But the Tsar ordered the army to fire live rounds upon the peaceful protesters. All over the city, the marchers came under fire from the soldiers. The number of casualties was at the very least in the hundreds, and possibly in the thousands, whilst tens of thousands were wounded. Tsar Nicholas II was henceforth known to his subjects as 'Nicholas the Bloody'. In a mere twenty-four hours, the situation had utterly changed: the workers who hours before had appealed to the Tsar for aid, now appealed to the revolutionaries for weapons.

The following day, barricades were thrown up in the streets of St. Petersburg and 160,000 workers came out on strike. The 1905 Revolution had begun, initiating months of strikes, demonstrations and rebellions, in which one layer after another would be drawn into the struggle. The movement initially raised economic demands, but increasingly political demands were also being called: for the downfall of the Tsarist regime and a constitutional assembly.

Luxemburg described the shift as follows:

> The sudden general rising of the proletariat in January under the powerful impetus of the St. Petersburg events was outwardly a political act of the revolutionary declaration of war on absolutism. But this first general direct action reacted inwardly all the more powerfully as it for the first time awoke class feeling and class-consciousness in millions upon millions as if by an electric shock. And this

---

5   Quoted in A. Woods, *Bolshevism: The Road to Revolution*, p. 179.

awakening of class feeling expressed itself forthwith in the circumstances that
the proletarian mass, counted by millions, quite suddenly and sharply came to
realise how intolerable was that social and economic existence which they had
patiently endured for decades in the chains of capitalism. Thereupon, there began
a spontaneous general shaking of and tugging at these chains.[6]

This spontaneous mass movement of solidarity with the workers in the
capital quickly spread across the breadth of the country. The revolutionary
movement quickly reached the Russian part of Poland, which formed at that
time one of the most industrialised parts of the Russian Empire. Between
14-20 January, the Polish capital, Warsaw, was paralysed by a revolutionary
general strike. On 16 January, various socialist groups called a demonstration
in which 100,000 people participated. The city was besieged by Russian
troops, who fired on the protesters. According to official reports, sixty-four
people were killed and sixty-nine wounded. The city was placed under martial
law. In the following months, Poland would also be shaken by strikes and
demonstrations.

The Social Democratic Parties and the Revolution

The movement was by no means initiated by any of the parties. It had arisen
spontaneously, and had caught the social democrats unprepared. Before
Bloody Sunday, the workers were sceptical of and even hostile towards
the revolutionaries, who they treated for the most part as outsiders and
troublemakers. But in twenty-four hours, the attitude of the workers changed
from one of hostility to enthusiasm.

The SDKPiL immediately welcomed the revolution and threw itself
into the struggle, with a programme drafted by Luxemburg. When the
revolution broke out in 1905, the SDKPiL would have numbered a couple
of hundred members at most. But the influence of the party grew rapidly
in the course of the revolution. By February 1906, its membership had
increased to about 30,000, despite the fact that the party was once again
illegal. Meanwhile, the number of workers organised in trade unions
expanded explosively.

The revolution also led to a split in the Polish Socialist Party (PPS), between
the nationalist wing led by Piłsudski (the future dictator of Poland), who
believed that victory could only be secured by the armed actions of a small core

---

6   R. Luxemburg, 'The Mass Strike, the Political Party and the Trade Unions', *Rosa
    Luxemburg Speaks*, p. 171.

of dedicated activists, and a wing that supported the revolutionary movement of the masses. At the congress of the PPS in March 1905, Piłsudski's wing lost control of the central committee, although he maintained control of the party's armed wing.

The Russian social democracy meanwhile was in poor shape, weakened by splits and arrests when the revolution broke out. The underground conditions of its work make it impossible to accurately guess their strength. Alan Woods, author of the book *Bolshevism: The Road to Revolution*, estimates that at the end of 1905, there were perhaps 8,400 "organised Bolsheviks", while the Mensheviks probably had about the same number of people. Their influence, however, was far greater than their numerical strength would suggest. Members of the party were recognised as local leaders in their factories and communities and, as such, the reality was that hundreds of thousands of workers were actually 'organised' under the leadership of the social democrats.

During the revolution, it became clear that when Rosa Luxemburg emphasised the conservatism of the party apparatus, her words certainly contained a grain of truth. This conservatism expressed itself in sections of the Bolshevik Party, specifically among what were called the 'committeemen'. These individuals were unable to adapt themselves to the changed situation. While Lenin now argued for the doors of the party to be opened wide to the revolutionary workers, drawing the latter in as quickly as possible to leading positions in the party, the committeemen continued to cling to the old methods, structures, and perspectives with which they had become familiar and comfortable.

Conservatism of the party apparatus was not an exclusive feature of Bolshevism. In all parties, a certain routine is built up, and indeed is absolutely necessary if an organisation is to work in any way effectively. But routine becomes a problem for the party when its leading layer clings to routine and finds itself unable to adapt once the situation is transformed. The Bolshevik committeemen took Lenin's words from 1903 as eternally given principles. They had become used to working in small, underground circles and thus had a hard time connecting with the broad masses. Yet that was precisely the task that was now being posed: in order to carry through a revolution, it is not enough to simply reach the most advanced layer of workers. The revolutionary party must connect with the masses that have entered the political stage. In 1905, the key to connecting with the masses was the St. Petersburg soviet.

In the 1905 Revolution, workers' councils, known as 'soviets',[7] appeared for the first time. Emerging from the strike committees that had led the movement, the soviets were made up of representatives elected by the workers themselves. In 1917, they would form the basis of the new workers' state, but they were no invention of Marx, Engels, Lenin, or anyone else. They were organs which, in 1905, were created on the initiative of the workers themselves to solve the problem of organising the struggle. In St. Petersburg, the home of the leading soviet to which everyone looked, delegates were elected from the factories on the basis of one deputy for every 500 workers. Representatives from the larger unions and workers' parties were also eventually invited. From here, the soviets spread to fifty cities in the course of the autumn of 1905.

While Lenin welcomed the soviets as the embryonic form of workers' power, members of the Bolshevik central committee in St. Petersburg were sceptical towards them. Rather than regarding the soviet as an organ uniting the masses – and therefore as an arena in which the Bolsheviks could fight to win influence over the broader mass of workers – they saw them as being in competition with the party. The Bolshevik leadership in St. Petersburg even went as far as moving a resolution demanding the soviet subordinate itself to the party. When the resolution was rejected, the Bolshevik delegates simply departed. Such behaviour on the part of these 'committeemen' was the height of sectarianism. The soviets united around themselves all those layers which had just awoken to political life through the struggle. They presented a golden opportunity for the social democrats to connect Marxist ideas with the politically uneducated masses. Lenin was furious with the behaviour of the 'committeemen', although he eventually managed to change the party's course. However, important time had been lost.

The Culmination of the Revolution

In October 1905, the revolution reached a new stage. The Tsar's government decided to convoke an advisory Duma,[8] the so-called Bulygin Duma. All of the socialist parties in Russia and Poland described it as a farce and boycotted it. At the beginning of October, the print workers of Moscow went out on strike. This soon spread, transforming into a wave of general strikes that swept over the whole Russian Empire. The Tsar, in an attempt

---

7   The Russian word 'soviet' literally translates to 'council' in English.

8   Duma – an ancient Russian word, virtually synonymous with *soviet*. During the reign of Nicholas II the State Duma was the name given to the national parliament. There were also local dumas, the equivalent of local councils.

to ward off the revolution, issued his 'October Manifesto', which promised a new constitution and a new, more effective Duma. At the same time, he granted amnesty to political prisoners and activists in exile. The formerly illegal revolutionary struggle could now be conducted out in the open, and the revolutionary leaders – who had to remain in exile during the first months of the revolution – could now return to Russia.

Trotsky, who arrived in Kiev in February, was the only exile to return at the beginning of the revolution, and it was he who played the most prominent role as leader of the St. Petersburg soviet. Martov arrived in Russia on 17 October, and Lenin on 4 November. Rosa Luxemburg, who was deeply involved in the debate on the question of the mass strike and the importance of the Russian Revolution then raging inside the SPD, initially remained in Germany. However, she soon felt that it would be impossible to write adequate articles and analysis without directly participating in the revolution and following the Polish and Russian newspapers. As a revolutionary, she felt the powerful draw of revolution, and so she too set off for Poland, albeit arriving considerably later.

The German leaders attempted to dissuade her from going. Bebel and Mehring[9] warned that this would be putting herself at personal risk. However, by pointing out that the danger to her life was, if anything, greater because she was a woman, they only served to stiffen her resolve to leave. Kautsky's arguments had a similar effect. He tried to convince her that the place of an intellectual was behind a desk, and that her role must be to remain in Germany, continuing their successful work radicalising the SPD. She shrugged all these objections off and, on 28 December 1905, Luxemburg left Berlin under the alias, Anna Matschke. On account of a rail workers' strike, she was forced to smuggle herself aboard a troop transport. The only civilian and woman on the train, she reached Warsaw on 30 December 1905. Although it was not yet clear to its participants, the revolution had in fact already reached its climax by this point, and the movement was in decline by the time Luxemburg reached Poland.

The forces of reaction were preparing a crackdown. The October Manifesto of the Tsar had been nothing but a manoeuvre to buy time in order to prepare

---

9   Franz Mehring (1846-1919) – long-standing member of the SPD, contributor to *Die Neue Zeit* and editor of *Leipziger Volkszeitung* between 1902-07. He moved towards a revolutionary position during the First World War, supporting Bolshevism and the October Revolution. Co-founder of the Spartacus League and the KPD, together with Rosa Luxemburg.

to crush the revolution. In the first month after the manifesto's publication, 4,000 people were murdered in pogroms[10] that targeted Jews, socialists, and intellectuals. On 2 December, the deputies of the St. Petersburg soviet were arrested, including its chairman, Leon Trotsky. The workers of St. Petersburg were exhausted, and the epicentre of the revolution moved to Moscow, where the workers mounted a general strike that developed into an armed uprising. As the uprising developed, it spread to other cities. But the Bolshevik Party was too weak to exert a decisive influence. The soviet vacillated. Finally, the uprising in Moscow was isolated and crushed. On 18 December, the leadership of the Moscow soviet was forced to call off the struggle and the uprising was over. Bloody repression and mass arrests followed. Outbreaks of armed uprisings happened in other places, but they were disconnected from one another and were all crushed.

Although it was difficult to accurately assess whether the revolution had suffered a final defeat or a mere temporary setback, Luxemburg had a feel for the direction events were heading in. She was of the opinion that the method of the general strike had played out its role by now, and that the only way forward would be on the basis of an armed uprising. In a letter to Luise and Karl Kautsky written on 20 December 1905 (Julian calendar), she wrote:

> To characterise the situation in two words (but only for yourselves): the general strike has just about *failed* – most of all in St. Petersburg, where the railway men made no real effort to carry it through [...] Everywhere people are hesitant and in a state of expectancy. The reason for all this is the simple circumstance that a *mere general strike alone* has ceased to play the role it once had. Now nothing but a direct, general fight on the streets can bring about the decision, but for this the right moment must be prepared more carefully. This expectant condition of affairs may therefore continue for a while, unless indeed some 'accident' – a new manifesto, etc. – brings about a spontaneous and sudden uprising.[11]

Beginning in March 1906, the Tsar launched a counter-revolutionary offensive. A wave of arrests, sometimes followed by summary execution, swept the country and the secret police stepped up their infiltration of the revolutionary organisations. Many of the SDKPiL's leaders were arrested, the rest returning to Krakow (at that time occupied by the Austro–Hungarian Empire), barring a few specialists in conspiratorial methods.

---

10 Pogrom – a violent riot directed at ethnic persecution and purging, particularly of Jewish people. Was also orchestrated as a political tool by the tsarist secret police.

11 R. Luxemburg, *Letters to Karl and Luise Kautsky from 1896 to 1918*, p. 98.

Luxemburg planned to return to Berlin in mid-March. However, on 4 March, Rosa Luxemburg and Leo Jogiches were swept up by the police. Initially, both managed to keep up their aliases: Anna Matsche and Otto Engelmann. But after the police searched the home of Rosa's sister and found photographs, hiding her identity became untenable. Jogiches managed to keep up his alias until mid-June. Luxemburg was crammed into a cell designed for one person along with thirteen others – luckily, all of them political prisoners. On 11 April, she was moved to the infamous Tenth Pavilion in the Warsaw Citadel. Here, her family was allowed to visit her and witnessed the abhorrent conditions of the prison with their own eyes. Much later, Rosa Luxemburg described the first visit from her brothers and sisters in the Warsaw Citadel in a letter to Sophie Liebknecht:

> There, one is brought out into an actual double cage of wire netting: that is to say, a little cage stands within a larger one, and you must converse through the moiré-like glimmer of the double mesh. On top of it all, since the meeting took place right after a six-day hunger strike, I was so weak that the captain of the fortress nearly had to carry me into the visiting room, and in the cage I had to hold onto the wire with both hands, which probably reinforced the impression of a wild animal in a zoo.
>
> The cage stood in a fairly dark corner of the room, and my brother pressed his face very close to the wire: "Where are you?" he asked over and over, wiping from his [glasses] the tears which kept him from seeing me.[12]

Luxemburg was convicted of serious crimes against the state. Her family did their best to free her, first by proposing an appeal to the Russian Prime Minister, which Luxemburg decidedly rejected. She likewise fiercely rejected appealing to the German consul, but her family nonetheless contacted the German authorities. Her brother travelled to Berlin to raise money for her bail. He succeeded in raising the required sum, most likely from the executive committee of the SPD, a fact of which Rosa was unlikely to have been aware at the time. Had she known, she would most likely have rejected the money so as to be free from any feeling that she owed the executive committee anything. On 8 July 1906, she was released on bail on the grounds of medical concerns. She was free, but she was not permitted to leave Warsaw.

Jogiches was accused of "plotting to overthrow by armed violence the monarchical form of government as laid down in the constitution" and,

---

12 R. Luxemburg, 'To Sonja Liebknecht, 18 February 1917', *The Letters of Rosa Luxemburg* [1978], p. 180.

ironically, of "trying to obtain the independence of Poland".[13] Jogiches was put on trial in January 1907, and sentenced to eight years of hard labour for high treason and military desertion. Nevertheless, he succeeded in fleeing shortly after the completion of his trial.

The revolution of 1905 had been defeated. However, it had not all been in vain. As mentioned, Lenin aptly described the 1905 Revolution as the dress rehearsal for the October Revolution of 1917. In that year, all leaders and parties were tested, and the dividing lines of the Russian and international labour movement were clearly drawn.

Luxemburg and the Bolsheviks

Rosa Luxemburg was finally permitted to leave Warsaw and go to Finland on 8 August 1906. In the second week of August 1906 she arrived in Kuokkala, where all the main leaders of the Bolshevik party were based. Here they could maintain close contact with the Russian capital from a position of relative safety. Whilst here, Luxemburg was able to devote a great deal of time to discussing the political and theoretical lessons of the revolution:

> […] Rosa Luxemburg spent much of her time with Lenin and his immediate Bolshevik circle. She had met him personally only once before, during 1901 in Munich, through the good offices of Parvus who, in the early halcyon days of *Iskra*, had been the only contact with the German Social Democrats which Russian conspiratorial caution had permitted. Now at last, after polemics and dislike at a distance, they got to know each other well. Evening after evening she sat in Lenin's ground-floor flat in the house of the Leiteisen family in Kuokkala and talked over the Russian revolution at length with Lenin, Zinoviev,[14] Kamenev and Bogdanov. She made a considerable impression on them; "the first Marxist who was able to evaluate the Russian revolution correctly and as a whole". A personal sympathy between Lenin and Rosa Luxemburg – based, like all of Lenin's friendships, on mutual intellectual respect – was born in this time and was to survive for six years until party differences drowned it once more in the froth of polemics. Even then a spark of personal sympathy always survived the renewed hostilities […][15]

The revolution had brought Luxemburg closer to the Bolsheviks while her view of the Mensheviks had grown more and more critical. According to

---

13 J. P. Nettl, *Rosa Luxemburg*, p. 359.

14 Grigory Zinoviev (1883-1936) – Bolshevik party leader, president of the Communist International 1919-1926.

15 Ibid., pp. 356-7.

Luxemburg, it was the Bolsheviks who had behaved as revolutionaries ought to behave, and she fundamentally agreed with their analysis of the situation. Finally, she agreed with the assessment of the Bolsheviks regarding the goal of revolution:

> If today the Bolshevik comrades speak of the dictatorship of the proletariat, they have never given it the old Blanquist meaning; neither have they ever made the mistake of *Narodnaya Volya*,[16] which dreamt of "taking power for itself" (*zachvat vlasti*). On the contrary, they have affirmed that the present revolution will succeed when the proletariat – all the revolutionary class – takes possession of the state machine. The proletariat, as the most revolutionary element, will perhaps assume the role of liquidator of the old regime by "taking power for itself" in order to defeat counter-revolution and prevent the revolution being led astray by a bourgeoisie that is reactionary in its very nature. No revolution can succeed other than by the dictatorship of one class, and all the signs are that the proletariat can become this liquidator at the present time.[17]

The quote above was a defence of the Bolsheviks' goal of the dictatorship of the proletariat[18] against an attack from Plekhanov who had accused the Bolsheviks in the 1905 Revolution of Blanquism. Here it is important to bear in mind that the term 'dictatorship of the proletariat' was taken from Marx, long pre-dating the era of Hitler and Stalin, and the connotations that are associated with the word 'dictatorship' today. On the contrary, the term was inspired by a practice from the oldest Roman Republic, in which the Republic would appoint a leader and give him absolute authority during extraordinary situations such as wars. This would last until he had completed his task but for no longer than six months. The dictatorship of the proletariat is a term referring to a transitional society, in which the working class has seized power and established itself as a ruling class. Using its control of the state, the proletariat would thus prevent the former ruling class from

---

16 *Narodnaya Volya* (*People's Will*) – Russian revolutionary organisation formed in 1879. Worked towards general democratic rights and the elimination of absolutism. Their means were, amongst others, terror against the top of society. In 1881, they killed Tsar Alexander II.

17 R. Luxemburg, 'Blanquism and Social Democracy', *Marxist Internet Archive* [website].

18 Nettl and others claim that Luxemburg did not support the dictatorship of the proletariat, but the quote above, as well as many others, prove that this is wrong. Luxemburg supported the idea of "the dictatorship of the proletariat" as it was put forward by the Bolsheviks.

reconquering its lost power and privileges. We can contrast this idea with the dictatorship of the bourgeoisie today, in which the bourgeoisie as a class is completely dominant, irrespective of whether the government takes the form of a parliamentary democracy or a military dictatorship.

Luxemburg declared herself to be in agreement with the Bolsheviks, and explained that the establishment of the 'dictatorship of the proletariat' had nothing in common with a coup conducted by a minority. The shared understanding of Luxemburg and Lenin was founded on the classic Marxist conception of the state, as described by Friedrich Engels in *The Origin of the Family, Private Property and the State*. Engels explained that, in the final analysis, the state can be reduced to "special bodies of armed men",[19] whose task it is to defend the property relations and dominant position of the ruling class. In all previous societies, the ruling class has constituted a small minority of the population: slave owners, feudal lords, capitalists. Their respective states ensured the class domination of a minority section of society. A workers' state would, on the contrary, for the first time in history, constitute a state in the interest of the majority. It would thus possess a quite distinct character to all forms of state that had preceded it. With the collectivisation of the means of production, a path would be cleared to a more extensive democracy, precisely because it would also encompass the economic sphere, which, under capitalism, is governed exclusively by the profit motive. With the abolition of class contradictions generally, the foundations of the state itself would disappear and as such it would start to wither away.[20]

Rosa Luxemburg's imprisonment prevented her from participating in either the SDKPiL's congress in June 1906, or in the unity congress of the Russian party in 1906, in which the Mensheviks – having been pushed to the left by the revolution – reunited once more with the Bolsheviks. At the 1906 congress, the SDKPiL too had joined the united party, and had supported the Bolsheviks on all of the most important political questions. Not until the party congress of the Russian Social Democratic Labour Party of 1907 in London could Luxemburg finally participate. In this congress, all the important leaders of the Russian movement participated: Plekhanov, Martov, Lenin and Trotsky among others were all in attendance, discussing the lessons of the 1905 Revolution.

---

19 V. I. Lenin, *State and Revolution*, p. 10.

20 For a more thorough introduction to the Bolsheviks' understanding of the workers' state, we refer to Lenin's *State and Revolution*.

Rosa Luxemburg made a long speech on behalf of the Polish organisation in which she presented the views of the Polish comrades. The vast majority of Luxemburg's speech was a razor-sharp critique of the Mensheviks, which can leave no doubt as to the fact that Rosa Luxemburg and the Polish comrades were on the side of the Bolsheviks. Luxemburg criticised the Mensheviks for having put their faith in the bourgeoisie and the liberal parties, and for surrendering the class independence of the proletarian struggle. According to Luxemburg, the Mensheviks had not pursued a revolutionary proletarian policy, but rather had subjugated the interests of the working class to those of the bourgeoisie and its parties. Rather than spurring on the movement, the Mensheviks had attempted to hold back the workers from any revolutionary initiative.

Luxemburg devoted special attention to Plekhanov in her contribution, criticising him in biting terms. In Luxemburg's opinion, Plekhanov had summed up the attitude of the Mensheviks magnificently when, in the wake of the revolution, he lamented, "they should not have taken up arms!" Rosa Luxemburg agreed with Lenin, who responded:

> On the contrary, we should have taken to arms more resolutely, energetically and aggressively: we should have explained to the masses that it was impossible to confine ourselves to a peaceful strike, that a fearless and relentless armed fight was indispensable.[21]

To the Mensheviks' critique of the Bolsheviks for being too "narrow minded" and "intolerant", Luxemburg responded that these features were simply an expression of the fact that the Bolsheviks were forced to defend the fundamental principle of the independent class politics of the proletariat against the opposition of the Mensheviks:

> You comrades of the right wing [Luxemburg is here referring to the Mensheviks – *MF*] complain at length about narrowness, intolerance, and a certain mechanistic disposition in the views of our comrades, the so-called Bolsheviks. [Cries: "Among the Mensheviks".] On that matter we agree with you completely. [Applause.]
>
> It is possible that Polish comrades, who are accustomed to thinking more or less in ways adopted by the West-European movement, find this particular steadfastness even more startling than you do. But do you know, comrades, where all these disagreeable features come from? These features are very familiar to someone acquainted with internal party relations in other countries: they represent the

---

21 Quoted in A. Woods, *Bolshevism: The Road to Revolution*, p. 265.

typical spiritual character of that trend within socialism that has to defend the very principle of the proletariat's independent class policy against an opposing trend that is also very strong. [Applause.]

Rigidity is the form taken by Social-Democratic tactics on the one side, when the other side represents the formlessness of jelly that creeps in every direction under the pressure of events. [Applause from the Bolsheviks and parts of the Centre.][22]

We can see then that Luxemburg was in agreement with the Bolsheviks as far as the goal of the dictatorship of the proletariat, and the necessity of an armed uprising was concerned. However, she also expressed a critique of the Bolsheviks, although not of a fundamental character: she criticised them for having placed too much emphasis on the technical rather than the political side of the revolution:

Of course, we think it necessary to clarify for the broad masses of the proletariat that their direct confrontation with the armed forces of reaction, a general popular uprising, is the sole outcome of the revolutionary struggle that can guarantee victory as the inevitable finale of its gradual development, although it is not within the capacity of Social Democracy to prescribe and prepare this outcome by technical means.[23]

Her critique is pointing towards the discussion of the relationship between the spontaneous movement of the masses and the role of the party, a discussion which we shall return to later in this chapter.

Luxemburg and the Permanent Revolution

In the Russian social-democratic movement, up to and beyond 1905, there was a lively discussion about the character of the Russian revolution. The Mensheviks believed that the revolution would be a bourgeois revolution, and on this account that the bourgeoisie must lead it, while the working class would be reduced to a supporting role, subordinating its own interests to those of the bourgeoisie.

The Bolsheviks were in full agreement with the Mensheviks on the idea that the tasks of the coming revolution were bourgeois and national-

---

22 R. Luxemburg, '"The Role of the Bourgeoisie and the Proletariat in the Russian Revolution", Speech to the Fifth (London) Congress of the Russian Social-Democratic Labour Party (25 May 1907)', in R. B. Day and D. Gaido (eds.), *Witnesses to Permanent Revolution*, p. 559.

23 Ibid., p. 557.

democratic. The tasks posed before the revolution were: the removal of the autocracy and the formation of a republic, the establishment of parliamentary democracy, the distribution of land to the peasantry, and the unification of the nation. However, this was where agreement ended. Disagreeing with the Menshevik conception of the role of the bourgeoisie in the movement, the Bolsheviks were of the opinion that the bourgeoisie would play a reactionary role. The working class, therefore, could in no way support the bourgeoisie, and had to firmly maintain complete class independence. Rather than tailing the bourgeoisie, the working class, in alliance with the peasantry, ought to take upon itself the role of eradicating the last vestiges of feudalism. That is, they must carry through a consistent democratic revolution. The Bolsheviks summed up their programme in the slogan: "the democratic dictatorship of the workers and peasantry".

But there was also a third position developed by the man who had led the St. Petersburg soviet during the revolution: Leon Trotsky. Trotsky agreed with the Bolsheviks that the bourgeoisie was utterly reactionary. However, he criticised their slogan of "the democratic dictatorship of the workers and peasantry". According to Trotsky, whilst Lenin and the Bolsheviks' slogan correctly expressed the need for a revolutionary alliance of the proletariat and the poor peasantry, it did not answer the question of which between the two would be the leading force in the revolution, thus determining its character and direction. Once the workers and peasants actually seized power, the contradictions between these two classes would reveal themselves. Indeed, that is precisely what happened after the October Revolution in 1917.

Trotsky did not believe that the future revolution in Russia would limit its scope to that of a bourgeois revolution. This idea, which he had begun formulating even before the 1905 Revolution, was developed by Trotsky to a far greater degree than any other contemporary Marxist, and has come to be known as the theory of 'permanent revolution'.

To give a brief summary of this idea: according to Trotsky, Marxists had to discard the schematic view, then dominant, that all countries must necessarily pass through the same stages of development: from feudalism, to capitalism, and then socialism. On a global scale, capitalism had developed into world imperialism, at the forefront of which were countries such as England and France. The domination of the world market forced all nations to enter into the web of global capitalist relations, irrespective of their present stage of development. This meant that a country like Russia could hardly follow the same path of development as the older capitalist nations, which had begun their process of development long before the rise of global imperialism. The backward countries were thrown into global capitalist relations at their given stage of development, despite the fact that they were yet to carry out their bourgeois revolutions. In a process that Trotsky termed 'combined and uneven development', the imperialist countries exported capital to and established industries in the less developed countries, and thus laid the foundations of modern industrial centres in the midst of backward, agrarian economies such as that of Russia.

In Russia, this meant that much of the bourgeoisie developed out of the old feudal aristocracy. It was often the aristocrat who established themselves as a capitalist, or else the two would be connected through old family ties. The enormous financial power of the imperialist countries meant that the Russian bourgeoisie was completely dependent on international capital, which thus came to own practically the entirety of Russia's industrial and financial sectors. At the same time, foreign investment in industry spurred the development of a sizeable proletariat. These factors combined to ensure that the bourgeoisie could never play a progressive role in the coming Russian Revolution. They could neither do away with the old aristocracy to whom they were connected – as the Great French Revolution had done – nor could they free the nation from the dominance of imperialism, to which they were likewise connected. At the same time, the working class had grown incomparably stronger than at the time of any of the classic bourgeois revolutions that had gone before. By the twentieth century, the bourgeoisie trembled with fear at the thought of arousing a revolutionary movement that would raise the working masses to their feet. On the contrary, the bourgeoisie would pose as defenders of the *status quo*, which formed the very foundation of their wealth and privileges. The Russian bourgeoisie was thus unable to lead a bourgeois, national-democratic revolution, the tasks of which would be the implementation of democracy, land reform, and the establishment of a nation state free from the domination of foreign imperialism. Only the proletariat could carry through the tasks of the bourgeois revolution. But once the proletariat was on the move, Trotsky explained that it would not stop at implementing the tasks of the bourgeois revolution against the opposition to the national bourgeoisie itself. The proletariat would not settle for formal equality but would demand social equality, and thus it would begin the tasks of the socialist revolution. In other words, the revolution would become permanent.

But the revolution would also become 'permanent' in another sense: it would have to spread internationally. Marx already explained that the global character of capitalism meant that socialism had to be international. But before Trotsky came forward with his theory of permanent revolution, no Marxist had yet foreseen that capitalism might break at its weakest link. Marx, who lived at a time when revolution and counter-revolution swept the heart of Europe, imagined that the socialist revolution would take place first in one of the most advanced capitalist countries. In the opinion of Leon Trotsky, conditions had changed since Marx's times and the socialist revolution could indeed begin in a backward country, but should it do so it was all the more paramount that it spread to the developed capitalist countries with their advanced level of technology, education, culture etc.

When Stalin began his crusade against Rosa Luxemburg in 1931, one of the accusations he levelled against her was that it was she who was behind the theory of the permanent revolution. As Trotsky pointed out, this was another of Stalin's lies. Trotsky himself rather than Luxemburg was the one behind this theory. Nonetheless, it is true that her analysis closely resembled that of Trotsky.

In his autobiography, *My Life*, Trotsky described how, at the 1907 congress, Rosa Luxemburg agreed with him on the theory of permanent revolution:

> On the question of the so-called permanent revolution, Rosa took the same stand as I did. In this connection, Lenin and I once had a half-humorous conversation in the lobby. The delegates stood about us in a close ring. "It is all because she does not speak Russian too well", he said, referring to Rosa. "But then, she speaks excellent Marxism", I retorted. The delegates laughed, and so did we.[24]

At the 1907 congress, Luxemburg sharply criticised the Mensheviks' conclusions that the working class ought to subordinate itself to the bourgeoisie and its parties. She lined up fully with the Bolsheviks and Trotsky in holding the view that the bourgeoisie and the liberal parties would play a counter-revolutionary role, completely agreeing that the proletariat had to play an independent role.

Luxemburg also agreed with Trotsky's critique of the Bolshevik position on the peasantry, and on the slogan of "the democratic dictatorship of the workers and peasants". In the opinion of Luxemburg and Trotsky, history had shown that the peasants cannot play an independent role and must follow one or other of the urban classes: the bourgeoisie or the proletariat. Luxemburg expressed her view as follows in her concluding remarks to the congress:

---

24 L. Trotsky, *My Life*, p. 178.

But precisely because they are utopian and incapable of fulfilment by their nature, peasant movements are completely unable to play any independent role and are subordinated in every historical context to the leadership of other classes that are more energetic and more clearly defined.[25]

It was obvious to Luxemburg that the peasantry must be brought under the leadership of the proletariat:

It is clear that political leadership of the chaotic peasant movement in Russia today, and the exercise of influence over it, are the natural historical responsibility of the conscious proletariat.[26]

To which Trotsky replied at the congress:

I am pleased to say that the point of view presented here by comrade Luxemburg on behalf of the Polish delegation is very close to the one that I have defended and continue to defend. Any possible differences between us are more a matter of individual nuances than of political direction. Our thinking moves on one and the same track of materialistic analysis.[27]

Both Luxemburg and Trotsky were later criticised by the Stalinists for 'ignoring the role of the peasantry', but this is a false accusation. Luxemburg and Trotsky believed, in opposition to the Mensheviks, that the peasants would play an objectively revolutionary role by demanding a solution to the land question, which, in the last analysis, could not be solved without a socialist revolution. Luxemburg summarised the revolutionary potential of the peasantry thus:

And in this still undifferentiated mass of the Russian peasantry, which the current revolution has put in motion, there are important strata that are not just our temporary political allies but also our natural future comrades. To disavow subordinating them even now to our leadership and our influence would be precisely an act of sectarianism that is unforgivable on the part of the revolution's leading detachment. […]

As for the peasantry, despite all the confusion and contradictoriness of its demands, and despite all the fog and ambiguity of its efforts, in the current revolution it is an objectively revolutionary factor because, by placing on the revolution's order of the day, in the most acute manner, the question of revolutionary land change,

---

25 R. Luxemburg, 'The Role of the Bourgeoisie and the Proletariat in the Russian Revolution'. *Witnesses to Permanent Revolution*, p. 564.

26 Ibid., p. 564.

27 Quoted ibid., p. 544.

it thereby poses a question that cannot be solved within the limits of bourgeois society and points beyond that society by its very nature.[28]

We can see then that there was agreement between Luxemburg and Trotsky on the question of the role of the peasantry, and on their attitude towards the Bolsheviks' slogan. Whether or not Luxemburg agreed with Trotsky's theory of the permanent revolution in its totality is somewhat less clear. She did not mention the theory by name, and when it came to describing the character of the revolution, she did so in terms that were not as clear as those of Trotsky. On numerous occasions she stated that the tasks of the revolution were bourgeois-democratic and that all talk of going beyond them was nonsense. In her article, 'Blanquism and Social Democracy', she wrote, for instance, that the proletariat would surely seize power, but that once in power, it would constitute a minority and thus power would shift to a constituent assembly elected by the people in its entirety.

But Luxemburg also stated many times that the Russian revolution would *not* simply be a bourgeois revolution. According to Rosa Luxemburg, the Russian Revolution of 1905 had closed a period of almost sixty years of peaceful parliamentary rule by the bourgeoisie, and had opened a transitional period from capitalist to socialist society. It made no sense to speculate as to how long this transitional period would last. Thus, according to Luxemburg, the revolution in Russia would have a character that would be *transitional* between that of the bourgeois revolutions of the past and the socialist revolution of the future:

> Thus, *in its content*, the present revolution in Russia goes far beyond previous revolutions, and, in its methods, it cannot simply follow either the old bourgeois revolutions or the previous – parliamentary – struggles of the modern proletariat. It has created a new method of struggle, which accords both with its proletarian character and with the combination of the struggle for democracy and the struggle against capital – namely, the revolutionary mass strike. In terms of content and methods, it is therefore a completely new type of revolution. Being formally bourgeois-democratic, but essentially proletarian-socialist, it is, in both content and method, *a transitional form* from the bourgeois revolutions of the past to the proletarian revolutions of the future, which will directly involve the dictatorship of the proletariat and the realisation of socialism.[29]

---

28 Ibid., p. 563.

29 R. Luxemburg, 'The Russian Revolution (20 December 1905)', in R. B. Day and D. Gaido (eds.), *Witnesses to Permanent Revolution*, p. 586.

Luxemburg believed, then, that the revolution in Russia would differ from earlier bourgeois revolutions first of all because the proletariat, led by the Social Democrats, would be at the fore, and because the struggles for formal bourgeois and proletarian-socialist demands would merge:

> The Russian proletariat, however, who are destined to play the leading part in the bourgeois revolution, enter the fight free from all illusions of bourgeois democracy, with a strongly developed consciousness of their own specific class interests, and at a time when the antagonism between capital and labour has reached its height. *This contradictory situation finds expression in the fact that in this formally bourgeois revolution, the antagonism of bourgeois society to absolutism is governed by the antagonism of the proletariat to bourgeois society, that the struggle of the proletariat to bourgeois society is directed simultaneously and with equal energy against both absolutism and capitalist exploitation,* and that the programme of the revolutionary struggle concentrates with equal emphasis on political freedom, the winning of the eight-hour day, and a human standard of material existence for the proletariat. This two-fold character of the Russian Revolution is expressed in that close union of the economic with the political struggle and in their mutual interaction which we have seen is a feature of the Russian events and which finds its appropriate expression in the mass strike.[30]

Luxemburg agreed with Trotsky, and Lenin for that matter, that the conditions for realising socialism in Russia were not present and that for this reason international revolution was necessary. She put forward the perspective that the Russian Revolution would be a "forerunner of the new series of proletarian revolutions of the West".[31] She was somewhat less optimistic than Trotsky, however, whose perspective was based on the Russian Revolution spreading, and the workers of the West coming to the aid of the Russian workers.

On the contrary, Luxemburg believed that a temporary defeat of the Russian workers was the most likely outcome:

> [...] I even think that if the Russian working class rises completely to its task, that is, if through its actions it carries revolutionary developments to the most extreme limit permitted by the objective development of social relations, then

---

30 R. Luxemburg, 'The Mass Strike, the Political Party and the Trade Unions', *Rosa Luxemburg Speaks*, pp. 201-2 (my emphasis – *MF*).

31 Ibid., p. 203.

what will almost inevitably await it at this limit will be a major temporary defeat.[32]

But she by no means took this to mean that social democrats should limit their work towards a revolution. In her opinion, "it is a poor leader and a pitiful army that goes in to battle only when it knows in advance that victory is in its pocket." The defeats were simply "inevitable historical steps that are leading to the final victory of socialism."[33]

Luxemburg and Trotsky differed as far as the possibility of a revolution in Russia spreading internationally was concerned. They therefore considered different likely outcomes of the revolution. Luxemburg thought the coming Russian Revolution would be a more isolated affair, as was the case in 1905. Trotsky, on the contrary, held the perspective that the coming revolution would spread internationally, as indeed it did in the years that followed the October Revolution of 1917.

In short, we can say that Rosa Luxemburg largely shared Trotsky's analysis as laid out in his theory of the permanent revolution, but she did not follow that analysis as consistently and far as Trotsky, and therefore did not draw such clear and far-sighted conclusions.

Regardless of their disagreements in 1905 and those that surfaced in subsequent years, when the Russian Revolution broke out in 1917, Lenin, Luxemburg and Trotsky were in agreement on all fundamental questions. In Russia in 1917, the theory of the permanent revolution was confirmed in practice. The bourgeoisie played a counter-revolutionary role. The working class took the leadership and it did not halt at the bourgeois-democratic tasks of the revolution. Rather, it moved on to the socialist revolution, seizing power in its own hands, under the leadership of the Bolsheviks, in the course of the October Revolution. And the Russian Revolution provided precisely the spark that ignited the world revolution, which Lenin, Trotsky and Luxemburg all emphasised was an essential factor in the survival of the revolution in Russia. There can be no question that Luxemburg would have harshly rejected Stalin's so-called theory of 'socialism in one country', which he put forward after Lenin's death in 1924. In fact, she would not have even been capable of conceiving of anyone putting such an idea forward and seriously calling it 'Marxist'.

---

32 R. Luxemburg, 'The Role of the Bourgeoisie and the Proletariat in the Russian Revolution'. *Witnesses to Permanent Revolution*, p. 566.

33 Ibid.

Strikes and Radicalisation in Germany

When the revolution broke out in Russia in early 1905, it was initially met with sympathy on the part of German SPD, although the party was not known for its sympathy or understanding of the Russian revolutionaries, their illegal work, and their internal political 'chaos' that contrasted so starkly with the 'order' prevailing in the German party. This opinion began to change especially when German authorities began persecuting Russian exiles. All across the country, meetings were held in solidarity with the revolution, with SPD leaders delivering fiery speeches, and financial collections being held. Amongst the German workers, who looked up to the example being set by the Russian Revolution, a clear process of radicalisation was underway.

Amidst the broader layers of the German working class too, something was stirring. In the first months of 1905, the number and intensity of strikes rose. In 1905, 507,964 workers participated in work stoppages, more than the entire decade of the 1890s, and more than the five previous years put together.[34] Under the influence of events in Russia, the class struggle in Germany became increasingly intense, whilst the connection between economic and political questions grew stronger – a point that Luxemburg described as a special characteristic of revolutionary periods. Simultaneously, a mass movement in the state of Prussia arose around the changing of electoral law, something that the SPD was particularly heavily focused on. In the course of this movement, the question was posed of using the general strike as a weapon. This was the first time the question of a general strike had been placed on the agenda in Germany as a means of political struggle.

The revolutionary movement in Russia and the escalating class struggle in Germany pushed the leadership of the SPD to the left. They became more open, for instance, to the idea of a general strike, termed a "political mass strike"[35] in Germany, being a legitimate tactical weapon in the class struggle. Already in 1904, the debate on the general strike had begun in *Die Neue Zeit*. Until then, the general strike had primarily been something that anarchists and syndicalists had argued for, and for that reason it had met strong opposition in social-democratic circles. In 1902, the Belgian workers

---

34 The numbers are from C. E. Schorske, *German Social Democracy, 1905-1917: The Development of the Great Schism*.

35 This assessment is made in C. E. Schorske, *German Social Democracy, 1905-1917: The Development of the Great Schism*. Therefore, I will not be distinguishing between mass strike and general strike.

had launched a general strike in an attempt to win the right to vote, and in 1903 the Dutch workers' movement had used the same weapon to fight an anti-strike law. Meanwhile, the Swedish social democrats had called a large protest strike in order to force a new electoral law through parliament. Even avid revisionists like Bernstein put forward the possibility of a general strike – although only ever as a defensive measure. The debate was no longer about whether a mass strike was possible, but whether the party leadership could call for it.

When the 1905 Russian Revolution broke out, the debate over reformism had just concluded in the SPD. The reformist line had, apparently, been defeated, and the line of Luxemburg and Kautsky had won. However, in the course of this entire debate, the trade union leaders remained more or less silent. Their opinion was that the theoreticians could debate as much as they liked, but ultimately the union leaders would continue with business as usual once all was said and done. But now the debate over the general strike was being raised not only in *Die Neue Zeit* but also at political meetings and among workers on the factory floor. It had become a direct threat to the 'pragmatic' plans of the trade union leaders who wished to get on with peaceful negotiations to the exclusion of all else.

The trade union leaders did what they could to stop the strikes from growing – fearful lest the movement run out of their control and threaten to sour their relationship with the employers at the negotiating table. In January 1905 the leaders of the miners attempted to prevent a large strike in the Ruhr district, while the central leadership of the trade unions did everything in its means to prevent the strike from spreading. When the union leaders started hearing talk of a general strike to force through electoral reform in Prussia – a political demand – they decided they had to take the offensive, which they did at the Trade Union Congress of May 1905 in Cologne. This was not the time for 'experiments', they cried. They threw up a host of practical objections: the unions were not strong enough; the workers would be unable to feed their families during the strike; and who could stop the employers from profiting from this political strike? No, it was not the time for strikes. It was time to keep working away to strengthen the labour organisations. That required peace and quiet. They summed up their opposition to the general strike with the phrase: "general strikes are general nonsense".[36]

Rosa Luxemburg became the main target of the union leaders. After all, this was the woman who had called their work a "Sisyphean labour", and who

36 J. P. Nettl, *Rosa Luxemburg*, p. 300.

now came out advocating a mass strike in Germany. This woman, this Pole, now came to their methodical, organised Germany with her revolutionary nonsense, and was spreading dangerous ideas and creating unrest. In July of 1905, before Luxemburg left for Poland to participate in the revolution, the leader of the miners, Otto Hue, wrote contemptuously in his trade union magazine:

> In Russia the struggle for liberty has been raging almost a year. We always have wondered why our experts on the 'general strike theory' don't take themselves off speedily to Russia, to get practical experience, to join in the battle. In Russia the workers are paying with their lives; why don't all those theoreticians, who anyhow come from Poland and Russia and now sit in Germany, France and Switzerland scribbling 'revolutionary' articles, get themselves on to the battlefield? High time for all those with such an excess of revolutionary zeal to take a practical part in the Russian battle for freedom, instead of carrying on mass-strike discussions from summer holiday resorts. Trying is better than lying, so off with you to the Russian front, you class-war theoreticians.[37]

Rosa Luxemburg was foremost among those for whom these poisonous barbs were intended. The revisionists joined in the chorus, as did the liberal press, who nicknamed her 'Bloody Rosa'. Rosa Luxemburg, as might be expected, picked up the gauntlet and threw herself into the struggle against the reformism of the labour leaders. She struck back first and foremost on the plane of theory. For the first time, she identified the trade union leaders as the most dangerous tool of reformism in the party. She criticised them for their complete misunderstanding of the social relations that had led to the mass strike in other countries, and for having a narrow national view that didn't extend beyond their own German nose:

> Belgium isn't worth studying… a latin, 'irresponsible' country, on which the German trade-union experts can afford to look down. Russia, well Russia, that 'savage land'… without organisation, trade-union funds, officials – how can serious, 'experienced' German officials possibly be expected to learn from there… even though precisely in Russia this mass-strike weapon has found unexpected, magnificent application, instructive and exemplary for the whole working-class world.[38]

In September of 1905, the SPD held its annual congress in Jena. Here, Rosa Luxemburg advanced her views on the mass strike. Bebel gave a three-hour

37 Quoted in J. P. Nettl, *Rosa Luxemburg*, p. 301.
38 Quoted ibid., p. 302.

long speech, which was fairly radical in words, but fairly vague as far as practical conclusions went. His sentiment was essentially: we must wait and see if our class enemies move against us, and only then will we respond to them.[39] Bebel, and the SPD executive committee with him, saw the mass strike as a purely defensive measure that might be taken in the case of an attack on the right to vote or some other basic democratic right.

Rosa Luxemburg believed that the attitude of the party executive committee was far too defensive on this question, but instead of attacking them openly she used the mass movement to put positive pressure on the leaders, putting them in a position where they would have to actually do what they said they would. This meant that, on the surface, there was no apparent disagreement between the executive committee and Luxemburg, and their line seemed to score victory at the congress. But things were not as one-sided as they appeared. Luxemburg wrote in a letter to Henriette Roland-Holst:[40]

> I certainly agree with you that Bebel's resolution deals with the problem of the mass strike very one-sidedly and without excitement. When we saw it in Jena, a few of us decided to mount an offensive during the discussion so as to nudge it away from a mechanical recipe for defence of political rights, and towards recognition as one of the fundamental revolutionary manifestations. However, Bebel's speech put a different complexion on things, and the attitude of the opportunists (Heine, etc.) did even more. On several occasions we, the 'far left', found ourselves forced to fight, not against him [Bebel], but with him against the opportunists, in spite of the important difference between Bebel and us… It was rather a case of joining with Bebel and then giving his resolution a more revolutionary appearance during the discussion… And in fact the mass strike was treated, even by Bebel himself – though he may have been unaware of it – as a manifestation of popular revolutionary struggle – the ghost of revolution dominated the whole debate, indeed the whole congress.[41]

Support for Luxemburg's position showed the growing radicalisation of SPD members. This was given a certain expression among the party tops who, for a time, moved to the left (at least in words). But the lines quoted above also demonstrate the paradox of Luxemburg's approach: she had 'won' the congress, in the sense that it supported her understanding of the resolution,

---

39 See ibid., p. 307.

40 Henriette Roland-Holst (1869-1952) – Dutch writer and socialist, in 1918 a member of the Dutch communist party.

41 Quoted ibid., p. 308.

but what difference did that make when that was not what the leaders really meant and, furthermore, when this political divergence was not brought out clearly in the eyes of the members of the party? The apparent agreement between the leaders of the SPD and the far-left wing fostered illusions in the radicalisation of the leaders. But as soon as pressure from the masses disappeared, the radical speeches of the party tops also stopped. The left wing of the party could point to a congress resolution, but to no avail – it was the leadership that determined the politics of the SPD and its actions in the real world, not resolutions. Luxemburg viewed the adoption of the resolution as a sign that the movement of the masses could push the leaders to the left, but it was soon revealed that this was not an expression of any real leftward turn among the leaders. Rather, she and the radical left wing had merely given the SPD leadership a left cover in the eyes of the membership.

The executive committee saw the Jena congress, first and foremost, as legitimising their four-year-long struggle against reformism. They used the occasion to remove the editorial board of *Vorwärts*, the party's central organ, which was mostly composed of reformists. In the end, six editors were removed and, on Bebel's recommendation, Rosa Luxemburg was appointed as one of the newspaper's new editors. From late October 1905 she began writing regularly for the paper, and in November and December she wrote almost daily of the revolutionary events taking place in Russia and Poland. But Luxemburg quickly grew disillusioned with the work at *Vorwärts* – the new editors were, in her opinion, mediocre and unable to write clearly and in a revolutionary manner. In December, she decided to quit her post at *Vorwärts*, travelling to Poland instead to throw herself into the Russian Revolution, as we have already seen.

And, as we know, her absence from Germany was prolonged by her imprisonment and her stay in Finland. In all, Luxemburg was away from Germany for nine months. In that period, a drastic shift took place at the top of the SPD. The Russian Revolution of 1905 was defeated and ceased to be a factor in the radicalisation of the German workers. Even prior to the defeat of the revolution, developments in Russia – with general strikes and insurrections – had already become a bit too 'revolutionary' for the party leaders and above all for the leaders of the trade unions. The strike movement inside Germany was now declining, and leftward pressure on the party leadership was therefore also easing. The latter now turned sharply right and drew close to the union leaders. However, enthusiasm for the revolution still ran high among the workers, and when Rosa Luxemburg returned to

Germany, she was in high demand as a speaker on those events at meetings across the country.

After her absence of nine months, Luxemburg left Kuokkala in Finland on 14 September 1906 to return to Germany. She was uncertain as to whether she might be arrested as soon as she set foot on German soil on account of the speech she had given at the Jena congress at the end of 1905. But she could not wait any longer. In Finland she had written a piece titled 'The Mass Strike, the Political Party and the Trade Unions' at the request of German social democrats in Hamburg, who were asking for it as a contribution to the debate for the party congress of the SPD in Mannheim, scheduled for 23-29 September 1906. Intended to summarise the lessons of the Russian Revolution for a German audience, the piece also delved into the German debate over the mass strike as a weapon in the class struggle. For Luxemburg, the lessons of the 1905 Revolution were not merely a Russian concern:

> Accordingly it appears, when looked at in this way, to be entirely wrong to regard the Russian Revolution as a fine play, as something specifically 'Russian', and at best to admire the heroism of the fighting men, that is, the last accessories of the struggle. It is much more important that the German workers should learn to look upon the Russian Revolution as *their own affair*, not merely as a matter of international solidarity with the Russian proletariat, but first and foremost, as a *chapter of their own social and political history*.[42]

On her way back from Finland, Luxemburg spent a couple of days in Hamburg in order to work with the publisher. She had sent the manuscript one month prior so that it could be ready for the congress, and did not expect to have to do anything other than the final proofreading. However, the executive committee of the SPD had stopped the publication. They demanded the printing blocks be destroyed (which was a normal precaution in case of police raids) and that the text be thoroughly watered down as a condition for its publication. The beginnings of the split between Rosa Luxemburg and the leadership of the SPD really begin from here. Karl Radek[43] later wrote that,

---

42 R. Luxemburg, 'The Mass Strike, the Political Party and the Trade Unions', *Rosa Luxemburg Speaks*, pp. 203-4.

43 Karl Radek (1885-1939) – joined the SDKPiL in 1904, took part in the 1905 Revolution in Warsaw. Moved to Germany, where he was active in the SPD left. Close to the Bolsheviks, he joined Lenin in Switzerland during the war and took part in the Zimmerwald conference in 1915. Moved to Russia after the October Revolution

"with [Rosa Luxemburg's] 'Mass Strike, the Political Party and the Trade Unions' begins the separation of the Communist movement from Social Democracy in Germany".[44]

The local political leadership in Hamburg – where the strike movement of 1905 had achieved its broadest sweep – were indignant at the interference of the SPD executive committee, and they ensured that the work was still released in its original form. On account of the delay of several days, it would not be circulated among delegates of the congress, but it lost none of its relevance in spite of this.

Party and Trade Unions

The executive committee of the SPD did not limit itself to attempting to stop the publication of Rosa Luxemburg's piece. They took extensive measures to prevent radical ideas and methods from gaining an influence within the party. In February 1906, they entered into a secret agreement with the trade union leadership, giving the trade unions official autonomy in all trade union related questions, including the question of strike action. This meant that the trade union leadership was de facto granted a right of veto over the methods the party could use, with which they would make liberal use of in the years that followed. Until this point, the industrial struggle had been seen as subordinate to the political struggle to change society more broadly.

The relationship between the political and the industrial aspects of the workers' movement was a central question of 'The Mass Strike, the Political Party and the Trade Unions'. Rosa Luxemburg took a sharp stance against this attempt to erect a divide between the two. In the first instance, she argued that it was nonsense to believe that a mass movement would seek the kind permission of the union leaders. If they took a stand against a mass struggle, they would be swept aside by the movement. Furthermore, attempts to insulate the industrial and political movements of the working class from one another would prove utterly artificial. Such attempts were the product of the parliamentary phase through which social democracy had passed. In the course of this stage in its development, the trade unions had simply been left to look after the economic struggle, while the social democracy had placed

---

to play a leading role in the Communist International. He attended the founding congress of the KPD and participated in the Spartacist uprising. Radek sided with Trotsky's Left Opposition, but eventually capitulated to Stalin. He was nevertheless framed in the Stalinist Purges and executed.

44 Quoted in J. P. Nettl, *Rosa Luxemburg*, p. 298.

all of its focus on the political struggle. The new agreement, in placing the political and industrial struggles on the same plane, actually served to raise the daily struggle for reforms above the struggle for socialism:

> The theory of the 'equal authority' of trade-unions and social democracy is likewise not a mere theoretical misunderstanding, not a mere case of confusion but an expression of the well-known tendency of that opportunist wing of social democracy which reduced the political struggle of the working class to the parliamentary contest, and desires to change social democracy from a revolutionary proletarian party into a petty-bourgeois reform one.[45] If social democracy should accept the theory of the 'equal authority' of the trade-unions, it would thereby accept, indirectly and tacitly, that transformation which has long been striven for by the representatives of the opportunist tendency.[46]

Luxemburg described the process that had taken place in the labour organisations at length. It had resulted in their bureaucratisation and the spread of a narrow, trade-unionist outlook, where the organisation itself had become the end goal. The trade-union leaders were therefore working against strikes and mass struggle because they feared that this would hurt the organisation:

> The specialisation of professional activity as trade-union leaders, as well as the naturally restricted horizon which is bound up with disconnected economic struggles in a peaceful period, leads only too easily, amongst trade-union officials, to bureaucratism and a certain narrowness of outlook. Both, however, express themselves in a whole series of tendencies which may be fateful in the highest degree for the future of the trade-union movement. There is first of all the overvaluation of the organisation, which from a means has gradually been changed into an end in itself, a precious thing, to which the interests of the struggles should be subordinated.[47]

This course of development meant that the leadership had come to focus narrowly on the smallest of reforms, celebrating them as advances, even though they were succeeded by a general degradation of workers' conditions:

---

45 Here Luxemburg has added a long footnote with a quote from one of the revisionists which shows their opinion of the mass strike. The footnote has not been included, as it can be found on p. 209 in *Rosa Luxemburg Speaks*.

46 R. Luxemburg, 'The Mass Strike, the Political Party and the Trade Unions', *Rosa Luxemburg Speaks*, p. 209.

47 Ibid., p. 214.

The trade-union leaders, constantly absorbed in the economic guerrilla war whose plausible task it is to make the workers place the highest value on the smallest economic achievement, every increase in wages and shortening of the working day, gradually lose the power of seeing the larger connections and of taking a survey of the whole position. Only in this way can one explain why many trade-union leaders refer with the greatest satisfaction to the achievements of the last fifteen years, instead of, on the contrary, emphasising the other side of the medal; the simultaneous and immense reduction of the proletarian standard of life by land usury, by the whole tax and customs policy, by landlord rapacity which has increased house rents to such an exorbitant extent, in short, by all the objective tendencies of bourgeois policy which have largely neutralised the advantages of the fifteen years of trade-union struggle.[48]

In their hunt for daily reforms, the trade-union leaders closed their eyes to the overarching limitations of capitalism. Yet, in the opinion of Luxemburg, the task of social democracy was precisely to use these daily struggles to draw out capitalism's limitations. This was precisely why the trade-union leaders of the SPD ended up wishing to free themselves from the control of the party and why they defended a revision of the theoretical foundations of social democracy:

> From the *whole* social-democratic truth which, while emphasising the importance of the present work and its absolute necessity, attaches the chief importance to the criticism and the limits to this work, the *half* trade-union truth is taken which emphasises only the positive side of the daily struggle.
>
> And finally, from the concealment of the objective limits drawn by the bourgeois social order to the trade-union struggle, there arises a hostility to every theoretical criticism which refers to these limits in connection with the ultimate aims of the labour movement. Fulsome flattery and boundless optimism are considered to be the duty of every 'friend of the trade union movement'. But as the social democratic standpoint consists precisely in fighting against uncritical parliamentary optimism, a front is at last made against the social democratic theory: men grope for a 'new trade-union theory', that is, a theory which would open an illimitable vista of economic progress to the trade-union struggle within the capitalist system, in opposition to the social-democratic doctrine.[49]

The agreement between the trade-union leaders and the party leaders constituted the first time that a division between the two sides of the

---

48 Ibid., p. 215.
49 Ibid.

movement had been established. It was quite clear that this was a concession to the narrow, reformist interests of the trade-union leadership. The agreement was initially hidden from party members precisely because the SPD leaders were aware that it constituted a breach in their former methods, and that the party members would not give such an innovation a warm welcome.

'The Mass Strike, the Political Party and the Trade Unions'

It was against this narrow viewpoint that was prevailing at the top of the German workers' movement that Rosa Luxemburg wrote 'The Mass Strike, the Political Party and the Trade Unions', as part of the debate over mass strikes in the German SPD.

Until 1905, the mass strike had been rejected as a social-democratic method of struggle because it was considered to be an anarchist method, focusing solely on the economic struggle and rejecting the political struggle. Furthermore, the mass strike had been viewed as a utopia because:

> [...] either the proletariat as a whole are not yet in possession of the powerful organisation and financial resources required, in which case they cannot carry through the general strike; or they are already sufficiently well organised, in which case they do not need the general strike.[50]

But Luxemburg argued that the situation had changed:

> For the first time in the history of the class struggle it [the 1905 Russian Revolution] has achieved a grandiose realisation of the idea of the mass strike and – as we shall discuss later – has even matured the general strike and thereby opened a new epoch in the development of the labour movement.[51]

This was not because Luxemburg had suddenly turned anarchist, on the contrary:

> The Russian Revolution, which is the first historical experiment on the model of the mass strike, not merely does not afford a vindication of anarchism, but actually means the *historical liquidation of anarchism*. [...]

> Anarchism has become in the Russian Revolution, not the theory of the struggling proletariat, but the ideological signboard of the counter-revolutionary lumpen-proletariat, who, like a school of sharks, swarm in the wake of the

---

50 Ibid., p. 156.

51 Ibid.

battleship of the revolution. And therewith the historical career of anarchism is well-nigh ended.[52]

According to Luxemburg, the mass strike cannot replace the political struggle for democratic rights, as the anarchists argue. In fact, the mass strike should become a *means* in the political struggle. For Luxemburg, the economic and the political struggles had to be linked up:

> On the other hand, the mass strike in Russia has been realised not as means of evading the political struggle of the working class, and especially of parliamentarism, not as a means of jumping suddenly into the social revolution by means of a theatrical coup, but as a means, firstly, of creating for the proletariat the conditions of the daily political struggle and especially of parliamentarism. The revolutionary struggle in Russia, in which mass strikes are the most important weapon, is, by the working people, and above all by the proletariat, conducted for those political rights and conditions whose necessity and importance in the struggle for the emancipation of the working class Marx and Engels first pointed out, and in opposition to anarchism fought for with all their might in the International.[53]

But in Germany, the trade union leaders were steadfast in their opposition to the use of the mass strike, even as a defensive weapon. They argued that the workers' organisations were not yet strong enough, and they presented a long list of objections: trade union membership was too low, strike funds were insufficient, etc. Luxemburg fiercely criticised their mechanistic manner of debating the question.

Luxemburg didn't limit herself to combating the arguments of the opponents of the mass strike alone. She also polemicised against that wing of the SPD that defended the idea of the mass strike but which saw in it a purely defensive measure that might be used if the government attacked the right to vote, for instance. That wing included the German party leadership and Bernstein. For them, the mass strike was reduced to a weapon completely under the control of the party and the trade unions. It became a 'mere appendage' to the parliamentary struggle rather than part of the revolutionary struggle to transform society.

In 'The Mass Strike, the Political Party and the Trade Unions', Rosa Luxemburg described concretely how the mass strike in Russia developed

---

52 Ibid., pp. 157-8.
53 Ibid., p. 158.

4. Mass Strike and Spontaneity

as a spontaneous movement of the masses themselves. The 1905 Revolution was the culmination of a strike movement that had developed over the course of years. The strike wave was not decreed by the party or the trade unions, but broke out when the workers' frustration had reached a critical level, at which point some apparently accidental question would become the straw that broke the camel's back. The revolution that began on Bloody Sunday was the culmination of this strike movement, and it began spontaneously. In the course of the movement, economic and political demands followed one after another, and the economic and political struggles merged together.

The main point that Luxemburg contended was that, contrary to the SPD leadership's conception, the mass strike is *not* something exclusively initiated and determined by the party and the trade unions as an appendage to the parliamentary struggle:

> The mass strike, as it appears for the most part in the discussion in Germany, is a very clear and simply thought out, sharply sketched isolated phenomenon. It is the political mass strike exclusively that is spoken of. What is meant by it is a single grand rising of the industrial proletariat springing from some political motive of the highest importance, and undertaken on the basis of an opportune and mutual understanding on the part of the controlling authorities of the party and of the trade unions, and carried through in the spirit of party discipline and in perfect order, and in still more perfect order brought to the directing committees as a signal given at the proper time, by which committees the regulation of support, the cost, the sacrifice – in a word, the whole material balance of the mass strike – is exactly determined in advance.[54]

She mocked the argument of the German labour leaders that the mass strike would destroy the labour organisations – on the contrary, she explained, the workers' organisations in Russia grew out of and emerged greatly strengthened by the mass strikes in the course of the revolution:

> [T]he apparently 'chaotic' strikes and the 'disorganised' revolutionary action after the January general strike [in Russia, 1905] are becoming the starting point of a feverish *work of organisation*. Dame History, from afar, smilingly hoaxes the bureaucratic lay figures who keep grim watch at the gate over the fate of the German trade unions. The firm organisations which, as the indispensable hypothesis for an eventual German mass strike, should be fortified like an impregnable citadel – these organisations are in Russia, on the contrary, already

---

54 Ibid., pp. 162-3.

born from the mass strike. And while the guardians of the German trade unions for the most part fear that the organisations will fall in pieces in a revolutionary whirlwind like rare porcelain, the Russian revolution shows us the exact opposite picture; from the whirlwind and the storm, out of the fire and glow of the mass strike and the street fighting rise again, like Venus from the foam, fresh, young, powerful, buoyant trade unions.[55]

For Luxemburg, both the opponents and the supporters of the Bernsteinian 'mass strike' stood on the "same platform". They understood it in the same – incorrect – way, as something that the party and the unions could "decide upon" and "forbid" as they pleased; "a kind of pocketknife which can be kept in the pocket clasped 'ready for any emergency', and according to the decision, can be unclasped and used."[56] Luxemburg argued that both sides had completely misunderstood the character of the mass strike.

> If, therefore, the Russian Revolution teaches us anything, it teaches above all that the mass strike is not artificially 'made', not 'decided' at random, not 'propagated', but that it is a historical phenomenon which, at a given moment, results from social conditions with historical inevitability.[57]

It was this mechanical conception, which reigned supreme in the highest echelons of the SPD, that Luxemburg took aim at. She counterposed the spontaneous movement of the masses against those political and trade union leaders who thought they could turn the class struggle on and off like a tap. She wished to shake the SPD out of its parliamentary routine, and bring it to the realisation that the revolutionary movement is something utterly removed from the orderly protest strikes on the pattern of May Day. A revolution is a deadly serious question for the working class. The idea of the mass strike then dominant in the SPD – of a limited protest strike, planned and organised down to the last-minute detail – loses all relevance in a genuinely revolutionary movement. In a revolution, it ceases to be enough for the masses to show their discontent and turn out to protest:

> It is precisely those factors which objectively facilitate the realisation of the demonstration strike after a preconceived plan and at the party's word of command – namely, the growth of political consciousness and the training of the proletariat – make this kind of mass strike impossible; today the proletariat in Russia, the

---

55 Ibid., p. 176.

56 Ibid., p. 159.

57 Ibid., pp. 160-1.

most capable vanguard of the masses, does not want to know about mass strikes; the workers are no longer in a mood for jesting and will now think only of a serious struggle with all its consequences.[58]

Luxemburg and the leaders of the SPD were speaking in completely different tongues. The leadership of the SPD viewed the strike as an orderly, time-limited, defensive measure. Meanwhile, Luxemburg considered the mass strike as one step in the revolutionary process, the logical conclusion of which was an uprising along the lines of that which had been seen in Moscow in 1905:

> By the logical internal development of progressive experience the mass strike this time changes into an open insurrection, to armed barricades, and street fighting in Moscow. The December days in Moscow close the first eventful year of the revolution as the highest point in the ascending line of political action and of the mass strike movement.

> The Moscow events show a typical picture of the logical development and at the same time of the future of the revolutionary movement on the whole: their inevitable close in a general open insurrection, which again on its part cannot come in any other way than through the school of a series of preparatory partial insurrections, which end in partial outward 'defeats' and, considered individually, may appear to be 'premature'.[59]

In Rosa Luxemburg's opinion, the argument of the labour leaders – that one had to calculate all the costs of a strike – was senseless in the context of a revolutionary period, when the workers have shown a readiness to make the ultimate sacrifice:

> The leading organisations in Russia certainly attempt to support the direct victims to the best of their ability. Thus, for example, the brave victims of the gigantic lockout in St. Petersburg, which followed upon the eight-hour day campaign, were supported for weeks. But all these measures are, in the enormous balance of the revolution, but as a drop in the ocean. At the moment that a real, earnest period of mass strikes begins, all these 'calculations' of 'cost' become merely projects for exhausting the ocean with a tumbler. And it is a veritable ocean of frightful privations and sufferings which is brought by every revolution to the proletarian masses. And the solution which a revolutionary period makes of this apparently invincible difficulty consists in the circumstances that such an

---

58 Ibid., p. 184.
59 Ibid., pp. 180-1.

immense volume of mass idealism is simultaneously released that the masses are insensible to the bitterest sufferings. With the psychology of a trade unionist who will not stay off his work on May Day unless he is assured in advance of a definite amount of support in the event of his being victimised, neither revolution nor mass strike can be made. But in the storm of the revolutionary period even the proletarian is transformed from a provident *pater familias* demanding support, into a 'revolutionary romanticist', for whom even the highest good, life itself, to say nothing of material well-being, possesses but little in comparison with the ideals of the struggle.[60]

A Particular Theory of Spontaneity?

Since her death, Luxemburg's 'The Mass Strike, the Political Party and the Trade Unions' in particular has been used to support the idea that 'Luxemburgism' exists as a distinct theory. In Frölich's opinion, the idea that Luxemburg had her own particular theory of spontaneity was invented by Zinoviev, when he was leading the Third (Communist) International, in 1921. The idea, later on, was repeated obsessively by the Stalinists. But Rosa Luxemburg in no way advanced a particular theory of the spontaneity of the masses.

As has been explained, she was responding to the reformist, mechanical understanding of the mass strike, prevalent at the top of the SPD, as a purely defensive measure. She described how the Russian Revolution arose and developed spontaneously. Her goal was to break the SPD's parliamentary routinism and politically rearm the party to face the tasks that a revolutionary situation would present by drawing the lessons from Russian Revolution and transposing them to Germany:

> In this way we arrive at the same conclusions in Germany in relation to the peculiar tasks of direction in relation to the role of social democracy in mass strikes, as in our analysis of events in Russia. [...]

> The social democrats are the most enlightened, most class-conscious vanguard of the proletariat. They cannot and dare not wait, in a fatalist fashion, with folded arms for the advent of the 'revolutionary situation', to wait for that which in every spontaneous peoples' movement, falls from the clouds. On the contrary, they must now, as always, hasten the development of things and endeavour to accelerate events. This they cannot do, however, by suddenly issuing the 'slogan' for a mass strike at random at any odd moment, but first and foremost, by making clear

---

60 Ibid., p. 189.

to the widest layers of the proletariat the *inevitable advent* of this revolutionary period, the inner *social factors* making for it and the *political consequences* of it. If the widest proletarian layer should be won for a political mass action of the social democrats, and if, vice versa, the social democrats should seize and maintain the real leadership of a mass movement – should they become, in a *political sense*, the rulers of the whole movement, then they must, with the utmost clearness, consistency and resoluteness, inform the German proletariat of their tactics and aims in the period of coming struggle.[61]

Contrary to the claims of the Stalinists, Rosa Luxemburg in no way rejected the role of the party in a revolutionary movement. Her point was merely that revolutions do not arise at the command of the party. Revolutions arise when the masses can no longer endure the old order:

It is sufficient in order to comprehend the foregoing to obtain an explanation of the question of the conscious direction and initiative in the mass strike. If the mass strike is not an isolated act but a whole period of the class struggle, and if this period is identical with a period of revolution, it is clear that the mass strike cannot be called at will, even when the decision to do so may come from the highest committee of the strongest social democratic party. As long as the social democracy has not the power to stage and countermand revolutions according to its fancy, even the greatest enthusiasm and impatience of the social democratic troops will not suffice to call into being a real period of mass strike as a living, powerful movement of the people. […]

Of course, even during the revolution, mass strikes do not exactly fall from heaven. They must be brought about in some way or another by the workers. The resolution and determination of the workers also play a part and indeed the initiative and the wider direction naturally fall to the share of the organised and most enlightened kernel of the proletariat. But the scope of this initiative and this direction, for the most part, is confined to application to individual acts, to individual strikes, when the revolutionary period is already begun, and indeed, in most cases, is confined within the boundaries of a single town. […]

During the revolution it is extremely difficult for any directing organ of the proletarian movement to foresee and to calculate which occasions and factors can lead to explosions and which cannot. Here also initiative and direction do not consist in issuing commands according to one's inclinations, but in the most adroit adaptability to the given situation, and the closest possible contact with the

---

61 Ibid., p. 200.

mood of the masses. The element of spontaneity, as we have seen, plays a great part in all Russian mass strikes without exception, be it as a driving force or as a restraining influence.[62]

According to Luxemburg, the party's task was to provide political leadership:

If, however, the direction of the mass strike in the sense of command over its origin, and in the sense of the calculating and reckoning of the cost, is a matter of the revolutionary period itself, the directing of the mass strike becomes, in an altogether different sense, the duty of social democracy and its leading organs. Instead of puzzling their heads with the technical side, with the mechanism of the mass strike, the social democrats are called upon to assume *political* leadership in the midst of the revolutionary period.

To give the cue for, and the direction to, the fight; to so regulate the tactics of the political struggle in its every phase and at its every moment that the entire sum of the available power of the proletariat which is already released and active, will find expression in the battle array of the party; to see that the tactics of the social democrats are decided according to their resoluteness and acuteness and that they never fall below the level demanded by the actual relations of forces, but rather rise above it – that is the most important task of the directing body in a period of mass strikes. And this direction changes of itself, to a certain extent, into technical direction. A consistent, resolute, progressive tactic on the part of the social democrats produces in the masses a feeling of security, self-confidence and desire for struggle; a vacillating weak tactic, based on an underestimation of the proletariat, has a crippling and confusing effect upon the masses. In the first case mass strikes break out 'of themselves' and 'opportunely'; in the second case they remain ineffective amidst direct summonses of the directing body to mass strikes. And of both the Russian Revolution affords striking examples.[63]

In all revolutionary movements, the spontaneous movement of the masses has played a determining role. Luxemburg didn't develop a particular 'theory', but merely gave a description of the revolution as was played out in Russia in 1905. Lenin by no means disagreed with Luxemburg's description of the spontaneous character of the revolution. In May 1917, in words that very much accord with Luxemburg's, Lenin said of the masses that they were "100 times more leftward than we [the revolutionaries] are".[64] And, in 'Lessons of

---

62 Ibid., pp. 187-8.

63 Ibid., pp. 189-90.

64 V. I. Lenin, 'Titbits for the "Newborn" Government', *LCW*, Vol. 24, p. 364.

the Moscow Uprising' he wrote: "The proletariat understood the development of the objective circumstances of the struggle, which demanded a transition from strike to uprising, earlier than its leaders."[65]

Luxemburg and Lenin differed on the question of *how* the party would exercise its leadership of the movement. As previously discussed, this disagreement was expressed at the 1907 congress of the Russian Social Democratic Labour Party, at which Luxemburg criticised the Bolsheviks for putting too much emphasis on the technical side of the uprising in the 1905 Revolution, while believing that they ought instead to have focused on giving the movement political leadership. In this sense, Luxemburg's approach to the revolution was abstract: the masses will move, and when they do it is up to the party to provide the correct political programme. From her experience in the SPD, focus on the practical side of organising was the hallmark of a conservative leadership that held back the movement of the masses. Instead of rejecting the bureaucratic character of the SPD, she rejected the technical, practical side of organising altogether as an evil in and of itself. Luxemburg seemed to believe that the movement of the masses itself would solve the problem of organisation and technical leadership.

Trotsky summed up Luxemburg's understanding as follows:

> There is no gainsaying that Rosa Luxemburg impassionately counterposed the spontaneity of mass actions to the 'victory-crowned' conservative policy of the German social democracy especially after the Revolution of 1905. This counterposition had a thoroughly revolutionary and progressive character. At a much earlier date than Lenin, Rosa Luxemburg grasped the retarding character of the ossified party and trade-union apparatus and began a struggle against it. Inasmuch as she counted upon the inevitable accentuation of class conflicts, she always predicted the certainty of the independent elemental appearance of the masses against the will and against the line of march of officialdom. In these broad historical outlines, Rosa was proved right. For the [German] Revolution of 1918 was 'spontaneous', that is, it was accomplished by the masses against all the provisions and all the precautions of the party officialdom. On the other hand, the whole of Germany's subsequent history amply showed that spontaneity alone is far from enough for success; Hitler's regime is a weighty argument against the panacea of spontaneity.

> Rosa herself never confined herself to the mere theory of spontaneity, like Parvus, for example, who later bartered his social revolutionary fatalism for the

---

65 Quoted in J. P. Nettl, *Rosa Luxemburg*, p. 333.

most revolting fatalism. In contrast to Parvus, Rosa Luxemburg exerted herself to educate the revolutionary wing of the proletariat in advance and to bring it together organisationally as far as possible. In Poland, she built up a very rigid independent organisation. The most that can be said is that in her historical-philosophical evaluation of the labour movement, the preparatory selection of the vanguard, in comparison with the mass actions that were to be expected, fell too short with Rosa; whereas Lenin – without consoling himself with the miracles of future actions – took the advanced workers and constantly and tirelessly welded them together into firm nuclei, illegally or legally, in the mass organisations or underground, by means of a sharply defined programme.

Rosa's theory of spontaneity was a wholesome weapon against the ossified apparatus of reformism. That it was often directed against Lenin's work of building up a revolutionary apparatus, reveals – to be sure, only in embryo – its reactionary features. With Rosa herself this occurred only episodically. She was much too realistic in the revolutionary sense to develop the elements of the theory of spontaneity into a consummate metaphysics. In practice, she herself, as has already been said, undermined this theory at every step. After the revolution of November 1918, she began the ardent labour of assembling the proletarian vanguard.[66]

When reading 'The Mass Strike, the Political Party and the Trade Unions', it is possible to come away with the impression that Luxemburg believed the role of the party was limited to waiting with folded arms until strikes break out, and then jumping in to give political leadership. Her attention was focused, as we've discussed, on politically rearming the SPD and the German workers. She explained how a revolutionary movement is very different from ordinary trade-union and parliamentary struggles, and that the party must be ready for it. But, as Trotsky was careful to point out, Luxemburg did not succumb to pure fatalism. She by no means relegated the party's role to that of merely reacting to the movement of the masses, placing all her faith in the latter. In Poland, she took part in building a strictly centralised party. In the final years of her life, she helped found the German Communist Party (KPD). In 1910 a mass movement for electoral reform erupted in Prussia, which she sharply criticised the SPD for failing to organise and lead. The difference between Luxemburg and Lenin lay in the fact that the latter had understood early on the need to build a strong and centralised organisation of educated Marxist cadres as the backbone of a revolutionary mass party. He

---

66 L. Trotsky, 'Luxemburg and the Fourth International', *Writings of Leon Trotsky: 1935-36*, p. 30.

had understood this *before* the revolution broke out, while Luxemburg only began this work whilst the German Revolution of 1918 was in progress – by which time it was too late.

As Trotsky explained, contained within Luxemburg's critique of the Bolsheviks' focus on the technical, practical side of organising, was a germ that – if elevated to a theoretical principle – would become reactionary. Incidentally, many so-called 'Luxemburgists' have focused solely on this theoretically weak side of Luxemburg. They have torn this side of her writings out of context, and have elevated it to the level of a novel and distinct 'theory'. The Stalinists too have nurtured this myth of a distinct 'Luxemburgist theory of spontaneity' and have counterposed it to their own representation of the party as infallible and in control at all times. As the spontaneous movement of the masses became a threat to the position of the Stalinist bureaucracy, so they sought to open up a divide between Luxemburg and Lenin.

Luxemburg's faith in the movement and revolutionary potential of the masses was thoroughly revolutionary. It represented a healthy reaction against the reformism that emanated from the tops of the German workers' movement, who substituted themselves for the movement of the masses, and who actually became the strongest pillar in support for bourgeois society. The weak side of Luxemburg's position meanwhile was already apparent in the course of the 1905 Revolution itself. The revolution was defeated precisely because the revolutionary organisations were too weak and the revolution insufficiently well organised. The general strike could certainly pose the question of power. In and of itself, however, it could not solve it, as Trotsky explained. The weakness of Luxemburg's position was further exposed at various points in the course of the victorious Russian Revolution of 1917, and in the defeats suffered by the German Revolution after 1918 and in 1923. The essential difference lay in the existence of a revolutionary party – the Bolshevik Party, in Russia – and the lack of such a party in Germany. In the latter case, the Communist Party was only founded *during* the revolution itself.

The success or defeat of a socialist revolution is intimately dependent on the question of leadership. It is impossible for a revolutionary situation to last forever. The working class cannot indefinitely be mobilised in constant struggle. The successful revolutionary conquest of power is a question of timing. If the moment is not seized – the moment where all of the forces of the working class are mobilised and its confidence is at its zenith, whilst the class enemy is simultaneously helpless and demoralised – should the workers fail to seize power in this narrow window of opportunity, the revolutionary momentum is lost, demoralisation sets in and the balance of class forces shifts. The opportunity is missed, and the revolution is defeated. In order to prevent this, the presence of a revolutionary party is crucial. But the revolutionary party cannot be summoned into existence during the revolution itself. It must be built *before* the revolution erupts. It is necessary to combine the 'spontaneous' movement of the masses with organisation, programme, perspective, strategy and tactics – in other words, with a revolutionary party led by experienced cadres.

Trotsky who, like Rosa Luxemburg, had sharply criticised Lenin in 1903 and who did not join the Bolshevik party until 1917, admitted openly that Lenin had been right and that he had been wrong on this question. Basing himself on the lessons of the Bolshevik Party in Russia, his 1924 pamphlet *Lessons of October* describes in detail how history had demonstrated the necessity of a revolutionary party and of a leadership trained for this task. Only combined with this factor could the proletariat hope to achieve victory in a revolutionary period:

> With respect to Germany, the case is quite a clear one. The German revolution might have been triumphant both in 1918 and in 1919, had a proper party leadership been secured. […]
>
> Without a party, apart from a party, over the head of a party, or with a substitute for a party, the proletarian revolution cannot conquer. That is the principal lesson of the past decade. It is true that the English trade unions may become a mighty lever of the proletarian revolution; they may, for instance, even take the place of workers' soviets under certain conditions and for a certain period of time. They can fill such a role, however, not apart from a Communist party, and certainly not against the party, but only on the condition that communist influence becomes the decisive influence in the trade unions. We have paid far too dearly for this conclusion – with regard to the role and importance of a party in a proletarian revolution – to renounce it so lightly or even to minimise its significance.
>
> Consciousness, premeditation, and planning played a far smaller part in bourgeois revolutions than they are destined to play, and already do play, in proletarian revolutions. In the former instance the motive force of the revolution was also furnished by the masses, but the latter were much less organised and much less conscious than at the present time. The leadership remained in the hands of different sections of the bourgeoisie, and the latter had at its disposal wealth, education, and all the organisational advantages connected with them (the cities,

the universities, the press, etc.). The bureaucratic monarchy defended itself in a hand-to-mouth manner, probing in the dark and then acting. The bourgeoisie would bide its time to seize a favourable moment when it could profit from the movement of the lower classes, throw its whole social weight into the scale, and so seize the state power. The proletarian revolution is precisely distinguished by the fact that the proletariat – in the person of its vanguard – acts in it not only as the main offensive force but also as the guiding force. The part played in bourgeois revolutions by the economic power of the bourgeoisie, by its education, by its municipalities and universities, is a part which can be filled in a proletarian revolution only by the party of the proletariat.

The role of the party has become all the more important in view of the fact that the enemy has also become far more conscious. The bourgeoisie, in the course of centuries of rule, has perfected a political schooling far superior to the schooling of the old bureaucratic monarchy. If parliamentarism served the proletariat to a certain extent as a training school for revolution, then it also served the bourgeoisie to a far greater extent as the school of counter-revolutionary strategy. Suffice it to say that by means of parliamentarism the bourgeoisie was able to train the social democracy so that it is today the main prop of private property. The epoch of the social revolution in Europe, as has been shown by its very first steps, will be an epoch not only of strenuous and ruthless struggle but also of planned and calculated battles – far more planned than with us in 1917.

That is why we require an approach entirely different from the prevailing one to the questions of civil war in general and of armed insurrection in particular. Following Lenin, all of us keep repeating time and again Marx's words that insurrection is an art. But this idea is transformed into a hollow phrase, to the extent that Marx's formula is not supplemented with a study of the fundamental elements of the art of civil war, on the basis of the vast accumulated experience of recent years. It is necessary to say candidly that a superficial attitude to questions of armed insurrection is a token that the power of the social democratic tradition has not yet been overcome. A party which pays superficial attention to the question of civil war, in the hope that everything will somehow settle itself at the crucial moment, is certain to be shipwrecked. We must analyse in a collective manner the experience of the proletarian struggles beginning with 1917. [...]

History secured for our party revolutionary advantages that are truly inestimable. The traditions of the heroic struggle against the tsarist monarchy; the habituation to revolutionary self-sacrifice bound up with the conditions of underground activity; the broad theoretical study and assimilation of the revolutionary experience of humanity; the struggle against Menshevism, against the Narodniks, and against conciliationism; the supreme experience of the 1905 Revolution; the theoretical study and assimilation of this experience during the years of counter-revolution; the examination of the problems of the international labour movement in the light of the revolutionary lessons of 1905 – these were the things which in their totality gave our party an exceptional revolutionary temper, supreme theoretical penetration, and unparalleled revolutionary sweep. Nevertheless, even within this party, among its leaders, on the eve of decisive action there was formed a group of experienced revolutionists, Old Bolsheviks, who were in sharp opposition to the proletarian revolution and who, in the course of the most critical period of the revolution from February 1917 to approximately February 1918, adopted on all fundamental questions an essentially social democratic position. It required Lenin, and Lenin's exceptional influence in the party, unprecedented even at that time, to safeguard the party and the revolution against the supreme confusion following from such a situation. This must never be forgotten if we wish other Communist parties to learn anything from us.

The question of selecting the leading staff is of exceptional importance to the parties of Western Europe. The experience of the abortive German October is shocking proof of this. But this selection must proceed in the light of revolutionary action. During these recent years, Germany has provided ample opportunities for the testing of the leading party members in moments of direct struggle. Failing this criterion, the rest is worthless. France, during these years, was much poorer in revolutionary upheavals – even partial ones. But even in the political life of France we have had flashes of civil war, times when the Central Committee of the party and the trade union leadership had to react in action to unpostponable and acute questions [...]. A careful study of such acute episodes provides irreplaceable material for the evaluation of a party leadership, the conduct of various party organs, and individual leading members. To ignore these lessons – not to draw the necessary conclusions from them as to the choice of personalities – is to invite inevitable defeats; for without a penetrating, resolute, and courageous party leadership, the victory of the proletarian revolution is impossible.

Each party, even the most revolutionary party, must inevitably produce its own organisational conservatism; for otherwise it would lack the necessary stability. This is wholly a question of degree. In a revolutionary party the vitally necessary dose of conservatism must be combined with a complete freedom from routine, with initiative in orientation and daring in action. These qualities are put to the severest test during turning points in history. We have already quoted the words of Lenin to the effect that even the most revolutionary parties, when an abrupt change occurs in a situation and when new tasks arise as a consequence, frequently pursue the political line of yesterday and thereby become, or threaten to become, a brake upon the revolutionary process. Both conservatism and revolutionary initiative find their most concentrated expression in the leading organs of the party. In the meantime, the European communist parties have still to face their sharpest 'turning point' – the turn from preparatory work to the actual seizure of power. This turn is the most exacting, the most unpostponable, the most responsible, and the most formidable. To miss the moment for the turn is to incur the greatest defeat that a party can possibly suffer. […]

Much has been spoken and written lately on the necessity of 'Bolshevising' the Comintern.[67] This is a task that cannot be disputed or delayed; it is made particularly urgent after the cruel lessons of Bulgaria and Germany a year ago. Bolshevism is not a doctrine (i.e., not merely a doctrine) but a system of revolutionary training for the proletarian uprising. What is the Bolshevisation of Communist parties? It is giving them such a training, and effecting such a selection of the leading staff, as would prevent them from drifting when the hour for their October strikes. "That is the whole of Hegel, and the wisdom of books, and the meaning of all philosophy…"[68]

1905: A Seminal Year

The 1905 Russian Revolution had provided invaluable lessons for the workers and especially for revolutionaries – both inside and outside of Russia. For Rosa Luxemburg, the lessons of the 1905 Revolution were decisive. She had experienced, in practice, the revolutionary movement of the masses. The revolution caused her to break with the Mensheviks, and placed her on the same side as Lenin and the Bolsheviks in the Russian party.

In the German SPD, likewise, 1905 caused initial dividing lines to be drawn. While Luxemburg and others on the left in Germany drew radical conclusions from the revolution and the strike movement, the tops of the SPD moved in the opposite direction, drawing closer to the reformists and the labour leaders. Luxemburg threw everything she had into defeating the reformism then spreading through the upper echelons of the German workers' movement.

Luxemburg's approach to the questions of organisation and the role of the party in a revolution remained abstract, and thus open to a potentially negative interpretation, whilst Lenin was extremely clear on these questions.

---

67 Comintern – the Communist (Third) International, founded in 1919.

68 L. Trotsky, *Lessons of October*, pp. 59-63.

However, the 1905 Revolution nevertheless placed them on the same side of the barricade on the essential question: the question of revolution. In subsequent years, the schism between revolutionaries and reformists widened in the international workers' movement. It was not until 1914, however, with the outbreak of the First World War, that this division really burst to the surface.

5. The Quiet Before the Storm

As the radicalising wave from the Russian Revolution and the German strike movement subsided, pressure eased on the leadership of the SPD. They were more than happy that the revolutionary unrest had died down. Now they could return their attention to the parliamentary work that was so dear to them. However, to Luxemburg and the most radicalised layers of the SPD nothing remained as it used to be. They had felt the touch of the Russian Revolution, and had drawn conclusions that were quite different to those drawn by the leaders of the SPD and the trade unions.

In the following years, it wasn't just the divide between Luxemburg and the party leadership as a whole that widened. In 1910, a break came in her relationship with Karl Kautsky, who had stood with her through thick and thin – particularly in the years building up to the 1905 Revolution.

The period between 1905 and the First World War was fairly calm. During this time, Luxemburg lectured at the new party school, wrote *The Accumulation of Capital*, and took up the political struggle against imperialism and the rising tide of nationalism at the head of the SPD. This degeneration was ultimately expressed in 1914 in the shameful betrayal of the SPD's support for the German bourgeoisie in the First World War.

The Party School and 'The Accumulation of Capital'

Luxemburg was not particularly active in the German party following her return from Russian-occupied Poland. In December 1906, she was sentenced to two months in jail for the speech she had delivered at the Jena congress, which she served until the summer of 1907.

In 1906, the SPD founded a party school in Berlin, with the participants selected by local party organisations and trade unions. They were, supposedly, of a political level such that they ought to be able to educate others. The school opened in November 1906, and from 1 October of the following year, having served her sentence, Luxemburg started teaching there. She taught political economy and economic history, and from 1911 she took over Franz Mehring's course on the history of socialism. Enjoying the work, Luxemburg was widely praised by the course's participants, who were by no means belonged to her wing of the party. Based on her lectures in political economy, and the studies which she undertook in preparation for them, she wrote two books: *Introduction to Political Economy*[1] and *The Accumulation of Capital*.

Through her lectures, Luxemburg encountered what she believed to be a shortcoming in the second volume of Marx's *Capital* regarding what is called the 'realisation' of surplus value. Determined to clarify the question, she put pen to paper. Following on from the Bernstein controversy, any attempt to 'correct' Marx, even by someone like Rosa Luxemburg, was certainly treading on thin ice.

Nonetheless, she proceeded to write a book based on the questions prompted by her studies, and the result was *The Accumulation of Capital*. The book deals with how surplus value is realised rather than how it is produced, a question which she believed Marx had not given a complete answer to. The whole book is based on a theoretical analysis, with little in the way of political conclusions, besides the characterisation she gives of imperialism. Given its highly theoretical character, and its analysis of Marx's schema from volume two of *Capital*, it must be said that Luxemburg's book is by no means easy to follow.

When it first appeared, the book created quite a stir, and it had no shortage of critics. Much of the criticism she faced was published in *Vorwärts* and other Social-Democratic newspapers. In response to this, whilst in prison, she wrote a shorter book entitled *The Accumulation of Capital: An Anti-Critique*, which was not published until 1921. Compared to the first book, it is a much easier read.

It seems that the original idea behind *The Accumulation of Capital* was not simply to address the problem of realisation, but also to examine the causes of imperialism, as the original work's subtitle indicates: 'A Contribution to an Economic Explanation of Imperialism'. In a letter to Konstantin Zetkin,[2] written in November 1911, Luxemburg wrote:

---

1 According to Paul Frölich, only fragments of this text were preserved.
2 Konstantin Zetkin (1885-1980) – Clara Zetkin's son and a friend of Luxemburg.

I want to find the *cause* of imperialism. I am following up the economic aspects of this concept… it will be a strictly scientific explanation of imperialism and its contradictions.[3]

However, it was the examination of these "economic aspects" that led her to re-evaluate what Marx had written in volume two of *Capital*, dealing with capital accumulation and what he called *extended* reproduction. She thus wrote:

I could not succeed in depicting the total process of capitalist production in all its practical relations and with its objective historical limitations with sufficient clarity. Closer examination of the matter then convinced me that it was a question of rather more than the mere art of representation, and that a problem remained to be solved which is connected with the theoretical matter of volume two of Marx's *Capital* and at the same time closely connected with present-day imperialist politics and their economic roots.[4]

She believed that Marx had not fully grasped the question on account of the fact that his work was still unfinished by the time of his death in 1883. It is certainly true that Marx never finished writing the three volumes of *Capital*, and the manuscripts for the last two volumes that he left behind were edited by Engels. But Luxemburg went a lot further than this. She believed that Marx had in fact been mistaken.

In *Capital*, Marx had attempted to lay bare the laws of motion of capitalism. The first volume deals with capitalist production and the creation of surplus value. It analyses the processes in the workplace, where commodities are produced, and surplus value arises from the unpaid labour of the working class. The second volume is concerned with the circulation of capital, and deals with market relations, where commodities are sold and surplus value is *realised* by the capitalists. The third volume, dealing with the capitalist system as a whole, draws all the threads together, and analyses the deepening contradictions of capitalism.

In volume two, Marx explains how surplus value is accumulated by the capitalists. In a letter to Engels, he explained:

In Book 1, lastly, we content ourselves with the assumption that if in the production of surplus value £100 becomes £110, the latter will *find already in existence* in the market the elements into which it will change once more. But now we investigate the conditions under which these elements are found at hand,

3 Quoted in J. P. Nettl, *Rosa Luxemburg*, p. 530.
4 Quoted in P. Frölich, *Rosa Luxemburg*, p. 135.

namely the social intertwining of different capitals, of component parts of capital and of revenue (=s).[5]

The question for Marx, which Rosa Luxemburg also took up, was: How do the capitalists sell the commodities they produce, when the working class only receives a part of the total value that it creates? While a portion is taken by the capitalists for their own consumption, where does the extra demand come from for accumulation? How do you resolve this problem of capitalism's reproduction on an increasingly expanded scale? Clearly, this is a rather complicated question.

To begin with, we need to understand Marx's approach. In volume one of *Capital*, he deals with *simple* reproduction, stripping everything down to its essentials (a 'pure' capitalism, so to speak), to show how exploitation exists and how surplus value is created in production, without taking into account production on an ever-expanding scale. Luxemburg quoted Marx:

> We here take no account of export trade, by means of which a nation can change articles of luxury either into means of production or means of subsistence, and *vice versa*. In order to examine the object of our investigation in its integrity, free from all disturbing subsidiary circumstances, we must treat the whole world as one nation, and assume that capitalist production is everywhere established and has possessed itself of every branch of industry.[6]

To clarify things, Marx assumes that there are only two classes and that capitalism forms a single, closed system. By investing in materials and equipment and purchasing labour-power, the capitalists set the productive process in motion. The end result is that all the value that goes into the production process is transferred to the commodities that are produced, while an additional amount of surplus value is also created. The total value created in production consists of *constant* capital (raw materials, unfinished goods, depreciation of machinery), which merely transfers its value to the finished product; *variable* capital (wages), which covers the maintenance of the workers; and surplus value (profit), which belongs to the capitalist.

Having produced surplus value, the commodities need to be sold so as to actually realise a profit. While surplus value is created in production, it is only

---

5   K. Marx, 'To F. Engels, 30 April 1868', *Marx and Engels Selected Correspondence*, p. 245.

6   K. Marx, *Capital*, Vol. 1, *Marx and Engels Collected Works* (Henceforth referred to as *MECW*), Vol. 35. p. 580, footnote 1.

realised through exchange on the market. In *simple* reproduction, realisation of surplus value presents no difficulties as the capitalists consume the total surplus value unproductively, namely they expend it on their personal needs and not on accumulating additional capital. The capitalist merely sells his product, pays the wages to his workers, covers his raw material costs and consumes the rest. He uses the revenues to replace the materials and the labour power needed to continue production, and in this way the cycle continues. But in simple reproduction, there is no *new* investment or increased capacity.

Marx divides the economy into two sectors: Department 1 (producing means of production) and Department 2 (producing means of consumption). If capitalism is to sustain itself, and even develop, it needs to maintain a balance between the two sectors of the economy. Therefore, in simple reproduction, the products of Department 1 must be equal to the constant capital required for the production processes of both Department 1 and Department 2. Were Department 1 to produce more machinery than is required by itself and Department 2, then there would be overproduction, and complete dislocation would ensue. Similarly, too few machines would create shortages and bottlenecks. Likewise, the products of Department 2 must be equal to the wages and surplus value of both departments combined, otherwise overproduction or scarcity would arise in this part of the market.

While this holds up well in regard to simple reproduction, in the case of expanded reproduction, matters become more complicated. No society can produce on the same scale year after year. Accumulation is a law of the capitalist economy. Under expanded reproduction, the surplus value is not, in large measure, unproductively consumed by the capitalist. Rather, it is used instead for expansion. Production proceeds therefore in "not a circle but a spiral".[7] Under such circumstances, the production of the means of production increases at a faster rate than the production of the means of consumption.

However, Rosa Luxemburg believed she detected a problem here. According to her, demand enabling such expansion (accumulation) cannot come from the working class, as the latter only needs to buy consumer goods. Nor can it come from the capitalists, who buy both consumer goods and capital goods from one another. She believed that in a *closed* system, as Marx assumed, capitalist accumulation is impossible. As Luxemburg writes:

---

7   K. Marx, *Theories of Surplus Value, MECW*, Vol. 32, p. 153. (Also see Marx's analysis of this in the unabridged 1967 edition of *Capital,* Vol. 1 by International Publishers, pp. 581, 627.)

Who then could be the buyer and consumer of that portion of commodities whose sale is only the beginning of accumulation? So far as we have seen, it can be neither the workers nor the capitalists.[8]

She then concedes, however, that the capitalists are consumers of the surplus, who use it for the extension of production and accumulation. But this, she maintains, doesn't solve the problem, only pushing it further into the future.

After we have assumed that accumulation has started and that the increased production throws an even bigger amount of commodities onto the market the following year, the same question arises again: where do we then find the consumers for this even greater amount of commodities? Will we answer: well, this growing amount of goods will again be exchanged among the capitalists to extend production again, and so forth, year after year?[9]

She describes this process as a "roundabout", revolving around itself in "empty space", which cannot explain accumulation.

As far as Luxemburg is concerned, the only solution to this "realisation problem" lies in the abandonment of the closed model of an economy based only on workers and capitalists. In other words, we need to abandon Marx's framework of analysis. She proceeds to look at other intermediary layers, such as civil servants, academics, artists, etc., as a possible solution, but discounts them, as their income is only derived from the redistribution of the existing consumption within the closed capitalist economy. She argues instead that the surplus value for accumulation can only be realised by the sale of commodities to *non-capitalist* countries, outside of the capitalist system. Of course, these areas are eventually conquered and absorbed, but this only reveals the limits of capitalism. This idea also provides Luxemburg with the economic explanation for imperialism.

Thus capitalism expands because of its mutual relationship with non-capitalist social strata and countries, accumulating at their expense and at the same time pushing them aside to take their place. The more capitalist countries participate in this hunting for accumulation areas, the rarer the non-capitalist places still open to the expansion of capital become and the tougher the competition; its raids turn into a chain of economic and political catastrophes: world crises, wars, revolution.[10]

---

8   R. Luxemburg, *The Accumulation of Capital – An Anti-Critique*, p. 56.

9   Ibid., p. 57.

10 Ibid., p. 60.

However, Luxemburg's criticism of Marx leads her to some dangerous conclusions. She believed that accepting the idea that capitalism creates its own market would rule out capitalist crisis and destroy the very foundations of Marxist economic theory.

> *First consequence:* if capitalist production can act limitlessly as its own consumer, i.e., production and market are identical, it becomes totally impossible to explain the periodic appearance of crises. [...]

> *Second consequence:* capitalist accumulation becomes (objectively) limitless once capitalist production has built a sufficient market for itself. As production will still grow, i.e., the productive forces will develop without limit, even when all mankind is divided into capitalists and proletarians, as there is no end to the economic development of capitalism, the one specifically Marxist foundation crumbles.[11]

She believes that to accept this proposition is to:

> [...] take refuge in the mist of pre-Marxist systems and schools which attempted to deduce socialism solely on the basis of the injustice and evils of today's world and the revolutionary determination of the working classes.[12]

The fact is, however, that Marx's analysis is absolutely sound. The expansion of capitalism and the creation of new markets accompanies the accumulation of capital. Contrary to what Luxemburg implies, this is not a concession to Say's Law, where every seller automatically brings their buyer to market, resulting in equilibrium and therefore the impossibility of crisis. On the contrary, as Marx explained, the very development of capitalism creates its own contradictions. Nevertheless, the capitalist system does in fact develop and expand. New demands are created within the system for capital and consumer goods. With additional constant capital invested in buildings and machines, there is also additional variable capital in the taking on of more workers. They receive wages and this means increased consumption. To admit the growth of one, means to admit the growth of the other. There is a chain of buying and selling, which interact with one another. In so doing, there exists a mutual interconnection between various branches of production, which results in the expansion of the market. But as Marx explains, within these processes there are contradictions. While capitalism strives to overcome them, they produce new contradictions on an ever-higher level. Eventually, the basis is laid for a crisis of overproduction. Overproduction of capital

---

11 Ibid., pp. 75-6.

12 Ibid., p. 76.

means an overproduction of commodities. This process does not invalidate the Marxist theory of crisis, but rather confirms it.

Luxemburg argues that if capitalism is able to sustain itself, as Marx explained, why is there a need to expand and conquer new markets elsewhere?

> *Third consequence*: when capitalist production builds itself a sufficient market and permits expansion of the total accumulated value, there appears another riddle of modern development: competition for the most distant markets and capital exports, the most dominant feature of modern imperialism. Indeed incomprehensible! Why all this fuss? Why conquer colonies, why the opium wars of the forties and sixties, why the squabble for swamps in the Congo, for Mesopotamian deserts? Capital should stay at home and earn an honest living. Krupp should go along and produce for Thyssen, Thyssen for Krupp, let them invest their capital in their own enterprises and expand them mutually, and so on and so on. The historical movement of capital, and with it modern imperialism, becomes quite incomprehensible.[13]

But here, Rosa Luxemburg is mixing things up. Marx proved in volume two of *Capital* that capitalist production is quite conceivable without foreign markets. However, at a certain point, production reaches a level when it can no longer remain within the limits of the nation state. As Lenin explained:

> Capitalism's need for a foreign market is by no means to be explained by the impossibility of realising the product on the home market, but by the circumstance that capitalism is in no position to go on repeating the same processes of production on the former scale, under unchanging conditions (as was the case under pre-capitalist regimes), and that it inevitably leads to an unlimited growth of production which overflows the old, narrow limits of earlier economic units.[14]

The capitalists cannot exist without accumulating and expanding, on pain of ruin. The inevitable concentration of capital increases the productivity of labour and increases output. Competition compels them to keep expanding production and search for new markets. With the development of capitalism comes the export of capital, which reaches its height in its imperialist stage. The conquest of new markets and sources of raw materials becomes an integral part of the system. Desperate for fields of profitable investment, the capitalists invest in foreign lands, exporting capital to countries where it can

---

13 Ibid., p. 77.

14 V. I. Lenin, *The Development of Capitalism in Russia*, LCW, Vol. 3, p. 590.

yield a higher rate of profit through the super-exploitation of the labour and resources of colonial and semi-colonial nations. However, this frantic search is not about *realisation* of value in commodities already produced, but which are unable to find a market in the imperialist nations. Rather, it is about exploitation and the search for surplus profit.

While Luxemburg denies the possibility of realisation of surplus value and accumulation within a closed system, Marx states that these are an absolute necessity, although they by no means develop in a harmonious manner. On the contrary, the whole process is saturated with contradictions.

> He[15] cannot therefore admit that the bourgeois mode of production contains within itself a barrier to the free development of the productive forces, a barrier which comes to the surface in crises and, in particular, in *overproduction* – the basic phenomenon in crises.[16]

This incidentally answers Luxemburg's assertion that the ability of capitalism to create markets eradicates crises. It does not. Marx adds:

> The contradictions inherent in the circulation of commodities, which are further developed in the circulation of money – and thus, also, the possibilities of crisis – reproduce themselves, automatically, in capital [...]

> But now the further development of the potential CRISIS has to be traced – the real crisis can only be educed from the real movement of capitalist production, competition and credit – in so far as crises arise out of the special aspects of capital which are *peculiar* to it as capital, and not merely comprised in its existence as commodities and money.[17]

The whole basis of Luxemburg's criticism of Marx is that capitalism cannot create its own market but must find some external source outside of capitalist commodity production. But this has been shown to be false. If capitalism couldn't create its own internal market, there would be an *immediate* and *permanent* crisis of overproduction from day one. This is clearly not the case. The capitalists overcome this problem by reinvesting the surplus created by the working class.

But even on Luxemburg's premise, if you could sell the surplus to non-capitalist consumers, you would also have to buy from them. The question is who would buy these imported commodities?

---

15 Here Marx is speaking of David Ricardo, the British classical economist.

16 K. Marx, *Theories of Surplus Value, MECW*, Vol. 32, p. 157.

17 Ibid., p. 143.

Luxemburg seems to confuse simple reproduction with extended reproduction, and ignores the contradictory dynamics of the system. Capitalism, after all, is a revolutionary system of production that sweeps aside everything in its path. As the *Communist Manifesto* explained, the capitalist mode of production revolutionised everything, and in the process created a world market.

Despite its revolutionary role, capitalist development is not harmonious, but anarchic and contradictory. As Engels stressed:

> Anarchy reigns in socialised production.
>
> But the production of commodities, like every other form of production, has its peculiar, inherent laws inseparable from it; and these laws work, despite anarchy, in and through anarchy. They reveal themselves in the only persistent form of social interrelations, i.e., in exchange, and here they affect the individual producers as compulsory laws of competition.[18]

The whole rationale of capitalism, its historic mission, is to take the surplus value created from the exploitation of the working class and plough it back into the expansion of industry. This eventually lays the material basis for a classless society, for socialism. The capitalists, under the whip of competition, are forced to raise the productivity of labour, resulting in an enormous development and expansion of the productive forces of industry, technique and science. With the growth of production, we have the expansion of the market, and also of consumption. Both are interconnected. This process takes place according to the laws of capitalist accumulation, which were outlined by Marx.

In *An Anti-Critique*, Luxemburg returns to her argument from *Reform or Revolution?* that the breakdown of capitalism forms a necessary link in the argument for socialism. The assertions of her critics – that expanded reproduction occurs within capitalism – in Luxemburg's view, meant giving up on the idea that socialism is an objective necessity, because it necessarily meant abandoning the idea that capitalism would inevitably break down:

> So the 'experts' are faced with having to choose between two alternatives. Either – as they deduce from Marx's models – capitalist production is identical with its market, and the historical materialist explanation for imperialism disappears, or capital accumulation can only take place in so far as customers can be found beyond capitalists and workers, in which case growing sales in non-capitalist strata and countries are the essential precondition for accumulation.[19]

---

18 F. Engels, *Anti-Dühring*, p. 322.

19 R. Luxemburg, *The Accumulation of Capital – An Anti-Critique*, p. 77.

Rosa Luxemburg makes some simple, but fundamental errors in her search for the answer to the so-called 'realisation problem'. Capitalists do indeed have to sell in order to realise the surplus value contained in the commodities that have been produced. However, their intention is not the accumulation of money, but rather to throw that money back into circulation in the form of new investments, which can be used to squeeze even more surplus value out of the working class. A hoard of money is not capital in the Marxist sense, but simply a product of money grabbing. Capital, in the sense understood by Marx, is value that is constantly being transformed into means of production for the exploitation of labour power, and thus for the creation of more surplus value. Capital sitting idle and remaining unused for the purpose of exploitation is merely 'lying fallow'.

The industrial capitalist, according to Marx:

> [I]s dominated by the same absolute drive to enrich himself as the hoarder, except that he does not satisfy it in the illusory form of building up a treasure of gold and silver, but in the creation of capital, which is real production.[20]

"Accumulation for accumulation's sake, production for production's sake: by this formula classical economy expressed the historical mission of the bourgeoisie", explained Marx.[21]

Where then does Marx's crisis of overproduction enter the picture? In *Anti-Dühring*, Engels explained that in every form of class society that has ever existed, the masses have been blighted by "underconsumption". Under capitalism the working class sells its labour power to the capitalist for wages. However, the secret is that, when put to work, labour power produces more value than its own value. This is the source of surplus value. Put another way, the working day can be divided between necessary labour-time and surplus labour-time. The necessary labour-time is that period when the worker produces value that covers their wages. The period of surplus-time is when the worker produces surplus value. Clearly the worker does not receive enough in wages to buy back the full value of their labour.

However, as explained, the capitalist class overcomes this problem by reinvesting the surplus value into means of production. As long as they continue doing so – even taking loans out in order to build new machines, factories, technology etc., in the hope that by expanding their capacity, they can expand their market share at their competitors' expense – the expansion

---

20 K. Marx, *Theories of Surplus Value*, MECW, Vol. 31, p. 179.
21 K. Marx, *Capital*, Vol. 1, MECW, Vol. 35, p. 558.

phase of the capitalist cycle will continue. In this way, workers are put to work, wages are paid, and so they can purchase consumer goods, while the capitalists purchase means of production. There is no overproduction. The problem is that all the new means of production which have been created must, over time, translate into more consumer goods. But the sales of these goods are limited by the restraints of the market, which in turn is limited by private ownership and production for profit – the majority of consumers are proletarians.

The hoarding of cash, which Luxemburg mistakenly regards as the final purpose of accumulation, only becomes widespread when the contradiction between the build up of productive capacity and a limited consumer market reaches a breaking point. We have a crisis of overproduction. At this point, the capitalists attempt to realise the value of their commodities by cutting prices and pull their capital out of circulation. Everyone attempts to sell their commodities without buying new ones. Circulation breaks down, prices collapse, and enormous amounts of value are destroyed. The crisis sets in.

Capitalist crises do not generally express themselves in the first instance in the consumer goods sector. The gap between this sector and realisation on the market is relatively short, and as such supply and demand maintain the market in relative balance. Furthermore, *in general*, crises are not triggered by sudden changes in patterns of consumption, which tend to remain stable. Instead, problems almost always initially express themselves in the reproduction process of capital. The industrial capitalist either sells to another capitalist, or a wholesaler if they produce consumer goods. They do not then wait for the consumer goods to fall into the hands of the final consumer before they plough their profits into new investments and new means of production. Only with a delay does the fact of overproduction make itself felt in the chain of production, at which point a crisis breaks out in the exchanges between capitalists. Realising that markets are over-saturated, capitalists demand immediate payment from one another. Having speculatively overinvested, long-term investments are now frozen. The credit markets collapse. From a factor propelling capital circulation forward, credit, as debt, becomes a direct hindrance. And finally, the workers find themselves being fired and their purchasing power now vanishes from the market, causing the consumer goods market to now collapse.

Had Luxemburg had access to Lenin's writings, she might have come across his polemical response to the Russian Narodniks[22] on this question, which

---

22 The Narodniks – a political movement in Russia in the late 1800s and early 1900s. They were made up of dedicated revolutionaries, primarily young people, who came

would have helped to clarify her views. What is striking about the economic theories espoused by the latter is how closely they resemble Rosa Luxemburg's own theory of capital accumulation. As Lenin explained:

> Do we deny that capitalism needs a foreign market? Of course not. But the question of a foreign market has *absolutely nothing to do with the question of realisation* [...] That is nonsense. A foreign market is needed because it is *inherent* in capitalist production to strive for *unlimited* expansion [...][23]

He explained that it was not so much the growth of consumption as the demands of production that expands the home market. Therefore, it is not necessary for a 'closed' capitalist economy to look ceaselessly for consumers beyond its borders, in the non-capitalist world. Capital accumulation itself creates new markets, although not without contradictions, as new, more powerful productive forces periodically produce greater, more gigantic crises of overproduction.

We can then see how imperialism is not fundamentally a product of the capitalists being unable to realise the value of their surplus of commodities, without which capital cannot accumulate, and that they therefore scour the world for foreign markets. First and foremost, imperialism – the highest stage of capitalism – is about the export of capital. That is to say, it is about building factories and new productive capacity in countries with a plentiful supply of cheap raw materials and labour power, and so where super profits can be made. Connected to this export of capital are other questions, such as the securing of maritime routes and sources of raw materials, colonial expansion, etc.

In chapter two, we described how and why Rosa Luxemburg bent the stick too far in her polemic with Bernstein, asserting that capitalism would meet with a final crisis, which would result in economic collapse. The same error in method that led Luxemburg to such a conclusion is at the heart of the misunderstanding that led her to the 'correction' of Marx that we have just examined. However, since 1915, the ideas contained in *The Accumulation of Capital* have had little impact. With the passage of time,

---

from the intelligentsia and had broken with their class background in order to go to the 'people'. What back then was called 'terrorist actions' was an important part of their political activity. This involved assassinations of high-level officials in the tsarist regime, including the tsar himself. Russian Marxism originated from this movement but simultaneously through a theoretical struggle against it.

23 V. I. Lenin, *A Characterisation of Economic Romanticism*, LCW, Vol.2, pp. 162-4.

reality has falsified Luxemburg's theory: capitalism today has settled in every part of the globe, and has not automatically collapsed in one great, final crisis. As Marx showed, expanded reproduction is simply an objective part of a closed capitalist system, and it has proceeded and continues to proceed without capitalism itself collapsing. The final overthrow of capitalism is not an automatic outcome of the purely economic development of capitalism, but rather is fundamentally dependent on the outcome of the class struggle.

A couple of years after the publication of Luxemburg's book, Lenin wrote *Imperialism: The Highest Stage of Capitalism*. In it, he makes no mention of Luxemburg's book, and yet he disproves some of her core arguments. Nevertheless, both Lenin and Luxemburg agreed that imperialism was an unavoidable consequence of the development of capitalism. This view was in sharp contrast with Kautsky's theory of 'ultra-imperialism', which stated that capitalism was embarking on a more peaceful and democratic stage beyond imperialism, simply by way of regulation. However, Lenin strongly disagreed with the fundamental idea contained in Luxemburg's *The Accumulation of Capital*, when he explained that imperialism was not characterised simply by the export of commodities, but rather by the export of capital. In Lenin's opinion, capitalism was not destined to simply collapse of its own accord, but needed to be consciously overthrown.

In *Imperialism*, Lenin gave a scientific and solidly-founded characterisation of imperialism and its causes, showing how, hand-in-hand, finance capital and the state conquer raw materials, markets, and spheres of influence, using both economic and military means.

Despite her errors on this question, the Stalinists have unjustly picked out *The Accumulation of Capital* as the source of all of Luxemburg's mistakes. They have claimed that her ideas regarding the collapse of capitalism necessarily led her to develop a 'theory of spontaneity', which in turn caused her to reject the building of the revolutionary party. The ultra-left Ruth Fischer,[24] one of the main architects of the Communist Party's crusade against Luxemburg, put it this way:

> The German party based its theory and practice in the main on Rosa Luxemburg's theory of accumulation, and this is the fount of all errors, all theories of spontaneity, all erroneous conceptions of organisational problems.[25]

---

24 Ruth Fischer (1895-1961) – leader of the Berlin branch of the German Communist Party, and was elected as party chair (together with Maslow) in 1924.

25 Quoted in J. P. Nettl, *Rosa Luxemburg*, p. 533.

As we have already discussed, there is no truth in the Stalinist claim that Luxemburg was a fatalist: by no means did she stand with her arms crossed waiting for capitalism to collapse of its own volition. On the contrary, she worked to prepare Social Democracy for the coming revolution, and would later begin the building of the German Communist Party. Despite the disagreements between Lenin and Luxemburg, they wrote a joint amendment for the World Congress of the Second International, which specifically dealt with imperialism. That is to say, as far as imperialism was concerned, they were in perfect agreement as to how the workers' movement ought to respond.

Luxemburg and Women's Suffrage

Before discussing the evolution of Rosa Luxemburg's relationship with the SPD – its leadership and Kautsky in particular – between the 1905 Revolution and the outbreak of the First World War in 1914, it is worth taking a short detour to discuss Luxemburg's position on the women's question. The reason why this detour is short is that, in truth, Luxemburg wrote very little on the question, although some of her more significant remarks on it belong to this period. When Rosa Luxemburg arrived in Germany in the 1890s, the SPD bureaucracy attempted to safely deal with this youthful firebrand by directing her exclusively towards work among women. But, as we saw, she was not to be so easily pigeonholed. She instead threw herself fully into the most important struggle of the day, which at that time was the struggle against revisionism. But, certainly, none of this is to say that she believed the women's question was unimportant. In November 1918, she wrote the following in a letter to her close friend Clara Zetkin who was responsible for this question in the SPD:

> I wait with longing for your article – [keep it] quite short! Don't put in a lot of work. We want to have your name [in our paper] right away. Write something perhaps about women, that is so important now, and none of us here understand anything about it.[26]

A speech at a social-democratic women's conference in May 1912 in Stuttgart offers one of the few occasions in which Luxemburg put forward her ideas on the women's question publicly. Speaking on 'women's suffrage and the class struggle', she unconditionally supported the demand for a woman's right to vote, showing how the women's struggle could not be separated from the class struggle:

26 R. Luxemburg, *The Letters of Rosa Luxemburg* [2013], p. 480.

A hundred years ago, the Frenchman Charles Fourier, one of the first great prophets of socialist ideals, wrote these memorable words: In any society, the degree of female emancipation is the natural measure of the general emancipation. This is completely true for our present society. The current mass struggle for women's political rights is only an expression and a part of the proletariat's general struggle for liberation. In this lies its strength and its future. Because of the female proletariat, general, equal, direct suffrage for women would immensely advance and intensify the proletarian class struggle. This is why bourgeois society abhors and fears women's suffrage. And this is why we want and will achieve it. Fighting for women's suffrage, we will also hasten the coming of the hour when the present society falls in ruins under the hammer strokes of the revolutionary proletariat.[27]

To Luxemburg, the struggle for women's suffrage was inseparably linked to the general struggle for a socialist revolution. She was therefore quite explicitly hostile to bourgeois women whom, she believed, would stand on the opposite side of the struggle to working-class women:

The women of the property-owning classes will always fanatically defend the exploitation and enslavement of the working people by which they indirectly receive the means for their socially useless existence.[28]

Luxemburg sharply demarcated between the struggle of working women and the bourgeois and petty-bourgeois women's movement:

In truth, our state is interested in keeping the vote from working women and from them alone. It rightly fears they will threaten the traditional institutions of class rule, for instance militarism (of which no thinking proletarian woman can help being a deadly enemy), monarchy, the systematic robbery of duties and taxes on groceries, etc. Women's suffrage is a horror and abomination for the present capitalist state because behind it stand millions of women who would strengthen the enemy within, i.e., revolutionary Social Democracy. If it were a matter of bourgeois ladies voting, the capitalist state could expect nothing but effective support for the reaction. Most of those bourgeois women who act like lionesses in the struggle against 'male prerogatives' would trot like docile lambs in the camp of conservative and clerical reaction if they had suffrage. Indeed, they would certainly be a good deal more reactionary than the male

---

27 R. Luxemburg, 'Women's Suffrage and Class Struggle', *Selected Political Writings of Rosa Luxemburg*, p. 222.

28 Ibid., p. 220.

part of their class. Aside from the few who have jobs or professions, the women of the bourgeoisie do not take part in social production. They are nothing but co-consumers of the surplus value their men extort from the proletariat. They are parasites of the parasites of the social body. And consumers are usually even more rabid and cruel in defending their 'right' to a parasite's life than the direct agents of class rule and exploitation.[29]

The Break with Kautsky

The year 1905 made a deep impression on Rosa Luxemburg. On the surface, however, nothing had changed – Luxemburg continued to enjoy a good relationship with the leadership of the SPD, and her Sunday dinners at the home of the Kautsky family continued. Nonetheless, disillusionment with the leadership of the SPD and with Karl Kautsky in particular had begun to develop. In early 1907, she wrote to Clara Zetkin:

> Since my return from Russia I feel rather isolated… I feel the pettiness and the hesitancy of our party régime more clearly and more painfully than ever before. However, I can't get so excited about the situation as you do, because I see with depressing clarity that neither things nor people can be changed – until the whole situation has changed, and even then we shall just have to reckon with inevitable resistance if we want to lead the masses on. I have come to that conclusion after mature reflection. The plain truth is that August [Bebel], and still more so the others, have completely pledged themselves to parliament and parliamentarianism, and whenever anything happens which transcends the limits of parliamentary action they are hopeless – no, worse than hopeless, because they then do their utmost to force the movement back into parliamentary channels, and they will ferociously defame as 'an enemy of the people' anyone who dares to venture beyond their own limits. I feel that those of the masses who are organised in the party are tired of parliamentarianism, and would welcome a new line in party tactics, but the party leaders and still more of the upper stratum of opportunist editors, deputies, and trade union leaders are like an incubus. We must protest vigorously against this general stagnation, but it is quite clear that in doing so we shall find ourselves against the opportunists as well as the party leaders and August. As long as it was a question of defending themselves against Bernstein and his friends, August and Co. were glad of our assistance, because they were shaking in their shoes. But when it is a question of launching an offensive against opportunism then August and the rest are with Ede [Bernstein], Vollmar, and

---

29 Ibid., pp. 219–20.

David against us. That's how I see matters, but the chief thing is to keep your chin up and not get too excited about it. Our job will take years.[30]

Rosa Luxemburg could already see quite clearly how the party leadership had gone over to reformism. Nevertheless, she persisted in her attempts to 'influence' the party, without yet organising an opposition around herself, neither as a network nor as a firmer organisation. The process that Luxemburg described in the letter to Zetkin only worsened in the years that followed. The reformism of the leadership would become increasingly flavoured with nationalism and an opportunistic adaptation to the imperialist interests of the German bourgeoisie.

In early 1907, the German government called an election. The 'Hottentot Election', as Luxemburg and others called it, was called as a result of questions relating to Germany's colonial possessions and foreign policy. The sitting government succeeded in making the election a nationalistic question of securing Germany's imperialist, colonial interests. They intended to use this as a means to attack the SPD, which was weak on this point. For the first time in its history, the SPD experienced a decline in votes, falling from eighty-one seats in the Reichstag to forty-three. The party leadership obsessed over this electoral defeat. In its wake, they toned down the party's revolutionary rhetoric and made concessions to nationalism in an effort to win back the votes they had lost.

This further accelerated the process of bureaucratisation and degeneration of the party. Revisionism, to which parts of the party apparatus had secretly converted, began spreading. The apparatus was increasingly expanded, the leaders having by and large given up on the idea of revolution, and having become completely absorbed in day-to-day work. To them, building the party became the goal in and of itself. Revolution, meanwhile, was viewed simply as a force of destruction. The creeping process of degeneration went on over a long period of time, through an accumulation of numerous small changes. Officially, the party resolutions were still binding and sounded quite radical, but reformism permeated the party's practical work and the outlook of its leadership. The extent to which reformism and bureaucratisation had penetrated the party would only become fully apparent when a sharp turn in the situation – namely, the outbreak of the First World War – ripped the cloak away from the party leaders' opportunism.

Rosa Luxemburg was working jointly with Karl Kautsky on *Die Neue Zeit*, when the two editors visited Lake Geneva in Easter of 1907. Their trip was

---

30 Quoted in J. P. Nettl, *Rosa Luxemburg*, p. 375.

designed to allow the two of them to work on the journal's politics, while allowing Luxemburg the opportunity to get much needed rest. It was here that Luxemburg's disillusionment with Karl Kautsky began setting in. Returning from the trip, she described Kautsky as "heavy, dull, unimaginative, and ponderous", and his ideas as, "cold, pedantic, and doctrinaire".[31] That her regard for Kautsky had begun declining was obvious from her letters at this time. Only later did she realise that this was the beginning of the end of their friendship. From 1908 onward, Sunday dinners at the Kautsky household increasingly became boring to Luxemburg. She increasingly regarded their conversation as little more than gossip. In June 1908, she wrote the following to a friend:

> Soon I shall be quite unable to read anything written by Karl Kautsky… It is like a disgusting series of spiders' webs… which can only be washed away by the mental bath of reading Marx himself…[32]

In late 1909, the political situation started brightening up somewhat: the right-wing bloc that had won the election in 1907 began falling apart. In Prussia, the so-called 'three-class' electoral system meant that the SPD received a mere six seats for its 600,000 votes, while the conservatives with 418,000 votes had received 212 seats. Dissatisfaction with this system had been rife for some time, and in 1910 a draft law for electoral reform was announced. However, it didn't in the least bit alter the electoral status of the great majority of voters. Rather, it simply moved a few groups – primarily academics – from the lowest voter class to the middle. The Social Democrats subjected the reform law to heavy criticism, and there was widespread discontent with the electoral reform law among the membership of the SPD. At the regional party congress in Prussia, where the question was debated, the party leadership suggested an alliance with different 'progressive' liberal groups in the Reichstag. But the mood among Prussian SPD members was far more radical. They regarded it as futile to conduct the campaign through a parliament that gave the Social Democrats such lousy representation. The congress, therefore, rejected the idea of an alliance with the liberals. In place of parliamentary manoeuvring, the congress decided to launch an "offensive for electoral rights" – i.e., a mass campaign to force through real electoral reform. The liberals were moving quickly to the right, while the ranks of the SPD were rapidly shifting to the left. The executive committee of the SPD

---

31 Quoted ibid., p. 376.
32 Quoted ibid., p. 411.

was thus left more or less isolated, along with the revisionist wing of the party which had also proposed cooperation with the liberals.

The release of the draft reform law by the government fired the starting pistol on what became a continuous series of protests and demonstrations that would gather every Sunday. The proposal was then adopted by the Prussian Landtag in March, but the Upper House proved unable to agree on the wording and, in the end, the reform was retracted all together. Meanwhile, the demonstrations organised by the social democrats continued unabated. Each Sunday, the protests grew, and there were clashes with the police. A number of strikes broke out in the mining and construction industries, organised by the trade unions. By 1910 almost 370,000 workers were involved in strike action, and in March of that year the political and economic demands started to merge.

Luxemburg was politically reinvigorated. She threw all her effort into the movement, writing articles and conducting a three-month-long speaking tour all over Germany. Given these circumstances, she paused her work at the party school. At the mass meetings at which she appeared, she was greeted with overwhelming enthusiasm.

As the movement reawakened, Luxemburg penned an article titled 'The Next Step' where she outlined what she believed were the next steps that the SPD ought to take. She encouraged the party to fan the flames of the strike movement, helping it advance and ensuring that it did not end in disillusionment. The next step of the party ought to have been to push forward towards a mass strike. Luxemburg called on the party to raise the political demand for a republic in order to radicalise the movement:

> Nevertheless, if the latest impressive street demonstrations already signify a welcome innovation in the outward forms of Social Democracy's struggle, and if at the same time they have set off a most powerful mass struggle for the right to vote in Prussia, then they for their part impose certain obligations on the party to whose initiative and leadership they are attributable. In view of the mass movement it has unleashed, our party must have a clear and definite plan of how it intends to continue the mass action which it has already begun. Street demonstrations, like military demonstrations, are usually only a prelude to the battle. There are cases in which demonstrations alone attain their end by intimidating the enemy. But apart from the undeniable fact that the enemy, in this case the unified reaction of the Junkers,[33] *haute* bourgeoisie and monarchists in Prussia and Germany, is not

---

33 Junker – "…(from Middle Low German *junkher*, literally 'young lord'), German noble title used since medieval times for young counts, and from the nineteenth century

in the least inclined to give in, demonstrations can exert an effective pressure only when they are backed up by the firm resolve and readiness to resort, if necessary, to stronger methods of doing battle. Above all we must be clear about what we intend to do if the street demonstrations prove inadequate to achieve their direct end.

The necessity of complete lucidity and determination in this regard has been proven by the party's experience until now. Two years ago we made the first attempts at street demonstrations in Prussia. Even then the masses proved equal to the situation, and enthusiastically followed the Social-Democratic rallying cry. Among the aroused masses one could sense a fresh breeze, a hope for new and more effective forms of struggle, a resolve not to be intimidated or to shrink from any sacrifice. And what was the end result? The party advanced no new demands and the action was not extended and continued. On the contrary, the masses were tacitly warned to desist, the general agitation ebbed away forthwith, and the whole affair in fact ran aground.

This first experiment might be an indication and a warning to our party that mass demonstrations have their own logic and their own psychology; to take these into account is an urgent necessity for politicians who wish to master them. For the expressions of the masses' will in the political struggle cannot be held at one and the same level artificially or for any length of time, nor can they be encapsulated in one and the same form. They must be intensified, concentrated and must take on new and more effective forms. Once unleashed, the mass action must go forward. And if at the acknowledged moment the leading party lacks the resolve to provide the masses with the necessary watchwords, then they are inevitably overcome by a certain disillusionment, their courage vanishes and the action collapses of itself.[34]

She submitted her article to the editorial board of the party newspaper, *Vorwärts*, as she believed that the official party organ was precisely the most appropriate place to discuss the tactic of the mass strike. But on 2 March, the

---

used, often disparagingly, as a description of German landlords in the old Prussian core provinces east of the Elbe. The Junkers were, for centuries, the most powerful social group in Prussia/Germany thanks to their power over their dependent peasants and their leading positions in the army and administration and in political life. The domination of the Junkers in the nineteenth and beginning of the twentieth century has been judged, particularly by social-liberal German historians, to be a substantial part in a particular German authoritarian tradition which helped the Nazis take power in 1933." (From denstoredanske.dk, accessed on 8 December 2018.)

34 R. Luxemburg, 'The Next Step', *Marxist Internet Archive* [website].

editors returned her article with a note stating that it had been decided that the question of mass strike should not be discussed at this time:

> We have regretfully to decline your article since, in accordance with an agreement between the party executive, the executive commission of the Prussian provincial organisation (of the SPD), and the editor, the question of mass strike shall not be elaborated in *Vorwärts* for the time being.[35]

Luxemburg then submitted her article to *Die Neue Zeit*, where her articles were usually given precedence. Karl Kautsky responded with kind words about how "beautiful and important" he found the article, and how he would very much like to publish it, albeit with his own answer to those points in her article that he disagreed with. However, he point-blank refused to publish that part of the article that raised the demand for a republic, which he was emphatically against. He claimed that the demand for a republic was an entirely new question, one which the SPD had not yet discussed, and which they therefore could not express a public position on. In the end, Kautsky returned Luxemburg's article, explaining that he could not publish an article that encouraged workers to use the mass strike, which he claimed would be doomed to inevitable failure. Having been rejected by Kautsky, Luxemburg immediately sent it on to several other newspapers, and in March it was printed in Konrad Haenisch's[36] paper in Dortmund, *Arbeiterzeitung*.

While Luxemburg travelled across the country speaking at mass meetings, Kautsky published his response to her article in his own piece, titled 'Now What?' Kautsky completely disagreed with Luxemburg's analysis of the situation. Among other things, he wrote:

> The excitement of the masses is not nearly sufficient for such an extreme course… but it was certainly great enough for the stimulus provided by Comrade Luxemburg to produce isolated attempts, experiments with the mass strike which were bound to fail.[37]

Kautsky's opinion was that the protests could continue, but that the party should not encourage them. Instead, the party should focus on the coming

---

35 Quoted in J. P. Nettl, *Rosa Luxemburg*, pp. 420-1.

36 Konrad Haenisch (1876-1925) – on the radical left wing of the SPD. Together with Rosa Luxemburg, he argued in 1910 that the party should make use of the mass strike. During the war he went over to the right wing of the party and spoke in support of the SPD's support for war credits in the Reichstag.

37 Ibid., p. 427.

election for the Reichstag, and the radicalisation of the workers could be harnessed to boost the vote for the SPD. For Kautsky, this would form a stepping stone to an absolute SPD majority, which for him was a stepping stone towards the revolution itself.

Rosa Luxemburg was furious with Kautsky, writing, "[Karl Kautsky] this coward who only has courage enough to attack others from behind, but I'll deal with him".[38] The final break between the two had now come.

From now on, three clearly distinct wings could be recognised inside the SPD: a right wing, made up of the party leadership; a centre, led by Kautsky; and a revolutionary left wing led, among others, by Luxemburg. This left would go on to form the core of the Spartacus League. When Luxemburg returned from her tour, she launched her counter-attack against Kautsky. A polemic now began in *Die Neue Zeit* and would last for a number of weeks.

The revisionists rejoiced. What had been the left wing of the party was now split. In open defiance of party decisions, the SPD leadership in the southern German state of Baden, who were notorious for their class collaboration in the federal parliament, proclaimed that they would continue to vote in favour of federal budgets. The revisionists were on the offensive and launched an attack on what they now saw as the divided 'Marxist wing'. Kautsky attempted to convince Luxemburg to set aside their disagreements in order to jointly combat the attacks of the opportunists. Luxemburg, however, refused. In her opinion, the time for sweeping disagreements under the carpet was over. From now on, her critique became particularly focused on Kautsky and the 'centre' of the party. This certainly did not help to mend her relationship with Kautsky. Not always elegantly, Kautsky tried to paint himself as the true heir of Marx against Luxemburg's radical left wing. He wrote:

> When we look at the Duchies of Baden and Luxemburg on the map we find that between them lies Trier, the city of Karl Marx. If from there you go left across the border, you come to Luxemburg. If you turn sharp right and cross the Rhine, you reach Baden. The situation on the map is a symbol for the situation of German Social Democracy today.[39]

To Luxemburg, the movement for electoral rights in Prussia and the situation in Baden were not two separate questions. She didn't simply see the behaviour of the Baden opportunists as a question of the violation of party discipline. For her, the opportunism in southern Germany was inseparably connected

---

38 Quoted ibid., p. 423.

39 Quoted ibid., p. 430.

with the overall state of the party. It was obvious to Rosa Luxemburg that all Kautsky and the party leadership had to offer about revolution were empty words. When their rhetoric was tested by events, it collapsed like a house of cards. Sharp criticism had to be directed at both the right and the so-called 'centre'. Luxemburg could already see how the so-called 'Marxism' of Karl Kautsky was little more than a theoretical cover for the reformism as practiced by the party leadership.

In the conflict between Luxemburg and Kautsky, most foreign social democrats were on the side of Kautsky. This even extended to Lenin and the Bolsheviks. Indeed, right up until 1914, Lenin regarded Kautsky as the foremost defender of Marxism in the International. But Lenin was geographically far removed from Germany. At such a distance, he was unable to discern the degeneration of the German party, and of Kautsky specifically. On the other hand, Luxemburg could witness this degeneration at close quarters, and was therefore able to assess the process much more clearly. When the final betrayal came in 1914, Lenin readily admitted that he had been wrong, and that Luxemburg had been right all along. His critique of Kautsky was all the more bitter as a result. In a letter to Shlyapnikov dated 27 October 1914, Lenin wrote:

> Rosa Luxemburg was right when she wrote, long ago, that Kautsky has the "subservience of a theoretician" – servility, in plainer language, servility to the majority of the Party, to opportunism. Just now there is *nothing* in the world more harmful and dangerous for the *ideological* independence of the proletariat than this rotten self-satisfaction and disgusting hypocrisy of Kautsky, who wants to smother and cover up everything, to tranquillise the awakened conscience of the workers by sophistries and pseudo-scientific chatter. If Kautsky succeeds in this, he will become the main representative of bourgeois corruption in the working-class movement.[40]

Luxemburg Alone

Rosa Luxemburg had criticised the party leadership before her break with Kautsky. The final break between her and Bebel – who until that point had fought her politically, but had nonetheless treated her well – came during the so-called Second Moroccan Crisis.[41]

---

40 V. I. Lenin, 'To A. G. Shlyapnikov', *LCW*, Vol. 35, pp. 167-8.

41 The First Moroccan Crisis took place in 1905 when the German emperor attempted to weaken French influence in Morocco and increase German presence. The crisis

In April 1911, the French government sent troops to Morocco, where it had imperialist interests, in order to assist the regime in defeating a rebellion. The German government attempted to exploit the situation to boost its own presence in the region, whilst also putting France's alliance with Great Britain to the test. The Germans first sent a gunboat, the *SMS Panter*, and then a cruiser to the harbour of Agadir. The French and British responded by rearming.

It was an event of international significance. As such, the secretary of the International, Camille Huysmans, circulated a notice to the parties of the International, requesting that they send their reactions to these events. It was also proposed that, should it come to it, a meeting be called so that the International could issue a joint response to the threat of war by the imperialist governments.

With Bebel absent from Berlin, an SPD secretary named Molkenbuhr answered Huysmans' call. His answer, however, was evasive. The German party leadership was absorbed in the coming Reichstag election, and their biggest fear was that a mood of national chauvinism might cut across the party, hurting its electoral prospects as it had in 1907. The party leadership therefore attempted to pass the question by in silence. They hoped that this expression of German imperialism might pass harmlessly by, without doing their electoral chances any harm. They therefore told Huysmans that they did not believe the question of Morocco should be allowed to overshadow domestic political questions, and as such it would be unnecessary for the International to call a meeting to discuss it.

Members of the SPD, however, were not prepared to let this pass in silence. In Berlin in particular, meetings were held and were well attended. A strong mood of opposition was expressed against the aggression of the German government. In the final week of July the crisis was approaching a climax, yet the party leadership still had not expressed any clear position on it.

As the representative of the SDKPiL's international bureau, Luxemburg also received a copy of Molkenbuhr's letter. For her, this was a principal question. The party had a duty to expose the imperialist politics of the German government and to oppose it.

On 24 July she decided to publish the correspondence between Huysmans and the Executive Committee of the SPD. In it, she severely criticised the

---

brought France and Germany to the brink of war, but it was averted by a conference where Germany was supported only by Austria–Hungary and thus had to give up on its demands.

party leaders for hoping to avoid the Moroccan question merely for the sake of an electoral campaign. She was emphatic that seats and votes for the SPD were *not* the priority. On the contrary, the electoral campaign itself ought to be a means for spreading social-democratic propaganda, above all on the crucial question of Morocco. The party ought to be resolute in its condemnation of German imperialism:

> Finally, the position of the Party Executive exhibits a general conception of the electoral struggle that does not appear entirely satisfactory to us. They say that we should restrict our agitation exclusively to matters of domestic policy, to questions of taxation and social legislation. But financial policy, the rule of the Junkers and the stagnation of social reform are organically bound up with militarism, naval policy, colonial policy, and with personal rule and its foreign policy. Any artificial separation of these spheres can only present an incomplete and one-sided picture of the state of our public affairs. Above all we should propagate socialist enlightenment in the Reichstag elections, but this we cannot do if we restrict our criticism to Germany's domestic circumstances, if we fail to depict the great international relationships, the growing dominance of capitalism, in all parts of the world, the obvious anarchy in every corner of the globe, and the major role played by colonial and global policy in this process. We must conduct our electoral agitation not as an abridged political primer reduced to a few simple points now 'in vogue', but as the socialist world view in all its comprehensiveness, richness and diversity.[42]

As Luxemburg made their correspondence public, the Executive Committee could no longer evade a discussion, and so they decided to go on the offensive. Launching a campaign aimed at Luxemburg personally, they hoped to divert the discussion at the party congress away from themselves and the principled questions involved, and make it instead about Rosa Luxemburg, her disloyalty, and her breach of party discipline. Luxemburg, however, would not back down from her criticism of the Executive Committee and the fact that they had tried to bury any discussion on such an essential question inside the party. A majority of the party membership, including even those on the right wing of the party, agreed with her critique of the leadership. But the strength of support for her position among the membership only increased the hostility of the party leadership, leaving her even more isolated.

Her opponents in the party now counted all of those who had been considered radicals back in 1909; the entire editorial board of *Die Neue*

---

42 R. Luxemburg, 'Concerning Morocco', *Marxist Internet Archive* [website].

Zeit; her colleagues of the party school and, naturally enough, the Executive Committee and most of the party apparatus. Luxemburg was more or less alone.

The Moroccan Crisis ended with German imperialism pulling back from the brink. However, it did manage to force through the demand that part of French-occupied Congo be ceded to German colonial control. Despite the fact that war was seemingly avoided, the crisis actually elevated the threat of war between the imperialist powers of Europe. Animosity between French and English imperialism on the one hand and German imperialism on the other was raised to a fever pitch.

The Reichstag elections of January 1912 represented another milestone on the SPD's path towards reformism. The vote for the party increased from 3,250,000 to 4,250,000, making it by far the largest party in Germany, with more than double the parliamentary seats as its closest competitor, 'The Catholic Centre'. But in the second round of the election, the SPD entered into an electoral alliance with the Progressive Party and the liberals. This allowed the progressives to win seats thanks to SPD votes, but it by no means provided any additional votes for the SPD.

Luxemburg criticised this alliance in no uncertain terms. For her, that the proletarian movement must maintain its class independence was paramount. Before the election, she had warned the SPD not to trust the right-wing parties. After the election it was quite obvious that the liberals had done nothing to live up to their agreement with the social democrats. But the electoral success of the SPD – the party's fraction in the Reichstag more than doubled – meant that the influence of the parliamentarians, who were increasingly being corrupted by the milieu in which they worked, became stronger, further accelerating the party's reformist degeneration.

Luxemburg's disappointment in the leadership grew, but she had not yet drawn the conclusion that flowed from this: that it was necessary to build an organised revolutionary wing. In the whole period prior to the outbreak of the First World War, the left wing of the SPD consisted of nothing more than a loose gathering of individuals.

Nonetheless, the germ of what would become the Spartacus League was forming precisely in this period. After the 1912 election, Luxemburg was surprised to receive the support of Franz Mehring, who had originally favoured the alliance with the liberals but who had grown critical of it. Here, the core of a new left wing in the SPD began crystallising. Luxemburg and Mehring had both written regularly for the *Leipziger Volkszeitung*, but when its editor changed, they soon found their articles were often rejected, or else had most of their radical passages deleted. As such, in late 1913 they began publishing the *Sozialdemokratische Korrespondenz* in cooperation with Marchlewski, which came out on a weekly basis. The paper would usually contain an editorial written by either Luxemburg or Mehring, and an economic note by Marchlewski. The initial idea was that the paper wouldn't have a large circulation, and that instead, local party newspapers could borrow articles from it and publish them themselves. In practice things didn't work out this way. Only four local newspapers printed articles from their paper.

In 1913, Bebel died and was replaced as party chairman by Friedrich Ebert, who would later become one of the principal gravediggers of the German Revolution. The most pressing political questions of the day were imperialism and the impending war, which now towered on the horizon. The entire party, including its left wing, now seemed to be gripped by a kind of apathy and disillusionment. Rosa Luxemburg refused to succumb to this mood. At a meeting on 16 September 1913 in Bockenheim, Luxemburg spoke for two hours on the struggle against imperialism. Among the many things that she touched upon, she also spoke out against the war and called for the workers to fight any attempt to drag them into it. In her speech, she is reported to have said the following: "If they think we are going to lift the weapons of murder against our French and other brethren, then we shall shout: 'We will not do it'."[43] This supposed utterance became the foundation of the public prosecutor's charge against Luxemburg for "public disobedience of the law". The case was heard at a court in Frankfurt on 20 February 1914.

Taking the stand in court, Luxemburg turned her defence into an attack against her accusers in the best revolutionary tradition. The fiery political speech that she delivered from the dock became an instant classic with SPD members, despite the leadership's opposition. The speech was printed in all the major party organs, including those that had refused to publish her articles of late. She again went on a tour, speaking at packed party meetings. Finally, she was convicted and sentenced to one year in prison. Her appeal against the sentence was rejected in October 1914, and in early 1915 she was brought in by authorities to serve out her sentence. After her initial conviction, the public prosecutors decided to comb through her speeches looking for further grounds to increase her sentence. They decided that she had also committed the crime of violating the honour of the German army by claiming that German soldiers were systematically maltreated. The lawsuit

---

43 Quoted in J. P. Nettl, *Rosa Luxemburg*, p. 481.

was supposed to be heard from 29 June to 3 July. The judge, however, decided to postpone the hearing because thousands of soldiers volunteered to testify to their ill treatment! The socialist press widely distributed the testimonies of these soldiers, exposing the German state. In the end, the case caused such an embarrassment for the government and the general staff that it was dropped entirely.

In the first six months of 1914, political and economic unrest flared up across Germany and Russia. The heavy weight of disillusionment was cast aside, and a new fighting spirit gripped the working class. Luxemburg once more posed the question of launching a mass strike – now as a weapon in the struggle against imperialism.

Polish and Russian Split

Since the 1905 Revolution, as well as being active in the SPD, Luxemburg had also participated in the Polish and Russian movements, regularly writing articles for their various party newspapers. However, she was increasingly withdrawing from the work of the Polish party. She did not participate in the Polish party congress of 1908, despite the fact that she did a lot of preparatory political work for it and that Jogiches had thoroughly discussed his main speech with her. Still, until 1911 she had been the main point of reference on theoretical questions in the Polish movement. She was the foremost writer for the Polish party's theoretical magazine, *Przeglad Socjaldemokratyczny*, and was Leo Jogiches' main source of advice on editorial questions. All articles went through her. Her role was nothing short of essential:

> To a large extent the reputation of the SDKPiL in the Russian party and beyond was due to the quality of this review; for a time it was probably the most interesting and stimulating of all Socialist publications in the Second International. The subjects treated ranged as widely as those in *Neue Zeit* but without the latter's pedantry and often excessively academic atmosphere. The Lenin–Trotsky debate on the nature of the revolution took place partly in the pages of the *Przeglad Socjaldemokratyczny* in the course of 1908.[44]

But her advice and opinions were increasingly ignored by the Polish party leadership, and her commitment was declining. In 1911 the Polish party split. This appeared, above all, to arise from discontent with the leadership, and especially the methods employed by Jogiches, who was regarded by many of the party's branches as having a dictatorial approach and a lack of regard for

---

44 Ibid., pp. 572-3.

internal party democracy.[45] Following the split, Luxemburg's involvement in the party declined further. In 1913 she published only one article in Polish. After that, she wrote none at all. In November 1916 the two Polish groups would reunite, and at the end of the war the left wing of the PPS would also fuse with them to form the Polish Communist Party. Both fusions took place with Luxemburg's approval, but she was not directly involved.

The good relationship that Luxemburg and Lenin had established in Finland after the 1905 Russian Revolution became closer still in the following years. Its culmination was a joint amendment that the two revolutionaries submitted to the world congress of the Second International in 1907.

> Though Rosa Luxemburg personally stood outside the Russian organisation and had no direct voice in its policies or feuds, her contact with the Bolsheviks and particularly with Lenin was not confined to public speeches of support. The consensus reached during the long sessions with him, Zinoviev, and Bogdanov at Kuokkala in the summer of 1906 were confirmed by the meetings in London and at the International congress at Stuttgart the following August.[46]

But when the Russian party experienced its final split between Mensheviks and Bolsheviks in 1912, Luxemburg and Lenin once more found themselves at odds. Jogiches and Luxemburg were against the split. Indeed, Luxemburg had a deep-rooted opposition to any kind of split in the social-democratic movement. Luxemburg wished to preserve party unity above all else. In her eyes, a split would be a sectarian mistake that would isolate revolutionaries from the masses. Lenin, however, was convinced that this split was absolutely necessary. A clear theoretical line of demarcation separated the reformists and revolutionaries in Russia. The revolutionary party had to be built on a solid theoretical foundation. This was not possible in unity with the Mensheviks, who constantly attempted to water down the party's revolutionary programme and to dissolve the party into an alliance with the liberal bourgeoisie.

During the 1912 split, Luxemburg was involved in a particular incident involving a sum of money that belonged to the Russian party. The fund was under the control of Kautsky, Mehring and Clara Zetkin and, naturally, all the factions in the Russian party tried to make a claim on it. As a contact between the German and Russian social democrats, Luxemburg was consulted about what to do with the money. She advised that it should not be given to

---

45 For a thorough examination see ibid., p. 571.
46 Ibid., p. 557.

the Bolsheviks, and that advice was followed. As could be imagined, such a decision provoked an angry reaction from Lenin and the Bolsheviks.

Nevertheless, Luxemburg's advice should not be read as a sign of her political support for Menshevism. On the contrary, the Mensheviks continued to regard Luxemburg as an ally of the Bolsheviks:

> To the Mensheviks Rosa Luxemburg was still quite simply Lenin's most active partisan in Germany [...] As late as February 1912, when relations between Lenin and Jogiches had already been broken off, Rosa Luxemburg still got Lenin's emissary Poletaev an introduction to Kautsky. Most important of all, she begged Jogiches on at least two occasions not to use the money as blackmail [...] As we shall see, she was not prepared to follow Jogiches into unbridled condemnation of Lenin after the dust-up in Paris,[47] not even when Lenin attacked her openly and specifically in 1912.[48]

The disagreements between Lenin and Luxemburg were several. Lenin moved to Krakow and supported the splitters from the Polish party, whilst at the same time Luxemburg did what she could to unify the Mensheviks and the Bolsheviks into a single party again. Through the International Socialist Bureau she pressured the Bolsheviks in order to unify the two wings. Here, for the first time in four years – and for the last – she agreed with Kautsky. The question of the money and of her agreement with Kautsky has later been used by the Stalinists to claim that she was on the side of the Mensheviks. But despite the disagreements between Lenin and Luxemburg, contact between the two was not broken off and they would, for instance, write in each other's press. As Nettl explained:

> Certainly they were close collaborators during these years, and much of their mutual respect was to survive their renewed political enmity. [...]
>
> SDKPiL policy [...] was to support the Bolsheviks *within* the Russian party; that is, on all issues save those which patently lead to organisational disintegration – the much feared split.[49]

And further:

---

47 This refers to a split in the Bolshevik group between Lenin and others on one side and those dubbed the "liquidators" (who Lenin accused of wanting to liquidate the party) on the other. Jogiches supported the liquidators against Lenin. For more, see: J. P. Nettl, *Rosa Luxemburg*, p. 348.

48 Ibid., p. 581.

49 Ibid., p. 559.

It should therefore not be wholly surprising to find that in 1912 personal contact between Rosa Luxemburg and Lenin still existed. At the end of February that year Lenin came to Berlin personally to succeed where Poletaev had failed, and carried out an assault on Kautsky for further payments of the trustee moneys. He took the opportunity of calling upon Rosa Luxemburg several times in two days. "Lenin was here yesterday and has been back four times today. I like talking to him, he is clever and educated – I like seeing his ugly mug... He found Mimi [Rosa's cat, whose approval of visitors was an essential preliminary to her mistress's sympathy] very imposing, a *barskii kot* [a lordly cat]." It was not until the row in the International Bureau at the end of 1913 that personal animosity really grew between them.[50]

The International Socialist Bureau processed the Russian organisational question in preparation of the coming world congress, where the question was due to be discussed by the whole International. But the Russian party question was never destined to be discussed by the International. While Luxemburg was at a meeting of the International leadership in Brussels, news arrived of the assassination of the archduke Franz Ferdinand and his wife in Sarajevo. By the time Luxemburg returned to Berlin, war was on the agenda.

---

50 Ibid., p. 591 (additions are made by Nettl).

6. The War

Despite years of assurances by politicians and diplomats all over Europe that peace was guaranteed, it had been obvious for decades that tensions between the great powers were building up beneath the surface. As capitalism entered into crisis, these tensions mounted further. The war was the military expression of the battle for resources, spheres of interest and colonial possessions, which the powerful states of Europe had been engaged in for a long time. On the one side were the old colonial powers, France and Great Britain, and on the other side there was Germany. Germany had arrived late on the scene of capitalist development, but in a relatively short space of time it had developed a strong industrial base. Now, possessing the military capacity to do so, it sought to seize a position of dominance on the world stage that corresponded to its economic and military might. The First World War was fundamentally a conflict between the great powers of Europe for the distribution and redistribution of markets and colonies.

It became apparent early on to the socialists of the Second International that war was looming. In the years preceding 1914, the question of the growing war threat was discussed many times over in the International. At the world congress in Stuttgart in August 1907, the fundamental position of the International was established – a position that the International would reaffirm on several succeeding occasions.

Rosa Luxemburg participated in the world congress of 1907 as a delegate of the SDKPiL, which gave her freedom from the discipline of the German party. As we have seen on several occasions, the highest wish of the German delegation was to somehow avoid any discussion of the war question and to avoid adopting any resolutions. At the congress, Luxemburg criticised the policy of the German party, and gave a speech which, in particular, included a sharp criticism of Bebel. On the question of imperialism, Luxemburg and Lenin were in agreement, on the basis of which they drafted and moved a joint amendment to the resolution on war. Lenin allowed Luxemburg to write the draft, and he gave her a Russian mandate in the commission.

> Lenin, who spent a lot of time with her at Stuttgart, had realised early on that his position was much like hers, and that she could represent it with greater experience and chance of success.[1]

The resolution began by establishing the fact that war is built into capitalism, and that the struggle against imperialism and war is inseparable from the struggle for socialism:

> Wars are therefore inherent in the nature of capitalism; they will only cease when capitalist economy is abolished, or when the magnitude of the sacrifice of human beings and money, necessitated only by the technical development of warfare, and popular disgust with armaments, lead to the abolition of this system.[2]

The amendment proposed by Luxemburg and Lenin committed the International to action in the case of war, and above all it committed the International to make use of the war to hasten the fall of capitalism. The amendment was inserted as the final two paragraphs of the resolution:

> In case of a threat of an outbreak of war, it is the duty of the working classes and their parliamentary representatives in the countries taking part, fortified by the unifying activity of the International Bureau, to do everything to prevent the outbreak of war by whatever means seem to them most effective, which naturally differ with the intensification of the class war and of the general political situation.

> Should war break out in spite of all this, it is the duty to intercede for its speedy end, and to strive with all their power to make use of the violent economic and political crisis brought about by the war to rouse the people, and thereby to hasten the abolition of capitalist class rule.[3]

The resolution and the amendment were adopted by large majorities. In 1914, however, both were simply thrown overboard.

---

1   J.P. Nettl, *Rosa Luxemburg*, p. 398.

2   Quoted ibid., p. 400.

3   Quoted ibid., p. 401.

4 August 1914 represents a landmark date in the history of the international workers' movement. On this date, through their actions, the leaders of the SPD passed a death sentence on the International. Three days earlier, Germany had declared war on Russia. On 4 August, the SPD's Reichstag fraction unanimously voted in favour of war credits to fund the war. They thus elected to support their own national bourgeoisie and its imperialist ambitions, rather than stand in solidarity with the workers of the world and fight to overthrow capitalism and imperialism. Already on 2 August the German trade union leaders had signed a 'no strike' agreement with the employers, banning strikes and lockouts as long as hostilities lasted. The German leaders were certainly not alone in their betrayal. Of the parties of the eight warring nations, only the British Independent Labour Party (ILP), the Serbian Social Democracy, and the Russian Mensheviks and Bolsheviks opposed the war and their own governments.

When the SPD gave its support to the German government's war credits, shockwaves were sent reverberating across the International. Luxemburg had observed the degeneration of the leadership of the SPD at close range, and yet even she had not anticipated such an immense betrayal. Lenin, who had not observed the degeneration at such close quarters, believed that the edition of *Vorwärts* outlining the SPD's support for war credits was a forgery of the German general staff. In a single stroke, the International collapsed. It was now dead as a tool for the world socialist revolution.

National chauvinism was whipped up by the ruling classes everywhere. The social-democratic leaders helped it along. The forces of internationalism were immediately reduced to next to nothing. At the first gathering of internationalist socialists in Zimmerwald, Switzerland, in 1915, Lenin dryly remarked that it would be possible to fit all the internationalists in the world into four stage-coaches. The first years of the war were years of pitch darkness for the revolutionaries.

The tops of the German SPD had been drifting in a national chauvinist direction for a long time. They had attempted to dodge the question of German imperialist aggression in Morocco, but a number of party leaders had gone further and openly advocated in favour of German colonial policy. Eduard David,[4] for instance, viewed German colonial politics as an "integral part of the universal cultural aims of the socialist movement."[5] When the war

---

4   Eduard David (1863-1930) – German social democrat, member of the Reichstag 1903-1918. Central supporter of the parliamentary truce during the war.

5   Quoted in P. Frölich, *Rosa Luxemburg*, p. 148.

broke out, the leadership of the SPD threw their support behind the German government. They argued that it was necessary to defend the fatherland against the encroachment of the barbaric Russian regime. The SPD Reichstag group defended their support for war credits using the following arguments:

> We are now facing the irrevocable fact of war. We are threatened by the horrors of invasion. The decision, today, is not for or against war; for us there can be but one question: by what means is this war to be conducted? Much, aye everything, is at stake for our people and its future, if Russian despotism, stained with the blood of its own people, should be the victor. This danger must be averted, the civilisation and the independence of our people must be safeguarded. Therefore we will carry out what we have always promised: in the hour of danger we will not desert our fatherland. In this we feel that we stand in harmony with the International, which has always recognised the right of every people to its national independence, as we stand in agreement with the International in emphatically denouncing every war of conquest. Actuated by these motives, we vote in favour of the war credits demanded by the Government.[6]

This patriotism seeped like a poison from the top of the party down to the local party leaders and editors. "National unity" became the party's watchword. Translated into practice, this meant a parliamentary truce and the cessation of all opposition as long as the war lasted. In return for yoking the workers to the war effort, the SPD and trade unions were permitted a continued existence, and the former was embraced into respectable bourgeois society. But the price of such acceptance and legality was the abandonment of everything the SPD had stood for until that point. These 'leaders' had sold their claim to defend the interests of the workers, and in exchange they had purchased a seat at the master's table. As the war developed, the terms of the parliamentary truce were expanded to include agreement on the suppression of the left wing of the SPD, as well as all other expressions among the German workers of a growing mood of discontent with the war.

The so-called 'centre' of the party around Karl Kautsky had written off the possibility of an outbreak of war. They had simply swallowed the assurances of the state officials at face value. Kautsky even developed his own theoretical cover for the chauvinism of the SPD leadership: he argued that violence and imperialist aggression were far from an inherent feature of capitalism. Rather, the violent expansionism that the world was witnessing was driven

---

6   Quoted in R. Luxemburg, *The Junius Pamphlet: The Crisis of the German Social Democracy, Rosa Luxemburg Speaks*, p. 270.

by particular groups of capitalists, such as the bankers, the arms industry etc. The capitalist class as a whole – and particularly heavy industry – he argued, on the contrary had an interest in peaceful capitalist development. This layer of the capitalist class must eventually turn against such violent imperialist politics, and return to the principles of free trade. Kautsky claimed that it was the duty of social democracy to appeal to the progressive section of the bourgeoisie and put the case for capitalism with a human face.

Kautsky deftly conjured away the betrayals of the International's leaders:

> [But] the International is not an effective tool in wartime; in essence it is an instrument of peace. Only in peacetime can it develop its full strength, and insofar as it is able to bring this strength to bear, it always works for peace.[7]

In other words, when class contradictions sharpened and events reached the point of workers being sent to slaughter other workers in the interest of national capital… according to Kautsky, the International simply ceased to be of any further use.

The Junius Pamphlet

In April 1915, while in prison, Rosa Luxemburg wrote a pamphlet under the title, *The Crisis of German Social Democracy*, later known more widely as the *Junius Pamphlet*. Luxemburg was persuaded by her comrades to write under a pseudonym to avoid further imprisonment, and as such she took the pseudonym, Junius, hence the pamphlet's name.[8] But upon release from prison, she realised that it actually had not been published owing to difficulties with the censors, and on account of the fact that those who were tasked with publishing it were either themselves in prison, or else had been drafted into the military. For this reason, the pamphlet didn't actually see the light of day until early April 1916 – over a year after it was written. When the pamphlet was finally published, the movement against the war had already matured. There was a real need for a concrete direction to be given and for the tasks of international social democracy to be spelled out. Luxemburg provided this direction in the form of the so-called 'Junius Theses', which were printed along with her longer text.

In her pamphlet, Luxemburg meticulously demonstrated that this was an all-round imperialist war, and that this was true for *all* the belligerent nations.

---

7   Quoted in P. Le Blanc, *Lenin and the Revolutionary Party*, p. 193.

8   Junius was a pseudonym used by an influential English pamphleteer in the eighteenth century, and perhaps also a reference to Lucius Junius Brutus, the legendary republican hero of ancient Rome

Even the smaller nations were merely subjugated to one or other of the larger imperialist nations' interests. The choice she posed before humanity was, "socialism or barbarism":

> This is the dilemma of world history, its inevitable choice, whose scales are trembling in the balance awaiting the decision of the proletariat. Upon it depends the future of culture and humanity. In this war imperialism has been victorious. Its brutal sword of murder has dashed the scales, with overbearing brutality, down into the abyss of shame and misery. If the proletariat learns from this war and in this war exert itself, to cast off its serfdom to the ruling classes, to become the lord of its own destiny, the shame and misery will not have been in vain.[9]

Bitterly criticising how the social democrats had fully endorsed this war by supporting their own national bourgeoisies, she exposed the hypocrisy of the social-democratic leaders. In particular, she pointed to how the actual result of their policies was diametrically opposed to the claimed ends for which they were pursuing them:

> German freedom, that same German freedom for which, according to the declaration of the Reichstag group, Krupp cannons are now fighting, has been endangered by this attitude of the social democracy far beyond the period of the present war. The leaders of the social democracy are convinced that democratic liberties for the working class will come as a reward for its allegiance to the fatherland. But never in the history of the world has an oppressed class received political rights as a reward for service rendered to the ruling classes. History is full of examples of shameful deceit on the part of the ruling classes, even when solemn promises were made before the war broke out. The social democracy has not assured the extension of liberty in Germany. It has sacrificed those liberties that the working class possessed before the war broke out.[10]

Luxemburg ripped apart each of the social democrats' arguments one by one. One such argument claimed that support for the war was necessary in order to stop Russian despotism in its tracks. But Luxemburg pointed out that if the leaders of the SPD *really* believed in the need to combat Russian despotism, they would throw their support behind the revolutionary activity of the Russian proletariat rather than behind the German bourgeoisie.

She also criticised the SPD leaders' claim that they supported the war as a war of national defence against foreign aggression. She showed, firstly, how

---

9 R. Luxemburg, *The Junius Pamphlet: The Crisis of German Social Democracy*, *Rosa Luxemburg Speaks*, pp. 269-70.

10 Ibid., pp. 297-8.

history has provided many examples where the bourgeoisie invoked foreign invasion in order to crush revolutionary movements. One such example was the Paris Commune of 1871. She also explained how the best defence against foreign invasion was not at all to put class struggle on hold but, on the contrary:

> The centuries have proven that not the state of siege, but relentless class struggle, is the power that awakens the spirit of self-sacrifice, the moral strength of the masses; that the class struggle is the best protection and the best defence against a foreign enemy.[11]

Luxemburg was not content to simply expose the hypocritical treachery of the SPD. She went on to describe what they ought to have done instead:

> Yes, socialists should defend their country in great historical crises, and here lies the great fault of the German social democratic Reichstag group. When it announced on 4 August, "in this hour of danger, we will not desert our fatherland", it denied its own words in the same breath. For truly it has deserted its fatherland in its hour of greatest danger. The highest duty of the social democracy toward its fatherland demanded that it expose the real background of this imperialist war, that it rend the net of imperialist and diplomatic lies that covers the eyes of the people. It was their duty to speak loudly and clearly, to proclaim to the people of Germany that in this war victory and defeat would be equally fatal, to oppose the gagging of the fatherland by a state of siege, to demand that the people alone decide on war and peace, to demand a permanent session of parliament for the period of the war, to assume a watchful control over the government by parliament, and over parliament by the people, to demand the immediate removal of all political inequalities, since only a free people can adequately govern its country, and finally, to oppose to the imperialist war, based as it was upon the most reactionary forces in Europe, the program of Marx, of Engels, and Lassalle.[12]

More concretely, she explained:

> The most elementary demand of national defence is that the nation takes its defence into its own hands. The first step in this direction is the militia; not only the immediate armament of the entire adult male populace, but above all, popular decision in all questions of peace and war. It must demand, furthermore, the immediate removal of every form of political oppression, since the greatest political freedom is the best basis for national defence. To proclaim these fundamental

---

11 Ibid., p. 304.
12 Ibid., p. 314.

measures of national defence, to demand their realisation, that was the first duty of the social democracy.[13]

Luxemburg had defended the idea of the mass strike throughout the preceding decade. She understood, however, that it would be an ultra-left mistake to now denounce the Social Democracy for having failed to simply call a mass strike, or even a revolution, the moment the war broke out. She understood that revolutions and mass strikes cannot be arbitrarily summoned at will. Nevertheless, she criticised the Social Democracy for failing to rally any opposition to the war whatsoever. Quite the contrary, the SPD actively assisted in whipping up the very mood of patriotic fervour that it now used as an excuse for not opposing the war in the first place. Instead, the Social Democracy ought to have exposed the real war aims of the imperialists, and should have advanced timely political slogans in order to foster serious opposition to the war among the masses. She was under no illusion that such a course of action would have immediately paid dividends, or that the Social Democracy could have immediately called upon mass support from its policies. But that was not the point:

> "Would the masses have supported the social democracy in its attitude against the war?" That is a question that no one can answer. But neither is it an important one. Did our parliamentarians demand an absolute assurance of victory from the generals of the Prussian army before voting in favour of war credits? What is true of military armies is equally true of revolutionary armies. They go into the fight, wherever necessity demands it, without previous assurance of success. At the worst, the party would have been doomed, in the first few months of the war, to political ineffectuality. [...]

> At first we would perhaps have accomplished nothing but to save the honour of the proletariat, and thousands upon thousands of proletarians who are dying in the trenches in mental darkness would not have died in spiritual confusion, but with the one certainty that that which has been everything in their lives, the international, liberating social democracy is more than the figment of a dream.

> The voice of our party would have acted as a wet blanket upon the chauvinistic intoxication of the masses. It would have preserved the intelligent proletariat from delirium, would have made it more difficult for imperialism to poison and to stupefy the minds of the people. The crusade against the social democracy would have awakened the masses in an incredibly short time.

---

13 Ibid., p. 312.

And as the war went on, as the horror of endless massacre and bloodshed in all countries grew and grew, as its imperialistic hoof became more and more evident, as the exploitation by bloodthirsty speculators became more and more shameless, every live, honest, progressive and humane element in the masses would have rallied to the standard of the social democracy. The German social democracy would have stood in the midst of this mad whirlpool of collapse and decay, like a rock in a stormy sea, would have been the lighthouse of the whole International, guiding and leading the labour movements of every country of the earth. The unparalleled moral prestige that lay in the hands of the German socialists would have reacted upon the socialists of all nations in a very short time. Peace sentiments would have spread like wildfire and the popular demand for peace in all countries would have hastened the end of the slaughter, would have decreased the number of its victims.

The German proletariat would have remained the lighthouse keeper of socialism and of human emancipation.[14]

Luxemburg rejected the SPD leaders' argument that you had to pick a side in the war. She clearly demonstrated how, no matter which side won, the only true winner would be imperialism:

Imperialism, and its servant militarism, will reappear after every victory and after every defeat in this war. There can be but one exception: if the international proletariat, through its intervention, should overthrow all previous calculations.[15]

To Luxemburg, the struggle against the war did not mean a struggle for a return to the *status quo ante*. Such a thing would have been a utopian dream. Besides which, it was precisely the pre-war conditions that led to the war in the first place. No, the proletariat had to take up battle against the source of war – imperialism:

The proletarian movement cannot reconquer the place it deserves by means of utopian advice and projects for weakening, taming or quelling imperialism within capitalism by means of partial reforms.

The real problem that the world war has placed before the socialist parties, upon whose solution the future of the working-class movement depends, is the readiness of the proletarian masses to act in the fight against imperialism. The international proletariat suffers, not from a dearth of postulates, programs, and slogans, but

---

14 Ibid., pp. 316-8.
15 Ibid., p. 323.

from a lack of deeds, of effective resistance, of the power to attack imperialism at the decisive moment, just in times of war. It has been unable to put its old slogan, war against war, into actual practice. Here is the Gordian knot of the proletarian movement and of its future.[16]

Lenin enthusiastically welcomed Luxemburg's pamphlet, although he had no knowledge of the true identity of its author:

> At last there has appeared in Germany, illegally, without any adaptation to the despicable Junker censorship, a Social-Democratic pamphlet dealing with questions of the war! […] Written in a very lively style, Junius' pamphlet has undoubtedly played and will play an important role in the struggle against the ex-Social-Democratic Party of Germany, which has deserted to the side of the bourgeoisie and the Junkers, and we heartily greet the author.[17]

Nonetheless, Lenin criticised what he believed to be the incompleteness of Junius' (i.e., Rosa Luxemburg's) arguments. He also emphasised two points where he believed the author had erred. Despite these criticisms, he emphasised that the errors were made with the best of intentions:

> Before proceeding with a criticism of Junius' faults and errors we must strongly emphasise that we do so for the sake of self-criticism, which is so necessary for Marxists, and of submitting to an all-round test the views which must serve as the ideological basis of the Third International. On the whole, Junius' pamphlet is a splendid Marxist work, and its defects are, in all probability, to a certain extent accidental.[18]

The first point that Lenin criticised was an argument which Luxemburg made in both the pamphlet and the 'Junius Theses': namely, that in the present imperialist epoch, national (i.e., non-imperialist wars) are impossible. According to Lenin, this is incorrect. He cited revolutionary wars or colonial wars for national liberation as possible examples. But Lenin believed such a mistake was understandable in the given context:

> It may be that this negation of national wars generally is either an oversight, or an accidental overstatement in emphasising the perfectly correct idea that the *present* war is an imperialist war, not a national war.[19]

---

16 Ibid., p. 324.

17 V. I. Lenin, 'The Junius Pamphlet', *LCW*, Vol. 22, p. 305.

18 Ibid., p. 306.

19 Ibid., p. 308.

Nonetheless, from this small mistake, incorrect conclusions could be drawn, and therefore Lenin felt it necessary to deal with the question. Whilst Junius was absolutely correct to argue that this was true of the First World War, Lenin argued that one could not rule out such national wars occurring in the future – for example, as a result of an uprising of the oppressed peoples in the colonies. It is unlikely that Rosa Luxemburg would have disagreed with this point. Lenin laid out his critique not simply for the sake of theoretical clarity, but also because of the potentially damaging consequences this argument could lead to in practice. It was correct, in Lenin's view, to refuse to support any of the belligerents in the First World War as all of the belligerents were imperialists or the proxies of imperialist powers. But ought we conclude from this that one must never support any side in any war? Or that one had to be against war as a matter of principle? Lenin answered:

> But the mistake is very harmful also from the standpoint of practical politics, for it gives rise to the absurd propaganda of 'disarmament', since it is alleged that there can be no wars except reactionary wars. It also gives rise to the even more ludicrous and downright reactionary attitude of indifference towards national movements. And such an attitude becomes chauvinism when members of the 'great' European nations, that is, the nations which oppress the mass of small and colonial peoples, declare with a pseudo-scientific air: "national wars are no longer possible!" National wars *against* the imperialist powers are not only possible and probable; they are inevitable, *progressive* and *revolutionary, though* of course, to be *successful,* they require either the concerted effort of huge numbers of people in the oppressed countries (hundreds of millions in our example of India and China), or a *particularly* favourable conjuncture of international conditions (e.g., the fact that the imperialist powers cannot interfere, being paralysed by exhaustion, by war, by their antagonisms, etc.), or the *simultaneous* uprising of the proletariat against the bourgeoisie in one of the big powers (this latter eventuality holds first place as the most desirable and favourable for the victory of the proletariat).[20]

Although it is probable that this point of difference partially reflects the differing views of Luxemburg and Lenin with regard to the right of nations to self-determination, Lenin said it would be "unfair to accuse Junius of being indifferent to national movements". In practice, Luxemburg had openly and actively opposed the colonial aspirations of the 'great German nation' in Morocco and elsewhere.

---

20 Ibid., p. 312.

The other point on which Lenin believed that Luxemburg was wrong, was on the question of the defence of the fatherland. Luxemburg dealt in the pamphlet with the SPD's argument that it was necessary to defend the fatherland. She criticised their actions, however, from the premise that their policy was actually ineffectual in achieving its aim. Lenin, however, believed that it was the very idea that the Social Democracy should be concerned about defending the capitalist fatherland that ought to be attacked. Lenin compared Luxemburg's arguments with the Menshevik theory of stages – i.e., that we must first raise the 'acceptable' demands, and only at a later, second stage can we raise socialism:

> In saying that class struggle is the best means of defence against invasion, Junius applies Marxist dialectics only halfway, taking one step on the right road and immediately deviating from it. Marxist dialectics call for a concrete analysis of each specific historical situation. It is true that class struggle is the best means of defence against invasion *both* when the bourgeoisie is overthrowing feudalism, and when the proletariat is overthrowing the bourgeoisie. Precisely because it is true with regard to *every* form of class oppression, it is *too general*, and therefore, *inadequate* in the present *specific* case. Civil war against the bourgeoisie is *also* a form of class struggle, and only this form of class struggle would have saved Europe (the whole of Europe, not only one country) from the peril of invasion. The 'Great German Republic' had it existed in 1914-16, would *also* have waged an *imperialist* war.

> Junius came very close to the correct solution of the problem and to the correct slogan: civil war against the bourgeoisie for socialism; but, as if afraid to speak the whole truth, he turned *back* to the fantasy of a 'national war' in 1914, 1915 and 1916.[21]

Lenin criticised Luxemburg for looking backwards rather than forwards when she posed a national programme against the imperialist war. By doing so she left the door ajar to those, such as the Mensheviks, who might wish to misuse her arguments to legitimise their own politics. While Lenin believed that her critique of the war was absolutely correct, he criticised her for stopping half way. Her slogan, "war against the war", pointed in the right direction, in Lenin's opinion. However, she failed to fully take the next step. Only the socialist revolution could offer a way forward. And the only way to secure that was by turning the imperialist war into a civil war of the proletariat against the bourgeoisie.

---

21 Ibid., pp. 316-7.

Lenin developed on what the tasks of Marxists were moving forward. First among those was the task of building a new International. Luxemburg also wrote about the need for a new International, but Lenin's central criticism was that she had not yet completely freed herself from the German Social-Democratic milieu. He was not speaking only or even particularly about the right wing of the party. He emphasised that it was most important of all to break completely from the so-called 'centre' of the party, focused around Kautsky. Using radical language but siding with the right wing in practice, this was all the more dangerous precisely because it sowed doubt in the minds of the workers and gave the right a left-wing cover. Kautsky's name only appeared twice in Luxemburg's entire pamphlet. Indeed, where she did mention him it was not to subject him to merciless criticism, but rather to hold up and contrast the current position of the SPD against something *correct* he had written about the struggle against imperialism back in 1907. According to Lenin, the magazine *Internationale*, which Luxemburg often wrote for, had a much clearer line on this question:

> The chief defect in Junius' pamphlet, and what marks a definite step backward compared with the legal (although immediately suppressed) magazine, *Internationale*, is its silence regarding the connection between social-chauvinism (the author uses neither this nor the less precise term social-patriotism) and opportunism. The author rightly speaks of the "capitulation" and collapse of the German Social Democratic Party and of the "treachery" of its "official leaders", but he goes no further. The *Internationale*, however, did criticise the "Centre", i.e., Kautskyism, and quite properly poured ridicule on it for its spinelessness, its prostitution of Marxism and its servility to the opportunists. This same magazine *began* to expose the role the opportunists by revealing, for example, the very important fact that on 4 August 1914, the opportunists came out with an ultimatum, a ready-made decision to vote *for* war credits in *any* case. Neither the Junius pamphlet nor the theses say *anything* about opportunism or about Kautskyism! This is wrong from the standpoint of theory, for it is impossible to *account for* the "betrayal" without linking it up with opportunism as a *trend* with a long history behind it, the history of the whole Second International. It is a mistake from the practical political standpoint, for it is impossible either to understand the "crisis of Social-Democracy", or overcome it, without clarifying the meaning and the role of *two trends* – the openly opportunist trend (Legien, David, etc.) and the tacitly opportunist trend (Kautsky and Co.).[22]

---

22 Ibid., pp. 306-7.

Despite the betrayal on 4 August, it was clear that Rosa Luxemburg still regarded herself as part of the SPD. Although she famously declared the party a "stinking corpse" following its great betrayal, throughout her pamphlet she nevertheless speaks on the party's crisis in the manner of a participant in an internal discussion, rather than as someone who has broken with the party, as Lenin noted. She compared the party's practice on the outbreak of the war and contrasted it with its earlier statements and practices. As *part* of the Social Democracy, she argued for the reform of the party and for a change in its policy, rather than of the necessity of a clean break with opportunism in the party in all its forms:

> But the German social democracy was not only the strongest body, it was the thinking brain of the International as well. Therefore the process of self-analysis and appraisement must begin in its own movement, with its own case. It is in honour bound to lead the way to the rescue of international Socialism, to proceed with the unsparing criticism of its own shortcomings.[23]

Lenin, on the contrary, argued that it was high time the revolutionary left wing in Germany drew the necessary conclusions and broke with the SPD. It was necessary to begin building an illegal organisation that openly proclaimed its revolutionary program:

> [...] Junius quite rightly says that a revolution cannot be "made." Revolution was on the order of the day in 1914-16, it was hidden in the depths of the war, was *emerging* out of the war. This should have been "*proclaimed*" in the name of the revolutionary class, and *its* programme should have been fearlessly and fully announced: socialism is impossible in time of war without civil war against the arch-reactionary, criminal bourgeoisie, which condemned the people to untold disaster. Systematic, consistent, practical measures should have been planned, which *could be carried out no matter what* pace the revolutionary crisis develops, and which would be in line with the maturing revolution. These measures are indicated in our Party resolution: 1) voting against war credits; 2) violation of "class truce"; 3) creation of an illegal organisation; 4) fraternisation among the soldiers; 5) support for all the revolutionary actions of the masses. The success of *all* these steps *inevitably* leads to civil war.[24]

This was the main difference between Lenin and Luxemburg. The collapse of the International had taken Lenin by surprise. However, he immediately

---

23 R. Luxemburg, *The Junius Pamphlet, Rosa Luxemburg Speaks*, pp. 264.

24 V. I. Lenin, 'The Junius Pamphlet', *LCW*, Vol. 22, pp. 317-8.

understood the extent of its degeneration, and concluded that a radical break was necessary, not only with the chauvinists of the right wing, but also the so-called 'centre' (Kautsky, Haase, Ledebour). Henceforth, a new International would have to be built. From 4 August 1914 Lenin's focus was above all on the education of the revolutionary cadres, i.e., that small minority that had stayed true to its internationalist, socialist principles in August 1914. The internationalists were extremely isolated from the masses. The latter had been overwhelmed by the nationalistic, defencist and patriotic mood that had swept Europe at the beginning of the war. Revolutionaries had to contend, therefore, with being isolated from and unable to reach the masses. In the midst of the patriotic frenzy, it was necessary to achieve clarity of thought regarding the key questions of the day: the war, its causes and its consequences. Lenin therefore expressed himself in the sharpest possible manner, with such slogans as "turn the imperialist war into a civil war", and unleashing a relentless polemic against pacifism (which would have led to impotence and paralysis), and at the same time against any concession towards defencism. Internally to Russia, he expressed opposition to capitulating to social patriotism through the slogan, "Russia's defeat is the lesser evil".

Few understood Lenin at this time. His slogans were met with distrust and scepticism even among the leadership of the Bolshevik party. Trotsky did not understand his position either, and criticised Lenin for being unable to connect with the masses. But that was not the point of his slogans. Lenin's slogans were given such sharp edges in order to slice away even the slightest hint of national chauvinism, which had penetrated the Second International to such a catastrophic extent, as was fully exposed by the events of 4 August. The cadres of the new International had to be re-educated on solid theoretical foundations and on the basis of the cleanest possible break from the chauvinism of the Second International. Not for the first time, Lenin went far to one extreme in his polemics in order to hammer his points home. This certainly left his statements open to misinterpretation if taken out of context and simply repeated in a simplistic or abstract way. Lenin's slogan that defeat was the lesser evil was simplified in a crude form, for example, by Zinoviev and taken to mean, "we are for the defeat of Russia". However, Lenin's position was that all belligerent sides in the imperialist war were reactionary. What Lenin advocated was the need for the Marxists to reject any form of national chauvinism, and to expose fully and firmly the reactionary, imperialist nature of the war and the forces that supported or capitulated to it. This was in order to win over the revolutionary vanguard to the perspective of international socialist revolution and organise them around an independent revolutionary programme rooted in the working class, which would then be capable of transforming the imperialist war in a revolutionary uprising of the masses.

The same ideas of irreconcilable opposition to chauvinism, defencism and any form of subordination of the revolutionary masses to the liberal bourgeoisie would be expressed through different words and slogans, but the content and Lenin's method would not change. The difference was that Lenin at this stage was not addressing just a very restricted circle of revolutionaries as in the previous period. Lenin recognised the change in the situation brought about by the Revolution and correspondingly set the task for the growing but still small forces of Bolshevism to connect to the masses and patiently explain, for example, that the change of regime had not changed the imperialist character of the war, and that an end to the war without annexations could be achieved only by a workers' government based on the power of the Soviets. Lenin summed up the tasks for the Bolshevik Party in the Revolution in the 'April Theses', securing the crucial political reorientation of the party in the new situation.

The problem was that in Germany, Luxemburg and her fellow revolutionaries lacked an organisation when the war broke out. Unlike Lenin, she had no organisation of cadres on which to focus her educational efforts. Instead, she wrote for the broad, undefined masses, posing the task as one of regenerating the SPD. Lenin concluded his critique of the *Junius Pamphlet* by pointing out precisely this weakness: the revolutionaries in Germany were isolated, although he noted that they were moving in the right direction:

> Junius' pamphlet conjures up in our mind the picture of a *lone* man who has no comrades in an illegal organisation accustomed to thinking out revolutionary slogans to their conclusion and systematically educating the masses in their spirit. But this shortcoming – it would be a grave error to forget this – is not Junius' personal failing, but the result of the weakness of *all* the German Leftists, who have become entangled in the vile net of Kautskyist hypocrisy, pedantry and 'friendliness' for the opportunists. Junius' adherents have managed, *in spite* of their isolation, to *begin* the publication of illegal leaflets and to start the war against Kautskyism. They will succeed in going further along the right road.[25]

The Left Wing of the SPD

In his critique, Lenin had touched upon a sore spot: the opponents of the war – the revolutionary left wing in the SPD – were few in number, isolated,

---

25 Ibid., p. 318.

and more akin to a loose network of like-minded individuals than a real organisation. But there *was* opposition to the war. On 3 August 1914, when the SPD's Reichstag fraction met to discuss whether or not to support the government's war credits, several of its members wished to vote against. Of the SPD's 110 Reichstag deputies, fourteen advocated voting against, including Karl Liebknecht. They were voted down, however, and their request to be exempted from party discipline was rejected. As a result, the entire SPD Reichstag fraction voted in favour of war funds on 4 August. From the outside, it looked like a united party in full support of the war.

Already by the very evening of that fateful vote, however, a small group of comrades of the left wing of the party gathered at Rosa Luxemburg's apartment to discuss the mighty tasks that lay ahead. At the outbreak of the war, Luxemburg thought that it might perhaps be possible to provide an impetus for a spontaneous outbreak of discontent among party members by publishing a manifesto signed by prominent individuals in the party. The main purpose of the meeting on the evening of 4 August was precisely to work out the details of such a manifesto. But only two party members of national prominence turned up: Franz Mehring and Paul Lensch, and the latter did not even wish to put his signature to anything. He would shortly thereafter desert to the side of the party leadership. Having already accepted party discipline over the question of war credits, Liebknecht too was unwilling to now break it. He too was unwilling to sign such a manifesto.

Yet Luxemburg still held onto the idea, sending out more than 300 invitations ahead of a new meeting. Only Clara Zetkin answered her call in the affirmative and without reservations.

It was characteristic of Rosa Luxemburg to hope that she might influence the party, if only she possessed the correct ideas. But the right wing was well-organised and controlled the entire party apparatus. Once again, it was shown that no matter how correct the left wing's analysis and slogans might be, they were no replacement for a real organisation of the revolutionaries. The course of the party, much less the course of history, could never be changed by appeals and manifestos alone.

To the rest of the world, it had seemed in August 1914 that the SPD was united. The first public expression of opposition to SPD's policies came in September, in the form of a statement signed by Karl Liebknecht, Franz Mehring, Clara Zetkin and Rosa Luxemburg. Luxemburg was the intellectual driving force of the group. But the group of SPD dissidents was heterogeneous, and it now became evident why it is precisely necessary to have an organisation of revolutionaries in place *before* great events unfold:

> In private Rosa gave full vent to her frustrations of getting the motley group of oppositionists together for any concerted and effective action. For their cohesion was a negative one, dislike of the attitude of the party, without any compensatory agreement on what to do instead. It was a rocking boat in which the foursome sailed into the official wind, and Rosa had her work cut out at the helm.

> "I want to undertake the sharpest possible action against the activities of the [*Reichstag*] delegates. Unfortunately I get little co-operation from my [collection of] incoherent personalities… Karl [Liebknecht] can't ever be got hold of, since he dashes about like a cloud in the sky; Franz [Mehring] has little sympathy for any but literary campaigns, [Clara Zetkin's] reaction is hysteria and the blackest despair. But in spite of all this I intend to try to see what can be achieved."[26]

The group around Rosa Luxemburg was a collection of individuals who, through different paths, had arrived on the left wing of the party, although each had a long history in the party. Besides Luxemburg herself, Karl Liebknecht, Franz Mehring, and Clara Zetkin were the most well-known members of the group.

Karl Liebknecht was the son of Wilhelm Liebknecht, one of the founders of the SPD. Karl was a lawyer by trade and an active organiser in the party. He was a man of action rather than a theoretician. He became particularly occupied by the struggle against militarism, and his 1906 pamphlet 'Militarism and Anti-Militarism' was officially adopted at the first social-democratic youth congress. For the trouble of writing it, Liebknecht was rewarded with eighteen months in prison, turning him into a symbol of the struggle of Social Democracy against militarism and war. He also became the object of a seething hatred from nationalists. He was particularly active in the youth organisation of the party, which he defended against the executive committee.

A few weeks after the war broke out, Liebknecht realised that he had made a mistake by voting for war credits. When the government demanded the Reichstag approve new war credits in early December, Liebknecht broke with party discipline and voted, alone, against granting new funds. His example immediately made Liebknecht a point of reference for everyone who opposed the war, both inside Germany and internationally. Within a short space of time, opposition to the war spread inside the SPD. Public meetings and

---

26 J. P. Nettl, *Rosa Luxemburg*, p. 611 (additions are made by Nettl).

protests were banned by the government. Their job was helped by the SPD leadership who did everything in their power to prevent meetings, whilst censoring the party's own press.

In February 1915, Liebknecht was called up for military service. However, he continued his revolutionary activity in the military, and in May 1915 he circulated a leaflet that raised the slogan 'The main enemy is at home!' This slogan and his brave stand in the Reichstag made Liebknecht the symbol of opposition to the war. In the words of the Marxist historian, Pierre Broué:

> History has essentially retained two names, those of Rosa Luxemburg and Karl Liebknecht, whom their shared struggle during the First World War and their tragic deaths during the same night of January 1919 were to link forever.[27]

Nonetheless, they were accompanied by other important leaders of the left.

Franz Mehring, born in 1846, had been at the centre of weekly meetings of the left wing in Berlin since as early as 1910. For a long time, he had been the editor of *Leipziger Volkszeitung*, and for a period he wrote editorials for *Die Neue Zeit*. However, in 1910 he broke with Kautsky and moved closer to Luxemburg. In December 1913, he and Luxemburg began publishing *Sozialdemokratische Korrespondenz* as a point of reference for the party's left wing.

Clara Zetkin, born in 1857, was the leader of the socialist women's organisation, and was the editor of its magazine, *Die Gleicheit*. She was linked to Luxemburg through close political and personal friendship.

The group that had gathered in Luxemburg's apartment on 4 August slowly began expanding to include others. Besides the four previously mentioned individuals, the work of the group was carried out by Jogiches, Marchlewski (Karski), Paul Levi (Luxemburg's lawyer since 1913), Meyer and Ströbel (both of whom were journalists for *Vorwärts*), and Wilhelm Pieck (vice-secretary of the party in Berlin, who had a number of useful contacts), as well as Paul Lange, Hermann and Käthe Duncker.

Besides Jogiches, none of them had much experience in conducting underground work. Nevertheless, after making contact with the Niederbarnim branch in Berlin, they began publishing illegal literature. The group had two purposes. First of all, they wished to break the silence and show that the party was not, in fact, united in its support for the war and, secondly, they aimed to build an organisation, although the reality was that it more closely resembled a network. By the middle of 1915, the group had established contacts in more

27 P. Broué, *The German Revolution, 1917-1923*, p. 28.

than 300 localities. Several local party leaders joined the group, and its first conference was held on 5 May at Pieck's apartment in Berlin.

Luxemburg had twelve months of jail time pending. She had been sentenced before the war but it had been postponed due to ill-health. The sentence was due to begin on 1 March 1915, but on the evening of 18 February, just before setting off to meet Clara Zetkin in order to plan out an international women's conference, she was suddenly arrested and thrown into the women's prison at Barnimstrasse in Berlin. There, she would secretly write the *Junius Pamphlet*, which she succeeded in smuggling out.

While Luxemburg was serving her sentence, *Die Internationale* was published for the first and only time in April 1915. In it, Luxemburg declared the SPD and the International dead. The magazine was edited by Luxemburg and Franz Mehring. Immediately, however, following its first edition, the magazine was banned and the public prosecutor accused Mehring, Luxemburg, Zetkin, the publisher and the owner of the printing house of high treason.

Most of the other left-wing leaders, much like Liebknecht and Luxemburg, were either imprisoned or conscripted. Clara Zetkin was arrested in July 1915 and was seriously ill by the time she was released in October of the same year.

Inside the SPD, however, opposition to the war was steadily growing. In June 1915, more than 750 well-known activists, editors of local party newspapers, trade union leaders and others signed a protest against the political line of the executive committee. The text had been written by Karl Liebknecht and those around him.

On 1 January 1916, the *Internationale* group (named after its short-lived publication) gathered for its first conference at Liebknecht's apartment. The twelve delegates at the conference adopted Luxemburg's *Junius Pamphlet* as the political foundation of the group, and on 19 March a larger conference was held with seventeen delegates from Berlin. The group decided to launch an underground newspaper named *Spartacus*, after the revolutionary leader of the slave rebellion that shook the Roman Empire. Members of the group soon came to be known as the Spartacists.

Other left-wing groups also emerged within the party. A secret conference was held in Easter 1916 by oppositionists from the socialist youth with the aim of splitting the youth organisation. The conference adopted Liebknecht's theses. The left succeeded in establishing a number of both legal and illegal magazines. The left wing had a wide influence locally in the SPD in several places, and in some areas it even formed a majority. Broué mentions

Pannekoek in Bremen, where there was an actual left wing, Marchlewski, Parvus and several others. For various reasons, including the long-term reverberations of the so-called 'Radek Affair',[28] these groups failed to link up in the first year of the war. They shared the belief that socialist revolution was the only answer to imperialism and war, and that the spontaneous action of the masses would be the decisive force. Nevertheless, they did not formally unite into a common faction or organisation.

From the factories in Berlin a left-wing group known as the 'Revolutionary Stewards' sprang up in the trade unions, led by the social democrat and leader of the Berlin metalworkers' branch, Richard Müller. The group worked semi-secretly and recruited dependable members from among Berlin's shop stewards. Out of all the left-wing groupings, theirs had the best contact with the workers. The core of their group never consisted of more than fifty people, but through delegate meetings they exerted influence over thousands and later hundreds of thousands of Berlin workers. Müller leaned towards the SPD 'centre', but many of the other group leaders were far closer to the Spartacists, with many later joining the Communist Party in 1919-20.

Within the SPD left, disagreements arose particularly over the question of whether to break away from the SPD and form an independent organisation, or whether to stay in the party. Luxemburg was firmly of the latter opinion. In her opinion, breaking with the SPD meant breaking with the masses, which she believed would reduce the revolutionaries to a sect. Amongst the aforementioned radical left groups, there were some who were opposed not only to the idea of splitting from the SPD, but even of formally forming an independent organisation, even as a faction inside the party:

---

28 The case is summarised in J. P. Nettl's *Rosa Luxemburg*, p. 316. During the split in the Polish party in 1911, an old and baseless accusation of theft was revived against Radek by the leadership of the SDKPiL, spearheaded by Jogiches, after he opposed them. He was excluded from the party, and the party also demanded that he be excluded from the SPD, arguing that he could not be excluded from one party in the International whilst remaining a member of another. The executive committee of the SPD used the accusation to rid itself of one of its strongest critics on the left. Luxemburg, who had no personal liking for Radek, supported the decision of the SPD executive committee in this case. Many on the left wing of the SPD were discontented with the behaviour of the Poles, and Lenin and Trotsky intervened in support of Radek as well. Radek later became a Bolshevik, and in 1918 he was sent to Germany as a representative of the new Soviet power in order to help the German left wing during the revolution.

The German left radicals had been in conflict for years with the authoritarian organisation of their own party. They concluded that centralisation was the main obstacle to the radicalisation of the masses and to the development of revolutionary activity. In this they disagreed with Lenin. They were aware that revisionism was advancing in the ranks of the Party, and particularly in its leadership. They knew that the trade-union bureaucrats and their conservative views were gaining influence in its leading bodies. However, they were convinced of the revolutionary character of the imperialist period, and were tireless critics of the opportunism of the leaders and of their authoritarian methods. Like Luxemburg, they believed that there were no recipes for organisation:

"We cannot secure ourselves in advance against all possibilities of opportunist deviation. Such dangers can be overcome only by the movement itself – certainly with the aid of Marxist theory, but only after the dangers in question have taken tangible form in practice."

This fundamental conception of activity, this identification of the Party with the mass movement, and their deep devotion to the organisation in which, despite its bureaucratic excrescences, they continued to see as the expression of the revolutionary social-democratic workers' movement, led them to reject the prospect of organising in a faction. They rejected the possibility of setting up, even in an informal and loosely-defined manner, a revolutionary tendency in German or international social democracy which would bring them into association with the Bolsheviks. Consequently they had even more reason to oppose any split in the Party or the International.[29]

In theory, the Spartacists favoured the founding of a new, Third International. In practice, they were not prepared to take steps towards preparing a split away from the SPD. They believed that the new International could only be formed on the basis of a mass movement. Until that movement broke out, they believed it was their task to remain inside the SPD, educating the masses through propaganda. When the internationalists who opposed the war met at the Zimmerwald conference of 1915, five Germans participated. Meyer and Thalheim represented the *Internationale* group. Borchardt was the only German who supported Lenin's position, advocating for a clear break with the Second International and the foundation of a new, communist International. The four other German participants voted with the majority of Zimmerwald delegates, who leaned towards centrism and pacifism, and who spoke in favour of re-establishing a reformed Socialist International.

---

29 P. Broué, *The German Revolution, 1917-1923*, pp. 39-40.

Opposition to the War and the Founding of the USPD

The leadership of the SPD, Kautsky included, covered up their support for the war by pointing to the patriotic wave that had swept Germany at the start of the war and the "apathy of the masses".

Kautsky certainly was not wrong when he noted that a patriotic wave swept the country at the outbreak of the war. That is usual at the outbreak of any war. It was certainly true that the SPD's support for the war met no resistance worthy of mention from the masses, or indeed from SPD ranks. But as Luxemburg pointed out, how could the masses have possibly expressed their opposition to the war? Their own organisation was now riding the patriotic wave. It was no coincidence that it was precisely in those sections of the party where left-wing opponents of the war were in the *leadership*, that opposition to the parliamentary truce and the party's support for the war were first expressed.

The parliamentary truce by which the SPD had bound itself stipulated that the party leaders must keep opposition within the party under control, and that strict limits must be placed on internal democracy. Already as of 5 August, for example, the executive had voted to postpone holding any new congress until after the war. One by one, the executive closed down all the party's radical local newspapers.

The war placed heavy burdens on the German working class, yet the social-democratic leaders assisted the German state in maintaining class peace. In the first two years of the war, food prices skyrocketed by 50 per cent, whilst wages remained stagnant. A lack of food and rationing were widespread. All workers were forced onto an absolute minimum diet. In the winter of 1915-16, ration cards entitled a person to 1.5 kilograms of bread, 2.5 kilograms of potatoes, 80 grams of butter, 250 grams of meat, 180 grams of sugar, and half an egg a week – and that depended on those wares even being available. The ration corresponds to one-third of the required calorie intake of an adult. Workers and soldiers were starving. Thousands upon thousands of young people were dying daily at the front lines, while the profits of the capitalist piled higher and higher.[30] The Reichstag adopted a new law that forced all men between the ages of seventeen and sixty to remain at their current job or else accept new employment assignments from the state. Everything that the social-democratic movement had achieved in previous years was rolled back with the help of the SPD leadership.

However, opposition began building. On 28 May 1915, more than 1,000 women protested for peace in front of the Reichstag. In autumn of the same

---

30 See ibid., p. 59.

year, protests erupted in Stuttgart and Leipzig. On 2 February 1916, there were protests in front of empty shops. The mood in society was changing, and social tensions were beginning to surface. Luxemburg could feel the change when she was released from prison in mid-February 1916, and found herself being welcomed with open arms by the workers of Berlin, and especially the women. She was immediately plunged into a whirlwind of meetings, speeches, and writing.

In May 1916, among others, she wrote an illegal leaflet titled 'A Dog's Policy'. The title made reference to the remarks of one of the leading SPD revisionists who compared Liebknecht to a dog that barks but does not bite. In it, she portrayed the SPD as bootlickers of the German government:

> A dog is someone who licks the boots of his master for serving him out kicks for many years.
>
> A dog is someone who gaily wags his tail in the muzzle of martial law and faithfully gazes up to his masters, the military dictators, quietly whining for mercy.
>
> A dog is someone who barks at a person – particularly in his absence – and who fetches and carries for his immediate masters.
>
> A dog is someone who, on the orders of the governments, covers the entire sacred history of a party with slime and kicks it in the dirt.
>
> Dogs are and always were the Davids, Landsbergs and comrades and they will get their well-earned kick from the German working classes when the day of reckoning comes.[31]

The Spartacists decided to test the degree of opposition in the working class by calling a demonstration on 1 May 1916 in the centre of Berlin. Thousands responded to the call. At the mass gathering, Liebknecht roused the assembled workers with the slogan: "Down with the government, down with the war!" He was immediately arrested. The Reichstag, including a majority of social-democratic deputies, voted to repeal his parliamentary immunity. But when Liebknecht's case came before the courts, 55,000 workers in Berlin's munitions factories and other workplaces came out on strike. This was the first political strike of the war, and it was organised by the Revolutionary Stewards.[32] Liebknecht was sentenced to two-and-a-half years in prison.

---

31 Quoted in J. P. Nettl, *Rosa Luxemburg*, p. 614.

32 Revolutionary Stewards [*Revolutionäre Obleute*] – An organisation of German shop stewards during the First World War, which opposed the war and acted independently of official trade unions and the SPD. Explained in more detail in pages 166-167.

After an appeal, his sentence was extended to four-and-half years. The regime escalated its repression, and multiple left-wing leaders were arrested. But the repression could not stop the rising wave of opposition. From the summer of 1916, the number of strikes and hunger riots steadily increased.

> Although the organised supporters of the *Spartakus* movement were still few in number, they were already making themselves heard. The Burgfrieden[33] had lost its taming force. The nationalist frenzy was at an end. The awakening was beginning.

> But German militarism took its revenge: many hundreds of *Spartakus* militants were arrested. The factories were 'combed out', and thousands conscripted in punishment, but as a result of this move revolutionary ideas were carried to all parts of the front. Increasingly severe sentences were passed, and mass trials took place. For the time being the military could credit itself with a victory. Because the political movement in the factories was temporarily robbed of its leaders, there were no protest actions when Liebknecht was sentenced by a higher military court to four years hard labour. However, his magnificent words, "No general ever wore a uniform with so much honour as I shall wear the convict's garb", made a deep impression on people.[34]

And then Luxemburg was arrested again. This time, however, she was not convicted by a court, but rather was placed under 'protective arrest' on 10 July 1916. She was told this was "for her own safety", but it meant that she was now detained without the right to appeal and without a release date. Not until the outbreak of the German Revolution in November 1918 would she be released. Initially, she was once more thrown into Barnimstrasse. However, suspicions that she was continuing a correspondence with her comrades on the outside led to the authorities increasing her isolation. In September 1916, she was moved to the police headquarters, which she described as pure hell. After a month-and-a-half there, she was transferred to the Wronke prison in the Province of Posen, where conditions were more bearable. The cell was open the entire day, and she had access to the prison garden. But in July 1917, she was transferred to Wrocław, where conditions were far harsher. But even under such constant persecution, Luxemburg was far from giving up her political work.

With many of the leaders now in prison, Jogiches took up the work of organising the Spartacists. He organised the regular publication of *Spartacus Letters*, most of the contents of which had been written by Luxemburg prior

33 Translator's note: *Burgfrieden* – the parliamentary truce.

34 P. Frölich, *Rosa Luxemburg*, p. 198.

to her detention. In its pages, the true character of the war was exposed, and both the right wing and the centre of the SPD were unsparingly criticised.

The growing influence of the Spartacus League was becoming an increasing cause of concern for the SPD centre. In a letter to the Austrian social-democratic leader Victor Adler, Kautsky wrote: "Extremism corresponds to the present needs of the uneducated masses. Today in the trenches, Liebknecht is the most popular man."[35] Lenin had been absolutely correct when he criticised Kautsky and the centre of the party as "lacking backbone", and for their submissiveness towards opportunism. Now the party's centre could feel itself being squeezed. It could feel that its support was at risk of slipping away towards those around Liebknecht and Luxemburg. As such, the centre concluded that they had to begin increasingly openly expressing opposition to the war. One of the leaders of the centre, Wurm, wrote to Kautsky on 21 April 1915:

> The editors of *Neue Zeit*, especially you [Kautsky], none the less have a duty to answer the attacks of the group I[nternationale]; silence will be taken as abandonment of the position… the fact remains that the I[nternationale] is now being distributed throughout Germany; thanks to the devoted work of Rosa's friends it was being handed out at all the local meetings [*Zahlabende*] in Greater Berlin last Tuesday. The masses are restive about the war and especially over the rising cost of living, they have no one on whom to vent their rage and since they can't get at the government the party becomes the scapegoat. That is the 'action' which Rosa is screaming for…[36]

Terrified that it would lose support to the Spartacists if it acted otherwise, the SPD centre began voicing public opposition to the war. Several of the old party leaders including Kautsky, Bernstein, and Hugo Haase (the chairman of the party and of the Reichstag group) signed a critique of the party executive committee. The executive committee, meanwhile, considered there to be an advantage in maintaining the centre as a loyal opposition. They gave the executive a left cover at a time of increasing opposition to the war among German workers. The executive decided therefore to open up a little room for opposition. In February 1915, it allowed Reichstag members who did not wish to vote in favour of war funds to absent themselves from the voting. On 20 March, Otto Rühle joined Liebknecht in voting against new war credits, while Haase and others left before the vote took place.

---

35 Quoted in P. Broué, *The German Revolution: 1917-1923*, p. 60.

36 Quoted in J. P. Nettl, *Rosa Luxemburg*, p. 638 (additions are made by Nettl).

When war broke out, those who took the position of the SPD centre supported the war but also claimed to favour a peace without annexations. Liebknecht denied that such a peace was possible as long as capitalism and imperialism continued to exist, and exposed the centre for deceiving the public. Liebknecht was vindicated early on in the war. When the executive committee declared openly that it supported the government's annexation policy in 1915, Bernstein, Kautsky and Haase, as the party's loyal opposition, wrote a manifesto laying out the position of the 'centre', which was published in the *Leipziger Volkszeitung*. They refrained from criticising the party's actions on 4 August 1914, and instead claimed that Germany's safety was now secured, and as such that it was high time the party ceased its support for the government and began campaigning for peace. The government took fright at the appearance of prominent names at the foot of the manifesto, and promptly shut the paper down. It was clear that the executive committee not only intended to support war credits but that its support extended to direct support for the annexationist programme of the government. This only increased opposition towards the granting of new war credits inside the SPD Reichstag fraction. When a new round of voting on the funding of the war took place on 29 December 1915, twenty-two SPD deputies absented themselves before the vote, whilst a further twenty stayed and voted against.

This was the first break between the executive committee and the centre. More and more sections of the party apparatus appeared to go over to the opposition. The executive committee responded by launching a massive campaign to regain control of the party. In October 1916, the executive committee, with the help of the military authorities, seized *Vorwärts*, the central organ of the party. The news was received angrily by the rank-and-file workers of the party in Berlin, who sympathised with the opposition. It had all become too much for Haase, and on 24 May 1916, he delivered a speech in the Reichstag condemning the restriction of civil rights during the state of emergency. A large minority of SPD deputies then joined him in voting against the renewal of the state of emergency. The SPD deputies then voted by a majority of fifty-three votes to thirty-three to immediately expel all those who voted against the extension of the state of emergency from the party's Reichstag fraction. The Reichstag group was now split in two. The thirty-three excluded deputies formed the *Socialdemokratische Arbeitsgemeinschaft* in the Reichstag – the precursor to the USPD.

The leaders of the centre and of the left wing by no means drew closer to each other politically on account of the split. On the contrary, the centre regarded itself as a counterpoint to the left wing, which was growing in influence. They believed that this growth was in turn assisted by the behaviour of the right wing of the party. On 28 February 1917, Karl Kautsky wrote to Victor Adler:

> The boy Karl has become a real menace [*fürchterlich*]. If we in the *Arbeitsgemeinschaft* had not appeared and proved that we too exist, the irresistibly growing opposition would simply have gone over to *Spartakus* altogether. If a break has been avoided and *Spartakus* held at bay, that is entirely to our credit. The right wing has not helped us but has only helped *Spartakus*.[37]

However, only in Berlin was there a clear line of differentiation between the centre and the Spartacists in the opposition, on account of the fact that it was in Berlin that the leaders of the two factions were based. In the rest of the country, the split occurred organically. Despite the theoretical differences, a national conference of the collective opposition in the SPD was organised on 7 January 1917 in Berlin on the initiative of the *Arbeitsgemeinschaft*. All of the oppositional tendencies were represented. Of the 157 present, thirty-five were Spartacists. Items on the agenda included the defence of party members threatened with expulsion, and the defence of opposition newspapers, yet no one proposed splitting from the SPD. Indeed, the majority rejected a proposal from the Spartacist, Meyer, to refuse the payment of party subscriptions on account of the fact that they feared such a move would lead to a split.

Luxemburg maintained her opposition to splitting from the SPD. On 6 January 1917, the day prior to the conference, she wrote the following in an article, which she managed to smuggle out of prison:

> Understandably and praiseworthy as the impatience and bitter anger of our best elements may be… flight is flight. For us it is a betrayal of the masses, who will merely be handed over helpless into the stranglehold of a Scheidemann[38] or a Leigen[39]… into the hands of the bourgeoisie, to struggle but to be strangled in the end. One can 'leave' sects or conventicles[40] when these no longer suit and one can

---

37 Quoted in ibid., pp. 659-60 (additions are made by Nettl).

38 Philipp Scheidemann (1865-1939) – member of the SPD in the Reichstag from 1898. Led the support of the SPD to the war in 1914, central leader of the party from 1913, and co-chairman of the party in 1917.

39 Carl Legien (1861-1920) – SPD Reichstag member. Throughout the war he displayed an unwavering chauvinism.

40 Conventicle – a religious gathering in a private home.

always found new sects and conventicles. But it is nothing but childish fantasy to talk of liberating the whole mass of proletarians from their bitter and terrible fate by simply 'leaving' and in this way setting them a brave example.[41]

The conference's only result was the decision to maintain "permanent contact" between the opposition groups in order to develop their influence "within the framework of the party statutes".[42] The SPD executive committee had other ideas, however, and on 16 January it announced that in holding its own conference, the opposition had "placed itself outside the party". It instructed all local organisations to exclude the "saboteurs" as quickly as possible. In the places where the executive committee held the majority, the minority was excluded. In the places where the oppositionists held the majority, the local organisations were excluded *en bloc* and new organisations were formed by people who were loyal to the executive. Ninety-one local organisations were excluded in this manner, and with them the great majority of party members in Berlin, Leipzig, Bremen, and Brunswick.

There was nothing the opposition could do but accept the established fact of a split. In the Easter of 1917 they met and formed the Independent Social Democratic Party of Germany (USPD). The SPD had been split almost right down the middle. 170,000 members stayed in the old SPD, while the newly-founded USPD took 120,000 members. Almost all of the party's pre-war leaders found themselves together in the USPD. The spectrum stretched from Luxemburg and Liebknecht on the one hand, to people like Haase, Bernstein, and Kautsky on the other. None of these leaders had wished for a split, nor had they prepared for one. There was no agreement on the political principles upon which the new party was founded.

The left wing in Bremen preferred an independent path and argued for the founding of a new party without the centrists. Others on the left, including some Spartacists, shared this opinion, arguing likewise for the building of a new revolutionary party. The choice taken by the Spartacists would decide whether such a course was possible. But the Spartacist leaders opted to join the USPD. They were afraid of being cut off from the masses and of being silenced by the authorities should they be deprived of the cover of a party with legal status. As such, the radical left groups across Germany remained divided: some outside and others inside the USPD. The entry of the Spartacists into the USPD also allowed the centrist leaders to shelter

41 Quoted ibid., pp. 656-7.
42 P. Broué, *The German Revolution: 1917-1923*, pp. 78-9.

under the colossal authority that Karl Liebknecht had won in his struggle against the war.

The USPD was clearly an extremely politically heterogeneous organisation. One wing, under the leadership of Kautsky and co., was striving to turn the clock back to the days of the pre-1914 SPD. The revolutionary wing, on the contrary, was grasping towards the formation of a real revolutionary party. The former defended the principle of 'defence of the fatherland', while the latter was fighting for an end to the war through a socialist revolution. The majority, however, favoured reviving the old SPD – which was underlined by the fact that the USPD adopted the old Erfurt programme of the SPD at its founding congress. Indeed, the only difference with the SPD of yesteryear was that the USPD had a much weaker apparatus and was far less centralised, a characteristic of the SPD that the majority blamed for its degeneration. The historian Carl Schorske[43] described the self-imposed limits of the USPD as follows:

> The Independents [USPD] thus deprived themselves of any organisational instrument by which the spontaneous mass actions of the revolution, once begun, could be unified and consolidated into a single political striking force. The frustrating experience of yesterday had blinded the revolutionary leaders of tomorrow.[44]

As mentioned, several of the radical left groups were strongly opposed to the decision of the Spartacists to join the USPD. In March 1917, radical left groups in Bremen, Hamburg, Hanover, and Rüstringen declared their intention to break with the centre and form an independent revolutionary party. However, there was a great deal of political confusion among these groups.

Nonetheless, despite the fact that confusion reigned in some parts of the left, at the same time new channels were forming through which Bolshevik ideas were beginning to make headway among sections of the German left. Many German *émigrés* in Switzerland had come into contact with the Bolshevik leaders also exiled there, including Lenin himself. They were impressed by the ideas of the Russian exiles. The Youth International, led by

---

43 Carl E. Schorske (1915-2015) – American cultural historian and professor emeritus at Princeton University. Author of *German Social Democracy 1905-1917: The Development of the Great Schism*.

44 C. E. Schorske, *German Social Democracy 1905-1917: The Development of the Great Schism*, p. 321.

Willi Münzenberg, smuggled Bolshevik literature into Germany. As such, many of the young activists of both the radical left groups outside the USPD as well as among the Spartacists, were increasingly influenced by Lenin's ideas. Paul Levi accepted an invitation to become a German representative in the bureau of the Zimmerwald Left, a position which brought him into close contact with the Bolsheviks. He soon returned to Germany, becoming an important leader of the Spartacus League.

So, despite seething opposition towards the war and towards the opportunism of the SPD leaders, the German revolutionaries had no organisation capable of leading the masses when the revolution broke out in Germany in November 1918. But before then, revolutionaries in Germany and the world over would be provided with a dazzling example: Russia's October Revolution.

7. The Russian Revolution

The Russian Revolution began on International Working Women's Day, on 23 February 1917 (Julian calendar). After five days of the Russian workers being mobilised on the streets, the Tsar was toppled. Nine months later, in October 1917, the workers had seized power. Rosa Luxemburg followed the events in Russia as closely as she possibly could from her prison cell, welcoming the revolution with enthusiasm, which was clearly demonstrated by her letters. This enthusiasm pervaded Luxemburg's attitude in the following period, which is evident even in the very text that is so often used to portray Luxemburg as an arch opponent of Bolshevism:

> In the present period, when we face decisive final struggles in all the world, the most important problem of socialism was and is the burning question of our time. It is not a matter of this or that secondary question of tactics, but of the capacity for action of the proletariat, the strength to act, the will to power of socialism as such. In this, Lenin and Trotsky and their friends were the *first*, those who went ahead as an example to the proletariat of the world; they are still the *only ones* up to now who can cry with Hutten:[1] "I have dared!"
>
> This is essential and *enduring* in Bolshevik policy. In *this* sense theirs is the immortal historical service of having marched at the head of the international proletariat with the conquest of political power and the practical placing of the problem of

---

1 Ulrich von Hutten (1488-1523) – German imperial knight who advocated the dissolution of Germany's ties with the papacy. In 1520 he published 'Arouser of the German Nation', which opens with his motto, "I have dared to do it", in which announced his support of Martin Luther.

the realisation of socialism, and of having advanced mightily the settlement of the score between capital and labour in the entire world. In Russia, the problem could only be posed. It could not be solved in Russia. And in *this* sense, the future everywhere belongs to 'Bolshevism'.[2]

Rosa Luxemburg saw the Russian Revolution as commencing the world socialist revolution. In sharp contrast to the SPD and the leaders of the Second International who had betrayed the workers, the Bolsheviks in Russia had cut a path forward towards the world socialist revolution.

But before we examine Luxemburg's assessment of these mighty events, we must first give them their appropriate context. As such, it is necessary to sketch the outlines of the revolution and the events of its first year. The subject matter we are dealing with constitutes perhaps the most denigrated chapter in world history. Retrieving the real course of events amidst all the lies that surround them is impossible without delving into the subject in some depth. As such, we assume a degree of patience from the reader.

The October Revolution

The October Revolution was the culmination of a process beginning nine months earlier on 23 February 1917. On this date, the women workers of Petrograd[3] decided that they had had enough: enough of the war; of the lack of food; of standing in endless breadlines in the freezing cold – in a word, they had had enough of their misery. They decided to strike, and the male workers soon joined them. In a matter of days, the movement had developed into a general strike in Petrograd. In just five days, the hated Tsar was forced to abdicate.

It was a movement that had erupted spontaneously. None of the parties were responsible for the initiative that had ended in the Tsar's downfall. The local Bolsheviks had even advised the women not to take action, believing that it was premature and would certainly be crushed. In its earliest stages, the movement lacked any organisation. The fact that the regime fell so swiftly before this spontaneous, elemental movement testifies as much to the degree of rottenness of the regime as to the strength of the movement.

---

2   R. Luxemburg, 'The Russian Revolution', *Rosa Luxemburg Speaks*, p. 395.

3   Petrograd – the most important city in Russia during 1917. Until 1914, the city was named St. Petersburg, but was renamed to do away with the apparent German-sounding name. In this chapter I have decided to use the name Petrograd as this was the name of the city during the events which we examine. The city was renamed to Leningrad in 1924, and re-renamed St. Petersburg in 1991.

On the evening of the Tsar's abdication, the old State Duma – a parliamentary body formally elected in 1912, but relegated to a purely consultative role by the Tsar – declared the formation of an unelected provisional government. Also on the same evening, a soviet was established in Petrograd by the leaders of the workers' parties, and a call was sent out for all workers and soldiers to elect deputies to the soviet, as they had done in 1905. This marked the beginning of a period that Lenin referred to as 'dual power', in which the government of the bourgeoisie and organs of workers' power (soviets), existed alongside each other. But, ultimately one class would have to triumph over the other. The interests of the working class and the bourgeoisie are diametrically opposed and utterly incompatible. Such a situation could not be sustained indefinitely.

The days that immediately followed the February Revolution, however, were days of rejoicing. The Tsar was gone, a number of democratic rights were implemented, and the revolutionaries could return home from exile. But as the days turned into weeks, and the weeks turned into months, it became clear to the masses that toppling the Tsar had not fundamentally changed society. The landlords still reigned in the countryside, while the majority of the peasants owned either no land whatsoever or else tiny plots that could not feed a whole family; workers had no bread; and last but not least, the hated war was continuing. The masses further radicalised. In the early days of the revolution, they placed their hopes in the moderate socialists – the Mensheviks and the Social Revolutionaries, who between them, had a majority in the soviets. By mid-April, the commitment foreign minister Milyukov had made to Russia's allies to continue the war to "its glorious conclusion" had been leaked, which provoked massive demonstrations of workers and soldiers. To stave off the crisis, after negotiations, six Socialist-Revolutionary and Menshevik ministers were included in the provisional government, with Alexander Kerensky as Minister of War. These ministers thus stood with one foot in each camp of the dual power. But the promises they made to the masses remained mere words. As such, the masses moved further to the left, towards the Bolsheviks.

The revolution found the most important Bolshevik leaders in exile, and those who were in Petrograd at the beginning of the revolution had a hard time orienting themselves politically. As in 1905, many of the old Bolsheviks, the so-called 'committeemen', initially suffered from a lack of clarity about the revolution. Stalin, along with Kamenev, was one of the first members of the Bolshevik central committee to return to Petrograd in 1917. The two immediately took over the editorial board of the Bolshevik newspaper, *Pravda*. Among other things, they used its pages to defend a position of conditional, critical support for the provisional government and the continuation of the war. Lenin, who was yet to return from his Swiss exile, became increasingly alarmed by the policies that the party was defending. Lenin wrote one letter after another to the Bolshevik central committee, later published in a collection with the title *Letters from Afar*. In them, he argued that the party must immediately withdraw its support from the provisional government and the war, and that it must advance an independent programme of the working class.

In April 1917, Lenin finally managed to return to Russia, just in time for a conference of the Bolshevik Party. There he put forward his famous 'April Theses', in which he explained that the first stage of the revolution was over. The time had arrived for the second stage: the struggle for the workers to seize power. The theses arrived like a thunderclap for the Bolshevik leadership, none of whom were as yet ready to subscribe to these views, and many openly opposed them. The perspective that Lenin outlined in the 'April Theses' closely resembled Trotsky's theory of permanent revolution. In fact, so close was the resemblance that some actually accused Lenin of having converted to Trotskyism. Indeed, Trotsky was in full agreement with Lenin's line, and in August of 1917, he joined the Bolshevik Party.[4]

According to Lenin, the task of the Bolsheviks was to win over the masses by "patiently explaining". He argued that the masses would compare the words and deeds of the moderate socialists through experience. In so doing, they would come to realise the limitations of these leaders. Such experience would teach the masses that they could only rely upon their own strength, and that they themselves had to seize power. Such an approach was summarised in Lenin's slogan, "all power to the soviets", which he raised precisely at a time when the moderate socialists held the majority and leading positions in the soviets. The message of the slogan was essentially: take the power that the masses have given you; match your fine words with deeds.

The tremendous influx of fresh revolutionaries into the party allowed Lenin to win the day at the April conference, despite opposition from large

---

4   By August 1917, Trotsky had been working closely with the Bolsheviks for months. However, in agreement with Lenin, he remained outside the party in order to win over the entire membership of the Mezhraiontsy (the 'Interdistrict' group, an organisation to which he and a couple of thousand others belonged) to the Bolsheviks. He was successful, and the whole group fused with the Bolsheviks in August 1917.

parts of the Bolshevik leadership. With time, however, experience taught most of the party leaders the correctness of Lenin's ideas. Between May and June, the 'socialist' ministers – and Kerensky in particular – played a key role in the attempt to revive the war effort. They supported the decision to launch a military offensive against Germany in spite of the extreme weariness and exhaustion of the soldiers at the front. The 'June offensive' was an unmitigated disaster, provoking huge territorial losses and open mutinies among the troops. Frustration in the provisional government grew. Strikes and demonstrations intensified, and peasant rebellions broke out in the countryside. The slogan "all power to the Soviets" became the main demand rising from the streets. The workers and soldiers of Petrograd in particular were running out of patience. In July, they decided to take to the streets in an armed demonstration to pressure the moderate socialists, who held the majority in the soviet, to move from words to deeds, and to keep their promises. But when they were given a clear choice, the 'socialist' ministers chose to side with the bourgeoisie. Soldiers were called in from the front to suppress the protests.

The Bolsheviks understood that the workers and soldiers in Petrograd had reached more advanced revolutionary conclusions than the rest of the working class, let alone the peasant masses in key parts of the country who also made up important sections of the army. These layers would follow suit, but more time was needed to win them over. A premature insurrection in Petrograd could still be isolated and crushed. For this reason, the Bolsheviks tried to dissuade them, but it became clear that the masses could not be held back. The Bolsheviks then decided to join the masses in order to ensure the greatest possible organisation and discipline in the protests. For two days the Petrograd workers and soldiers conquered the streets, displaying their sheer determination, though the movement was short of an open insurrection. However, as soon as 'trusted' troops could be mustered from the front, the government responded with bloody repression. They accused the Bolsheviks of treason and attacked them as 'German agents'. The party was banned. Armed reactionaries, including the Black Hundreds, were used to put down any resistance. Trotsky was arrested, whilst Lenin and the other Bolshevik leaders were forced into hiding.

The setback suffered by the Bolsheviks turned out to only be temporary – a price they had to pay in order to maintain and strengthen their connection with the revolutionary masses. At the time, however, this was not at all obvious, and it seemed to many that the revolution was lost and that counter-revolution would surely be victorious. The situation changed dramatically when the arch-reactionary commander-in-chief of the armed forces, Kornilov, marched his troops on Petrograd in late August in an attempt to seize power and crush the soviets. Kornilov's attempted coup had acted, in the words of Marx, as the "whip of the counter-revolution", which spurred the revolution onward once more. The provisional government, now headed by Kerensky and led by the moderate socialists, had to come crawling before the Bolsheviks, pleading for help to stop Kornilov. The Bolsheviks accepted, demanded and organised the arming of the Petrograd workers, and took a decisive lead in the struggle against the counter-revolution. However, they also used the occasion to expose the powerlessness of Kerensky and the provisional government. Kornilov was beaten back by the efforts of the Bolsheviks. This further radicalised the masses and increasingly drove them behind the Bolsheviks. The scales were tipped, in one soviet after another, in the direction of Bolshevik majorities. They could now expect to win a majority at the forthcoming All-Russian Congress of Soviets, due to meet in October.

The revolution was approaching its climax. The masses were mobilised and confident. The ruling class was demoralised. It was clear to Lenin, Trotsky and some of the other Bolshevik leaders that the current situation could not last much longer. Either the workers would launch an uprising and seize power, or else inaction would pave the way for demoralisation, momentum would once more swing back to the ruling class and the counter-revolution would enact its bloody vengeance as it had after the 1905 Revolution and the Paris Commune fifty years earlier.

The revolution had to take a decisive step forward. On the eve of the opening of the Congress of Soviets, the Bolsheviks organised an armed uprising in Petrograd. Strategic points in the city were occupied by revolutionary soldiers and workers under the command of the Petrograd soviet. But long before the insurrection, the Bolsheviks had already won over the majority of workers and soldiers in Petrograd.

On 25 October, representatives from soviets all over Russia gathered in Petrograd for the second[5] All-Russian Congress of Soviets. This was no mere

---

5   The first All-Russian Congress of Soviets was convened in Petrograd between 16 June and 7 July. In spite of the mood in Petrograd shifting dramatically in favour of the Bolsheviks, culminating in the movement of the 'July Days', the composition of the All-Russia congress still reflected a clear majority in support of the provisional government and the Socialist-Revolutionary and Menshevik parties. Bolshevik

gathering of career politicians. On the contrary, the Soviet Congress directly represented the workers and soldiers of Russia. It was a democratic gathering, the only historical precedent with which it could hitherto be compared was the Paris Commune of 1871. At the congress there was a clear majority for the Bolsheviks and the Left Socialist Revolutionaries. The latter represented a left-wing split from Kerensky and the Socialist Revolutionary Party, which had been the dominant force among the revolutionary oriented rural petty bourgeoisie and peasants in the period from February to October, but which was now divided between a right wing, representing the richer peasants and the intelligentsia of the cities, and a left wing representing the far more revolutionary poor peasants and agricultural workers.

The Bolsheviks placed a simple proposal before the Congress of Soviets: the congress was to put an end to the dual power period by seizing power into its own hands. The Left Socialist Revolutionaries supported the Bolshevik demand for soviet power. When the Mensheviks and Right Social Revolutionaries realised they were in a minority, they walked out of the congress. The congress, however, continued in their absence. It now voted to officially depose the provisional government. In its place it elected the new All-Russian Central Executive Committee – a kind of parliament, but one in which the representatives could be recalled by the Congress of Soviets and whose deputies received no more than the wage of a skilled worker; and a new Soviet government – the Council of People's Commissars. The Congress immediately issued an appeal to all the warring nations to begin negotiations for a peace without annexations, and a resolution distributing the land among the peasants. World history was being written. From the Congress, the revolution spread across Russia and far beyond its borders, like a wildfire on a parched landscape.

In the history textbooks, the October Revolution is often portrayed as a bloody affair. The Russian Civil War that followed it certainly was blood-soaked and violent, as wars generally are. What is remarkable about the October Revolution, however, is just how peaceful it actually was. It is said that more people died during the filming of Eisenstein's reproduction of the storming of the Winter Palace for the 1927 film *October* than died in the actual storming of the Winter Palace. Such a peaceful seizure of power was

---

resolutions for the Soviets to assume power and end the war were voted down in favour of support for the socialist ministers in the government and the continuation of the war without annexations. It elected an All-Russian Central Executive Committee with the Menshevik Chkheidze as president.

possible on account of the work that the Bolsheviks had conducted before the insurrection. Through meetings and discussions, they had won the great majority over to the side of the revolution, and particularly the workers and soldiers of Petrograd. A revolutionary situation cannot last long. Given such a crisis, the presence of a revolutionary party is essential. And it was precisely the presence of the Bolshevik Party in Russia in 1917 that secured the victory of the revolution, and furthermore that its victory was organised and disciplined, and therefore, peaceful.

Year One of the Revolution[6]

The October Revolution, however, could not achieve miracles nor wish away its problems. In many ways, it was not until the seizure of power was effected that the difficulties really began. It is precisely these difficulties that Luxemburg examines in her famous article about the Russian Revolution. In order to understand Luxemburg's approach to the questions, and on account of the extent to which her writings on the question have been manipulated since her death, it is necessary to subject the events of the first year of the Russian Revolution to examination.

The Bolsheviks had seized power in a country that was economically devastated. Even prior to the First World War, on numerous measures, Russia was far more backward than the advanced capitalist countries. The vast majority of the population still lived in the countryside under semi-feudal conditions, farming with the same methods their families had used for centuries. The war, however, had ripped the sons of the peasantry from the land, and had forced them into the army, where they joined millions of others in the enormous meat grinder that was the First World War. On top of the war, much of the country's productive capacity had collapsed. The result was a population living on the bare minimum of subsistence.

Furthermore, despite the fact that the old ruling class had been deposed by the revolution, the capitalists, nobles, and officers were not about to accept the loss of their power, fortunes, and privileges without a fight. They initiated a bloody war against the country's new rulers, in which they were able to count upon the support of the imperialist powers. The latter landed

---

6 This section is based on '*Den nye sovjetmagt og borgerkrig – hvad der virkelig skete*' ('The New Soviet Power and the Civil War: What really happened') written by Jonas Foldager in *Den Russiske Revolution og Borgerkrig – da arbejderne tog magten* (*The Russian Revolution and Civil War – When the Workers Seized Power*). A more detailed examination of the first year of the revolution is given in this text.

twenty-one foreign armies onto the soil of the new Soviet Republic in order to reinstate the old ruling class and crush the new Soviet power. The fact that the revolution not only held out against this overwhelming enemy but emerged victorious, demonstrated precisely the level of support it enjoyed among the Russian people.

The Bolsheviks not only inherited a devastated economy, they also inherited a state apparatus which was falling to bits. The army and the civil administration were in a state of dissolution. The new Soviet Republic had to start over. The art of administering an entire nation, state apparatus, army and economy had to be learnt overnight – something the old ruling class had had centuries to get to grips with. Without having had so much as a moment to breathe and consolidate its rule, the new regime was immediately thrown into the fire.

Immediately upon assuming power in October, the soviet government had to navigate a particularly tricky question: what to do about the Constituent Assembly? The Provisional Government had postponed convening the Constituent Assembly time and again. The Bolsheviks, meanwhile, had raised this slogan for years, even prior to the revolution, in opposition to the tsarist dictatorship. The Bolsheviks conceived the Constituent Assembly as a step forward in comparison with the dictatorship of a tsar or an unelected bourgeois Provisional Government.

However, the entire period from February to October 1917 had above all shown that bourgeois parliamentarianism was utterly incapable of delivering peace or bread to the peasants, and that the two forms of state power – bourgeois parliament and workers' soviet democracy – that is, a situation of dual power, could not coexist side by side. Nonetheless, under pressure from more moderate elements in the Soviet regime, and on account of the fact that the Bolsheviks had indeed raised this demand for many years, elections to the Constituent Assembly were called shortly after the October Revolution. All parties participated in them – the Bolsheviks included – but each held very different expectations. The bourgeoisie had given up entirely on the idea of a bourgeois democratic regime. Instead, they unanimously favoured installing a 'strongman' in power in the form of some type of military dictatorship. The petty bourgeoisie and its political representatives in the form of the Socialist Revolutionaries, meanwhile, placed all their hopes in the Constituent Assembly. Through it, they imagined they would become the ruling parliamentary party on the morrow.

Indeed, a majority of votes cast in the Constituent Assembly elections went to the Socialist Revolutionaries. More than 36 million people voted, of whom about 13 per cent voted for the bourgeois parties (the Cadets, etc.), 4 per cent for the Mensheviks, 25 per cent for the Bolsheviks, and 58 per cent for the Socialist Revolutionaries.[7]

But history had overtaken the Constituent Assembly. The election to the Constituent Assembly was based on electoral lists that the parties had drawn up prior to the October Revolution. As such, whilst the Socialist Revolutionaries went into the election with the list of a once unified party, by the time the elections took place, the party had actually split in two. One half, the right wing, was fiercely opposed to the new Soviet regime. The left wing, on the contrary, supported the October Revolution. By the end of 1917, there were seven Left Socialist Revolutionary commissars in the Soviet government, the Council of People's Commissars. From a membership point of view, the Socialist Revolutionaries had more or less split down the middle. The right wing found its support primarily in the upper echelons of the party and in its apparatus, while the left wing had a majority among the rank-and-file membership. On the electoral lists, therefore, the right wing made up three quarters of the party's candidates. This gave a majority in the Constituent Assembly to enemies of the October Revolution, but this was not reflective of opinion in the Socialist Revolutionary party or in the country at large.

The Bolsheviks and Left Socialist Revolutionaries therefore put an ultimatum to the Constituent Assembly at its opening session (in early January 1918): that it broadly acknowledge the decisions of the Congress of Soviets on the decrees of peace, land for the peasants, etc. When this ultimatum was rejected, the two parties left, and the assembly was closed shortly thereafter.

In essence, the question of the Constituent Assembly was a question of either defending the new Soviet power or of returning to the unstable pre-October situation of dual power. The period from February 1917 to the October Revolution had demonstrated the impossibility of the organs of power of two hostile classes coexisting side by side. One would have to choose between workers' power – as expressed through the soviets, or the rule of the bourgeoisie – as expressed through the Constituent Assembly. Had the Soviet power accepted the Constituent Assembly, it would have amounted to annulling the results of the October Revolution and handing power back to the bourgeoisie and the landlords, a course of action which was certainly not favoured by the workers and peasants. The Constituent Assembly lacked

7   See V. Serge, *Year One of the Russian Revolution*, pp. 138-9.

any social base, and even the most anti-communist of historians have been forced to admit that only a thin layer even noticed its dissolution. The vast majority of the population – the peasants – wanted land and peace. For the satisfaction of their demands, they looked towards the soviets.

Shortly after the October Revolution, the bourgeoisie, together with the Allied powers, began planning the overthrow of the new Soviet power. In the army, the revolution expressed itself in a conflict between the mass of lower ranking soldiers and the high command and senior officers. The result was the same almost everywhere – the counter-revolutionary command fled to the slightly less hostile Don region in order to regroup their forces, which were composed largely of Junkers and officers. With the assistance of the imperialist powers, they began building up counter-revolutionary armies across Russia – the so-called 'White Armies' – with the purpose of exterminating the Bolsheviks and all vestiges of the revolution, such that the workers would not dare to rise up for many generations to come.

On the other side of the class divide stood the Soviet government, which lacked any army whatsoever. The soldiers had begun demobilising even before the October Revolution. The Russian Revolution was born out of the First World War, with one of the foremost demands put forward by the Russian masses being that of peace. As such, the new Soviet government's first action was precisely to send out an appeal for all warring nations to commence peace negotiations to attain a general, democratic peace without annexations. Russia's allies in the war – France and Great Britain – met the Soviet government's appeal for peace with silence. Only Germany, which was at war with Russia, responded, and in December a truce was declared, preceding peace negotiations that would take place at Brest-Litovsk. After initial unsuccessful negotiations led by Adolph Joffe, Trotsky was charged with leading the Soviet delegation.

The representatives of the new soviet Republic were faced with a daunting task. De facto, the Russian army was in a state of complete dissolution. The soldiers had not waited to demobilise, and had simply abandoned their positions, leaving the road to Petrograd wide open. The Soviet government possessed no force capable of stopping a German advance against the capital, which would inevitably end with the crushing of the revolution. Peace negotiations were the only option if the Soviet power wished to survive. The Germans, however, made ghastly demands. Not only did they reject the Bolsheviks' demand that all colonies and annexed territories be released, they themselves demanded that the Soviet regime surrender immense amounts of territory. These territories included several of the Baltic countries, and the majority of modern-day Belarus and Ukraine. In all, it was demanded that 215,000 square kilometres of land, including the most economically important regions of the former Russian Empire, and no less than 20 million Soviet citizens, who had also risen in revolution, be handed over to the German emperor. On top of this, the Germans also demanded that Russia pay 3 billion roubles in war reparations. To concede to such demands would have left the road from Warsaw to Petrograd wide open. The Soviet delegation rejected the German demands, but they were forced to continue negotiations. What alternative did they have? They had no army with which to continue fighting.

The Bolsheviks used the peace negotiations very deftly. All the negotiations were recorded in shorthand and publicised. These tactics allowed the Bolsheviks to use the negotiations as a platform to shout over the heads of the German General Staff to the workers of Germany and the rest of the world. From Brest-Litovsk, the Russian delegation appealed to the workers of the world to rise up and seize power for themselves as the Russian workers had done.

The negotiations generated a massive wave of disagreement within the Bolshevik Party and the Soviet government. The 'left wing' of the Bolsheviks demanded that the Soviet government reject peace and instead pursue a revolutionary war against the German empire. The Bolsheviks were not pacifists, and they certainly did not rule out revolutionary war if such methods could bring aid to the revolutionary movements in other countries. For them, the world revolution was a consideration that came before all else. But this was a practical question – with which troops were the Soviets to fight such a war? Lenin argued that accepting the German conditions was the only option because continuing the war had simply become impossible. But he also believed that it would be necessary to provoke a breakdown in negotiations in order to make it obvious to the workers, and particularly those in the Allied countries, that there was no alliance between the new Soviet government and Germany. It had to be clear to all that the soviets had not accepted these atrocious conditions voluntarily, but that German imperialism had forced them at gunpoint. In this way, they could reject the smears of the bourgeois media that the Bolsheviks were German agents and that Soviet Russia and Germany were allies. Trotsky's position, summarised in the slogan, "neither war nor peace", won a majority in the Soviet government.

On 10 February 1918, Trotsky therefore read aloud a statement to the German delegation on behalf of the Soviet government, informing them that Russia had demobilised its army but would not sign the peace deal. The

German emperor was unsure of how to respond to such an unorthodox move. Everything pointed towards carrying through an offensive to crush the young workers' state, but the emperor vacillated. He was unsure whether the Germans could secure their supply lines for an invasion of Russia, but he was also fearful of how such an invasion would impact the morale of the German soldiers. In the end, he settled on launching an offensive against 'Bolshevism'. As soon as the German offensive started, the Russians telegraphed the Germans and accepted the peace conditions. But the Germans were no longer in a hurry. Instead, they added further demands to their list. This included the demand that the Russians stop agitating among German troops; that the Russian army be demobilised; that the Soviets recognise the Ukrainian People's Republic (the response of the counter-revolutionaries to the Ukrainian soviet); and that Finland and the Åland Islands be surrendered, which de facto meant surrendering the Finnish revolution that had just begun. Although they protested, the Russians nevertheless signed the Treaty of Brest-Litovsk. Now no one could be in any doubt that there was no alliance between Soviet Russia and Germany. After its signing, the peace deal drew criticism not only from a wing of the Bolshevik Party, the 'left communists' led by Bukharin and Radek, but also from the Bolsheviks' allies, the Left Socialist Revolutionaries, who withdrew from the Council of People's Commissars. They remained in the All-Russian Central Executive Committee but it now became clear that possibilities for cooperation between the Left Socialist Revolutionaries and the Bolsheviks had become extremely strained.

Simultaneously, the counter-revolutionary White forces in Finland gave a demonstration of what awaited the revolutionary workers once reaction succeeded. The Finnish workers had seized power in early 1918, but their Social Democratic leadership vacillated and attempted to remain within the framework of bourgeois democracy. Counter-revolutionary forces mobilised for a counter-offensive, with the support of volunteers from Sweden, Denmark and elsewhere. After the Treaty of Brest-Litovsk, the Russians were officially compelled to pull out of Finland, leaving the Finnish workers to fight alone. They fought bravely, but could not resist the overwhelming counter-revolutionary forces supported by 20,000 German soldiers. The White forces showed extreme brutality. Their victory was followed by bloody revenge – membership of a workers' organisation (party, trade union, etc.) meant imprisonment, and shop stewards in the workers' movement were executed. In total, the counter-revolutionary White Terror is estimated to have killed 30,000 people. This was an important lesson in class warfare. The victorious propertied classes know that in the wake of a revolutionary situation, they can only re-establish their class rule by drowning the revolution in blood and crippling the working class for decades to come.

The counter-revolutionary bloodshed in Finland commenced in April 1918. Until that point, the soviets in Russia had not resorted to political terror. Acts of retaliation were limited to rank-and-file soldiers and sailors settling accounts with their own officers. In Finland, and subsequently everywhere in Russia where the Whites got the upper hand, they clearly demonstrated to the Russian masses what awaited them if they were victorious – workers, communists, and indeed all opponents were rounded up and imprisoned or executed, and pogroms were unleashed against Jews. (It is estimated that the White Volunteer Army of Denikin killed 120,000 Jews alone in its pogroms). The brutal crackdown of the Whites pushed many neutral layers of the population over to the side of the Reds, in the following months and years, as the civil war progressed.

However, the counter-revolutionary war waged by the Whites had just begun. It was supported financially and by direct military intervention by all the imperialist powers against the Revolution. The bourgeois press in Russia, which still operated openly and legally after the October Revolution, started a hysterical campaign in the spring of 1918 to sow panic. In May, they reported that the Germans were sending forces to Moscow and Petrograd, and that the Bolsheviks were contemplating forming a coalition government with them. In response to this clearly slanderous campaign, proceedings were initiated against about a dozen bourgeois newspapers, which were made illegal along with a couple of Socialist Revolutionary newspapers.

The situation in Russia was desperate. Hunger was widespread, and Soviet-controlled regions were surrounded on all sides by counter-revolutionary forces. This was the backdrop against which a number of restrictions of democratic rights were carried out in the first year of the revolution. Once the German offensive started, all newspapers that showed hostility to the revolutionary defence or sympathy towards the German invaders were closed.

As hunger spread, some layers of the population became open to the propaganda of the counter-revolutionaries. In some places there were even uprisings. The revolution was hanging by a thread. In reality there was wheat, but it was hoarded by wealthy peasants because the money with which the government was offering to buy their grain was considered worthless. As such, in order to feed the cities, the Bolsheviks were forced to organise armed divisions of workers, which were sent out to the countryside to collect surplus grain from the wealthier peasants. Thus began a civil war in the countryside in order to secure wheat for the hungry workers in the city and at the front.

After the seizure of power by the counter-revolution in Ukraine, which had been torn out of the control of the Soviets by the Treaty of Brest-Litovsk, a counter-revolutionary campaign was initiated across all of Russia. Until the end of April 1918, the Mensheviks and the Socialist Revolutionaries had officially opposed armed struggle against the soviets. Now, however, they gave direct assistance to the armed rebellion of the counter-revolution.

The soviet system had proved to be exceptionally democratic. In the soviets, questions were discussed and decided upon by elected representatives, and all parties that did not actively fight against the soviet power were afforded full freedom. The third All-Russian Congress of Soviets in January 1918, among other measures, approved the *Declaration of Rights of the Working and Exploited People* as a basis of the Soviet Constitution and established the Russian Soviet Federative Socialist Republic. Mensheviks and Right Socialist Revolutionaries used the Congress to openly vent their opposition to the revolutionary measures. An extraordinary fourth Congress was convened in March to ratify the Brest-Litovsk treaty, which was vehemently opposed for different reasons by Left Socialist Revolutionaries, Mensheviks and Right Socialist Revolutionaries. But when the Mensheviks and the Right Socialist Revolutionaries actively joined the civil war on the side of counter-revolution, the Bolsheviks responded by putting forward a resolution excluding from the soviets all those parties that encouraged civil war and allied themselves with the enemy. This was obviously a necessary step. It is hard to imagine what bourgeois government would ever allow armed parties fighting against their system to operate legally, even more so in a war situation. The Left Socialist Revolutionaries, however, now took another step towards a break with the Bolsheviks, voting against the resolution. Nonetheless, it was still passed, and the counter-revolutionary 'socialist' parties were ejected from the soviets.

In July 1918, delegates gathered for the fifth All-Russian Congress of Soviets. The Bolsheviks held the majority with 773 out of 1,164 delegates. The leader of the newborn Red Army, Leon Trotsky, put forward a resolution proposing harsh measures against anyone continuing to encourage war with Germany. A fierce debate erupted. The Left Socialist Revolutionaries had not only been dissatisfied with the Treaty of Brest-Litovsk – they were even more hostile to the policy of the Bolsheviks towards the peasants. The Bolsheviks had attempted to ally themselves with the poorest peasants, while the base of support of the Left Socialist Revolutionaries was among the middle layer of the peasantry. The Left Socialist Revolutionaries were hostile to grain requisitions and wanted to continue the war with Germany to reconquer grain-producing regions. At the same time, they were hostile to the Whites because the middle peasants were also harshly oppressed under the old tsarist regime. They accused the Bolsheviks, among other things, of impoverishing the peasants and of being in league with the Germans. During the congress, news arrived of the murder of the German ambassador, Count Mirbach, in Moscow. The assassination had been carried out by Left Socialist Revolutionaries who served in the secret police, the Cheka, with the intention of provoking a war with Germany. At the same time, the Left Socialist Revolutionaries occupied the central postal office in Moscow, and from there sent out telegrams declaring the decisions of the Council of People's Commissars void, and proclaiming the Socialist Revolutionary Party to be the only governing party. That is to say, they attempted to carry out a coup. This led to armed clashes in which the uprising was defeated. Thus, the alliance between the Bolsheviks and the Left Socialist Revolutionaries came to an end, and the latter broke up as a party. The Congress resumed its work on 9-10 July after the uprising was defeated and resolved to ban the Left Socialist Revolutionary Party, leaving the door open to all Socialist Revolutionary organisations that would disown the actions of their party's Central Committee.

The civil war raged on. On all fronts, the White armies advanced with a great deal of support from the European powers. A joint English–American–French expeditionary force landed in Murmansk on 2 July; Japanese and American forces landed in Vladivostok, and the Czechoslovak Legion[8] took control along the Volga and in the Urals. Behind the advancing lines of the Whites, workers and 'Reds' were summarily executed; captured cities were purged, and the Whites attempted to terrorise the population into submission.

---

8 The Czechoslovak Legion was part of the Tsarist army. It was composed of Czech and Slovak volunteers enrolling to fight against Austria-Hungary. Their demobilisation from the Ukrainian front was agreed with the Soviet authorities in February 1918, but it was cut across by the German offensive, prior to the signing of the Brest-Litovsk treaty. The Legion's retreat towards the Urals converted its very existence into a complicating factor in the extremely chaotic situation of the Civil War, which led the Legion to link up with the White armies. The fall of Austria-Hungary in November 1918 and the proclamation of Czechoslovak independence prompted the Legion to open negotiations with the Red Army to seek further retreat and evacuation by sea via Vladivostok. This was completed in September 1920.

The rich peasants withheld their wheat from the cities, where hunger was rampant. The soviets were isolated. The White armies enjoyed the support of twenty-one armies of foreign intervention, sent by the world's mightiest imperialist powers. The revolution was hanging by a thin thread indeed.

A few weeks later, in August 1918, the Socialist Revolutionaries attempted to assassinate Lenin, who was gravely wounded. Meanwhile, an attempt to assassinate Uritsky, the chairman of the Cheka in Petrograd, was successful. As such, the Bolsheviks' decision to institute the so-called 'Red Terror' in autumn 1918 – in which food saboteurs and supporters of the counter-revolution were summarily executed – was not taken on a whim. Rather it was a desperate and defensive measure in response to the White Terror in the context of a class war that was being fought to the death.

The fact that one soviet party after another went over to the counter-revolution left power in the soviets concentrated in the hands of the Bolsheviks, who were now the only ruling party. This was not a desirable situation, but it was nevertheless the product of a long chain of causes and effects. The perspective of the Bolsheviks was to hold on until the world revolution came to the rescue of the Russian workers. If they allowed the counter-revolution to win, it would not only lead to a fascist dictatorship in Russia, it would also demoralise the international working class. Defeat in Russia would have thus tremendously strengthened counter-revolution internationally.

Meanwhile, Rosa Luxemburg was languishing in jail. Her enthusiastic support for the October Revolution is documented in her letters to Luise Kautsky as early as November 1917. She followed the Russian events as closely as she could for the following twelve months until her release from prison. However, her access to direct and accurate information was extremely limited. As she admitted in a letter she wrote from Breslau prison to her comrade Julian Marchlewski at the end of July 1918, information "reaches me only third-hand [about] the actual state of affairs [in Soviet Russia]".[9]

In the same letter, she expressed the concern that the "spectre of an alliance [of the Bolsheviks] with the 'Middle Kingdom' [Germany] seems to become ever more threatening".

Such extreme concern was at the centre of an article Luxemburg wrote later, in September, titled 'The Russian Tragedy'. Her fear was based on the idea that the concessions to Germany that the Bolsheviks had been forced to grant at Brest-Litovsk, and their subsequent retreats in the months that followed, although forced upon them because of the military weakness and isolation

---

9 R. Luxemburg, *The Letters of Rosa Luxemburg* [2013], p. 466.

of the Revolution, had objectively strengthened German imperialism, thus postponing the perspective of revolution in Germany.

Luxemburg's fears of such a capitulation were unjustified and she later dropped them altogether. However, she never blamed the Bolsheviks for what she considered to be important mistakes. She put the blame of the impossible situation facing the Russian revolutionaries squarely on the shoulders of the leaders of the German Social Democracy for their betrayal.

Her standpoint had nothing to do with the scepticism of the detractors of Bolshevism. It was the standpoint of a revolutionary whose exclusive concern was to fight for the best conditions that would guarantee the triumph of the international proletariat in the socialist revolution.

In the autumn of 1918, Rosa Luxemburg wrote the draft of a longer article, which she herself did not publish, but which was published posthumously and has subsequently been used to present a distorted image of her view of the Russian Revolution and the Bolsheviks. This article was titled 'The Russian Revolution'.

The Misuse of Luxemburg's 'The Russian Revolution'

The Russian Revolution was a tremendous source of inspiration for workers all over the world. For the first time, the workers managed to seize power, to hold it, and to take the first steps towards building a socialist society. Among the first steps of the new Soviet government, for instance, following the land reform and the appeal for peace was the establishment of legal equality for men and women. The right to divorce and abortion was legalised. Russia showed the whole world that society does not need capitalists, landlords or bankers in order to function. Quite the contrary, in fact.

It is no wonder then that a deluge of literature has been and continues to be published in order to smear the Russian Revolution. The sole aim of this literature is to scare workers and youth away from attempting to change society. But these smears do not merely originate from the bourgeoisie. Many so-called left-wingers have also engaged in the same slander campaign, and in their efforts, Rosa Luxemburg is often held aloft in what is a reformist crusade against Lenin, Bolshevism, and the Russian Revolution.

As mentioned above, Luxemburg wrote a long article about the October Revolution titled 'The Russian Revolution'. It is always from this article that quotes are drawn as ammunition for this campaign. Luxemburg wrote this piece from her prison cell in the autumn of 1918 as the young Soviet regime, as we have seen, faced a dire situation, with restrictions on democratic rights applied as a result of the civil war. If one reads Luxemburg's articles in their entirety, it is clear that she was fully conscious of the dire situation in Russia. There is no evidence at all to suggest that Luxemburg was opposed to the October Revolution. Quite the contrary. The very article begins and ends with unconditional support of the Bolsheviks and the October Revolution.

In the beginning of the article, after a scathing critique of the Mensheviks and their political equivalents in Germany represented by Kautsky, she writes the following lines about the Bolsheviks and the October Revolution:

> In this situation, the Bolshevik tendency performs the historic service of having proclaimed from the very beginning, and having followed with iron consistency, those tactics which alone could save democracy and drive the revolution ahead. All power exclusively in the hands of the worker and peasant masses, in the hands of the soviets – this was indeed the only way out of the difficulty into which the revolution had gotten; this was the sword stroke with which they cut the Gordian knot, freed the revolution from a narrow blind-alley and opened up for it an untrammelled path into the free and open fields.

> The party of Lenin was thus the only one in Russia which grasped the true interest of the revolution in that first period. It was the element that drove the revolution forward, and, thus it was the only party which really carried on a socialist policy. It is this which makes clear, too, why it was that the Bolsheviks, though they were at the beginning of the revolution a persecuted, slandered and hunted minority attacked on all sides, arrived within the shortest time to the head of the revolution and were able to bring under their banner all the genuine masses of the people: the urban proletariat, the army, the peasants, as well as the revolutionary elements of democracy, the left wing of the Socialist-Revolutionaries.

> The real situation, in which the Russian Revolution found itself, narrowed down in a few months to the alternative: victory of the counter-revolution or dictatorship of the proletariat – Kaledin[10] or Lenin. Such was the objective situation, just as it quickly presents itself in every revolution after the first intoxication is over, and as it presented itself in Russia as a result of the concrete, burning questions of peace and land, for which there was no solution within the framework of 'bourgeois' revolution.

> In this, the Russian Revolution has but confirmed the basic lesson of every great revolution, the law of its being, which decrees: either the revolution must advance

---

10 Alexey Kaledin (1861-1918) – leader of the Don Cossacks and active in the Kornilov coup. Participated in the formation of the counter-revolutionary White armies at the beginning of the civil war. Shot himself in January 1918.

at a rapid, stormy, resolute tempo, break down all barriers with an iron hand and place its goals ever farther ahead, or it is quite soon thrown backward behind its feeble point of departure and suppressed by counter-revolution. To stand still, to mark time on one spot, to be contented with the first goal it happens to reach, is never possible in revolution. And he who tries to apply the home-made wisdom derived from parliamentary battles between frogs and mice to the field of revolutionary tactics only shows thereby that the very psychology and laws of existence of revolution are alien to him and that all historical experience is to him a book [sealed] with seven seals. [...]

The 'golden mean' cannot be maintained in any revolution. The law of its nature demands a quick decision: either the locomotive drives forward full steam ahead to the most extreme point of the historical ascent, or it rolls back of its own weight again to the starting point at the bottom; and those who would keep it with their weak powers half way up the hill, drags it down irredeemably into the abyss.

Thus it is clear that in every revolution only that party capable of seizing the leadership and power has the courage to issue the appropriate watchwords for driving the revolution ahead, and the courage to draw all the necessary conclusions from the situation. This makes clear, too, the miserable role of the Russian Mensheviks, the Dans,[11] Tseretelis,[12] etc., who had enormous influence on the masses at the beginning, but, after their prolonged wavering and after they had fought with both hands and feet against taking over power and responsibility, were driven ignobly off the stage.

The party of Lenin was the only one which grasped the mandate and duty of a truly revolutionary party and which, by the slogan – "All power in the hands of the proletariat and peasantry" – insured the continued development of the revolution.

Thereby the Bolsheviks solved the famous problem of "winning a majority of the people", which problem has ever weighed on the German Social-Democracy like a nightmare. As bred-in-the-bone disciples of parliamentary cretinism, these German Social-Democrats have sought to apply to revolutions the home-made wisdom of the parliamentary nursery: in order to carry anything, you must first have a majority. The same, they say, applies to a revolution: first let's become a "majority". The true dialectic of revolutions, however, stands this wisdom of

11 Fyodor Ilyich Dan (1871-1947) – Menshevik, member of the Presidium of the Petrograd soviet prior to the October Revolution.

12 Irakli Tsereteli (1881-1959) – Menshevik, after the February Revolution a member of the executive committee of the Petrograd soviet. From May 1917 minister in the provisional government.

parliamentary moles on its head: not through a majority, but through revolutionary tactics to a majority – that's the way the road runs.

Only a party which knows how to lead, that is, to advance things, wins support in stormy times. The determination with which, at the decisive moment, Lenin and his comrades offered the only solution which could advance things ("all power in the hands of the proletariat and peasantry"), transformed them almost overnight from a persecuted, slandered, outlawed minority whose leader had to hide like Marat[13] in cellars, into the absolute master of the situation.

Moreover, the Bolsheviks immediately set as the aim of this seizure of power a complete, far reaching revolutionary program; not the safeguarding of bourgeois democracy, but a dictatorship of the proletariat for the purpose of realising socialism. Thereby they won for themselves the imperishable historic distinction of having for the first time proclaimed the final aim of socialism as the direct program of practical politics.

Whatever a party could offer of courage, revolutionary far-sightedness and consistency in an historic hour, Lenin, Trotsky and all the other comrades have given in good measure. All the revolutionary honour and capacity which western Social-Democracy lacked was represented by the Bolsheviks. Their October uprising was not only the actual salvation of the Russian Revolution; it was also the salvation of the honour of international socialism.[14]

This quote illustrates Luxemburg's opinion of the October Revolution and the Bolsheviks with all the clarity that anyone could wish for. The critiques that she raises beyond this point in the article are connected to concrete aspects of Bolshevik policy following October: on the land question, the national question, and restrictions to democracy. We will deal with these concrete criticisms later.

It must be noted that Luxemburg did not write this article for publication. Luxemburg sent an unfinished draft of it to Paul Levi, who had taken over the editing of the *Spartacus Letters* following the arrest of Jogiches in March 1918. Attached to the draft was a note, stating: "I am writing this pamphlet only for you and if I can convince *you* then the effort isn't wasted."[15] The article was not published until years after Luxemburg's death, being released to the public by Levi in 1922 who by that time had been excluded from

---

13 Jean-Paul Marat (1743-93) – Jacobin, active during the French Revolution (note by Frölich).

14 R. Luxemburg, 'The Russian Revolution', *Rosa Luxemburg Speaks*, pp. 372-5.

15 Quoted in J. P. Nettl, *Rosa Luxemburg*, p. 698.

the Communist Party. In short, it is an incomplete text that was written by Luxemburg for the purpose of private discussion, and above all to clarify her own thoughts.[16] Furthermore, it should be noted that it bears the marks of having been written whilst Luxemburg herself was in prison, at a time where she therefore had only limited access to detailed information and could not exchange views openly with her comrades about what she thought.[17]

To take one example, we can see this in the critique she levels at the Bolsheviks for some of their harsher actions, such as the restrictions on democracy and the Red Terror. Her criticisms are abstract and without context, despite the fact that she continually emphasises in the same article that the choices that the Bolsheviks face cannot be separated from the concrete situation and that they are the result of an "inevitable chain of causes and effects":

> Everything that happens in Russia is comprehensible and represents an inevitable chain of causes and effects, the starting point and end term of which are: the failure of the German proletariat and the occupation of Russia by German imperialism.

---

16 There are a lot of myths concerning this article and different representations of Luxemburg's purpose in writing it. Before Luxemburg wrote 'The Russian Revolution' she had, in September 1918, written a shorter article, 'The Russian Tragedy', which criticised the Bolshevik acceptance of the Brest-Litovsk peace with Germany and its consequences. According to Nettl, she wrote another critical article which the editors of the *Spartacus Letters* refused to print out of concern that Luxemburg's criticism could be used to undermine the Bolsheviks. After this, Paul Levi visited Rosa Luxemburg in prison and convinced her not to publish the long article which she planned to write. According to Nettl, this was the first time in a decade that Luxemburg had been convinced not to print something she had written. According to Frölich, Luxemburg did not write the article for publication but in order to "convince her comrades and for her own understanding". Exactly how and why the article was written, we will probably never know, but the more important question is its political content.

17 During the summer of 1917, Rosa Luxemburg had been moved from Wronke to Breslau prison, where conditions were much harsher. She was dependent on the newspapers for information on the events in Russia, and the government had worked out strict instructions for the press regarding its reporting on Russia. With regards to the October Revolution, the order was: "all that explains or praises the proceedings of the revolutionaries in Russia must be suppressed." (Quoted in J. P. Nettl, *Rosa Luxemburg*, p. 680.)

It would be demanding something superhuman from Lenin and his comrades if we should expect of them that under such circumstances they should conjure forth the finest democracy, the most exemplary dictatorship of the proletariat and a flourishing socialist economy. By their determined revolutionary stand, their exemplary strength in action, and their unbreakable loyalty to international socialism, they have contributed whatever could possibly be contributed under such devilishly hard conditions.[18]

The article ends as it began: with glowing praise for the Bolsheviks:

The Bolsheviks have shown that they are capable of everything that a genuine revolutionary party can contribute within the limits of historical possibilities. They are not supposed to perform miracles. For a model and faultless proletarian revolution in an isolated land, exhausted by world war, strangled by imperialism, betrayed by the international proletariat, would be a miracle.

What is in order is to distinguish the essential from the non-essential, the kernel from the accidental excrescences in the politics of the Bolsheviks. In the present period, when we face decisive final struggles in all the world, the most important problem of socialism was and is the burning question of our time. It is not a matter of this or that secondary question of tactics, but of the capacity for action of the proletariat, the strength to act, the will to power of socialism as such. In this, Lenin and Trotsky and their friends were the *first*, those who went ahead as an example to the proletariat of the world; they are still the *only ones* up to now who can cry with Hutten: "I have dared!"

This is essential and *enduring* in Bolshevik policy. In *this* sense theirs is the immortal historical service of having marched at the head of the international proletariat with the conquest of political power and the practical placing of the problem of the realisation of socialism, and of having advanced mightily the settlement of the score between capital and labour in the entire world. In Russia, the problem could only be posed. It could not be solved in Russia. And in *this* sense, the future everywhere belongs to 'Bolshevism'.[19]

Nothing in this assertion can be twisted to sound like Luxemburg being in any way in opposition to either the October Revolution or the Bolsheviks. The reformists are *only* able to use her against the October Revolution and the Bolsheviks by ripping her quotes out of their context and in such a way distorting her words to say the exact opposite of what she is actually saying.

---

18 R. Luxemburg, 'The Russian Revolution', *Rosa Luxemburg Speaks*, p. 394.

19 Ibid., p. 395.

For those who still have doubts, all we can do is encourage them to read her article in its full extent.

This positive approach to the revolution is fundamental to the meaning of Luxemburg's article, as evidenced by the fact that she chose to open and close the article in such a manner. It was between these two extracts, in the context of the words of praise we have just quoted, that Luxemburg put forward her concrete criticisms, which we will now examine.

The Land Question

The first point of critique that Luxemburg aimed at the Bolsheviks was their policy with regards to the land question. She contended that, despite their own wishes, the Bolsheviks by their policy had inadvertently ended up supporting the counter-revolution and thus weakened the prospects of the revolution. In her opinion, a socialist policy towards the land question must rest on two prerequisites: the nationalisation of the land of the large landlords, and the fusion of agriculture with industry:

> In the first place, only the nationalisation of the large landed estates, as the technically most advanced and most concentrated means and methods of agrarian production, can serve as the point of departure for the socialist mode of production on the land.[20]

The small peasant could keep his land, according to Luxemburg, and through the power of example would become convinced of the benefits of economies of scale. A prerequisite of this would be:

> [T]hat the separation between rural economy and industry which is so characteristic of bourgeois society, should be ended in such a way as to bring about a mutual interpenetration and fusion of both, to clear the way for the planning of both agrarian and industrial production according to a unified point of view.[21]

How this would be practically administered, however, was unimportant in Luxemburg's opinion. The more important point was that this would only be made possible through the prior nationalisation of large and medium landed property.

Luxemburg did not blame the Bolsheviks for not yet having commenced such reforms on account of the fact that they had many other problems which they were struggling against:

---

20 Ibid., p. 375.

21 Ibid., p. 376.

That the Soviet government in Russia has not carried through these mighty reforms – who can reproach them for that! It would be a sorry jest indeed to demand or expect of Lenin and his comrades that, in the brief period of their rule, in the centre of the gripping whirlpool of domestic and foreign struggles, ringed about by countless foes and opponents – to expect that under such circumstances they should already have solved, or even tackled, one of the most difficult tasks, indeed, we can safely say, *the* most difficult task of the socialist transformation of society! Even in the West, under the most favourable conditions, once we have come to power, we too will break many a tooth on this hard nut before we are out of the worst of the thousands of complicated difficulties of this gigantic task![22]

She criticised the Bolsheviks on account of the fact that she believed the measures they had implemented did not "lead in the direction of that fundamental prerequisite for a later socialist reform of agriculture" but rather pointed in the opposite direction, and furthermore, that they "even [cut] off the way to such measures; [they pile] up insurmountable obstacles to the socialist transformation of agrarian agriculture".

Luxemburg criticised the Bolsheviks for increasing the number of owners of private property rather than nationalising it:

The seizure of the landed estates by the peasants according to the short and precise slogan of Lenin and his friends – "*Go and take the land for yourselves*" – simply led to the sudden, chaotic conversion of large landownership into peasant landownership. What was created is not social property but a new form of private property, namely, the breaking up of large estates into medium and small estates, or relatively advanced large units of production into primitive small units which operate with technical means from the time of the Pharaohs.[23]

Furthermore, she believed that the chaotic manner in which land division had been conducted would reinforce the class divide in the countryside rather than erasing it. She believed that the end result would be "to the *disadvantage* of the interests of the proletariat and of socialism".[24]

She explained that the tactics of the Bolsheviks were certainly apt for winning over the peasants to the revolution, and that the latter may even attach their fortunes to those of the new government as a result. "But", Luxemburg said, "it had two sides to it; and the reverse side consisted in the

22 Ibid.
23 Ibid., p. 377.
24 Ibid.

fact that the direct seizure of the land by the peasants has in general nothing at all in common with socialist economy". In her opinion, it would turn the future socialisation of agriculture into "a question of opposition and of struggle between the urban proletariat and the mass of the peasantry". Her conclusion was clear:

> The Leninist agrarian reform has created a new and powerful layer of popular enemies of socialism on the countryside, enemies whose resistance will be much more dangerous and stubborn than that of the noble large landowners.[25]

From the above critique, we are left in no doubt that her intention was not at all to weaken the new regime, but to rather strengthen it and ease the transition to socialism. She was correct in pointing out the dangers and limitations of the Bolshevik policy, which would be demonstrated in the following years in the growth of an antagonism between the countryside and the city, which grew throughout the course of the civil war until it finally reached a breaking point. In order to forestall a break between the peasantry and the proletariat, the Bolsheviks were forced to introduce the New Economic Policy (NEP) in 1921, which reintroduced an open market in agricultural produce.

It should be noted that, viewed in the abstract, Luxemburg certainly had a point. But concretely, matters were not so simple. As Rosa Luxemburg herself pointed out, the Bolsheviks had no other options given the way things stood. Following her own reasoning, her critique would have read with greater consistency had it been reformulated as a warning, which is incidentally corroborated by the fact that this article was indeed only half-finished.

It should also be added that Luxemburg did not seem to be too well acquainted with the Bolshevik's actual land policy, a fact which is understandable considering that she was imprisoned. The Bolsheviks had not, as she alleged, created more private property. In the course of the spring and summer of 1917, Russia had been shaken by peasant uprisings. The provisional government, led by the moderate socialists, had attempted to put down these rebellions. The Bolsheviks, meanwhile, directly adopted the programme of the Socialist Revolutionaries on the land question, which essentially amounted to telling the peasants: "Seize the land of the landlords and church and divide it among yourselves". The Bolsheviks had made it clear that they intended to carry this out and that they would secure land for the peasants. This was how the majority of the peasantry was won to the side of

---

25 Ibid., p. 378.

the October Revolution, which was an absolute necessity in a country like Russia where the majority of the population were themselves peasants. And, indeed, once in power, they carried through their promises.

However, the Bolsheviks did not distribute the land as private property. They nationalised the land and confiscated the largest landed estates and distributed it among the peasants under the control of local soviets. The decree on land distribution was one of the first decrees adopted at the second All-Russian Congress of Soviets in October 1917. It contained the following formulation:

> "The landlord's property in the land is annulled immediately and without any indemnity whatever. The landlord, appanage, monastery and church estates with all their goods and chattels are given in charge of the town land committees and county soviets of peasant deputies until the Constituent Assembly. The confiscated property is *placed as a national possession under the protection of the local soviets*. The land of the rank-and-file peasants and rank-and-file Cossacks is protected against confiscation."

And:

> The collated instructions read: "The right to private property in the land is annulled for ever." "The right to use the land is accorded to all citizens… desiring to cultivate it with their own labour." "Hired labour is not permitted." "The use of the land must be equalised – that is, the land is to be divided among the toilers according to local conditions on the basis of standards either of labour or consumption."[26]

What the practical results of this policy would be were not obvious in October 1917, but according to Trotsky, this was quite intentional. He answered Rosa Luxemburg's critique as follows:

> A great many people, and not only enemies but friends, have failed to understand this far-sighted, and to a certain extent pedagogical, approach of the Bolshevik Party to the peasantry and its agrarian programme. The equal distribution of the land – objected Rosa Luxemburg for example – has nothing in common with socialism. The Bolsheviks, it goes without saying, had no illusion upon this point. On the contrary, the very construction of the decree bears witness to the critical vigilance of the legislator. Whereas the collated instructions say that all the land, both that of the landlords and the peasants, "is converted into national property", the basic decree does not commit itself at all as to the new form of property in

---

26 Quoted in L. Trotsky, *History of the Russian Revolution*, Vol. 3, pp. 1174-5 (my emphasis – MF).

the land. Even a none too pedantic jurist would be horrified at the fact that the nationalisation of the land, a new social principle of world-historic importance, is inaugurated in the form of a list of instructions adjoined to a basic law. But there was no reactionary slovenliness here. Lenin wanted as little as possible to tie the hands of the party and the soviet power *a priori* in a still unexplored historic realm.

Here again he united unexampled audacity with the greatest caution. It still remained to determine in experience how the peasants themselves would understand the conversion of the land into "the property of the whole people". Having made so long a dash forward, it was necessary to fortify the positions also in case a retreat should become necessary. The distribution of the landlord's land among the peasants, while not in itself a guarantee against bourgeois counter-revolution, made impossible in any case a feudal-monarchic restoration.

It would be possible to speak of socialist perspectives only after the establishment and successful preservation of the proletarian power. And this power could preserve itself only by giving determined co-operation to the peasant in carrying out his revolution. If the distribution of the land would strengthen the socialist government politically, it was then wholly justified as an immediate measure. The peasant had to be taken as the revolution found him. Only a new régime could re-educate him – and not at once, but in the course of a generation, with the help of a new technique and a new organisation of industry. The decree together with the instructions meant that the dictatorship of the proletariat assumed an obligation not only to take an attentive attitude toward the interests of the land labourer, but also to be patient of his illusions as a petty proprietor. It was clear in advance that there would be a number of stages and turning-points in the agrarian revolution. The collated instructions were anything but the last word. They represented merely a starting-point which the workers agreed to occupy while helping the peasants to realise their progressive demands, and warning them against false steps.

"We must not ignore", said Lenin in his speech, "the resolutions of the lower ranks of the people, even though we are not in agreement with them… We must give full freedom to the creative capacity of the popular masses. The essence of the thing is that the peasantry should have full confidence that there are no more landlords in the country, and let the peasants themselves decide all questions and build their own life." Opportunism? No, it was revolutionary realism.[27]

So, according to Trotsky, the policy of the Bolsheviks was concretely determined out of concern for the revolution: only by winning over the peasants, could the revolution be victorious.

---

27 Ibid., pp. 1176-7.

At least as important as the forms of property ownership was the question of the material foundation on which this ownership was based. Not only had the methods of agriculture themselves remained unchanged for centuries, but the infrastructure of the country had been laid to waste by four years of total destruction in the course of the World War. Nothing was working. Everything had to be rebuilt from scratch. To implement socialist forms of property, that is, collective, industrialised agriculture, in a situation in which the factories were understaffed, the White armies were closing in around Petrograd, and when one could barely send a letter from the capital to the countryside, was pure wishful thinking. The Bolsheviks therefore realised that socialist forms of property in the countryside first and foremost depended on the consolidation of Soviet power, the development of industry in the cities, and the spreading of the revolution internationally to the developed capitalist nations. On this perspective, the Bolsheviks and Luxemburg were in complete agreement. It was the firm conviction of the Bolsheviks that their policy regarding the land question was the one that opened the road to such a perspective. Without it they would never have won over the peasants and there would have been no revolution.

The Right of Nations to Self-Determination

No one familiar with Luxemburg's views can be surprised to learn that on the national question she criticised the Bolsheviks for sticking to their slogan of the "right of nations to self-determination" after coming to power. As with the other slogans of the Bolshevik party, this policy did not remain a dead letter. It too was carried into practice.

Luxemburg did not pull any punches. She called the thesis on the right of nations to self-determination "opportunism" and "hollow, petty-bourgeois phraseology and humbug".[28] Her arguments were the same as those she had raised earlier: the national question was simply exploited by the petty bourgeoisie and the bourgeoisie. She criticised the Bolsheviks for a policy which she believed gave the counter-revolution a powerful tool in its fight against the new soviet regime:

> Instead of striving, in the true spirit of the internationalist class policy that they represented in other matters, for the tightest union of the revolutionary forces of the entire territory of the Russian Empire, to defend tooth and nail the integrity of the Empire as a hotbed of revolution, to place the unity and inseparability of the

---

28 R. Luxemburg, 'The Russian Revolution', *Rosa Luxemburg Speaks*, p. 379.

proletarians of all nations in the sphere of the Russian Revolution as the supreme commandment of politics, and to oppose all particular nationalistic aspirations, the Bolsheviks, through their roars of nationalist phrase mongering concerning the "right to self-determination to the point of secession", have, quite to the contrary given the bourgeoisie in all peripheral countries the most desirable, most brilliant pretext for their counter-revolutionary efforts, and have virtually delivered them a banner under which to carry this out. Instead of warning the proletarians in the peripheral countries against any form of separatism as a bourgeois trap, and instead of nipping separatist tendencies in the bud with an iron fist – the use of which in this case would be in the true spirit of the dictatorship of the proletariat – they have rather confused the masses in all the peripheral countries with their slogan and delivered them to the mercy of the demagogy of the bourgeois classes. Through this nationalist demand they have themselves prepared and brought about the disintegration of Russia, and thus handed the enemy a knife to stab into the heart of the Russian Revolution.[29]

As with the land question, she criticised Bolshevik policy for not going far enough. With their slogan of the right of nations to self-determination, the Bolsheviks hoped to win over the peoples in the oppressed nations to the side of the revolution. The result, according to Luxemburg, would be the opposite – it would lead to the breakdown and dissolution of Russia, and would therefore strengthen the main enemy of the revolution: imperialism, particularly German imperialism, which would do everything in its power to crush the revolution:

> While Lenin and his comrades clearly expected that, as champions of national freedom even to the extent of "separation", they would turn Finland, the Ukraine, Poland, Lithuania, the Baltic countries, the Caucasus, etc., into so many faithful allies of the Russian Revolution, we have instead witnessed the opposite spectacle. One after another, these 'nations' used the freshly granted freedom to ally themselves with German imperialism against the Russian Revolution as its mortal enemy, and, under German protection, to carry the banner of counter-revolution into Russia itself.[30]

As described earlier, Luxemburg did not believe that there could be anything progressive in the struggle for national independence. She therefore believed

---

29 R. Luxemburg, *Zur russischen Revolution*, Chapter 3, *Marxist Internet Archive* [Website], our translation.

30 R. Luxemburg, 'The Russian Revolution', *Rosa Luxemburg Speaks*, p. 380.

that the Bolshevik policy on the question could have no other result than to strengthen the bourgeoisie of the 'border states'. She wrote off Ukrainian nationalism, for instance, as nothing more than a:

> [M]ere whim, a folly of a few dozen petty-bourgeois intellectuals without the slightest roots in the economic, political or psychological relationships of the country; it was without any historical tradition.[31]

Trotsky responded to this critique in his *History of the Russian Revolution*:

> When Rosa Luxemburg, in her posthumous polemic against the programme of the October Revolution, asserted that Ukrainian nationalism, having been formerly a mere 'amusement' of the commonplace petty-bourgeois intelligentsia, had been artificially raised up by the yeast of the Bolshevik formula of self-determination, she fell, notwithstanding her luminous mind, into a very serious historic error. The Ukrainian peasantry had not made national demands in the past for the reason that the Ukrainian peasantry had not in general risen to the height of political beings. The chief service of the February Revolution – perhaps its only service, but one amply sufficient – lay exactly in this, that it gave the oppressed classes and nations of Russia at last an opportunity to speak out. This political awakening of the peasantry could not have taken place otherwise, however, than through their own native language – with all the consequences ensuing in regard to schools, courts, self-administration. To oppose this would have been to try to drive the peasants back into non-existence.[32]

If the Bolsheviks had carried out Luxemburg's policy of "nipping separatist tendencies in the bud with an iron fist",[33] to the people of the oppressed nations, they would have appeared as mere continuators of tsarist, Great Russian chauvinism and national oppression. Unity cannot be forced upon an oppressed people. Luxemburg was afraid that the national separatist movements and the Bolshevik policy would lead to the downfall of the revolution. In fact, the exact opposite occurred. The February Revolution politically awakened the masses of the oppressed nations for the first time. The formal equality they achieved during the February Revolution did not satisfy them, and instead it simply underlined the degree of the real, national oppression that they suffered. The provisional government's rejection of the

---

31 Ibid., p. 382.

32 L. Trotsky, *History of the Russian Revolution*, Vol. 3, p. 898.

33 R. Luxemburg, *Zur russischen Revolution*, Chapter 3, *Marxist Internet Archive* [Website].

right to self-determination drove the oppressed nations into revolt against the regime and helped accelerate its downfall. Only by securing the right to self-determination, up to and including separation, did the Bolsheviks win the trust and sympathy of the masses of the oppressed nationalities. And this support was key to securing the Bolshevik victory against the counter-revolution. Rather than leading to a disintegration of the soviet state, it aided its victory in Russia as well as among the oppressed nations.

On the Dissolution of the Constituent Assembly

The reformists tend to most frequently use those parts of Rosa Luxemburg's critique that relate to the dissolution of the Constituent Assembly and the restrictions that the Bolsheviks introduced on democracy.

Luxemburg criticised the Bolsheviks' assertion that the electoral registers for the Constituent Assembly were out of date, thus rendering them unreflective of the situation in Russia post-October Revolution. In reply, she suggested that the Bolsheviks might have simply called new elections:

> But one cannot help wondering how such clever people as Lenin and Trotsky failed to arrive at the conclusion which follows immediately from the above facts. Since the Constituent Assembly was elected long before the decisive turning point, the October Revolution, and its composition reflected the picture of the vanished past and not of the new state of affairs, then it follows automatically that the outgrown and therefore still-born Constituent Assembly should have been annulled, and without delay, new elections to a new Constituent Assembly should have been arranged. They did not want to entrust, nor should they have entrusted, the fate of the revolution to an assemblage which reflected the Kerenskyan[34] Russia of yesterday, of the period of vacillations and coalition with the bourgeoisie. Hence there was nothing left to do except to convoke an assembly that would issue forth out of the renewed Russia that had advanced further.[35]

According to Luxemburg, there would have been no problem in electing a Constituent Assembly using outdated registers that were unreflective of the situation in Russia after the revolution. She believed that the pressure of the masses would correct the lopsided composition of the democratic institutions:

---

34 Alexander Kerensky (1881-1970) – Socialist Revolutionary who became Minister of Justice after the February Revolution, then Minister of War, and finally Prime Minister of the Provisional Government and supreme commander of the Russian military. Fought against the soviet regime after the October Revolution.

35 R. Luxemburg, 'The Russian Revolution', *Rosa Luxemburg Speaks*, p. 385.

According to Trotsky's theory, every elected assembly reflects once and for all only the mental composition, political maturity and mood of its electorate just at the moment when the latter goes to the polling place. According to that, a democratic body is the reflection of the masses at the end of the electoral period, much as the heavens of Herschel always show us the heavenly bodies not as they are when we are looking at them but as they were at the moment they sent out their light-messages to the earth from the measureless distances of space. Any living mental connection between the representatives, once they have been elected, and the electorate, any permanent interaction between one and the other, is hereby denied.

Yet how all historical experience contradicts this! Experience demonstrates quite the contrary: namely, that the living fluid of the popular mood continuously flows around the representative bodies, penetrates them, guides them. How else would it be possible to witness, as we do at times in every bourgeois parliament, the amusing capers of the 'people's representatives', who are suddenly inspired by a new 'spirit' and give forth quite unexpected sounds; or to find the most dried-out mummies at times comporting themselves like youngsters and the most diverse little *Scheidemaennchen* suddenly finding revolutionary tones in their breasts – whenever there is rumbling in factories and workshops on the street.

And is this ever-living influence of the mood and degree of political ripeness of the masses upon the elected bodies to be renounced in favour of a rigid scheme of party emblems and tickets in the very midst of revolution? Quite the contrary! It is precisely the revolution which creates by its glowing heat that delicate, vibrant, sensitive political atmosphere in which the waves of popular feeling, the pulse of popular life, work for a moment on the representative bodies in the most wonderful fashion. It is on this very fact, to be sure, that the well-known moving scenes depend which invariably present themselves in the first stages of every revolution, scenes in which old reactionaries or extreme moderates, who have issued out of a parliamentary election by limited suffrage under the old regime, suddenly become the heroic and stormy spokesmen of the uprising.[36]

---

36 Ibld., pp. 385-6. From here on, Luxemburg gives examples from the classic bourgeois revolutions, beginning with the English: "The classic example is provided by the famous 'Long Parliament' in England, which was elected and assembled 1642 and remained at its post for seven whole years and reflected in its internal life all alterations and displacements of popular feeling, of political ripeness, of class differentiation, of the progress of the revolution to its highest point, from the initial devout skirmishes with the Crown under a Speaker who remains on his knees, to the abolition of the House of Lords, the execution of Charles and the proclamation of the republic."

Luxemburg failed to follow her own logic consistently. In the same article she argued both that only the seizure of power by the soviets offered a way forward, and yet at the same time that the soviets must exist side by side with a Constituent Assembly, that is, alongside a parliamentary assembly. According to Luxemburg, the movement of the masses would exert the necessary pressure on the Assembly, even though its composition was not reflective of the revolutionary mood. It was a rehash of her argument that the pressure of the masses would push the leadership of the SPD to the left. But the pressure of the masses did not solve the problem with the leadership – neither in the workers' movement, nor in parliament – as Luxemburg herself would come to realise in practice in the course of only a few short months. When the revolution broke out in Germany, Rosa Luxemburg would be posed with the same problems. Under those circumstances, when she was at the centre of a mass movement rather than isolated in a prison cell, she altered her opinion. She came to realise that in practice there is no middle road between bourgeois democracy and workers' councils. The two cannot exist side by side.

When workers' and soldiers' councils were formed in the most important cities of Germany in November 1918 (which we will deal with in greater depth in the next chapter), the leadership of the SPD attempted to derail the revolution and drown out the councils by calling a constituent National Assembly. Luxemburg stood firm and rejected the National Assembly (i.e., Constituent Assembly) as historically outdated. In November 1918 she wrote and published the following words, which indirectly critique the very stance she defended just a couple of months earlier:

> The National Assembly is an outmoded legacy of bourgeois revolutions, an empty shell, a requisite from the time of petty-bourgeois illusions of a 'united people' and of the 'liberty, equality, fraternity' of the bourgeois State.

> To resort to the National Assembly today is consciously or unconsciously to turn the revolution back to the historical stage of bourgeois revolutions; anyone advocating it is a secret agent of the bourgeoisie or an unconscious spokesman of petty-bourgeois ideology.

> The struggle for the National Assembly is carried on under the war-cry of 'democracy or dictatorship'. Even socialist leaders obediently adopt these slogans of counter-revolutionary demagogues without noticing that this alternative is a demagogic falsification.

> Today it is not a question of democracy or dictatorship. The question that history has placed on the agenda is: bourgeois democracy or socialist democracy? For

the dictatorship of the proletariat is democracy in a socialist sense. It is not a matter of bombs, coups d'état, riots or 'anarchy', as the agents of capitalist profit dishonestly make out; rather, it is the use of all the means of political power to realise socialism, to expropriate the capitalist class – in the interests and through the will of the revolutionary majority of the proletariat, that is, in the spirit of socialist democracy.

Without the conscious will and action of the majority of the proletariat, there can be no socialism. In order to intensify this consciousness, to steel this will, to organise this action, a class organ is necessary: a national council of the urban and rural proletarians.

The convocation of such a representative body of labour in place of the traditional National Assembly of the bourgeois revolutions is in itself an act of the class struggle, a break with the historical past of bourgeois society, a powerful method of arousing the proletarian masses, a first open and abrupt declaration of war against capitalism.

No evasions, no ambiguities – the die must be cast. Yesterday parliamentary cretinism was a weakness; today it is an ambiguity; tomorrow it will be a betrayal of socialism.[37]

When the question posed itself concretely, Rosa Luxemburg was left in no doubt: the National Assembly (Constituent Assembly) and the councils could not coexist. One power would have to triumph over the other. So, when the reformists of our day attempt to use Luxemburg's critique of the dissolution of the Constituent Assembly in Russia to condemn the supposedly 'undemocratic' Bolsheviks, presenting her as an advocate of a parliamentary road to socialism, they can do so only by concealing the fact that she changed her own opinion only a couple of months later.

Restrictions on Democracy and Terror

As well as criticising the dissolution of the Constituent Assembly in her article, Luxemburg also criticised the restriction of democratic rights that the Bolsheviks gradually introduced in the course of 1918, including restrictions on the freedom of the press and freedom of assembly, among other things. According to Luxemburg, such a course of action threatened to strangle the political life of the country and thus the revolution itself. The latter, Luxemburg explained, depends upon the full participation of the masses, which itself is predicated on an extensive democracy:

---

37 R. Luxemburg, 'The National Assembly', *Marxist Internet Archive* [Website].

Socialism in life demands a complete spiritual transformation in the masses degraded by centuries of bourgeois rule. Social instincts in place of egotistical ones, mass initiative in place of inertia, idealism which conquers all suffering, etc., etc. No one knows this better, describes it more penetratingly; repeats it more stubbornly than Lenin. But he is completely mistaken in the means he employs. Decree, dictatorial force of the factory overseer, draconian penalties, rule by terror – all these things are but palliatives. The only way to a rebirth is the school of public life itself, the most unlimited, the broadest democracy and public opinion. It is rule by terror which demoralises.

When all this is eliminated, what really remains? In place of the representative bodies created by general, popular elections, Lenin and Trotsky have laid down the soviets as the only true representation of political life in the land as a whole, life in the soviets must also become more and more crippled. Without general elections, without unrestricted freedom of press and assembly, without a free struggle of opinion, life dies out in every public institution, becomes a mere semblance of life, in which only the bureaucracy remains as the active element. Public life gradually falls asleep, a few dozen party leaders of inexhaustible energy and boundless experience direct and rule. Among them, in reality only a dozen outstanding heads do the leading and an elite of the working class is invited from time to time to meetings where they are to applaud the speeches of the leaders, and to approve proposed resolutions unanimously – at bottom, then, a clique affair – a dictatorship, to be sure, not the dictatorship of the proletariat but only the dictatorship of a handful of politicians, that is a dictatorship in the bourgeois sense, in the sense of the rule of the Jacobins[38] (the postponement of the Soviet Congress from three-month periods to six-month periods!) Yes, we can go even further: such conditions must inevitably cause a brutalisation of public life: attempted assassinations, shooting of hostages, etc. [...]

This is an overpowering objective law from which no party can be exempt.[39]

She criticised Lenin and Trotsky for introducing the dictatorship of the party in place of the dictatorship of the proletariat:

The basic error of the Lenin–Trotsky theory is that they too, just like Kautsky, oppose dictatorship to democracy. 'Dictatorship or democracy' is the way the question is put by Bolsheviks and Kautsky alike. The latter naturally decides

---

38 This is a reference to the period in which the Jacobins, the most radical wing in the French Revolution, held power in 1793-94.

39 R. Luxemburg, 'The Russian Revolution', *Rosa Luxemburg Speaks*, pp. 391-3

in favour of 'democracy', that is, of bourgeois democracy, precisely because he opposes it to the alternative of the socialist revolution. Lenin and Trotsky, on the other hand, decide in favour of dictatorship in contradistinction to democracy, and thereby, in favour of the dictatorship of a handful of persons, that is, in favour of dictatorship on the bourgeois model. They are two opposite poles, both alike being far removed from a genuine socialist policy. The proletariat, when it seizes power, can never follow the good advice of Kautsky, given on the pretext of the 'unripeness of the country', the advice being to renounce socialist revolution and devote itself to democracy. It cannot follow this advice without betraying thereby itself, the International, and the revolution. It should and must at once undertake socialist measures in the most energetic, unyielding and unhesitant fashion, in other words, exercise a dictatorship, but a dictatorship of the *class*, not of a party or of a clique – dictatorship of the class, that means in the broadest possible form on the basis of the most active, unlimited participation of the mass of the people, of unlimited democracy.[40]

She continues with remarks that have become iconic for all those wishing to turn her words against Lenin, Trotsky, and the Bolsheviks:

Freedom only for the supporters of the government, only for the members of one party – however numerous they may be – is no freedom at all. Freedom is always and exclusively freedom for the one who thinks differently. Not because of any fanatical concept of 'justice' but because all that is instructive, wholesome and purifying in political freedom depends on this essential characteristic, and its effectiveness vanishes when 'freedom' becomes a special privilege.[41]

Luxemburg pointed to real problems when she described the emptying of the soviets and the fact that the Bolsheviks were left as the only ruling party. But what was the alternative? To allow the counter-revolution to win? The fact of the matter was that every other party had, one by one, sided with the counter-revolution in the civil war and had taken up arms against the soviet regime. Civil war and hunger had depopulated the cities, and with them the soviets. Ultimately, however, only victory in the civil war could bring the masses once more into activity.

Luxemburg had real concerns, but the manner in which the reformists use them is utterly false. They manipulate her article in order to apparently 'prove' that she had prophetically established the 'inevitable' connection between the

40 Ibid., p. 393.
41 Ibid., pp. 389-90.

regime of Lenin and the Bolsheviks and the Stalinist dictatorship that came later. But Stalin's dictatorship had nothing at all to do with the first years of the young Soviet state led by Lenin and the Bolsheviks. In the wake of the October Revolution, the soviet regime operated democratically. Purely local questions were settled by the local soviets themselves, whilst questions of national and international importance were settled in the central soviet. Here, everyone, including Lenin himself, had to fight to defend their point of view if they wanted to win the majority for their ideas and proposals. Full freedom existed for all of the political parties, with exception of the Black Hundreds – a fascist party responsible for pogroms against Jews and left-wingers. The restrictions introduced by the Bolsheviks limiting democratic rights – including the banning of parties – were the product of the pressure of the civil war. As such, they were regarded as temporary measures that would be lifted once the war ended. Even during the civil war, however, there were lively, democratic discussions and disagreements inside both the Bolshevik Party and the soviets.

The young soviet state and the one-party dictatorship established following Stalin's rise to power were like oil and water. A bloody chasm separates the two regimes: Stalin exterminated everyone who was in any way connected with the Bolshevik Party during the revolution. The rise of Stalin and the bureaucracy in Russia cannot be traced back to some congenital defect in Leninism and Bolshevism. Rather, it owes its origins to the fact that the Russian Revolution was isolated in a backward country. This was the reason why the revolution degenerated. This was why a bureaucracy could take power. In 1924, it was Stalin who first voiced the counter-revolutionary interests of the rising soviet bureaucracy by formulating the idea of 'socialism in one country'. From the very beginning, the Bolsheviks on the contrary had maintained that the Russian Revolution must spread to the developed capitalist nations, or else it would perish. This was a perspective that was fully shared by Luxemburg herself:

> It is not Russia's unripeness which has been proved by the events of the war and the Russian Revolution, but the unripeness of the German proletariat for the fulfilment of its historic tasks. And to make this fully clear is the first task of a critical examination of the Russian Revolution.

> The fate of the revolution in Russia depended fully upon international events. That the Bolsheviks have based their policy entirely upon the world proletarian revolution is the clearest proof of their political far-sightedness and firmness of principle and of the bold scope of their policies.[42]

---

42 Ibid., p. 368.

It was precisely the isolation of the Russian Revolution that gave rise to all the maladies that we've discussed. And, indeed, Luxemburg herself explained that in the given circumstances, the tough measures of the Bolsheviks were wholly understandable:

> Yes, dictatorship! But this dictatorship consists in the *manner of applying democracy*, not in its *elimination*, but in energetic, resolute attacks upon the well-entrenched rights and economic relationships of bourgeois society, without which a socialist transformation cannot be accomplished. But this dictatorship must be the work of the *class* and not of a little leading minority in the name of the class – that is, it must proceed step by step out of the active participation of the masses; it must be under their direct influence, subjected to the control of complete public activity; it must arise out of the growing political training of the mass of the people.
>
> Doubtless the Bolsheviks would have proceeded in this very way were it not that they suffered under the frightful compulsion of the world war, the German occupation and all the abnormal difficulties connected therewith, things which were inevitably bound to distort any socialist policy, however imbued it might be with the best intentions and the finest principles. [...]
>
> Let the German Government Socialists cry that the rule of the Bolsheviks in Russia is a distorted expression of the dictatorship of the proletariat. If it was or is such, that is only because it is a product of the behaviour of the German proletariat, in itself a distorted expression of the socialist class struggle. All of us are subject to the laws of history, and it is only internationally that the socialist order of society can be realised.[43]

The Purpose of the Critique

We have seen how Luxemburg criticised the Bolsheviks for giving the land to the peasants and for carrying the "right of nations to self-determination" into practice. Both points of critique were made out of a fear that the Bolsheviks' actions would weaken the revolution. On the question of the dissolution of the Constituent Assembly, Luxemburg changed her opinion, as we have seen. And on the restriction of democratic rights, she was of the opinion that they flowed from "an inevitable chain of causes and effects". Above everything else, Luxemburg was *in favour* of the October Revolution. Luxemburg's critique of the October Revolution and the Bolsheviks came from a revolutionary standpoint. She was concerned with understanding how the revolution is spread and its complete victory could be assured.

---

43 Ibid., pp. 394-5.

Warszawski, who had been Luxemburg's close collaborator in the course of many years in Poland, later published a letter that she had sent towards the end of November 1918 regarding the relationship between the SDKPiL and the Russian Revolution:

> If our party [SDKPiL] is full of enthusiasm for Bolshevism and at the same time opposed to the Bolshevik peace of Brest-Litovsk, and also opposes their propagation of national self-determination as a solution, then it is no more than enthusiasm coupled with the spirit of criticism – what more can people want from us?

And she continues:

> I shared all your reservations and doubts, but have dropped them in the most important questions, and in others I never went as far as you. Terrorism is evidence of grave internal weakness, but it is directed against internal enemies, who… get support and encouragement from foreign capitalists outside Russia. Once the European revolution comes, the Russian counter-revolutionaries lose not only this support, but – what is more important – they must lose all courage. Bolshevik terror is above all the expression of the weakness of the European proletariat. Naturally the agrarian circumstances there have created the sorest, most dangerous problem of the Russian revolution. But here too the saying is valid – even the greatest revolution can only achieve that which has become ripe [through the development of] social circumstances. This sore too can only be healed through the European revolution. And this is coming.[44]

Warszawski evaluated Luxemburg's letter in the following terms:

> We have seen the opinions which Rosa Luxemburg stated in her pamphlet were no longer her opinions from November 1918 and until her death. All the same, in spite of the errors and incompletions of her work, it is revolutionary work. Rosa Luxemburg's criticism differs from opportunistic criticism because it can never harm the cause or the party of revolution, it can only enliven it and help it – because it is revolutionary criticism.[45]

Rosa Luxemburg was no enemy of Lenin, the Bolsheviks, and the Russian Revolution. On the contrary, in the Russian Revolution she was on the same side of the barricades as the Bolsheviks. Any attempt to argue otherwise is utterly dishonest and a complete distortion of her thinking, as Frölich also contends:

---

44 Quoted in J. P. Nettl, *Rosa Luxemburg.*, pp. 716-7 (additions are made by Nettl).
45 Quoted ibid., p. 717.

Never at any time did she have the intention of launching a campaign against the Bolsheviks. She was always sparing with her hymns of praise, but she never spoke of people or of a party with so much enthusiastic approval as she did of the Bolsheviks in this work. It is a myth, and one which has been sedulously spread by the reformists, to say that she condemned the whole Bolshevik policy, including the October Revolution, and that she rejected the idea of the proletarian dictatorship, and thereby justified the policy of the Mensheviks. Her pamphlet leaves no room for doubt.[46]

The idea that the revolutionary movement is a monolith, devoid of internal debate and hostile to critique shares nothing with the genuine Marxist tradition and the heritage of Bolshevik Party under Lenin and Trotsky. Only later, under Stalinism, did the communist parties take on this character. However, this would certainly pass as an accurate description of the SPD in 1918. By no means coincidentally, Luxemburg was fully convinced that Lenin and Trotsky would receive her critique in a positive manner, and that a critical approach was the only approach by which anything could be learnt from the revolution:

> There is no doubt either that the wise heads at the helm of the Russian Revolution, that Lenin and Trotsky on their thorny path beset by traps of all kinds, have taken many a decisive step only with the greatest inner hesitation and with the most violent inner opposition. And surely nothing can be farther from their thoughts than to believe that all the things they have done or left undone under the conditions of bitter compulsion and necessity in the midst of the roaring whirlpool of events, should be regarded by the International as a shining example of socialist policy toward which only uncritical admiration and zealous imitation are in order.

> It would be no less wrong to fear that a critical examination of the road so far taken by the Russian Revolution would serve to weaken the respect for and the attractive power of the example of the Russian Revolution, which alone can overcome the fatal inertia of the German masses. Nothing is farther from the truth. An awakening of the revolutionary energy of the working class in Germany can never again be called forth in the spirit of the guardianship methods of the German Social Democracy of late-lamented memory. It can never again be conjured forth by any spotless authority, be it that of our own 'higher committees' or that of 'the Russian example'. Not by the creation of a revolutionary hurrah-spirit, but quite the contrary: only by an insight into

---

46 P. Frölich, *Rosa Luxemburg*, p. 211.

all the fearful seriousness, all the complexity of the tasks involved, only as a result of political maturity and independence of spirit, only as a result of a capacity for critical judgement on the part of the masses, whose capacity was systematically killed by the Social-Democracy for decades under various pretexts, only thus can the genuine capacity for historical action be born in the German proletariat. To concern oneself with a critical analysis of the Russian Revolution in all its historical connections is the best training for the German and the international working class for the tasks which confront them as an outgrowth of the present situation.[47]

According to Luxemburg, it would be utopian to believe that one could make a revolution in which nothing could be criticised, especially in such difficult circumstances as those of Russia in 1917. The purpose of her critique was to make clear that primary responsibility for solving the problems that the Russian Revolution faced rested upon the shoulders of the international proletariat:

Clearly, not uncritical apologetics but penetrating and thoughtful criticism is alone capable of bringing out treasures of experiences and teachings. Dealing as we are with the very first experiment in proletarian dictatorship in world history (and one taking place under the hardest conceivable conditions, in the midst of the world-wide conflagration and chaos of the imperialist mass slaughter, caught in the coils of the most reactionary military power in Europe, and accompanied by the most complete failure on the part of the international working class), it would be a crazy idea to think that every last thing done or left undone in an experiment with the dictatorship of the proletariat under such abnormal conditions represented the very pinnacle of perfection. On the contrary, elementary conceptions of socialist politics and an insight into their historically necessary prerequisites force us to understand that under such fatal conditions even the most gigantic idealism and the most storm-tested revolutionary energy are incapable of realising democracy and socialism but only distorted attempts at either.

To make this stand out clearly in all its fundamental aspects and consequences is the elementary duty of the socialists of all countries; for only on the background of this bitter knowledge can we measure the enormous magnitude of the responsibility of the international proletariat itself for the fate of the Russian Revolution.[48]

47 R. Luxemburg, 'The Russian Revolution', *Rosa Luxemburg Speaks*, pp. 369-70.
48 Ibid., pp. 368-9.

According to Luxemburg, that the Bolsheviks undertook the actions they did was completely understandable. Problems would only arise through uncritical imitation of the Russian Revolution:

> The danger begins only when they make a virtue of necessity and want to freeze into a complete theoretical system all the tactics forced upon them by these fatal circumstances, and want to recommend them to the international proletariat as a model of socialist tactics. When they get in their own light in this way, and hide their genuine, unquestionable historical service under the bushel of false steps forced on them by necessity, they render a poor service to international socialism for the sake of which they have fought and suffered; for they want to place in its storehouse as new discoveries all the distortions prescribed in Russia by necessity and compulsion – in the last analysis only by-products of the bankruptcy of international socialism in the present world war.[49]

The sharp formulations that Lenin and the Bolsheviks used to justify the political measures that had been forced upon them evidently made Luxemburg nervous. Lenin himself explained on several occasions how he would tend to take his argument to the limit. In his polemics he would occasionally even go a bit too far to the other extreme in order to hammer home an important point. Luxemburg's main purpose was to ward off German revolutionaries from attempting to mechanically apply the lessons of the Russian Revolution to German conditions. She hoped to prepare German workers and revolutionaries for the coming revolution by way of her critique:

> To concern oneself with a critical analysis of the Russian Revolution in all its historical connections is the best training for the German and the international working class for the tasks which confront them as an outgrowth of the present situation.[50]

Luxemburg emphasised that blame for the situation in which the Bolsheviks now found themselves lay squarely with the SPD. Measures, which were wholly comprehensible in the circumstances, were forced upon the Bolsheviks because the SPD had betrayed the world socialist revolution and had become a tool of reaction in supporting the imperialist world war. The Bolsheviks were forced into a corner, according to Luxemburg, because the German workers had not yet carried through their own revolution. She was fully in accord with the leading Bolsheviks, who predicted that the latter would not

---

49 Ibid., pp. 394-5.
50 Ibid., p. 370.

be able to hold onto power for much longer, much less construct socialism, should the revolution in Russia remain isolated. The Russian Revolution had the role of being the spark that would ignite the world revolution. A revolution in the developed capitalist countries, especially in Germany, would save the young Soviet power. Together they could then begin the task of building a new socialist society.

In a letter to Luise Kautsky dated 19 December 1917, Luxemburg wrote from Breslau:

> Yes, the Bolsheviks! Of course they don't please me either with their peace-fanaticism.[51] But after all – *they* are not to blame. They are in a straight jacket, and have merely the choice between two beatings and are choosing the lesser. *Others* are responsible for the fact that the devil profits by the Russian revolution… Therefore let us sweep before our own doors. On the whole events there are glorious and will have incalculable results.[52]

The Russian Revolution would indeed become the spark that lit a revolutionary conflagration whose flames would spread all the way to Germany. Before long, Luxemburg herself was thrown into the cauldron of revolution. Soon, she would be confronted directly with the problems posed by a revolutionary situation – not from her prison cell armed with nothing other than her pen, but in practice, as she wrote one month earlier expressing her true revolutionary spirit: "I am expecting many other great things during the coming years, only I should prefer to admire history not merely from behind iron bars."[53]

---

51 Luxemburg probably refers to the armistice between Russia and the Central Powers
   concluded on 15 December, which would lead to the negotiations at Brest-Litovsk.

52 R. Luxemburg, *Letters to Karl and Luise Kautsky from 1896 to 1918*, pp. 214-5.

53 Ibid., p. 207.

8. *The German Revolution*

Russia was not alone among the nations of Europe in being shaken by revolution towards the end of the war. The same violent social contradictions and crisis of the regime could be found in all the belligerent nations. Similar conditions created similar revolutionary results. On 9 November, a workers' and soldiers' council was set up in Berlin. The German Revolution had begun.

The revolutionary crisis expressed itself first at the top of society, as is so often the case in history. The autocratic regime could feel the earth shift beneath its feet and, in the words of the minister Hintze, sought to "forestall an upheaval from below by a revolution from above."[1]

By introducing certain democratic reforms, and forming a government encompassing the majority parties in the Reichstag, the bourgeoisie hoped to avert revolution. On 3 October, the cousin of the emperor, Prince Max von Baden, was appointed chancellor. In order to cover the left flank of the new government, ministerial portfolios were granted for the first time ever to social democrats: Phillip Scheidemann and Gustav Bauer. The latter were drawn into government only in order to give the regime stability and to confuse the working class – a tactic that has been used effectively on numerous occasions ever since.

It was clear, however, that a new government was insufficient to stem the revolutionary tide. The SPD leaders were of the opinion that revolution was now inevitable unless the emperor himself abdicated. Konrad Haenisch of the SPD expressed their fears well in a personal letter:

---

1   Quoted in P. Broué, *The German Revolution 1917-1923*, p. 130.

The problem is to resist the Bolshevik Revolution, which is rising, ever more threatening, and which means chaos. The Imperial question is closely linked to that of Bolshevism. We must sacrifice the Kaiser to save the country.[2]

The SPD also urged that political prisoners be granted amnesty as quickly as possible in order to convince the workers that the new government was sincere in its promise to 'democratise'. The release of Karl Liebknecht was particularly important if the new government wished to avoid the latter being converted into a martyr of the movement. The SPD had their way and Liebknecht was released on 21 October, with 100 other political prisoners released over the following days. On 23 October Liebknecht arrived in Berlin where he was received by a crowd numbering thousands. He immediately threw himself into the struggle, giving a speech in the very same square where he was arrested two years earlier. In that speech, he praised the Russian Revolution and spoke of the coming proletarian revolution in Germany.

His speech expressed the perspectives of the Spartacists who, at their conference on 7 October, judged the situation in Germany to be revolutionary. They declared their solidarity with the Russian Revolution and elaborated a programme that included a number of demands, including: the abolition of forced labour; an end to the state of emergency; cancellation of all war loans; the expropriation of the banks, mines and factories; a shorter working week; the transfer of responsibility for discipline in the army to delegates elected by soldiers; the right of soldiers to organise and hold meetings; and the abolition of the monarchy. In order to realise this programme, the conference called for "the formation of councils of workers and soldiers where they do not already exist".[3]

For its part, the USPD immediately offered Liebknecht a seat on the party's leading body. This, they hoped, would assist the party in walking a political tightrope by borrowing some of Liebknecht's enormous prestige. As a precondition, however, Liebknecht demanded that the party call a congress, certain that the membership would reject the former policy of the USPD leaders. The leadership rejected this demand, and so Liebknecht remained outside the party. Instead, he began working more closely with the Revolutionary Stewards (*Revolutionäre Obleute*).

Despite the fact that hundreds of political prisoners had been set free, Rosa Luxemburg remained in prison for a further few weeks. The amnesty did

---

2   Quoted in P. Broué, *The German Revolution: 1917-1923*, p. 144.

3   Quoted ibid., pp. 131-2.

not extend to those under so-called 'protective custody'. To remain behind bars whilst events beyond the prison walls were rapidly accelerating was pure torture for Luxemburg. On 18 October 1918 she wrote to Sophie Liebknecht from her prison cell:

> The conversations under surveillance, the impossibility of discussing what really interests me, by now has become so annoying that I would rather forego all visits until we can see each other as free human beings.
>
> After all, it can't last much longer.[4]

Only on 9 November, when the revolution reached Breslau, where she was imprisoned, would Rosa Luxemburg finally be released.

The November Revolution

The number of strikes taking place across Germany was on the rise throughout 1918. As far back as April 1917 Germany was rocked by a second wave of strikes against the war with 200,000 workers coming out in Berlin and Leipzig. In January 1918, it was followed by Germany's largest wartime strike in which more than a million workers from the armament factories downed tools in protests against the conditions being forced upon the Bolshevik government during the Brest-Litovsk negotiations. The Revolutionary Stewards were principally responsible for its organisation. On the back of the defeat of the strike, more than 100,000 strikers were enrolled into the army and sent to the front. Lenin later said that these events marked a change in the mood of the German proletariat. This was the build up to the German Revolution, which erupted in early November 1918, beginning with a mutiny of the sailors of Kiel.

The peace treaty signed at Brest-Litovsk in March 1918 had given the German regime a small amount of breathing space and, with renewed energy, the German army conducted an assault on the Western Front led by General Ludendorff. The push quickly ran out of momentum, however. In the course of the offensive, 300,000 German soldiers were killed and, by the summer, the German army was encountering serious problems on the Western Front.

By September 1918, even the German general staff had come to realise the necessity of pursuing peace negotiations with the Allied Powers. Despite this, they then ordered a North Sea offensive on 28 October. The aim of this

---

4 R. Luxemburg, 'To Sonja Liebknecht, Breslau, 18 October 1918', *The Letters of Rosa Luxemburg* [1978], p. 256.

offensive, regardless of its outcome, was to salvage the honour of the German navy by demonstrating its courage. However, the tens of thousands of sailors whose lives the admirals were gearing up to sacrifice were not quite ready to die to save their officers' honour.

The crew of the dreadnought battleships Thüringen and Helgoland refused to up-anchor. The sailors had mutinied. Rapidly, the mutiny spread to other ships. The admiralty of the fleet demanded that the mutiny be crushed and, in the face of being sunk by torpedo boats, the crew surrendered. Roughly 1,000 men were arrested and now faced the danger of being executed. However, the repression did not nip the revolution in the bud. On the contrary, it escalated it. In the harbour cities of Wilhelmshaven and Kiel, the workers refused to deliver provisions for the ships and the sailors made contact with the workers. On 3 November, a demonstration was held in Kiel at which nine were killed and twenty-nine were wounded.[5] The snowball was now rolling – by this point, there was no way back for the sailors. In the evening, meetings were held on the ships. The officers were disarmed and arrested by their subordinates, and the soldiers elected representatives that organised as a network. The red flag was hoisted above the warships. The mutiny spread across the length and breadth of the 100,000-man strong German fleet.

The revolution spread at the speed of light around the rest of Germany. On 6 November, workers' and soldiers' councils seized power in Hamburg, Chemnitz, Magdeburg, Braunschweig, Frankfurt, Cologne, Stuttgart, Nuremberg, and Munich. On 9 November, a workers' and soldiers' council was set up in Berlin. In the morning on that same day, fliers calling for an uprising were distributed at every workplace in Berlin. The workers held meetings all over the city and marched from the industrial areas towards the city centre. The revolution happened peacefully. Most of those soldiers deployed against the movement were quickly convinced not to shoot the protesters. Only four people died, one of whom was a Spartacist.

As in Russia, the workers' and soldiers' councils in Germany were a spontaneous creation of the movement that emerged from the need to coordinate and organise the struggle. As in Russia, delegates were directly responsible to those who elected them and could be recalled at any moment. Delegates enjoyed no privileges, and as such there was no careerism. What had emerged was the germ of true workers' democracy.

The SPD was desperate to prevent 'Russian conditions' coming home to Germany. Above all, they wished to lead the revolution into safe channels.

---

5 The figures in this section are from P. Broué, *The German Revolution, 1917-1923.*

But in order to do so, they were obliged to tail the movement to a certain extent, lest they lose the support that they had among the workers. The SPD leaders were aware from early on that the situation was getting out of hand. Therefore, even before the revolution arrived in Berlin, they placed an ultimatum before the government: either the emperor abdicated before 8 November, or else the SPD would not be held responsible for what might follow.

At the same time, the SPD proposed forming a government with the USPD. Their aim in attempting to drag the latter into government was to use the USPD's authority among left-wing workers to keep the movement under control. The leaders of the USPD were slow to respond to the advance. While this proposal was under discussion, the SPD called a meeting with Max von Baden,[6] who informed the social democrats to their surprise that the emperor had abdicated. Before announcing this news, Max von Baden had directly posed the question to Ebert, the leader of the SPD: could he rely on his support in fighting the revolution should the emperor abdicate? Ebert responded: "If the Kaiser does not abdicate the social revolution is inevitable. I do not want it – in fact, I hate it like sin."[7] With this assurance, Max von Baden transferred the office of chancellor to Ebert. The leaders of the USPD, meanwhile, were utterly divided, and the question of participating in the government or otherwise was postponed to the following day.

In Berlin, a protest of workers arrived at the Reichstag building at which the social democrat, Scheidemann, was eating lunch in the canteen. He was unable to evade addressing the assembled workers, and gave a short, impromptu speech from the balcony. The mood was clearly extremely radical, and Scheidemann was afraid of losing the trust of the masses. He therefore proclaimed the republic from the Reichstag balcony, and named Ebert chancellor. Upon learning what had happened, Ebert was furious – he was of the firm opinion that the SPD had no wish to proclaim a republic. Meanwhile, from another balcony, addressing another crowd assembled at the Imperial Palace at almost exactly the same time, Liebknecht proclaimed the *socialist* republic. However, events had not gone this far yet.

On the evening of 9 November, hundreds of representatives of the armed workers met in Berlin. They appealed for mass meetings to be held in all the factories and barracks the following day at ten o'clock, at which

---

6 Prince Maximilian of Baden (1867-1929) – briefly served as the last chancellor of the German Empire in November 1918.

7 Quoted in R. Sewell, *Germany 1918-1933: Socialism or Barbarism*, p. 98.

representatives would be elected – one for every 1,000 workers, and one for each battalion. They would then reconvene on the same day at four o'clock at Busch Circus with the purpose of appointing a revolutionary government.

The masses held power in their hands. But as in Russia in February 1917, they did not know what to do with it. A vacuum had opened up, and the leadership of the SPD emerged – in the beginning at least – as that political force that was the best prepared and most clear in exactly how it would fill this vacuum. During the night of 9-10 November, the SPD mobilised support among the soldiers for the meeting the following day. The infantrymen, who were typically recruited from among the peasantry, were more politically backward than the workers, and the majority of them supported the SPD. By moving quickly, the SPD managed to mobilise many of its supporters for the meeting of the workers' and soldiers' council the following day.

On 10 November, 1,500 delegates assembled for the planned meeting at Busch Circus. A mood of excitement ran through the gathering. Shortly before the meeting assembled, the vacillating USPD finally notified the SPD that they would indeed be willing to form a government with them. Each party appointed three ministers, which they called 'people's commissars' as a nod to the overwhelming mood in support of the Russian Revolution among the German workers. Ebert, Scheidemann, and Landsberg were nominated by the SPD, and Dittmann, Haase, and Barth were nominated by the USPD. The composition and nature of the new government was fiercely debated by the delegates in Busch Circus. The SPD had successfully whipped up the soldiers against any and all opposition towards the new government. Every time a delegate spoke up against it, they were drowned out by the same chorus from the armed soldiers: "Unity, unity!"

Even Liebknecht was met with the same shouts when he spoke against the proposed government and exposed the SPD as being representatives of the counter-revolution:

> [...] these people who today are with the Revolution, and were its enemies only the day before yesterday [...] The counter-revolution is already on the move, it is already in action, and is here in our midst.[8]

The revolution had awoken millions to political life, the majority of whom had never been politically active before. As in Russia, the awakened masses turned first to those political parties that they already knew. In Russia, following the

---

8   Quoted in P. Broué, *The German Revolution 1917-1923*, p. 153.

February Revolution, power was handed over to the Mensheviks and Social Revolutionaries. In Germany, the masses initially followed the SPD, and to a lesser extent the USPD. Only on the basis of practical experiences could the broader masses learn that neither the leadership of the SPD nor the USPD could solve their problems.

At the meeting in Busch Circus, the delegates decided to elect an executive committee for the newly formed workers' and soldiers' council. The initial list put before the delegates actually included a majority of USPD representatives on account of the fact that this was the party that enjoyed the highest level of support among factory workers. Among others, the list included Liebknecht and Luxemburg. But at the behest of the SPD, the soldiers obstructed this proposal, demanding that an executive committee be formed on the basis of an equal number of representatives of both parties. If this demand was not met, they threatened to withdraw from the council and form their own. Such methods were successful in forcing through an executive composed of twelve soldiers' representatives under the influence of the SPD, and six SPD and six USPD representatives of the workers. Liebknecht, whose name had been proposed on this list, refused to participate in protest at the serious breach of basic democratic procedure. Six further representatives were chosen from among the revolutionary delegates as non-party 'independents'. The meeting also acknowledged the proposed government. The result was a government made up of the SPD and the USPD, *alongside* an executive committee of the workers' and soldiers' councils composed of representatives of the exact same parties. The newly elected executive committee of the workers' and soldiers' council immediately handed power over to the six 'people's commissars' who headed the new government. As Pierre Broué explained:

> Thus the second day of the German Revolution found the Majority Social Democrats [the SPD – *MF*], who had done their utmost to prevent it, winning an indisputable victory. Their leader Ebert, Chancellor of the Reich by the grace of Max of Baden, People's Commissar by that of the general staffs of the two Social-Democratic Parties, found his position endorsed by the first assembly of the councils in the capital, so that he became, at one and the same time, head of the legal government and of the revolutionary government![9]

The news was met with enormous enthusiasm by the workers of Russia. Radek later described the scenes in Moscow:

---

9 Ibid., p. 154.

Tens of thousands of workers broke out into wild cheers. I have never seen anything like it. Late in the evening, workers and red soldiers were still parading. The world revolution had come. Our [Soviet Russia's][10] isolation was at an end.[11]

The new government carried through a series of reforms, including freedom of assembly, the repeal of censorship, and the promise to implement a six-hour working day commencing on 1 January 1919. They even promised to nationalise various companies. The SPD regarded its role as being that of stabilising the situation, and hemming the movement into the limits strictly imposed by capitalism. To the workers, they presented themselves as radicals, while behind the scenes they based themselves on the old state apparatus and, in particular, the army. Ebert entered into an alliance with the general staff to jointly combat Bolshevism and maintain 'law and order'.

Luxemburg immediately welcomed the revolution but at the same time issued a warning. In *Die Rote Fahne* (the newspaper of the Spartacists which recommenced publication on 18 November after some difficulties) she wrote:

> What is called for now is not jubilation at what has been accomplished, not triumph over the beaten foe, but the strictest self-criticism and iron concentration of energy in order to continue the work we have begun. For our accomplishments are small and the foe has not been beaten.[12]

The monarchy had been toppled, but Luxemburg was careful to warn against the belief that the monarchy was the real enemy. No, the real enemy was the imperialist bourgeoisie. In the same article she wrote:

> What has been achieved? The monarchy has been swept away, supreme governing power has been transferred into the hands of the workers' and soldiers' representatives. But the monarchy was never the real enemy; it was only a facade, the frontispiece of imperialism. […] The monarchy, like every bourgeois government, was the executive of the ruling classes. The imperialist bourgeoisie, the rule of the capitalist class – this is the criminal who must be held accountable for the genocide.

For Luxemburg, the goal of the revolution was not the establishment of a bourgeois-democratic regime, but the carrying through of the socialist revolution:

---

10 Radek was the representative of Soviet Russia.
11 Quoted ibid., p. 155.
12 R. Luxemburg, 'The Beginning', *Marxist Internet Archive* [website].

The abolition of the rule of capitalism, the realisation of the social order of socialism – this and nothing less is the historical theme of the present revolution.[13]

And the road to socialism passed directly through the workers' and soldiers' councils.

The path of the revolution follows clearly from its ends, its method follows from its task. All power in the hands of the working masses, in the hands of the workers' and soldiers' councils, protection of the work of revolution against its lurking enemies – this is the guiding principle of all measures to be taken by the revolutionary government.

Luxemburg posed a number of concrete demands to advance the movement: for new elections to the workers' and soldiers' councils; a national congress of the councils; the organisation of the agrarian proletariat and the smallholding peasants; the formation of a proletarian Red Guard and a workers' militia; and the confiscation of dynastic wealth and large properties for the purpose of feeding the hungry. Beyond these points, she advanced the call for a workers' world congress to be called immediately in Germany in order to "emphasise clearly and distinctly the socialist and international character of the revolution", in distinction to the SPD–USPD government, which had taken the opposite course.

By the end of the first week of the revolution, the revolutionary workers had handed power over to the SPD – the very same party that had stood in opposition to the revolution. But in Luxemburg's opinion, this was a wholly understandable state of affairs:

The picture of the German revolution corresponds to the inner ripeness of the German situation. The government of the German revolution at its present stage is in the hands of Scheidemann and Ebert.[14]

The revolution had only just begun, but:

[…] revolutions do not stand still. Their vital law is to advance rapidly, to outgrow themselves. It is already being driven forward by its inner contradictions from this initial stage. The situation can be comprehended as a beginning, as a condition untenable over the long haul. […]

What happens next is not in the hands of the dwarfs who would hold up the course of the revolution, who would put a spoke in the wheel of world history. It

---

13 Ibid.

14 Ibid.

is the realisation of the ultimate goal of socialism which is on today's agenda of world history.[15]

The National Assembly and the Workers' and Soldiers' Councils

A period characterised by dual power had begun. On the one hand, there was the government. On the other, there were the workers' and soldiers' councils. It was obvious that both could not coexist alongside one another in the long run. As in Russia, sooner or later the question would have to be posed: *either* the workers would seize power through the councils and break the repressive machine of the bourgeois state apparatus; *or* the bourgeoisie would triumph and the counter-revolution would swing into action, crushing the workers' and soldiers' councils.

The leadership of the SPD didn't have the least intention of doing away with capitalism. Their goal was the establishment of a bourgeois parliamentary democracy. The old state apparatus remained intact, and the SPD wished to preserve and protect it whilst it could, once again, establish itself in power unchallenged. Given their immediate predicament, the SPD leaders leaned on the most backward layers of the soldiers, who were essentially peasants in uniform. The SPD focused on the call for what they named a 'National Assembly', but which functionally would serve as a constituent assembly. They intended that such an assembly should undermine the soldiers' and workers' councils, causing the latter to dissolve. The USPD were less clear in their intentions. Some within the party believed that the councils and the National Assembly ought to exist side by side. Meanwhile, the revolutionary left wing argued that the councils had to seize power alone.

For their part, the Spartacists roundly rejected the call for a National Assembly, denouncing the SPD's insistence upon the demand as an attempt to derail the revolution by eliminating the soldiers' and workers' councils. In their programme, 'What Does the Spartacus League Want?', written by Luxemburg, they put forward the demand for the "[e]limination of all parliaments and municipal councils, and the takeover of their functions by workers' and soldiers' councils".[16] The Spartacists posed the choice point-blank: *either* the workers' and soldiers' councils, *or* the National Assembly.

---

15 Ibid.

16 R. Luxemburg, 'What Does the Spartacus League Want?', *Selected Political Writings of Rosa Luxemburg*, p. 373.

In an article dated 20 November 1918, Luxemburg described the National Assembly as "an outmoded legacy of bourgeois revolutions, an empty shell" and a "detour", which would help the elements that would betray the revolution:

> What is gained, then, with this cowardly detour called the National Assembly? The bourgeoisie's position is strengthened; the proletariat is weakened and confused by empty illusions; time and energy are dissipated and lost in 'discussions' between the wolf and the lamb; in a word, one plays into the hands of all those elements whose intent is to defraud the proletarian revolution of its socialist goals and to emasculate it into a bourgeois democratic revolution.[17]

According to Luxemburg, therefore, anyone who promoted the National Assembly was effectively acting as "a secret agent of the bourgeoisie or an unconscious spokesman of petty-bourgeois ideology." She believed it was "a ridiculous petty-bourgeois illusion" to imagine that one could implement socialism through parliament:

> The moment the great National Assembly decides to realise socialism fully and completely, to extirpate the rule of capitalism root and branch, at that moment the struggle begins. Once the bourgeoisie is touched in the heart – and its heart beats from within a fire-proof safe – it will fight a life-and-death battle for its rule and will develop thousands of open and covert methods of resistance against the socialist measures.

> All this is inevitable. All this must be fought through, warded off, beaten down – with or without the National Assembly. The 'civil war' which some have anxiously tried to banish from the revolution cannot be dispelled. For civil war is only another name for class struggle, and the notion of implementing socialism without a class struggle, by means of a majority parliamentary decision, is a ridiculous petty-bourgeois illusion.[18]

The National Congress of Councils

A national congress of workers' and soldiers' councils was convened in Berlin on 16 December, which took place over five days. The congress gathered representatives from the local workers' and soldiers' councils across Germany and was elected on the basis of one delegate per 1,000 workers, or per one battalion. Here too, the SPD focused its energy on building support for its call for the National Assembly.

---

17 R. Luxemburg, 'The National Assembly', *Marxist Internet Archive* [website].
18 Ibid.

The overwhelming majority of delegates at the congress supported the SPD. Of the 488 delegates, 289 supported the SPD, 90 supported the USPD amongst whom there were ten Spartacists, and the Bremen left also had a further ten delegates.[19] The composition of the congress was in many ways out of step with the situation in the proletarian centres. This was due to several factors: the rules for electing delegates had been established regionally, and the SPD knew how to exploit them. The soldiers, who politically lagged behind the workers from the factories, had a relatively higher representation, which was expressed in the fact that, of the 488 delegates, only 187 were workers. Meanwhile, a total of 95 delegates employees of the trade unions or parties, and particularly of the SPD.

Neither Liebknecht nor Luxemburg, on the other hand, were delegates. In Berlin, rules for the election of delegates clearly stated that only if a person actually worked at a factory or belonged to a military unit could they be elected as its representative. The proposal for Liebknecht and Luxemburg to be invited as guests (as were six members of the provisional government and several other prominent leaders such as Karl Kautsky) was placed twice before the congress, but was rejected by large majorities on both occasions. The influence of the SPD prevailed, and they were certainly not prepared to welcome the presence of these two revolutionaries.

The mood of the workers from the larger cities, however, was much more radical than that of the congress. This was particularly evident in Berlin. Together with the Revolutionary Stewards, the Spartacists were able to mobilise a demonstration of 250,000 people in the capital under the banner of very radical slogans in order to pressure the congress delegates. The demonstration was far larger than that organised by the SPD in support of the congress. Again, on 18 December, while the congress was still ongoing, the Spartacists and the Revolutionary Stewards organised another huge protest and a number of strikes. The congress, however, remained unmoved.

The SPD focused all of its energies on ensuring that the congress of councils' main clarion call was for elections to a National Assembly. To no one's surprise, they easily achieved this. The decision of the congress to explicitly oppose "council power" also demonstrated the SPD's majority at the gathering. On the surface, the situation appeared to be rather paradoxical: the revolutionaries were arguing in favour of "all power to the workers' and soldiers' councils", while the congress of these very same workers' and soldiers'

---

19 The remaining delegates either came from different political groups or did not have a defined political affiliation.

councils had just rejected seizing power, and had instead handed it over to the government.

But the revolution had only just begun. A large section of the masses continued to follow the lead of the SPD, thus enabling the latter to attain its large majority at the congress. However, as events unfolded over time, the masses were radicalising. Even during the congress, the fact that the SPD was not in complete control was quite evident. A series of other resolutions passed that were far more radical than the policy of the SPD. For instance, the council congress adopted multiple resolutions demanding the abolition of the standing army and the establishment of a peoples' militia, which passed by large majorities. Resolutions were adopted demanding the abolition of all signs of rank in the army, for the election of all officers by the soldiers with the right of immediate recall, and for the transfer of responsibility for discipline in the army to the soldiers' councils. These were demands that were all sternly opposed by the general staff, with whom the SPD were closely connected.

In many ways, the period of November 1918 to January 1919 resembled the spring of 1917 in Russia, where the masses had secured the overthrow of the Tsar but were beginning to realise that nothing had fundamentally changed in their own lives. In Germany, the workers had toppled the Kaiser, but here too, society had fundamentally remained unchanged. In response to this growing realisation, the German workers came out on strike with demands for improved conditions. Luxemburg's perspective was that these strikes would sharpen the class struggle and expose the leaders of both the USPD and the SPD:

> The conclusion to be drawn is not only that during the second act of the revolution strikes will become increasingly frequent but, further, that strikes will become the central feature and the decisive factor of the revolution, thrusting purely political questions into the background. You understand that the inevitable consequence of this will be that the economic struggle will be enormously intensified. The revolution will thus come to the point at which it will be no joke to the bourgeoisie. The bourgeoisie are quite agreeable to mystifications in the political domain, where masquerades are still possible, where such creatures as Ebert and Scheidemann can pose as socialists; but they are horror-stricken where profits are concerned. When it comes to that, they will present the alternative to the Ebert–Scheidemann government: either put an end to the strikes, stop this strike movement which threatens to strangle us; or we have no more use for you.[20]

---

20 R. Luxemburg, 'Our Program and the Political Situation', *Selected Political Writings of Rosa Luxemburg*, pp. 397-8.

At the outset of the revolution, the SPD and the centrists of the USPD had enjoyed the highest levels of support among the German masses. The Spartacists were far from having won the masses to a revolutionary programme. Incidentally, their perspective was that they would only win the majority at the culmination of the revolution:

> The victory of the Spartacus League comes not at the beginning, but at the end of the Revolution: it is identical with the victory of the great million-strong masses of the socialist proletariat.[21]

But the Spartacists were trailing behind when the revolution first erupted: they had no revolutionary organisation. Such an organisation would have to be built in the midst of the revolution itself.

The Counter-Revolution

While the SPD supported the revolutionary process in words, behind the scenes they were preparing a counter-revolutionary offensive to finally bring an end to the 'anarchy' of the revolution. As early as November, when the first revolutionary wave was beginning to ebb, the German general staff and Ebert jointly hatched a plan to besiege Berlin with counter-revolutionary forces. Two divisions under General Groener's leadership would march into Berlin, seize power from the workers' and soldiers' councils, establish a puppet government and disarm the Spartacists.

But before Groener's troops could arrive in Berlin, another coup attempt unfolded. Reactionary troops marched to Ebert's office on 6 December and proclaimed him president, although he would eventually decline the post offered to him. Another group of reactionary soldiers simultaneously arrested the Executive Committee of the workers' and soldiers' councils, primarily consisting of USPD members. Meanwhile, other government troops razed the office of the Spartacists' newspaper, *Die Rote Fahne*, arresting Liebknecht, and attacking a protest led by Spartacists, killing sixteen people. The attempt backfired. Furious sailors and workers spontaneously marched against the troops, freeing the arrested members of the Executive Committee. The coup was scuppered.

The main organ of the SPD played down these events, throwing blame onto a few individuals in the army and on the Spartacists, whom they accused of having provoked the incident. The Spartacists responded by organising

---

21 R. Luxemburg, 'What Does the Spartacus League Want?', *Selected Political Writings of Rosa Luxemburg*, p. 376.

protests and strikes against the coup attempt. The Berlin working class gave vent to its anger in a 150,000-strong protest of armed workers and soldiers on 8 December. The Spartacists put out an urgent appeal:

> Workers, soldiers, comrades! Attention! The revolution stands in great danger! Be on your guard! Our most vital interests are at stake! Everything for the revolution and socialism!

> Everything – even life! Defeat the attack! Down with the conspirators! Long live socialism! In the future, the final victory will be ours![22]

General Groener's detachment – the shock troops of the counter-revolution – began arriving in Berlin in the days that followed, and they were welcomed by Ebert. But the soldiers began fraternising with the radicalised workers. The counter-revolution was losing its grip on the soldiers and it had to give up on its aim of disarming the workers. Their commander-in-chief, General Lequis, admitted that "the influence of the extraordinary propaganda of the Spartacists is making itself felt".[23] The generals had to pull back and wait for a more opportune moment. Momentum was still with the revolution. But there could be no doubting the intentions of the generals: they wished to implement a military dictatorship.

However, the rank-and-file soldiers of the army were increasingly demobilising themselves – they were sick and tired of war and simply returned home. The regime could not trust the regular troops, and as such it came increasingly to depend upon the Freikorps – volunteer forces drawn from the most reactionary layers of society. Many of them had fought on the side of the counter-revolution against the Bolsheviks in Russia. Now they hoped to cleanse Germany of Bolshevik influence. Incidentally, many of those who would later form the backbone of Hitler's fascist *Sturmabteilung* ('stormtroopers', or SA) would be drawn from the Freikorps.

In Berlin, the revolutionary unrest continued. There were continuous strikes and protests. The government regarded the capital as being completely infected with anarchy. All Ebert's efforts were directed towards the restoration of 'law and order'. Once again, Ebert and the military decided to launch a renewed counter-revolutionary campaign. The occasion for implementing their plans came on 23 and 24 December, when the regular army clashed with revolutionary sailors from the People's Naval Division. The People's Naval Division was primarily composed of sailors from Kiel, who had arrived in

---

22 Quoted in R. Sewell, *Germany 1918-1933: Socialism or Barbarism*, p. 127.
23 Quoted in P. Broué, *The German Revolution: 1917-1923*, p. 230.

Berlin and established themselves at the centre of the capital in order to defend it from reaction. Their presence was the cause of much apprehension on the part of the government, which regarded them as a threat to its authority. The government therefore resolved to withhold the sailors' wages, hoping that doing so would cause their organisation to disintegrate.

The angry sailors responded by kidnapping the Prussian social democratic minister Otto Wels, whom they held ransom until their salary was paid. But negotiations with the government broke down, and Ebert ordered regular troops to intervene and free Wels. Shortly after the sailors had received Ebert's ultimatum, government troops began bombarding them with artillery. A part of the building that had been occupied by the sailors was damaged, killing more than ten. Their deaths only inflamed the sense of outrage felt by the workers and soldiers of Berlin, a large crowd of whom surrounded and fraternised with the government soldiers. The latter vacillated. Several of them laid down their arms and refused to follow the commands of their officers – the government could no longer trust its troops and as such the attack on the sailors was brought to a chaotic end. The sailors had won, and they were paid what they were owed. The general staff were seething and demanded revenge for this humiliating defeat. According to official sources, in the days that followed, troops loyal to the government killed 156 people.

The workers were in uproar at the deployment of soldiers against the Kiel sailors defending the revolution and, on 29 December, the USPD withdrew from the government in protest at the "bloodbath". The government was plunged into crisis. The SPD had lost its left cover. The USPD ministers who quit their posts were replaced by SPD ministers, which included Gustav Noske – the man who would style himself as the "bloodhound" of the counter-revolution. The government was now even weaker than it had been and as such was ever more dependent on the general staff.

The creation of a new government, composed exclusively of right-wing social democrats, gave further encouragement to the counter-revolution. The witch hunt of the Spartacists had begun. The SPD was an active participant in this, spreading smears through its newspaper, *Vorwärts*, among other things.

The smear campaign was particularly focused on Liebknecht and Luxemburg, the two most well-known leaders of the Spartacists.

Enormous posters were thrown up, which had messages such as:

Workers! Citizens!
The downfall of the Fatherland is imminent!
Save it!

It is not being threatened from without, but from within:
By the Spartacist Group.
Strike its leader dead!
Kill Liebknecht!
You will then have peace, work and bread!
Signed: Soldiers from the Front.[24]

A murderous mood was whipped up against Liebknecht, Luxemburg, and the Spartacists, in which they were accused of being bloodthirsty instigators of violence and anarchy, and the sole cause of all the problems in the country. The question of killing Liebknecht and Luxemburg was openly discussed, and a bounty was placed on their heads.

Bloody Rosa?

The German press had long presented Luxemburg as 'bloody Rosa'. Such propaganda only increased from this point on. But Luxemburg had no desire to see the revolution carried through a bloodbath. In 'What Does the Spartacus League Want?', she describes the Spartacist view on violence and terror:

> The proletarian revolution requires no terror for its aims; it hates and despises killing. It does not need these weapons because it does not combat individuals but institutions, because it does not enter the arena with naïve illusions whose disappointment it would seek to revenge. It is not the desperate attempt of a minority to mould the world forcibly according to its ideal, but the action of the great massive millions of the people, destined to fulfil a historic mission and to transform historical necessity into reality.[25]

Luxemburg was absolutely clear that a socialist revolution had nothing in common with a coup carried out by a minority – on the contrary, it was a vast movement of the overwhelming majority. However, this by no means meant that she harboured pacifist illusions about the peaceful character of the revolution. Instead, she placed blame for any violence that should ensue squarely on the shoulders of the ruling class:

> But the proletarian revolution is at the same time the death knell for all servitude and oppression. That is why all capitalists, Junkers, petty bourgeois, officers, all

---

24 Quoted in R. Sewell, *Germany 1918-1933: Socialism or Barbarism*, p. 130.

25 R. Luxemburg, 'What Does the Spartacus League Want?', *Selected Political Writings of Rosa Luxemburg*, p. 370.

opportunists and parasites of exploitation and class rule rise up to a man to wage mortal combat against the proletarian revolution.

It is sheer insanity to believe that capitalists would good humouredly obey the socialist verdict of a parliament or of a national assembly, that they would calmly renounce property, profit, the right to exploit. All ruling classes fought to the end, with tenacious energy, to preserve their privileges. […] [T]hey all shed streams of blood, they all marched over corpses, murder, and arson, instigated civil war and treason, in order to defend their privileges and their power.

The imperialist capitalist class, as the last offspring of the caste of exploiters, outdoes all its predecessors in brutality, in open cynicism and treachery. […] [I]t will turn the country into a smoking heap of rubble rather than voluntarily give up wage slavery.[26]

But Luxemburg did not respond by turning the other cheek or by giving up in advance. On the contrary, she argued for decisive action to break the resistance of the counter-revolution:

All this resistance must be broken step by step, with an iron fist and ruthless energy. The violence of the bourgeois counter-revolution must be confronted with the revolutionary violence of the proletariat. Against the attacks, insinuations, and rumours of the bourgeoisie must stand the inflexible clarity of purpose, vigilance, and ever ready activity of the proletarian mass. Against the threatened dangers of the counter-revolution, the arming of the people and disarming of the ruling classes. Against the parliamentary obstructionist manoeuvres of the bourgeoisie, the active organisation of the mass of workers and soldiers. Against the omnipresence, the thousand means of power of bourgeois society, the concentrated, compact, and fully developed power of the working class.[27]

The ruling class has always tried to ward off the masses from rebellion through fearmongering. Their message is: rebellion will mean violence and bloodshed – something all normal-thinking people naturally wish to avoid. But throughout history, it has always been the ruling classes who have unleashed bloodshed and violence. They have put down revolutions with the utmost brutality, with the intention of beating down the working class so frightfully that the memory persists and a new rising becomes impossible for generations. The ruling class showed in the course of the Paris Commune, the Russian Revolution, and again in the German Revolution that it will stop at

---

26 Ibid., pp. 370-1.
27 Ibid., p. 371.

precisely nothing to defend its power and privileges. If the counter-revolution gains victory, it will drown the revolution in blood. It will seek to crush the workers' hope and deter the masses from taking the road of revolution ever again.

The outbreak of revolution is something that lies completely outside the control of revolutionaries. Rather, it depends upon objective conditions. But once they do break out, the stronger the revolutionary organisation the greater its chance of ensuring the revolution is carried through in an organised and disciplined manner – and therefore the likelihood and degree of bloodshed is minimised. And, most importantly of all, a strong revolutionary organisation is the best guarantee of a revolution's victory and of the defeat of the counter-revolution, which would otherwise seek to drown it in blood.

The Spartacists

Upon the outbreak of the German Revolution, the Spartacists were far from being in a position of strength. Radek had travelled to Germany as a representative of the Soviet government for the council congress, but was refused entry at the border. He nevertheless managed to cross into Germany illegally and arrived on 20 December 1918. Upon his arrival, one of his first actions was to meet with the Spartacists, where he received quite a jarring picture of the situation. He described the impression in his diary:

> How many people had we at the congress [the workers' and soldiers' councils' congress – *MF*]? There was not even a *Spartakus* caucus. [...] And in the Berlin Workers' and Soldiers' Council? There too we had no organised group. In the provinces things were better here and there. In Bremen we had managed to capture a substantial portion of the council under the command of Knief. In Chemnitz, Brandler was working. "And how large is our organisation in Berlin?" I asked. "We are only collecting our forces. When the revolution began we did not have more than fifty people organised in Berlin."[28]

There were no more than fifty Spartacists in Berlin and maybe a couple of thousand in the whole of Germany when the revolution broke out. Beginning from a very low level, they were thus forced to commence the construction of an organisation in the middle of the revolution itself. On 11 November – two days after the arrival of the revolution in Berlin – the Spartacists held a conference in which they officially decided to change their name from the *Internationale* Group to the Spartacus League. At the same conference they

---

28 Quoted in J. P. Nettl, *Rosa Luxemburg*, p. 747.

also elected a leadership – the *Zentrale* – which consisted of Liebknecht, Luxemburg, Mehring, Jogiches, Ernst Meyer, Hermann and Käthe Duncker, Wilhelm Pieck, Paul Levi, Paul Lange, Thalheimer, and Eberlein. They also laid the plans for publishing a daily newspaper, a theoretical magazine, magazines for women and youth, a propaganda publication for the soldiers, and a press bulletin. Considering their strength, this was a very ambitious plan – one which was never destined to be carried out.

The day before, on 10 November, a group of armed Spartacists had occupied the printing house of the *Berliner Zeitung* in order to print their own newspaper, *Die Rote Fahne* (*The Red Flag*). The paper was published on 11 November, but the owner of the printing house appealed to the government and the Executive Committee of the councils, and it was not published again until 18 November – and at a very steep price to boot. All the energy of the Spartacists was thrown into publishing a daily newspaper. Luxemburg was the paper's editor, and all articles went through her. In these months – from her liberation from prison by the revolution until she was murdered – the revolution completely engulfed her in hectic activity.

The Spartacists had contact with almost all the important centres outside Berlin. But to a large extent, they remained a more-or-less loose network, organised around a small core of leaders, rather than a real organisation:

> Nowhere did the Spartacists form an organised faction, nowhere did they undertake systematic work to build their faction or even an organised tendency either in the workers' councils or in the USPD, where their work rested on the propaganda of *Die Rote Fahne* and on the prestige and activity of their most prominent members. At the same time, however, the League [The Spartacists] held to its conception of revolutionary agitation and moving the masses into action, and worked to mobilise the broad masses of workers whose spontaneous action it hoped to enlighten and inspire. To this effect it organised many meetings and demonstrations.[29]

At the beginning of the revolution, the Spartacists remained part of the USPD. Luxemburg's perspective was to win support and members from the party and – in the long term – to win the majority of the party over. Liebknecht had also argued in favour of this perspective, particularly on account of the fact that the Revolutionary Stewards were also a part of the USPD. The party drew in a broad layer of those who had been radicalised by the revolution, and particularly the workers of the larger cities.

---

29 P. Broué, *The German Revolution: 1917-1923*, p. 203.

On behalf of the Soviet government and with the prestige of the Bolsheviks behind him, Radek argued that the Spartacists had to break with the USPD and form their own party. Luxemburg was very sceptical – she continued to fear isolating herself from the masses. On the other hand, many of the younger Spartacists wanted to form a new party because, in their eyes, that was precisely what 'real revolutionaries' like the Bolsheviks would do. But to Lenin and the Bolsheviks, the question of an independent party was not a matter of principle. Rather, it was a tactical question. Organising the revolutionaries independently, however, was a matter of necessity.

In reality, the main problem was not so much whether the revolutionaries were organised in their own party or as a faction inside the USPD. The main problem was that they lacked a cadre organisation – an organisation of revolutionaries educated and tested not only in Marxist theory but in tactics, the lessons of Bolshevism and the Russian Revolution, etc. Initially, such an organisation might have been formed as a faction inside the USPD. Under such circumstances, that might have meant that a mass split in the USPD, in which a large part of the membership went over to the Communists, would have taken place much earlier. In the end, that split took place in October 1920. How events might have unfolded differently under other circumstances is impossible to tell. The essential point is that the lack of a revolutionary organisation at the outbreak of the revolution gave rise to enormous difficulties for Luxemburg and her fellow revolutionaries.

The Spartacists drew in the most radicalised individuals and groupings. They were all honest revolutionaries, but they were also young, politically uneducated, and impatient. They looked to the Russian Revolution, but then equated Bolshevism with armed uprising. They knew little of Lenin's approach to party building, nor the tactics and slogans that the Bolsheviks raised in the period from February to October 1917, and even less about the period that preceded it. For them, the lesson of Bolshevism could more-or-less be summed up in the following words: proclaim the revolutionary party and the masses will follow. But things had not been so easy in Russia.

In his book *'Left-Wing' Communism, an Infantile Disorder*, published in 1921, Lenin attempted to educate these young, impatient layers among the Communists whom he described as "ultra-left":

> Would it not be better if the salutations addressed to the Soviets and the Bolsheviks were *more frequently* accompanied by a *profound analysis* of the reasons *why* the

Bolsheviks have been able to build up the discipline needed by the revolutionary proletariat?[30]

Lenin generalised the lessons of the history of Bolshevism in the following terms:

> Only the history of Bolshevism during the *entire* period of its existence can satisfactorily explain why it has been able to build up and maintain, under most difficult conditions, the iron discipline needed for the victory of the proletariat.
>
> The first questions to arise are: how is the discipline of the proletariat's revolutionary party maintained? How is it tested? How is it reinforced? First, by the class-consciousness of the proletarian vanguard and by its devotion to the revolution, by its tenacity, self-sacrifice and heroism. Second, by its ability to link up, maintain the closest contact, and – if you wish – merge, in certain measure, with the broadest masses of the working people – primarily with the proletariat, *but also with the non-proletarian* masses of working people. Third, by the correctness of the political leadership exercised by this vanguard, by the correctness of its political strategy and tactics, provided the broadest masses have seen, *from their own experience*, that they are correct. Without these conditions, discipline in a revolutionary party really capable of being the party of the advanced class, whose mission it is to overthrow the bourgeoisie and transform the whole of society, cannot be achieved. Without these conditions, all attempts to establish discipline inevitably fall flat and end in phrase-mongering and clowning. On the other hand, these conditions cannot emerge at once. They are created only by prolonged effort and hard-won experience. Their creation is facilitated by correct revolutionary theory, which, in its turn, is not a dogma, but assumes final shape only in close connection with the practical activity of a truly mass and truly revolutionary movement.[31]

The youth among the Spartacists had no experience of revolutionary work, having been radicalised by – and to a certain extent, dazzled by – the revolution itself. They wished to see the abolition of the old system and everything connected to it, including the old parties, organisations and trade unions, and for them, it could not come fast enough. For this layer of young people, revolutionary tactics could be more-or-less summed up in one word: forward! And these layers naturally pushed for the founding of a new Communist Party.

---

30 V. I. Lenin, *'Left-Wing' Communism: An Infantile Disorder*, *The Classics of Marxism: Volume Two*, pp. 107-8.

31 Ibid., p. 108.

The Spartacists were supported by the Bremen left radicals who formed a new organisation, the International Communists of Germany (IKD), on 23 November. They enjoyed a certain influence in Bremen, especially among the workers of the shipyards and the harbour. They remained outside the USPD, but they were quite aware that they were too few in number to form the core of a new party, instead giving critical support to the Spartacists and declaring their willingness to support every initiative by the latter towards the establishment of an independent revolutionary organisation, breaking with the centrists of the USPD. The left radicals in Hamburg also joined the IKD. This new organisation, however, was characterised by ultra-left tendencies. When the left radicals in Dresden, for instance, found themselves in a minority in the workers' and soldiers' council on 16 November, they abandoned it, declaring it to be a counter-revolutionary council.

Luxemburg remained hesitant over the question of founding a new party. But the Spartacists were increasingly clashing with the USPD leadership. At a meeting of USPD members in Berlin on 15 December, following shortly on the back of the national congress of councils, the Spartacists raised their demand for an extraordinary party congress. This was rejected by the USPD leadership, which feared to do so lest it lose its majority to the growing left wing.

The meeting discussed the entire political situation then unfolding. Haase put forward the policy of the USPD leadership, defending the party's cooperation in government with Ebert and Scheidemann, and advancing the idea that the councils had a place *alongside* a constituent assembly. Luxemburg was the main speaker in opposition to the leadership, and she launched a fierce attack against Ebert's government and the USPD's participation in it. She agreed with Haase that the masses supported Ebert and the government. But she laid responsibility for that fact at the feet of Haase and the leadership of the USPD. It was precisely their cooperation in government with the SPD that had given the latter legitimacy rather than exposing them.

The USPD leadership manoeuvred in such a way as to have the Spartacist proposal voted down. They replied to Luxemburg's call for an extraordinary congress with a resolution from Haase, stating that the main focus of the party ought to be the National Assembly election – artificially creating an opposition between two proposals that were not at all in conflict with one another. Luxemburg lost the vote, with 185 votes cast in favour of her resolution, against 485 cast in favour of Haase's. Haase used the occasion to call upon the Spartacists to walk out of the party. The USPD was on the verge of an explosion. Similar votes took place across Germany, with revolutionary delegates putting forward similar motions to that moved by Luxemburg, and in most cases, the vote ended up splitting the USPD into two camps of almost equal size. Scepticism towards the USPD leadership was also developing among the Revolutionary Stewards, whom the Spartacists hoped to be able to win over to the formation of a new party, thus securing the support of the most advanced layer of workers in Berlin: the factory leaders.

The Berlin meeting of USPD delegates had not brought an extraordinary congress any closer to realisation. Meanwhile, pressure for a split with the USPD was growing among the Spartacist rank-and-file. As early as 14 December, the Spartacists had published their own programme, 'What Does the Spartacus League Want?', co-authored by Luxemburg and Levi. On 22 December, the Spartacists issued an ultimatum to the leadership of the USPD demanding they put out the call for a party congress within three days to be held before the end of the month. When the leadership of the USPD predictably rejected the demand, the Spartacists called their own separate congress, in the course of which the Communist Party would be founded.

Founding of the Communist Party

In a revolutionary situation, the consciousness of the masses changes rapidly. But in order for the working class to seize power, history has demonstrated that a revolutionary party able to lead the masses is necessary. Luxemburg was faced with a difficult task. What had taken the Bolsheviks two decades to build, she now had to build in a couple of months. It is next to impossible to build a revolutionary organisation in the midst of the revolution itself. And yet, that was the task.

Luxemburg was eventually convinced of the necessity of founding a new party, although Jogiches was opposed to doing so. She was nevertheless against calling the party 'communist'. In her opinion, it would have been preferable to call the party 'socialist' as doing so, she believed, would make it easier to win over members of the socialist parties in the Second International. She was concerned that by taking on the name 'communist' the new party would be too closely connected with the Russians, which would scare some away. She was very cautious, and her orientation was towards the ranks of the Second International. Lenin, meanwhile, argued that a firm break with social chauvinism in all its colours was an absolute necessity, and that the name 'communist' was therefore far preferable. However, Luxemburg's proposed name was voted down by the *Zentrale* – the Spartacist leadership – which instead adopted the name 'communist'. On 29 December, the Spartacists decided, by eighty votes for and three votes against, to leave the USPD.

The following day, 129 delegates from the Spartacists, the Free Socialist Youth, and the IDK met and founded the Communist Party of Germany, the KPD. The 'Spartacists' moniker nevertheless continued to be used colloquially.

In her speech, 'Our Program and the Political Situation', Luxemburg outlined the new party's political principles and its analysis of the situation. She explained how a thread connected the party all the way back to Marx and Engels and the *Communist Manifesto*, and how the SPD had degenerated from its revolutionary roots. It was high time, in Luxemburg's opinion, for revolutionaries to jettison the legacy of the SPD.

> Our program is deliberately opposed to the standpoint of the Erfurt Program; it is deliberately opposed to the separation of the immediate, so-called minimal demands formulated for the political and economic struggle from the socialist goal regarded as a maximal program. [...] For us there is no minimal and no maximal program; socialism is one and the same thing: this is the minimum we have to realise today.[32]

She explained that the first phase of the revolution had commenced on 9 November when the workers and soldiers had shown the way forward and formed councils, but this was over now. The weakness of the revolution meant that power had begun to slip from their hands. This phase had been marked by illusions: among the proletarians and soldiers of "unity under the banner of so-called socialism"; and among the ruling class that the Ebert–Scheidemann government could hold back the workers with the help of the soldiers. These illusions were now shattered:

> One and all, [these illusions] have now been dissipated into nothingness. It has been shown that the union between Haase and Ebert–Scheidemann under the banner of "socialism" serves merely as a fig leaf for the veiling of a counter-revolutionary policy.[33]

She explained it was wholly positive that the illusions dissipated. A new phase must then open, in which support increasingly tends to drain from the government – not only from the workers, but also from the petty bourgeoisie and the soldiers. On the other hand, the bourgeoisie itself will also lose its

---

32 R. Luxemburg, 'Our Program and the Political Situation', *Selected Political Writings of Rosa Luxemburg*, p, 387.

33 Ibid., p. 391.

faith in the government. As such, Luxemburg explained, the government would go over to the side of undisguised counter-revolution in the coming period: "they are sailing under full steam into the second phase, that of the declared counter-revolution, or, as I may even say, that of the restoration of the earlier pre-revolutionary conditions."[34] But, she concluded, this could only lead to a sharpening of the class struggle:

> The circumstances will force Ebert and Scheidemann to the expedient of dictatorship, with or without the declaration of a state of siege. But this, however, as an outcome of the previous development, by the mere logic of events and through the operation of the forces which control Ebert and Scheidemann, will imply that during the second act of the revolution a much more pronounced opposition of tendencies and a greatly accentuated class struggle will take place. ["*Hear! Hear!*"] This intensification of conflict will arise, not merely because the political influences I have already enumerated, dispelling all illusion, will lead to a declared hand-to-hand fight between the revolution and the counter-revolution; but rather because the flames of a new fire are spreading upward from the depths of the totality, the flames of economic struggles.[35]

She proved to be completely correct in her prognosis that counter-revolution was rearming itself. But in her speech to the founding congress of the party, Luxemburg was sure to warn against belief in an inevitable or easy victory. She attempted to instil a sense of reality into the minds of the young communists, and to awaken them to the difficulties that they would meet. The entire ruling class, with the help of the state apparatus and especially the tops of the SPD, would do everything in its power to fend off the revolution. The communists were still far from enjoying the support of the majority of the masses. True, the workers in the cities had become radicalised, but the revolution was yet to make itself felt in the countryside:

> In the form that I depict it, the process may seem rather more tedious than one had imagined it at first. It is healthy, I think, that we should be perfectly clear as to all the difficulties and complications of this revolution. For I hope that, as in my own case, so in yours also, the description of the difficulties of the accumulating tasks will paralyse neither your zeal nor your energy. On the contrary, the greater the task, the more will we gather all of our forces. And we must not forget that the revolution is able to do its work with extraordinary *speed*. I make no attempt

---

34 Ibid., pp. 394-5.
35 Ibid., pp. 395-6.

to prophesy how much time will be needed for this process. Who among us cares about the time; who worries, so long only as our lives suffice to bring it to pass.[36]

Ultra-Left Tendencies

The majority of the delegates at the founding congress of the Communist Party were young. Three quarters of them were under the age of thirty-five years old, and only one (Jogiches) was older than fifty. Half of them were industrial workers. Characteristic of the young members of the new party was a tendency towards ultra-leftism. Frölich described the party's composition:

> The Spartacus League was a loose organisation of a few thousand members only. Its core was the old Left Wing of Social Democracy, a Marxist *elite* schooled in Rosa Luxemburg's tactical ideas. The majority of the Socialist Youth joined forces with the League, which then recruited additional supporters amongst the many young people who had been driven to the Left Wing of the working-class movement by their opposition to war. During the war years, all these elements had run risks and incurred dangers quite new to the working-class movement in Western Europe. They were all enthusiastic adherents of the Revolution, though many of them still had very romantic ideas about it.[37]

When Karl Radek had arrived in Germany in mid-December 1918, he was shocked by the shrill tone that the Spartacists struck:

> Dirty and ragged, I feverishly bought a copy of *Rote Fahne*. As I drove to the hotel I looked the paper over. I was seized with alarm. The tone of the paper sounded as if the final conflict were upon us. It could not be more shrill. If only they can avoid overdoing it! …

> It was the question of how to relate to the National Assembly that sparked controversy… It was a very tempting idea to counter-pose the slogan of the councils to that of a National Assembly. But the congress of councils itself was in favour of the National Assembly. You could hardly skip over that stage. Rosa and Liebknecht recognised that… But the party youth were decidedly against it, "we will break it up with machine guns".[38]

One of the first debates at the founding congress of the new party was precisely that discussion on whether to participate in the election to the

---

36 R. Luxemburg, 'Our Program and the Political Situation', *Selected Political Writings of Rosa Luxemburg*, pp, 407-8.

37 Quoted in R. Sewell, *Germany 1918-1933: Socialism or Barbarism*, p. 134.

38 Quoted ibid., p. 112.

National Assembly. Paul Levi put forward the case of the leadership: despite the fact that the German bourgeoisie intended to use the National Assembly to liquidate the revolution with the help of the SPD, the communists had to participate in the elections, as they had now been called by the councils. The elections would draw the focus of the masses' attention towards the National Assembly for months to come, and the communists had to exploit this fact. There was widespread disagreement from young delegates towards the proposal to participate in the election, and indeed Levi faced repeated interruptions by hecklers when trying to move the proposal.

Luxemburg had sharply condemned the National Assembly as a diversion, and had contrasted it with the workers' and soldiers' councils. However, she agreed with Levi and the rest of the leadership that, once the workers' and soldiers' councils had called National Assembly elections, the Communists had no choice but to participate in them and present their political programme if they were serious about attempting to reach the masses.

But Luxemburg and the rest of the leadership were unable to convince the majority of the members of the new-born Communist Party of the correctness of this tactic. As such, their proposal to participate in the elections was voted down. Luxemburg answered the congress in the following terms:

> We understand and value the motives from which stems the opposition to the executive's point of view. Our pleasure is, however, not wholehearted. Comrades, you take your radicalism rather too easily. With all our stormy impatience we must not lose the necessary seriousness and the need for reflection. The Russian example against the Constituent [Assembly] does not apply. When the Constituent [Assembly] was driven out, our Russian comrades already had a Trotsky–Lenin government. We still have Ebert–Scheidemann.[39]

On the surface, it might seem as though the young communists had simply followed the example set by revolutionary Russia. Had the Bolsheviks not dissolved the Constituent Assembly? But, as Luxemburg pointed out, the difference was that the Bolsheviks had dissolved the Constituent Assembly *after* they had won the majority in the soviets, and *after* the soviets had seized power through an insurrection and a Soviet Congress. In Germany, a majority of the masses still supported the SPD and the USPD, and this majority still regarded the calling of the National Assembly as a step forward. The task of the communists was, therefore, still that of winning over the workers from the grip of the SPD and the USPD. The young communists had not

---

39 Quoted in J. P. Nettl, *Rosa Luxemburg*, p. 757 (additions are made by Nettl).

yet acquainted themselves with the lessons of Bolshevism. As Lenin later explained in *'Left-Wing' Communism, an Infantile Disorder*:

> At the beginning of the period mentioned [February to October 1917 – *MF*], we did *not* call for the overthrow of the government but explained that it was impossible to overthrow it *without* first changing the composition and the temper of the Soviets. We did not proclaim a boycott of the bourgeois parliament, the Constituent Assembly, but said – and following the April (1917) Conference of our Party began to state officially in the name of the Party – that a bourgeois republic with a Constituent Assembly would be better than a bourgeois republic without a Constituent Assembly, but that a "workers' and peasants'" republic, a Soviet republic, would be better than any bourgeois-democratic, parliamentary republic. Without such thorough, circumspect and long preparations, we could not have obtained victory in October 1917, or have consolidated that victory.[40]

And:

> In the first place, contrary to the opinion of such outstanding political leaders as Rosa Luxemburg and Karl Liebknecht, the German "Lefts", as we know, considered parliamentarism to be "politically obsolete" even in January 1919. We know that the "Lefts" were mistaken.[41]

The boycott of the National Assembly by the KPD isolated the party from the masses, who looked towards these elections, especially because they were the first since universal suffrage had been introduced. Despite the communists' boycott there was an 83 per cent turnout – the highest in German history.

On the question of how to approach the government, the young communists likewise adopted an ultra-left attitude. They believed that the Communist Party had to put forward the slogan of toppling the Ebert–Scheidemann government. At the congress, Luxemburg warned them against the belief that this would actually solve anything. The government could not simply be toppled. It had to be undermined from below by the movement of the masses. Purely putting forward the slogan of toppling the government without being in a position to replace it with something could not advance the movement so much as a millimetre. This would become clear just a couple of weeks later.

---

40 V. I. Lenin, *'Left-Wing' Communism: An Infantile Disorder*, *The Classics of Marxism: Volume Two*, p. 114.

41 Ibid., p. 145.

It would be unfair to blame the young communists themselves entirely for their ultra-left tendency. In the articles she had written, Luxemburg herself argued very forcefully against the calling of the National Assembly as well as against the government. She personally understood the necessity of connecting with the masses and that therefore the Communists needed to adopt a flexible approach regarding both the government and the National Assembly. However, she had done little in the way of educating the young communists in terms of how to actually connect with the masses.

The ultra-left trend was also expressed at the party congress in two further motions that proposed to make membership of the trade unions and membership of the newly founded Communist Party incompatible. The delegates moving these motions called upon the communists to leave the unions, and furthermore to do everything in their power to work against them, as they were dominated by the right-wing Social Democrats. With great difficulty, the Communist Party leadership managed to avoid a vote on this question by referring it to the party's trade union commission.

The leadership of the party understood that a boycott of the trade unions would mean serious isolation from the masses. Precisely in the manner Luxemburg had described the events that unfolded in Russia in 1905, the revolutionary movement that swept across Germany politically awakened great masses of the population for the first time, and these masses poured into the trade unions, which are the most basic form of workers' organisation. Before the revolution, the membership of the trade unions numbered about 1.5 million. By the end of December 1918, that figure had risen to 2.2 million, and by the end of 1919 it stood at a staggering 7.3 million members. According to the leadership of the Communist Party, it was the task of communists to work inside the trade unions, and through them to connect to the masses and wrest political influence away from the social democrats. But a whole year would pass before the KPD decided to actively work inside the SPD-dominated unions on account of the opposition among the rank-and-file.

Throughout the duration of the founding party congress, negotiations were ongoing with the representatives of the Revolutionary Stewards. The latter were worried about the ultra-left tendencies visible among the communists. They therefore posed a number of demands as a precondition for their joining the party, which included: that the decision to boycott the elections must be scrapped; that there should be parity on the commission dealing with the party programme; and that all references to 'Spartacus' or 'Spartacist' be removed from the party name. As Broué notes, these were demands that no old Bolshevik, and probably no old Spartacists, would object to.

> But, to the majority of the Congress, they were not acceptable, and their ironic attitude towards these negotiations was, moreover, one of the symptoms which Radek found to be most alarming.[42]

The result was that the Revolutionary Stewards remained outside the new Communist Party and continued to be attached to the USPD. This was a hard blow that seriously weakened the communists. The Revolutionary Stewards were the group that enjoyed the best contacts with the workers in the factories of Berlin and so, without them, the communists had no real foothold within the industrial working class. For the most radical workers of the factories in Berlin, it likewise meant that they lacked a revolutionary political leadership, leaving them under the influence of the vacillating left leaders of the USPD.

Luxemburg was quite aware of the problem, but it didn't cause her too much concern. She likened the problems that the party was facing to the wailing of a new-born child. She wrote to Clara Zetkin, describing the leadership's defeat over its proposal to participate in the constituent assembly:

> Our 'defeat' was merely the triumph of a somewhat childish, half-baked, narrow-minded radicalism. In any case that happened at the beginning of the conference. Later contact between us [the executive] and the delegates was established … an entirely different atmosphere [*Resomanz*] than at the start. … *Spartakisten* are a fresh generation, free from the cretinous traditions of the 'good old party'. … We all decided unanimously not to make the matter into a cardinal question [*Kabinettsfrage*] and not to take it too seriously.[43]

Despite the young party's evident weaknesses, the foundation of a communist party in Germany had a huge impact internationally. The Russian party was no longer alone, and it renewed feelings of hope that the isolation of the young Soviet republic would soon be broken. Finally, a party that fully *supported* the Russian Revolution existed, and it clearly posed the choice:

---

42 P. Broué, *The German Revolution, 1917-1923*. p. 224.

43 Quoted in J. P. Nettl, *Rosa Luxemburg*, p. 758 (additions are made by Nettl).

In this hour, socialism is the only salvation for humanity. The words of the *Communist Manifesto* flare like a fiery *menetekel*[44] above the crumbling bastions of capitalist society: Socialism or barbarism![45]

The party was founded but it was far from being in a position to lead the working class to power. Luxemburg and the rest of the leadership could do nothing but wait and hope that events would confirm their correctness before the young members, and that the latter would learn through their own experience, giving up their ultra-left tendencies. The problem was that the revolution had only just begun, and time was not on the side of the communists. The counter-revolution in Germany, led by the Social Democrats, was far better organised than its Russian counterpart had been in 1917. The counter-revolution did not simply sit and wait for events to take their course. Instead, shortly after its foundation, the young party would be tested by the counter-revolution.

The 'Spartacist Uprising'

The ruling class and the leadership of the SPD had grown impatient. The revolutionary unrest had lasted for too long and, as far as they were concerned, it was high time for the counter-revolution to swing into action. But the workers had also grown impatient – particularly in Berlin – and they sensed that power was slipping from their hands. Growing impatience on both sides set the stage for what would come next: events that have since been dubbed the 'Spartacist Uprising', despite the fact that the Spartacists neither initiated nor organised the movement.

The situation had grown dire by the beginning of January 1919 – the USPD had just withdrawn from government and there were rumours that a military coup was being hatched. Meanwhile, the witch hunt against the Spartacists continued apace. The general staff and the Social-Democratic ministers were preparing a bloody showdown with the Spartacists who had campaigned for the toppling of the government since the Communist Party's foundation. The SPD and the general staff intended to put a halt to the revolution and prepare the way for their own kind of military 'solution' to

---

44 Menetekel – a sign of impending doom. Derived from the "writing on the wall" that appears in Daniel 5:25-29: "*Mene Tekel*" – "God has numbered the days of your reign and brought it to an end; You have been weighed on the scales and found wanting."

45 R. Luxemburg, 'What Does the Spartacus League Want?', *Selected Political Writings of Rosa Luxemburg*, pp. 367-8.

the crisis. The new minister of defence, the Social Democrat Gustav Noske, was to lead the offensive of the counter-revolutionary forces.

It was a secondary question that gave the government its occasion for a clash with the revolution: the dismissal of Emil Eichhorn from his post as the left-wing chief of police of Berlin. Eichhorn was a member of the USPD, and he was regarded as being a threat to the government for having organised a left-wing police force of some 2,000 workers and soldiers loyal to the revolution. His dismissal served two purposes: on the one hand, the government would rid itself of a left-wing chief of police, but more than this, his dismissal might also serve to provoke the left-wing workers of Berlin. The government counted on the workers rising up as a pretext for its sending in the military to crush their rebellion.

A number of false accusations against Eichhorn were conjured up, and on 4 January he was told to step down. Eichhorn, however, refused, claiming that he enjoyed the support of the masses, that he answered to the revolution itself and would only step down if the revolution demanded it.

In the evening of 4 January, the leadership of the KPD met to discuss the government's provocation. It decided that a response was necessary, but that it would be crazy to attempt to topple the government in the given circumstances. Instead, they proposed calling a general strike. Broué quotes an unnamed communist who was present and later recorded his memories of the meeting:

> There was complete agreement on how to appreciate the situation. Everyone present thought that it would be senseless to try and take over the government: a government supported by the proletariat would not have lasted for more than a fortnight. Consequently, the members of the *Zentrale* [KPD leadership – *MF*] all agreed that they had to avoid any slogans which necessarily would have meant overthrowing the government at that time.[46]

Luxemburg was of the opinion that even if they managed to topple the Ebert government, doing so would be pointless, as the rest of Germany was not ready to follow the workers of Berlin. It was a situation that, in many ways, resembled the July Days in Russia in 1917. Now, in January 1919, it was the workers of Berlin who were about to rush ahead without the support of the rest of the country.

When the Executive Committee of the USPD learned of the dismissal of Eichhorn, it immediately adopted a resolution in support of him. A

---

46 Quoted in P. Broué, *The German Revolution, 1917-1923*, p. 240.

meeting was convened between the USPD leaders, the representatives of the Revolutionary Stewards, and the leaders of the KPD in order to discuss united action. The three groups decided to call a protest on 5 January. On that day, hundreds of thousands of workers came out into the streets of Berlin and marched on the police headquarters.

Meanwhile, armed workers occupied the editorial offices of *Vorwärts* – they had not yet forgiven the SPD for 'stealing' their newspaper. They were talked round to abandoning their occupation, but only a short while later the offices were occupied a second time. The situation was repeated at the offices of the bourgeois papers and other buildings including, briefly, the Reichstag itself, were also occupied by the workers. Whilst the events had not been organised by the Spartacists, many of the participants were indeed Spartacists. Beyond a shadow of a doubt, provocateurs would also have been present in the crowds. However, the events of that week undoubtedly reflected the mood of frustration among the workers of Berlin.

The next day, 500,000 people took to the streets – many of them armed. In many factories, workers came out on strike. This was one of the largest single protests of the revolution. The situation was reaching its climax. The Social-Democratic minister, Gustav Noske, later wrote:

> Great masses of workers… answered the call to struggle. Their favourite slogan "Down, down, down" (with the government) resounded once more. I had to cross the procession at the Brandenburg Gate, in the Tiergarten, and again in front of general staff headquarters. Many marchers were armed. Several trucks with machine guns stood at the Siegessaule. Repeatedly, I politely asked to be allowed to pass, as I had an urgent errand. Obligingly, they allowed me to cross through. If the crowds had had determined, conscious leaders, instead of windbags, by noon that day Berlin would have been in their hands.[47]

With the masses in the streets, the representatives of the USPD, KPD (Pieck and Liebknecht), and the Revolutionary Stewards met to discuss the next steps. They had no plan and no idea of the direction they should lead the masses.

The same anonymous communist quoted above described the situation:

> The masses were there very early, from nine o'clock, in the cold and the fog. The leaders were in session somewhere, deliberating. The fog grew heavier, and the masses were still waiting. But the leaders deliberated. Midday came, bringing hunger as well as cold. And the leaders deliberated. The masses were delirious

---

47 Quoted in R. Sewell, *Germany 1918-1933: Socialism or Barbarism*, p. 146.

with excitement. They wanted action, something to relieve their delirium. No one knew what. The leaders deliberated. The fog grew thicker, and with it came twilight. The masses returned sadly homeward. They had wanted some great event, and they had done nothing. And the leaders deliberated. They had deliberated in the Marstall. They continued in the police headquarters, and they were still deliberating. The workers stood outside on the empty Alexanderplatz, their rifles in their hands, and with their light and heavy machine guns. Inside the leaders deliberated. At the police headquarters, the guns were aimed, there were sailors at every corner, and in all the rooms overlooking the street there was a seething mass of soldiers, sailors and workers. Inside the leaders were sitting, deliberating. They sat all evening, and they sat all night, and they deliberated. And they were sitting at dawn the next morning – and still deliberating. The groups came back to the Siegesallee again, and the leaders were still sitting and deliberating. They deliberated and deliberated and deliberated.[48]

At the meeting, a 'revolutionary committee' was established, with representatives of the USPD, the KPD, and the Revolutionary Stewards. It was led by Georg Ledebour, Karl Liebknecht, and Paul Scholze.

The leaders were overwhelmed by the enormity of the movement and felt that the time was right for an offensive. They received a message – which was later shown to be dubious – that they could count on military support in a number of places. In this atmosphere, a resolution was passed concerning the toppling of the government, but it was never issued. Liebknecht found himself carried away by the mood and supported the proposal. In the end, the only concrete proposal to come from this committee was the call for renewed protests the next day, on 6 January.

However, by the following day, a cooler mood prevailed in the committee and its revolutionary illusions were dissipating. It was obvious that, whilst the majority of the workers of Berlin were ready to strike and protest, they were not yet inclined towards an armed uprising. By the evening of 6 January, the movement was in decline. Both the central and executive committee of the workers' and soldiers' councils in Berlin approved of Eichhorn's dismissal. The Social Democrat Noske installed himself at the headquarters of the Freikorps and prepared his counter-attack. The vacillating leaders had allowed the movement's peak to pass it by.

In the revolutionary committee, there was now a majority that favoured opening negotiations with the government, a proposal that Liebknecht

---

48 Quoted in P. Broué, *The German Revolution, 1917-1923*, p. 242.

opposed. The USPD, nonetheless, unilaterally initiated negotiations of its own on the night of 6-7 January. They wished to secure a ceasefire in which the occupied buildings could be evacuated. The strength of the government grew by the hour in proportion to the dying down of the movement, and it therefore opted to protract the negotiations. Liebknecht visited the workers who had occupied *Vorwärts* and declared that, in opening negotiations, the USPD had betrayed the movement – the only choice left was to fight to the end. On 8 January, negotiations broke down and the government announced that it would retaliate with force. A 'social-democratic' army unit consisting of two regiments of six companies each was organised and billeted at the Reichstag building. Meanwhile, the revolutionaries had established a league of red soldiers who now appealed to the armed workers, calling on them to take to the streets. Events had arrived at the brink of civil war. But whilst violent clashes were erupting on the streets of Berlin, overwhelming majorities at mass meetings in the factories were calling for an end to the fighting.

On 8 and 9 January, government forces retook several occupied buildings and laid siege to the offices of *Vorwärts* with orders to take the building – if necessary, by force. In the evening of 10 January, while negotiations were still ongoing, one of the negotiators, Ledebour from the USPD, was arrested, along with the Communist leader Ernst Meyer.

In the morning of 11 January, government forces began firing upon the *Vorwärts* building. After a firefight lasting two hours, the occupiers hoisted the white flag and sent a delegation to negotiate their surrender. The members of the delegation were immediately arrested. The rest were given 10 minutes to surrender. A number of the prisoners were summarily executed.

The Communists were in a state of crisis. Radek spoke in favour of the party calling for a retreat, appealing for the workers to return to work and to begin a campaign for new elections to the workers' councils. Luxemburg agreed that a retreat was necessary but she was of the opinion that the Communists could not call for such a retreat openly, as doing so would give the USPD leaders the excuse they needed to capitulate to the government.

Luxemburg made a critical assessment of the uprising. She regarded positively the fact that "the broadest masses of the proletariat in Berlin and the main centres of revolution beyond the kingdom", had realised that the choice was either: abandon socialism or chase the Ebert–Scheidemann government from power. But the movement also showed weakness – *how* was the fight to be continued? On 8 January 1919, she wrote:

But what is yet far from clear, in which the weakness and immaturity of the revolution is still evident, is the question of *how* the struggle to get rid of the Ebert government should be carried out, *how* one translates the inner maturity that the revolution has already reached into deeds and power relations. Nothing has revealed these weaknesses and deficiencies as clearly as the last three days.[49]

She sharply criticised the bodies that stood at the head of the masses during the January uprising. Specifically, she condemned the Revolutionary Stewards and the leadership of the USPD in Greater Berlin for leaving the masses to themselves. They had entered into negotiations with the same government that they were in open struggle against without consulting the masses. The masses were out on the street, but, she explained, there was a lack of the necessary leadership:

> When the masses have been called on the streets and are on alert, you must clearly tell them what to do or at least what is being done and planned by friend and foe. In times of revolutionary crisis, the masses should of course be on the street. They are the only safeguard, the only security for the revolution. When the revolution is at risk – *and it is now more than ever!* – then it is the duty of the proletarian mass to be on guard where their power is expressed: on the street! Their presence, their mutual contact, is already a threat and a warning to all evident and hidden enemies of the revolution: Beware![50]

Luxemburg called for action, not words:

> The experience of the last three days is loudly calling on the leaders of the workers' movement: Don't deliberate endlessly! Do not negotiate! Take action![51]

Although she was not openly critical of the KPD's own representatives who were among the "leaders of the workers' movement", the story goes that when Luxemburg subsequently met with Liebknecht at the party office after a meeting of the revolutionary executive committee, she exclaimed furiously: "But Karl, how could you, and what about our programme?"[52]

Radek was sternly critical of the KPD. In a letter to the party leadership written on 9 January, he pointed out that the party had, quite correctly,

---

49 R. Luxemburg, 'Neglected Duties', *Politiske skrifter*, p. 310 (quotes from the Danish translation of 'Neglected Duties' have been translated into English by the author).

50 Ibid., pp. 311-2.

51 Ibid., p. 313.

52 Quoted in J. P. Nettl, *Rosa Luxemburg*, p. 767.

written in its programme, 'What Does the Spartacus League Want?', that it would only seek to take power once it had won over a majority of the workers to its position. That was not yet the case. He was particularly critical of the party's representatives in the revolutionary committee:

> In this situation, the action on which the revolutionary delegates decided on Saturday, as a reply to the attack by the social-patriotic government upon the police headquarters, should have had the character only of an act of protest. The proletarian vanguard, exasperated by the policy of the government and badly led by the revolutionary delegates, whose political inexperience made them unable to grasp the relation of forces in the Reich as a whole, has in its zeal transformed the movement of protest into a struggle for power. This permits Ebert and Scheidemann to strike a blow at the movement in Berlin which can weaken the movement as a whole.[53]

Radek insisted that the Communists had to honestly and openly inform the masses of their retreat, and thereby limit the damage:

> The only force able to call a halt and to prevent this disaster is you, the Communist Party. You have enough perspicacity to know that this struggle is hopeless. Your members Levi and Duncker have told me that you know this… Nothing can stop him who is weaker from retreating before a stronger force. In July 1917, we [the Bolsheviks – *MF*] were infinitely stronger than you are today, and we held back the masses with all our might, and, when we did not succeed, with a tremendous effort we then led a retreat from a hopeless struggle.[54]

But the leaders of the KPD, including Luxemburg, assessed the situation differently. She evaluated the movement in her article 'Order Prevails in Berlin' – which would turn out to be her last. She wrote that it was natural that the movement had ended in defeat. The defeat was mainly on account of the political immaturity of the mass of soldiers, which was in itself a "symptom of the common immaturity of the German revolution". But at the same time, she said the workers could have acted no differently given the provocation of the government:

> Faced with the shameless provocation of the Ebert–Scheidemanns, the revolutionary working class was *forced* to take up arms. Yes, it was *a matter of honour* for the revolution to repel the attack immediately and with all due

---

53 Quoted in P. Broué, *The German Revolution, 1917-1923*, p. 251.
54 Quoted ibid.

energy, lest the counter-revolution be encouraged to advance further, and lest the revolutionary ranks of the proletariat and the moral credit of the German revolution in the International be shaken.[55]

The KPD and Luxemburg did not believe that the movement was yet ready to overthrow the government. It must be said, however, that alongside her pointed attacks on the government, Luxemburg's articles also expressed a point of view, prevalent inside the KPD, which posed perhaps the greatest obstacle for further advance of the revolution.

According to Luxemburg, the workers could have acted in no other way than by taking up arms in resistance against the provocation to the revolution. It was a matter of saving the "honour of the revolution" and of not encouraging the counter-revolution to take new steps forward. According to Luxemburg, the revolution could only advance. She could not conceive of the possibility of a temporary, tactical defensive action. Rather, the final victory would be prepared by a series of defeats:

> Now it is an internal law of the life of the revolution never to stand still in inaction, in passivity, once a step has been taken. The best parry is a forceful blow. Now more than ever this elementary rule of all struggles governs each step of the revolution.[56]

Here we see a clear contradiction between Luxemburg's position, and the advice of Radek and the tactics of the Bolsheviks. In July 1917, the Bolsheviks had attempted to convince the workers of Petrograd *not* to take to the streets lest they become isolated. When they failed to do so, they participated in the demonstrations, side by side with the workers, and attempted to give the demonstrations the utmost organisation and discipline. When it became apparent that they could not take a stand against the counter-revolution, they organised a retreat in the most orderly fashion possible. Radek wrote to the KPD Central Committee to convince them that a withdrawal organised by the party would prove far less demoralising than encouraging further struggle, which could only end in defeat.

In his advice, Radek drew upon the lessons of the Bolsheviks from 1917. The Bolsheviks did not go all out to mobilise the masses in the streets when they regarded the conditions as unripe for victory. Rather, they attempted to hold them back whilst simultaneously educating the masses and winning

---

55 R. Luxemburg, 'Order Reigns in Berlin', *Selected Political Writings of Rosa Luxemburg*, p. 412.

56 Ibid.

them over politically. Of course, this by no means meant that the Russian Revolution was without its struggles and defeats. But the Bolsheviks attempted to minimise defeats to the degree that they could, and as such won the trust of the masses through their honest assessment of the situation and by clearly stating things as they stood. By such means, the Bolsheviks were able to organise the seizure of power once the time arose for it and the balance of power tipped in their favour.

Rosa Luxemburg could not bring herself to call a retreat, although it was obvious to her that, for now, the struggle could not be won. According to Luxemburg, the defeat was not just down to a lack of maturity on the part of the revolution, but was also down to the question of the leadership of the movement. She was convinced, however, that the masses would correct these shortcomings:

> The leadership failed. But the leadership can and must be created anew by the masses and out of the masses. The masses are the crucial factor; they are the rock on which the ultimate victory of the revolution will be built. The masses were up to the task. They fashioned this 'defeat' into a part of those historical defeats which constitute the pride and power of international socialism. And that is why this 'defeat' is the seed of our future triumph.[57]

The Murders

The SPD and the counter-revolutionary troops stepped up their witch-hunt against Luxemburg and Liebknecht. It was no longer safe for them to sleep at home. Instead, they had to keep moving, sleeping at different hotels and at accommodation provided by supporters. On 13 January, the SPD's newspaper *Vorwärts* printed a poem accusing the Spartacist leaders of cowardice, hiding while workers were killed:

> Many hundreds of corpses in a row,
> Proletarians,
> Karl, Rosa and Co.,
> Not one of them is there,
> Proletarians.[58]

Luxemburg knew she was in grave danger. As early as 25 December she wrote to Clara Zetkin that she had received "urgent warning from 'official

---

57 Ibid., p. 415.
58 Quoted in J. P. Nettl, *Rosa Luxemburg*, p. 770.

sources' that the assassins are looking for Karl and myself and we shouldn't sleep at home…"[59] Although they were aware of the danger, Luxemburg and Liebknecht refused to leave Berlin and go into hiding. They felt it was their duty to stay with the workers. This decision would prove fatal.

After the July Days in Russia, the Bolsheviks were in a similar situation: the party was banned and arrest warrants were issued for several of the party leaders. Lenin wanted to appear in court and use the trial to represent the political views of the Bolsheviks. But his fellow party members persuaded him to hide in Finland. This had nothing to do with cowardice: it was a matter of practical necessity.

Countless examples throughout history have demonstrated that the presence of a revolutionary party is vital in a revolutionary situation. Within that party, the role of leadership is paramount. Men and women cannot act beyond the limits imposed by their material conditions – no matter how much the revolutionaries want to, they cannot create revolutions. But when the masses move, parties and even individuals can play a decisive role in determining a revolution's outcome. Lenin, for instance, was crucial to the outcome of the Russian Revolution. In October, when the Bolsheviks were discussing whether to launch an insurrection, parts of the party leadership were still putting up resistance. It was the intervention of Lenin, whose authority within the party was enormous, that overcame this resistance. His authority was not authority in the military sense of the term. Rather, it was a moral and political authority built over decades, in the course of which Lenin's ideas and analysis had been put to numerous practical tests.

Thus, Trotsky described the authority Lenin held in the Bolshevik Party:

> Numerous puny sects and splinter groups, peddling their own cheap little offerings, often deliver sweeping repudiations of authority in principle. In its place we hear them praising abstract principles of democracy. It is of course an axiom that a revolutionary party is not revolutionary unless it is democratic – i.e., grounded in majority rule concretely, and not abstractly. But that does not eliminate the problem of authority and what it represents. For us, it is the distillation of experience, that is, the accumulated lessons learned from past battles and defeats. In the Bolshevik Party, not only the personal prestige of Lenin, but the prestige of its leaders collectively made up the authority of the Central Committee. […]
>
> Tempered and tested by experience, authoritative leaders represented a tremendous accumulation of capital for the Party. In moments of doubt, hesitation or lack of

---

59 Quoted ibid., p. 759.

clarity, the words of experienced leaders focus the attention of the Party on the essential issues, eliminating misunderstandings and errors without much friction and waste of time. Moreover, on occasions where immediate action is required, when there is little time to debate the matter before the Party and take a decision, the leader with the necessary authority is able to take responsibility even when the fate of the Party is at stake. Having carefully weighed all the circumstances, the Party's confidence in him and his confidence in the Party will normally [ensure] approval for his actions.

It is likewise true that such authority not only streamlines deliberations within the Party, but there is a danger that this may also weaken critical thought within the Party and lead to an over-confidence towards the Party's leading bodies. [...]

Needless to say, the solution to this problem is not the complete denial of all authority. All the processes that we are analysing are rooted by their very nature in the contradictions of real life. The problem should be solved in such a way as to allow the replacement of one leader by another more qualified. [...]

The genius of Lenin was expressed in the fact that he pioneered new historical methods. [...]

However, men like Lenin are not born in a vacuum. His authority was not imbibed with his mother's milk, nor was it inspired by school textbooks and church prayers. Every Bolshevik, from Lenin's closest collaborators to the provincial comrades, had to convince themselves of the superiority of Lenin's ideas and methods through the experience of countless discussions, political events, and concrete actions.[60]

Beyond a shadow of a doubt, Luxemburg was the individual who enjoyed the highest political authority in the newly founded German Communist Party, an authority that she had built up through many years of experience, and one that could not simply be replaced. She was perhaps the only leader who might have been able to overcome the ultra-left tendencies within the party. Only on the basis of overcoming these infantile tendencies could the party connect with the masses, on the basis of which the German Revolution might have finally been crowned with victory. But history was destined to play out differently.

On 12-13 January, Luxemburg and Liebknecht were residing first at an apartment in Neukölln, Berlin, and then with a sympathiser in Wilmersdorf. It was here that they were arrested on the evening of 15 January, together with Pieck, who was also in the apartment. They were taken to Hotel Eden,

---

60 L. Trotsky, *Stalin*. p. 678-80.

the Freikorps headquarters, where they both endured rough treatment. Liebknecht was brought out first. On the way out, he was struck on the back of the head with a rifle belonging to a soldier named Otto Runge. He was driven to the Tiergarten park, where he was shot. Afterwards, the soldiers claimed that he had been killed "during an escape attempt".

Luxemburg was next. She too received a blow to the head from the butt of a rifle, after which she was placed in a waiting car, and shot in the head. Her body was thrown into the Landwehr Canal in Tiergarten and wasn't found until late May.[61]

The main leaders of the German Revolution were murdered in cold blood. The counter-revolution had severed the head of the revolutionary movement.

There was no serious attempt to hold the guilty responsible for their murders. In May, a parody of a trial was held, during which a soldier named Horst von Pflugk-Harttung admitted that he had shot Liebknecht "while trying to escape". However, Pflugk-Harttung was acquitted with great applause. Kurt Vogel, who was responsible for the entire operation, admitted that he had thrown Rosa Luxemburg's body in the canal in Tiergarten, but claimed that another had shot her. The jury could not decide if she had already died from the blow to the head, and Vogel faced only two years and four months in jail. He escaped from prison, however, and fled to Holland, where he stayed until things cooled down. He then returned to Germany a free man. Runge, who had slaughtered the prisoners, was sentenced to two years in prison.

The Communists threw political responsibility for the murders onto the SPD, and it became a line of blood that has divided Social Democrats and Communists ever since. Whether the order came from the top of the SPD has not been established. There can be no doubt, however, that the SPD leadership helped whip up an atmosphere which clearly revealed the government's attitude and so would have given encouragement to those who directly orchestrated the killings. The soft penalties testify to this fact. Political responsibility rests solely with the leadership of the SPD. They betrayed the

---

61 In the past few years, some doubt has been cast on whether the body in the canal really was that of Rosa Luxemburg. The discovery of a body in the basement of the Charité hospital resembling Luxemburg has raised a number of questions. Whilst we may not be certain about the fate of her corpse, this does not alter the fundamental point which is amply proven: that Luxemburg was murdered by the counter-revolution. See, for example, Comenetz, 'Mysterious Berlin corpse probably Rosa Luxemburg', *Reuters* [website].

revolution and they were responsible for the murders of Liebknecht and Luxemburg.

> [N]o direct responsibility of any Social-Democratic leader can be established. But their moral responsibility is overwhelming. Two days before, *Vorwärts* had published what was nothing less than a call for the murder of "Karl, Rosa and partners, not one dead, not one, amongst the dead". It was men gathered, armed, and in the end protected by Noske and the Social-Democratic ministers who carried out the assassinations. Scheidemann was to say: "You see how their own terrorist tactic has done for them themselves!"[62]

The murders were received with shock and anger. During a meeting that same day, the workers' and soldiers' council of Berlin expressed its profound disgust and protested the government's excessive use of terror in the wake of its victory over the Communists. The revolutionary movement did not end with the murders on 15 January and so the government initiated a terrorist campaign in which several Communist leaders were arrested and murdered, among whom Leo Jogiches, Rosa's life-long comrade, killed on 10 March. Demonstrations and uprisings were crushed with the utmost brutality and thousands of workers were killed in clashes with the army and the Freikorps under the leadership of the SPD.

For now, the counter-revolution had brought the revolution to a halt and murdered its leaders. But the 'order' that they had apparently established was merely temporary. The words of Rosa Luxemburg's last article were almost prophetic in its prediction of the mighty revolutionary struggles that were still to come in the years that followed:

> "Order reigns in Berlin!" You stupid lackeys! Your "order" is built on sand. The revolution will "raise itself up again clashing", and to your horror it will proclaim to the sound of trumpets:
>
> *I was, I am, I shall be!*[63]

---

62 P. Broué, *The German Revolution, 1917-1923*, p. 257.

63 R. Luxemburg, 'Order Reigns in Berlin', *Selected Political Writings of Rosa Luxemburg*, p. 415.

Final Considerations: The Eagle

Rosa Luxemburg dedicated her entire adult life to the fight for world socialist revolution, a goal for which she ended up giving her life. The picture painted of Luxemburg as the proponent of a 'soft', 'democratic' socialism in opposition to Lenin's 'tyrannical dictatorship' is an abuse of history – a distortion without any basis.

Luxemburg was one of the first individuals to take cognisance of and take up arms against the reformist degeneration of the SPD. She saw more clearly than anybody else, including Lenin, how reformism had infected not only the right wing of the party, but also many of those so-called 'Marxists' like Kautsky, who could use revolutionary language but whose radicalism went no further than mere words. For a long time she was alone in her struggle against the party's degeneration, until finally the rot became obvious to all and sundry: on 4 August 1914, when the SPD leaders openly betrayed the working class. She fought tooth and nail against every attempt to water down the party's revolutionary programme, and predicted that the moment social democracy gave up on the historical task of socialist revolution, it would give up its very right to existence. It would end up as little more than a pillar propping up capitalism. This perspective has been wholly confirmed today, when the social-democratic parties have degenerated to a degree that far surpasses anything seen in Luxemburg's time. Most of these parties are either implementing bourgeois austerity policies or have shown that they would gladly do so if handed the reins of government.

Despite her revolutionary ideas and uncompromising struggle against reformism, Luxemburg has been adopted – quite unjustifiably – by those who stand to the left of the unalloyed reformism of today's social democracy, but whose own politics are soft and opposed to the revolutionary politics of Lenin. In the opinion of this author, this is nothing short of a crime against Luxemburg's life and everything she fought and died for. Not only did Rosa Luxemburg condemn the openly reformist leaders of the social-democratic movement, she also condemned and fought against that section of the left wing of the party that sounded radical and revolutionary, but whose radical rhetoric provided cover for a reformist, 'soft' approach. Such was the case with Kautsky. Rosa Luxemburg would turn in her grave if she knew just how her name and authority are used today to justify reformism, softness, and anti-revolutionary ideas.

Rosa Luxemburg's actions and ideas were, are, and will remain revolutionary to the core. All she said and did – including her mistakes – came from a revolutionary perspective. On all questions, she took the side of the working class and the revolution. Her disagreement with Lenin in 1904 on the organisational question of the Russian party is latched upon time after time by those wishing to portray Luxemburg as anti-Leninist. The small detail that she changed her mind is, of course, left out in the course of the myth-making.

After the 1905 Revolution, she was in no doubt that the Bolsheviks were correct in their struggle against the Mensheviks, i.e., on the question of the revolution itself. Of those things she had written in 1904 in criticism of Lenin and the Bolsheviks, she would later write in 1906:

> [T]hat belongs to the past – a distant past, since today life is proceeding at a dizzying speed. These errors have been corrected by life itself and there is no danger they might recur.[1]

Her critique of the conduct of the Bolsheviks following the October Revolution was also, more or less, dispelled by the experience of the German Revolution. Here, Rosa Luxemburg was faced with many of the same concrete questions that the Bolsheviks had faced. For the Constituent Assembly or for the workers' and soldiers' councils? When faced with the choice, Luxemburg was in no doubt: only the seizure of power by the workers' and soldiers' councils, following the Russian example, offered a way forward. She showed that she was more than capable of revising her stance, and when faced with a task

---

1   R. Luxemburg, 'Blanquism and Social Democracy', *Marxist Internet Archive* [website].

concretely, she was instinctively drawn to a correct revolutionary position. In Poland, she rightly fought against Polish nationalism. But despite criticising the Bolshevik policy in defence of the right of nations to self-determination, which she wrongly believed could only assist the nationalists, she did not hesitate in condemning the German national chauvinism expressed by the SPD leadership in the midst of the Moroccan Crisis and in the run up to the First World War. When faced *concretely* with the same problem that Lenin and the Bolsheviks had faced, she took the same course.

Only by ripping quotes out of context can we sustain the myth that Luxemburg opposed the October Revolution and the Bolsheviks. Luxemburg celebrated the October Revolution and those who led it, despite her criticisms, which pertained to particular questions. This is how she expressed her general position:

> The Bolsheviks have shown that they are capable of everything that a genuine revolutionary party can contribute within the limits of historical possibilities. [...]
>
> In this, Lenin and Trotsky and their friends were the first, those who went ahead as an example to the proletariat of the world [...]
>
> This is essential and *enduring* in Bolshevik policy. In *this* sense theirs is the immortal historical service of having marched at the head of the international proletariat [...][2]

Once more, when the question of the necessity of a revolutionary organisation posed itself concretely, she likewise changed her mind. Once the German Revolution broke out, she realised that building a revolutionary party was imperative. But the problem was that it was too late to begin this task in the middle of the revolution. And that was her gravest mistake: she failed to understand in time the necessity of building a revolutionary party based upon a cadre of professional revolutionaries. As early as 1905, she clearly recognised how the leadership of the SPD had degenerated and she fought tooth and nail against its degeneration. But she did not draw the conclusion that flows from this fact: that a revolutionary faction had to be built within the party. Had she built such an organisation of cadres in 1905 and the succeeding years – that is, an organisation comprising revolutionaries steeped in Marxist theory and endowed with rich practical experience – the German working class would have been in a much stronger position. It would have meant that when the war broke out, and above all when the German Revolution broke

---

2   R. Luxemburg, 'The Russian Revolution', *Rosa Luxemburg Speaks*, p. 395.

out, the backbone of a mass revolutionary party would have been in place. The presence of such a party would have decisively changed the outcome of the revolution, and thus world history itself.

Why did Rosa Luxemburg not build such a party in time? An answer to that question can only be given if we understand the history of the period and the trajectory of her own life. In the SPD, she had seen how the bureaucracy had grown strong and taken control of the party and the movement. The SPD bureaucracy played the most conservative role, straining every fibre of its being to hinder the initiative of the working class. In the end, upon the outbreak of war, it crossed over to direct betrayal of the working class. During the revolution it played an even more counter-revolutionary role, if such a thing is possible. Luxemburg's distrust and opposition to the SPD apparatus was therefore wholly understandable and well-founded. Instead, she placed unwavering confidence in the spontaneous movement of the masses. Indeed, only the movement of the masses could transform the world, as Luxemburg well understood. But her belief that the movement of masses alone would automatically resolve the problem of revolutionary leadership was misplaced. The Russian Revolution, and the German Revolution that followed it, both showed – albeit one positively and the other negatively – why a revolutionary leadership must necessarily be built *before* the revolution breaks out. What is needed is a leadership that can not only give the movement a correct political programme, but which is also strong enough to reach the entire working class with its ideas and win sufficient political authority among them, such that, in the end, it can organise the seizure of power itself. It takes years to build such an organisation. The cadres have to be educated. The leadership has to be built, it must be tested in practice and go through a rigorous process of selection. Only in this way can its political authority in the working class be developed. It is Lenin's greatest merit that he managed to build this necessary leadership, in the form of the Bolshevik Party, *before* the revolution broke out in Russia. Unfortunately, Luxemburg began the process of building the revolutionary party too late.

But hindsight is a marvellous thing. At the time, Lenin alone really understood the necessity of constructing a revolutionary party. He managed to build such a party capable of leading the October Revolution: the Bolshevik Party. It was a party that was unique up until that point in history: no one had built anything like it before. As such, Rosa Luxemburg had few lessons upon which to draw. But whilst we may excuse Rosa Luxemburg for that reason, those who have come after cannot be so easily excused for committing the same mistakes. Those on the left who refuse to build a revolutionary party, and in so doing claim they are following the path of Rosa Luxemburg, draw upon her weak side, emphasising this alone, ripped from its historical context. They do not account for – or else consciously ignore – the fact that she drew other conclusions based upon her experience, and that, in the midst of the German revolution, she began the task of building the party.

This was the essential – and fatal – difference between Rosa Luxemburg and Lenin. But to make the leap from this to the idea that Luxemburg was an anti-Leninist Marxist is, at best, an expression of ignorance and, at worst, a complete lie. Luxemburg and Lenin both fought for the seizure of power by the working class and the establishment of the dictatorship of the proletariat. They shared the perspective that the Russian Revolution must spread – that it was impossible to build socialism in one country. For both, the only salvation for mankind lay in the world socialist revolution.

Rosa Luxemburg was not afraid of disagreements or polemics – even of the very harshest character. She disagreed with Lenin on several occasions. It is the considered belief of this author that on most of those occasions Lenin was right and Luxemburg was wrong. But those disagreements by no means made Luxemburg 'anti-Leninist'. Lenin, incidentally, also had no hesitations in his characterisation of Luxemburg. Following her death, he explained how she was one of the first to grasp the real significance of the 1905 Revolution:

> Thus the fundamental questions (Soviet power and the dictatorship of the proletariat) that are now engaging the minds of class-conscious workers all over the world were posed in a practical form at the end of 1905. *While such outstanding representatives of the revolutionary proletariat and of unfalsified Marxism as Rosa Luxemburg* [my emphasis – MF] immediately realised the significance of this practical experience and made a critical analysis of it at meetings and in the press, the vast majority of the official representatives of the official Social-Democratic and socialist parties – including both the reformists and people of the type of the future 'Kautskyites' [...] – proved absolutely incapable of grasping the significance of this experience and of performing their duty as *revolutionaries*, i.e., of setting to work to study and propagate the lessons of this experience.[3]

---

3 V. I. Lenin, 'A Contribution to the History of the Question of the Dictatorship', *LCW*, Vol. 31, pp. 341-2.

Yes, Luxemburg had her disagreements with Lenin. But these were disagreements between two sincere revolutionaries over how to best secure the victory of the world socialist revolution. After Luxemburg's death, Lenin summarised the points on which the two had disagreed:

> Rosa Luxemburg was mistaken on the question of the independence of Poland; she was mistaken in 1903 in her appraisal of Menshevism; she was mistaken on the theory of the accumulation of capital; she was mistaken in July 1914 when, together with Plekhanov, Vandervelde, Kautsky and others, she advocated unity between the Bolsheviks and Mensheviks; she was mistaken in what she wrote in prison in 1918 ['The Russian Revolution' – *MF*] (she corrected most of these mistakes at the end of 1918 and the beginning of 1919 after she was released).[4]

To acknowledge that Luxemburg was occasionally wrong by no means entails rejecting her credentials as a Marxist or a revolutionary. Nor does it imply that we cannot learn anything from her life and ideas. In *'Left-Wing' Communism: An Infantile Disorder*, Lenin wrote:

> What applies to individuals also applies – with necessary modifications – to politics and to parties. It is not he who makes no mistakes that is intelligent. There are no such men, nor can there be. It is he whose errors are not very grave and who is able to rectify them easily and quickly that is intelligent.[5]

The notion of a 'flawless' revolutionary and a 'flawless' party was the invention of Stalinism. It implies blind obedience to such a 'flawless' leader. Far from guaranteeing that revolutionaries will not make mistakes, it instead guarantees that they will not learn from them. The idea of the flawless leader was invented precisely to give cover to the fatal mistakes of the Stalinist bureaucracy and of its 'supreme' leader – mistakes that they had no intention of understanding or correcting. However, the fact that Lenin believed Luxemburg made mistakes did not change his fundamental view of her, which he expressed in the words of a Russian proverb:

> "Eagles may at times fly lower than hens, but hens can never rise to the height of eagles." […]
>
> [I]n spite of her mistakes she was – and remains for us – an eagle. And not only will Communists all over the world cherish her memory, but her biography and

---

4   V. I. Lenin, 'Notes of a Publicist', *LCW*, Vol. 33, p. 210.

5   V. I. Lenin, *'Left-Wing' Communism, an Infantile Disorder, The Classics of Marxism: Volume Two*, p. 124 note.

her *complete* works [...] will serve as useful manuals for training many generations of Communists all over the world.[6]

Trotsky too took up the defence of Luxemburg's revolutionary legacy. In an article titled 'Hands off Rosa Luxemburg!' he said of her disagreements with Lenin:

> If one were to take the disagreements between Lenin and Rosa Luxemburg in their entirety, then historical correctness is unconditionally on Lenin's side. But this does not exclude the fact that on certain questions and during definite periods Rosa Luxemburg was correct as against Lenin. In any case, the disagreements, despite their importance and at times their extreme sharpness, developed on the bases of revolutionary proletarian policies common to them both.[7]

Trotsky was in no doubt that her theoretical legacy belonged to the Fourth International as the successor of Bolshevism:

> The latest spontaneity confusionists have just as little right to refer to Rosa as the miserable Comintern bureaucrats have to refer to Lenin. Put aside the incidentals which developments have overcome, and we can, with full justification, place our work for the Fourth International under the sign of the "three L's", that is, not only under the sign of Lenin, but also of Luxemburg and Liebknecht.[8]

Today, we continue to honour the legacy of the heroic revolutionary, Rosa Luxemburg. We do so not by converting her into a mere symbol. Rather, we can best honour her legacy by carrying it on into our time. More than a century after her murder, capitalism has found itself in a dead end. Revolution – and counter-revolution – are on the order of the day. We are all the more duty-bound, therefore, to familiarise ourselves with Luxemburg's life and ideas; to learn from her best sides – her tireless struggle for the socialist world revolution, her unwavering faith in the will and ability of the working class to change society. We must build the revolutionary organisation that she began, but was tragically unable to finish constructing before her life was cut short by the reactionary Freikorps. Such an organisation is vital to ensure that the future struggles of the working class will not share the same fate that befell the German Revolution. Such an organisation will guarantee that they will end

---

6   V. I. Lenin, 'Notes of a Publicist', *LCW*, Vol. 33, p. 210.

7   L. Trotsky, 'Hands off Rosa Luxemburg!', *Writings of Leon Trotsky: 1932*, p. 136.

8   L. Trotsky, 'Luxemburg and the Fourth International', *Writings of Leon Trotsky: 1935-36*, p. 32.

in victory. This is the only monument worthy of Rosa Luxemburg's towering legacy, because Rosa Luxemburg was a revolutionary to her core and that is the legacy that we must defend.

Postscript

Liebknecht and Luxemburg were not the only people murdered by the counter-revolution. In the months that followed their deaths, several other leaders of the newly-founded Communist Party were also murdered. After Rosa Luxemburg's death, Leo Jogiches threw all his energy into investigating her murder and ensuring that those guilty were convicted. But, just a couple of months later, in March 1919, he too fell victim to the Freikorps. The counter-revolution had succeeded in severing the head of the young Communist Party. However, it failed to stop the onrush of the German working class. After Luxemburg's death, the German Revolution continued for several years. Indeed, the German workers had several opportunities to seize power in that time.

In late January 1919 the scheduled elections to the National Assembly were held. The USPD received 2.5 million votes, while the SPD received 11.5 million. Following the decision at its founding congress, the KPD boycotted the elections. Despite the SPD continuing to enjoy the support of broad layers of the working class, the workers continued to shift to the left in the early part of 1919. In more and more workers' councils, SPD delegates were replaced by USPD members and Communists. In February, 1,500 delegates met for a joint meeting of all the workers' and soldiers' councils in Berlin. The composition of the assembly showed just how far the balance of forces had changed: the USPD and KPD now held the majority, while the SPD was reduced to a minority. Resolutions were passed, and the meeting raised a series of demands, including the organisation of a workers' militia and the abolition of the Freikorps. With 90 per cent of delegates voting in favour of calling a general strike to achieve their demands, in twenty-four hours, Berlin was paralysed by a general strike. Strikes, demonstrations and uprisings also erupted in other cities across Germany. In Munich, a workers' republic was declared and, for a short while, the Communists held power in much of southern Bavaria.

However, the counter-revolution was also rearming. SPD Minister of Defence, Gustav Noske, ordered 30,000 Freikorps soldiers to smash the general strike. Despite the fact that the strike was drawing to a close by 9 March, the Freikorps continued their campaign of terror. By the time the smoke had cleared, between 2,000 and 3,000 workers were dead. In other German cities too, the Freikorps began a reign of terror. The workers' and soldiers' councils were dissolved using brute force. In Munich alone, upward of 1,000 workers were killed by the forces of counter-revolution. By the summer of 1919, every single workers' council in cities across Germany had been smashed by the counter-revolution. But the revolution was not yet defeated, and the bloody setback it had received remained, as yet, only temporary.

When the immediate threat of revolution subsided, the capitalists believed that it was time to take back full control. They had been forced to grant enormous concessions to save the system from complete overthrow. For the ruling class, part of the plan of returning to some kind of 'normality' also meant jettisoning the Social-Democratic government of Ebert, Scheidemann and Noske. Their job was done. They had played their part as a break on the movement and in executing thousands of revolutionary workers. Now the real masters – the capitalists – demanded complete control. Several plans were hatched by the general staff to launch coups against the government, but it wasn't until March 1920 that they finally felt strong enough to carry their plans through to victory. These were the events that came to be known as the Kapp Putsch.

On 13 March 1920, 12,000 soldiers marched into Berlin to establish a military dictatorship. Wolfgang Kapp, a founder of the Fatherland Party, was declared chancellor. Noske ordered the Reichswehr officers to smash the rebellion of the general staff but they refused. The government fled Berlin. Suddenly, the bureaucrats of the SPD, USPD, and the trade unions realised that now it was *their* lives that were on the line. They therefore appealed to the workers to fight the military coup and to defend the republic. The workers mobilised *en masse* against the counter-revolution. A general strike brought Berlin to a complete standstill. The young KPD adopted a sectarian line at first, and called on the workers to adopt a neutral stance, arguing that what was unfolding was a struggle between two "counter-revolutionary camps". But within twenty-four hours the KPD was forced to change its position as it became obvious that the Berlin workers supported the strike to a man. The Communists had little choice other than to participate in the struggle. The coup attempt brought the working class across the country to its feet in a massive counter-mobilisation. Mass protests even drove the military out of many cities. The workers started to arm themselves and red militias were established. In one giant sweep, the attempted counter-revolutionary coup was crushed beneath the overwhelming might of the united, battle-ready working class. While the Kapp Putsch was defeated, once again, the movement of the working class failed to reach its full potential owing to the lack of a strong, revolutionary leadership. Momentum was lost, and the movement ebbed.

The SPD, however, emerged from the struggle massively discredited.[1] As such, the USPD began growing by leaps and bounds in terms of both membership and votes. At the election in June 1920 the USPD doubled its number of votes compared to 1919, receiving almost 5 million, while its membership grew to 800,000. The rank-and-file of the USPD began moving sharply to the left. As early as March 1919, at a party conference, the USPD declared itself in favour of the dictatorship of the proletariat and a soviet government. By December 1919, it broke with the Second International and opened negotiations with the newly-established Third (Communist) International. In October 1920, the majority of the USPD decided to join the new International, after which fusion negotiations commenced between the USPD and the KPD. The KPD had also grown in the same period – from between 3,000 and 4,000 members at its founding conference to 78,000 in the wake of the Kapp Putsch. Following its fusion with the USPD, the Communist Party finally became a mass party with over half-a-million members.

However, this was by no means the end of the ultra-left tendencies that had marked the Communist Party since its inception. The leadership remained inexperienced and was growing impatient. In 1920, Lenin wrote his classic text, *'Left-Wing' Communism: an Infantile Disorder*, which was aimed

---

1 In the 1920 election, the SPD's vote halved, plummeting to 5,614,000 votes. After 1920, governments were formed through various coalitions of the SPD and bourgeois parties. The SPD leader, Ebert, nevertheless remained president until his death in 1925.

particularly against these ultra-left tendencies in the German Communist Party. Unfortunately, many of the leaders of the International shared the impatience of the German leaders and urged them to take premature action. The result was what came to be known as the 'March Action' in March 1921. The Communist Party leaders who advocated this theory of the 'offensive' believed that action by the vanguard of the proletariat – the KPD – would 'electrify' the rest of the working class, jolting it into action.

The German Communist leaders had resolved that it was high time to launch a 'revolutionary offensive'. The moment to launch the offensive, according to them, arose during a conflict in central Germany where the army was deployed against the striking miners and to disarm workers who had kept their weapons after the Kapp Putsch. Beginning on 27 March 1921, the KPD called the workers to action and launched a number of more-or-less isolated and desperate actions that posed little threat to the ruling class. The intention was to ignite a new revolutionary movement of the German working class. In the course of these armed actions, communists in Hamburg went as far as occupying the harbour and several factories. But the KPD leadership had completely misread the mood of the working class. A mass movement cannot be brought into existence by artificial means. Outside the mining regions of central Germany, the workers were not yet ready for an uprising. The KPD members who came out on the streets therefore ended up engaging in isolated armed struggles with the police. These engagements led to the death of hundreds of communists, whilst thousands more of the best revolutionary workers were imprisoned. The debacle was for nothing, and 200,000 workers left the KPD in protest at the 'March Action'.

The 'offensive' served to widen the divide between communists and the reformist workers who had remained in the SPD. The failure of the campaign made it clear that the final struggle for power was not on the agenda and that capitalism had succeeded in stabilising itself, at least for a time. Lenin and Trotsky therefore demanded a change of focus in the Third International: from the immediate fight for power, towards the task of winning over the masses. In the course of the debate in the Third International, Lenin and Trotsky won a majority for the tactic of the 'united front'. In essence, this directed the communists to seek unity with the reformist organisations *for the achievement of concrete, practical goals*, in the course of the workers' daily struggles. By engaging alongside reformist workers, the communists could prove that they were the best and most uncompromising class fighters. They could engage in a dialogue with these workers, and patiently explain the limitations of the politics of the reformist parties. In this manner, the communists would be able to win over these reformist workers. This united front tactic *did not* imply that the communists ought to surrender their revolutionary programme, or abstain from criticising the reformist leaders. The task, however, was to prove the correctness of the communists' ideas through the masses' own experience. This turn in the International and in the German party brought the decline in membership to an end, and allowed the KPD to once more build up its influence and standing.

After its defeat in the war, the 'victor's peace' drawn up by Britain and France in the Treaty of Versailles of June 1919 forced Germany to surrender a significant chunk of its industrial base to France. France annexed the Saar mines and Alsace-Lorraine, along with its 2 million inhabitants and two-thirds of Germany's iron production. The southern part of Silesia with its industries and mines were given to Poland, and Denmark received the northern part of Schleswig. The victors in the war charged a hefty payment for their victory: not only did they annex large parts of Germany's territory, they also demanded enormous war reparations which Germany was unable to pay. In January 1923, the German state ran out of cash. A couple of days later, French troops invaded the Ruhr – the heart of industrial Germany, an area then responsible for 80 per cent of its steel production and 71 per cent of its coal production.

The French occupation created a wave of anger that swept across Germany. Half a million people protested in Berlin. Under the pressure of the masses, the government organised a campaign of 'passive resistance'. Workers in the Ruhr were asked not to cooperate with the French and to make their occupation as difficult as possible.

The emptying of Germany's treasury also meant that the state had to finance its expenses through the printing of money. Inflation exploded. In June 1922, one US dollar could be exchanged for 300 marks. In December of the same year, the exchange rate had risen to 8,000 marks, and by January 1923 to no less than 18,000 marks. Not only did this mean a collapse in living standards for the working class – the petty bourgeoisie were even more severely crushed. Then, in 1923, hyperinflation set in. In 1918, the price of a loaf of bread was 0.63 marks, in July 1923 it had increased to 3,465 marks, in September to 1.5 million marks, and in November to 201 billion marks. The mark lost any meaning. It was not worth the paper it was printed on. Wages could not keep pace with this dizzying ascent. At the same time, the struggle against the French occupation was evolving into a bitter class struggle with strikes, general strikes, and rebellions erupting.

The German workers increasingly turned to the Communist Party, seeking a radical solution to their desperate situation. A revolutionary situation was quickly maturing in Germany. But, unlike in March 1921, when the leadership of the German Communist Party was attempting to push too far ahead of events, they now lagged seriously behind. The class struggle was once more becoming extremely intense and bitter. In August, the government was forced to resign. Trotsky, who had led the Revolutionary Military Committee that had organised the practical seizure of power in Russia in October 1917, urgently advised the German communists to name the day for an armed insurrection. To hesitate now would be fatal. Although the KPD had secretly built up a military organisation over the course of the year, the leadership rejected Trotsky's appraisal of the situation. They were backed by other leaders of the Third International, including Stalin, Zinoviev, and Radek, who advised the KPD to hold back.

But the situation was reaching fever pitch and, at last, the KPD began preparing a national general strike as a springboard for an uprising. In Saxony and Thuringia, the Communists joined the Social Democrats in the regional state governments on a radical, socialist programme. This action was utterly unacceptable to the central government, and troops were sent to Saxony to put down the workers. The final showdown was rapidly approaching, but the communist leaders continued to hesitate. In the end, they gave way to the counter-offensive of the national Social-Democratic leaders against the revolutionary wave. At the very last moment, the KPD called off the uprising. In Hamburg, however, the local communists had not received the message cancelling the uprising. For three days, hundreds of brave communists fought the police in the northern port town. But Hamburg was completely isolated, and all the forces of counter-revolution nationally could be focused on this single city. The rebellion was crushed with the utmost brutality.

Prevarication had caused the Communist Party to miss its chance. The result was the most terrible kind of defeat – a defeat without having waged a battle. It caused widespread demoralisation among the German workers and communists. It was made worse by the fact that there was never an attempt by the party to honestly evaluate what had gone wrong. Instead, blame was placed on a couple of leaders who were made into scapegoats and excluded from the party.

The 1923 defeat had serious consequences internationally – especially in the Soviet Union. For years, the Russian workers had endured the most inhuman levels of suffering and deprivation due to the isolation of the revolution. They were clinging to the perspective that the world revolution would come to their aid. The defeat in Germany killed this hope. It made clear that the isolation of the Russian Revolution would persist for some time. This was more than the Russian workers could take. Apathy took hold among the Russian masses. Upon this basis, Stalin and the rising soviet bureaucracy began to wrest power from the working class in order to concentrate it in their own hands. Stalin's anti-Marxist 'theory' of building "socialism in one country" reflected the needs of the bureaucracy, and fed on the disillusionment after the German defeat.

The Stalinist degeneration in the Soviet Union spread to every party of the Communist International, with fatal consequences.

The repeated defeats suffered by the German working class, and the many mistakes of the Communist Party leaders not only demoralised the German working class – it also led to disenchantment among the petty bourgeoisie. In the period from 1918 to 1923, these layers had been inclined to look to the working class, but their expectations had been badly disappointed. When the economy experienced a further collapse in the course of the Great Depression, the German petty bourgeoisie was no longer inclined to place its hopes in the working class. On the contrary, it now looked in precisely the opposite direction for a lead.

By 1928, Stalin and the bureaucracy had launched the policy of the so-called 'Third Period' across the Communist International. They claimed that capitalism had entered its final crisis and that it was only a matter of time before it collapsed under the weight of its own contradictions. Stalin identified the social democrats, who the communists labelled 'social fascists', as the greatest obstacle to the socialist revolution. In Germany, this insane policy had the practical consequence that the communists first and foremost fought against the social democrats, rather than the fascists, who had emerged as a growing force, lavishly sponsored by the ruling class. In fact, the communists even directly cooperated with the Nazis on several occasions in order to break up social-democratic meetings.

Hitler and the Nazis cynically played upon the desperation of the ruined petty bourgeoisie in order to elevate themselves to power in 1933. They were able to do so without facing any serious resistance from either the social democrats or the communists, who were busy fighting one another. And yet, the members of both parties were among the first victims of Hitler's hangmen after the Nazis seized power.

There can be no doubt that the victory of the German workers in the revolutionary period between 1918-23 would have utterly changed world history. The enormous natural resources of soviet Russia would have been combined with the industry and the educated working class of Germany. The victory of the German working class would have meant that the process of bureaucratic degeneration of the Soviet Union would have been reversed and a genuinely revolutionary Communist International would have developed as a powerful beacon of hope and galvanised the oppressed masses throughout the capitalist world. It would also have given a massive impetus to revolution in other countries across Europe and beyond. Instead, the defeat of the German Revolution paved the way for Hitler and Nazism in Germany, and for the Stalinist degeneration of the revolution in the Soviet Union.

History has proven Rosa Luxemburg's prediction to be absolutely correct: the choice before humanity was indeed "socialism or barbarism". The defeat of the revolution led to Hitler, to the Holocaust, and to the slaughter of 60 million people in the Second World War. We have a duty to learn from Rosa Luxemburg's revolutionary legacy and to do our part to ensure that, in the revolutionary epoch opening up, history will not repeat itself. This time the working class must be victorious.

Glossary

Organisations

ADGB (Allgemeiner Deutsche Gewekschaftsbund): German Confederation of Trade Unions. Associated with the SPD.

Comintern: See 'Third (Communist) International'.

Freikorps (Free Corps) Right-wing gangs of mercenaries often made up of war veterans and associated with the military. The Freikorps were established by the old general staff and financed by the Ministry of War. They were used by Noske to crush the revolution from 1919, and were behind the murder of Rosa Luxemburg and Karl Liebknecht.

KPD (Kommunistische Partei Deutschlands, Communist Party of Germany): Founded in December 1918, primarily by the Spartacus League, it was led by Karl Liebknecht, Rosa Luxemburg and others. It fused with the left wing of the USPD in December 1920 to form the United Communist Party of Germany (VKPD), although the word 'United' was dropped from its name soon thereafter.

Left Opposition: Founded by Trotsky in 1923 in order to fight the growing bureaucracy in Russia. The Left Opposition was expelled from the Russian Communist Party in 1927. The International Left Opposition, the forerunner of the Fourth International, was founded in 1930.

Left-Radicals: Based in Bremen. Joined the Spartacists in late 1918 to found the KPD.

PPS (Polska Partia Socjalistyczna, Polish Socialist Party): Founded in 1892 at a congress of all Polish socialists in exile. The PPS unified all Polish socialist *émigré* groups, as well as groups inside Russian-occupied Poland. Luxemburg and Jogiches joined the party but split from it in 1893 to found the SDKPiL. In 1906, another split took place between the Left Faction and the right-wing Revolutionary Faction, led by Józef Piłsudski. Piłsudski would later go on to become the dictator of Poland. The left wing of the party went on to join the SDKPiL in founding the Communist Party of Poland in 1918.

Reichstag (Diet of the Realm): The German parliament.

Reichswehr (Realm Defence): The regular army of the Weimar Republic. The Reichswehr was composed of regular units and the Freikorps.

Revolutionary Stewards (Revolutionäre Obleute): An organisation of German shop stewards that emerged in the course of the First World War. They opposed the war and acted independently of the official trade unions and the SPD.

SA (Sturmabteilung, Stormtroopers): The original paramilitary organisation of the German National Socialist Workers' Party (Nazi Party). Its origins can be traced back to the Freikorps that were used against workers and communists during the German Revolution.

SDKPiL (Socjaldemokracja Królestwa Polskiego i Litwy, The Social Democracy of the Kingdom of Poland and Lithuania): Founded in 1893 as the Social Democracy of Poland, the party originated as a split from the PPS. The core of the organisation initially included Rosa Luxemburg, Leo Jogiches, Marchlewski (Karski), and Warszawski (Warski). In 1899, it fused with the Union of Workers in Lithuania, thus changing its name to The Social Democracy of the Kingdom of Poland and Lithuania (SDKPiL). The SDKPiL joined the Russian Social Democratic Labour Party (RSDLP) in 1907 and gained two representatives on the central committee. Together with other groups, it founded the Communist Party of Poland in 1918.

Second International (or Socialist International): Founded in 1889 as the successor to the First International that had been founded by Marx and Engels in 1864. In 1914, almost all national sections of the International supported 'their own' imperialist governments in the First World War, and the International collapsed. It was revived as a thoroughly reformist organisation in 1923.

Spartacus League (Spartakusbund): Named after Spartacus, the leader of the famous slave rebellion against ancient Rome. It began its existence as a revolutionary tendency in opposition to the war inside the SPD from 1914. Its members included Rosa Luxemburg, Karl Liebknecht, Clara Zetkin, Franz Mehring and Leo Jogiches. They would later leave the SPD and join the USPD in 1917. The Spartacists then split from the USPD and founded the KPD in December 1918.

SPD (Sozialdemokratische Partei Deutschlands, The Social Democratic Party of Germany): Often referred to as 'Social Democrats' or, after the split in the party in 1917 (see 'USPD'), as 'majority Social Democrats'. The party was originally founded in 1875 as a fusion between two socialist groups: one comprising supporters of Ferdinand Lassalle, and the other around August Bebel and Wilhelm Liebknecht, known as the 'Eisenach Party'. The SPD was considered to be the leading Marxist party in the Second International, with more than a million members in 1914.

Third (Communist) International, or 'Comintern': Organised under the leadership of Lenin as the revolutionary successor to the Second International and a tool for the world socialist revolution. It was founded in March 1919, and in the course of its first four congresses it developed and implemented the ideas and methods of Bolshevism on the world arena. From its fifth congress in 1924 to its dissolution in 1943 it came under the control of the Stalinist bureaucracy, and was gradually converted into little more than a tool of Stalin's foreign policy.

USPD (Unabhängige Sozialdemokratische Partei Deutschlands, The Independent Social Democratic Party of Germany): Also known as the 'independents', the USPD was founded in April 1917 by the opposition which had been expelled from the SPD. The party participated in the provisional government from November to December 1918. In 1917 the party had 120,000 members, growing to 750,000 members by 1919. In 1920 the majority of the party joined the KPD. The minority returned to the SPD in 1922.

Zentrale: The Executive Committee of the KPD.

Papers

Die Neue Zeit (The New Times): The theoretical journal of the SPD from 1883 to 1923.

Die Rote Fahne (*The Red Flag*): Initially the newspaper of the Spartacists, and later of the KPD.

Sprawa Robotnicza (*The Workers' Cause*): Political organ of the SDKPiL. Founded in 1893 by Leo Jogiches and Rosa Luxemburg, its editor.

Vorwärts (*Forward*): Central newspaper of the SPD for many decades. Founded in 1876.

Individuals

Adler, Victor (1852-1918): Austrian Social Democrat. One of the founders of the Social-Democratic movement in Austria.

Baden, Prince Max von (1867-1929): Replaced Emperor Wilhelm II as German chancellor for two months in 1918, during which time the war ended and the Weimar Republic was founded.

Bauer, Otto (1881-1938): Leader of the so-called 'Austro-Marxists', he played a leading role in the Social Democratic Party of Austria (SPÖ). Leader of the party in 1918. Went into exile following the February Uprising of 1934.

Bebel, August (1840-1913): One of the founders of the SPD. Official chairman of the party from 1892 to 1913.

Bernstein, Eduard (1850-1932): Leading German Social Democrat. The first person to give a theoretical expression to reformism in the Second International. His revisionism was harshly opposed by Rosa Luxemburg. Bernstein opposed the war from a pacifist point of view, but was also opposed to the German Revolution. He was one of the founders of the USPD in 1917, but re-joined the SPD in 1920.

David, Eduard (1863-1930): German Social Democrat. Member of the Reichstag between 1903-18 and a key advocate of the 'parliamentary truce' during the war.

Duncker, Hermann (1874-1960): Member of the SPD, during which time he was among the publishers of *Die Internationale* and a member of the Spartacus League. Later a founder of the KPD and member of the party's Central Committee. Married to Käthe Duncker.

Duncker, Käthe (1871-1953): Member of the SPD, during which time she was among the publishers of *Die Internationale* and a member of the

Spartacus League. Later a founder of the KPD and member of the party's Central Committee. Married to Hermann Duncker.

Eberlein, Hugo (1887-1941): Member of the SPD in 1906. Opposed to the war in 1914. Member of the Spartacus League and the Central Committee of the KPD. Delegate at the first congress of the Third International, played a leading role in the Comintern. Went into exile in the Soviet Union in 1933, where he was arrested by the GPU during the Moscow trials. Stalin intended to hand him over to Hitler, but he died in prison in 1941.

Ebert, Friedrich (1871-1925): Leading member of the SPD from the right wing of the party. Advocated a chauvinist position during the war. Chancellor in 1918. Between November 1918 and December 1919 he was chairman of the workers' and soldiers' councils' Executive Committee. Worked with the general staff of the army to crush the revolution. President of Germany from 1919 to 1925.

Eichhorn, Emil (1863-1925): Former glass worker. Eichhorn worked for the SPD from 1893 and was leader of the party's press bureau between 1908 and 1917. A member of the USPD from 1917 to 1920. His dismissal as Berlin chief of police – an office he was given in 1918 – provoked the so-called 'Spartacus Uprising'. He joined the KPD in 1920 and died in 1925.

Eisner, Kurt (1867-1919): Editor of *Vorwärts* from 1900 to 1906. Initially supported the war but went over to a pacifist opposition. Founded the USPD in Munich and was imprisoned in January 1918. Led the November Revolution in 1918 in Bavaria, where he was made prime minister. Was murdered by the monarchist Anton Graf von Arco auf Valley in February 1919.

Fischer, Ruth (1895-1961): Joined the Social Democratic Party of Austria (SPÖ) at the age of nineteen and was one of the first members of the Austrian Communist Party in 1918. Led an ultra-left opposition in the KPD after she moved to Berlin. Leader of the KPD from 1924 to 1925 but was expelled in 1926. She later became an anti-communist.

Frölich, Paul (1894-1953): Joined the SPD at the age of eighteen and was part of the far-left wing of the party. Elected to the Central Committee of the KPD at its founding congress. He was expelled from the KPD in 1928 and joined Brandler's KPO (the right-wing opposition within the Communist Party). Later joined the centrist SAP (*Socialistische Arbeiderspartij*) in Belgium.

Went into exile after nine months in a concentration camp in 1933. Returned to West Germany and re-joined the SPD in 1950.

Haase, Hugo (1863-1919): SPD member of the Reichstag from 1897, and co-chairman of the party from 1911 to 1916. Initially opposed to war credits in 1914 but followed party discipline until 1916 where he voted against new credits. Co-chairman of the USPD in 1917 and member of the Council of People's Commissars from November to December 1918. He was murdered by a monarchist in 1919.

Haenisch, Konrad (1876-1925): On the radical left wing of the SPD. Argued along with Luxemburg in 1910 in favour of the party using the mass strike as a means of struggle. Shifted rightwards during the war as part of a nationalist wing in the party and advocated that the SPD support war credits in the Reichstag.

Hanecki, Yakov (1879-1937): Known in Russia as Ganetsky. Real name Jakub Fürstenberg. Active in the Polish social democracy from 1896 and later became a communist. Close collaborator with Lenin. Worked for the Stalinist regime after Lenin's death until he was sentenced to death in 1937.

Huysmans, Camille (1871-1968): Belgian social democrat. Member of the Belgian parliament from 1910-1965. Secretary for the Second International from 1905-1922. Prime minister from 1946-1947. Minister of Education from 1947-1949.

Jaurès, Jean (1859-1914): Leader of the French Socialist Party in 1902. Assassinated in 1914 after having opposed the war.

Jogiches, Leo (1867-1919): Commonly known by the party name Jan Tyszka. Active in the revolutionary movement from an early age. Close collaborator of Rosa Luxemburg, who was also his partner for many years. One of the founders of the Polish revolutionary social democracy and active in the Polish Revolution of 1905. Fled to Germany in 1907 and became a Spartacist organiser during the war. Member of the Central Committee of the KPD since the founding congress. Arrested and murdered by Freikorps in March 1919.

Kapp, Wolfgang (1858-1922): Founder of the far-right German Fatherland Party in 1917. He led the coup attempt of 1920, which attempted to re-establish the monarchy and establish a military dictatorship.

Kautsky, Karl (1854-1938): One of Engels' collaborators, he was founder and editor of Die Neue Zeit. Friend and collaborator of Rosa Luxemburg's until 1910. He was considered the main theoretician of Marxism until 1914, when he refused to oppose war credits and acted as a cover for the right-wing of the SPD. When he broke with the SPD in 1917 and became one of the founders of the USPD, he was on the right of the new party. He opposed the socialist revolution in Germany and returned to the SPD in 1922.

Kautsky, Luise (1864-1944): Social Democrat. Close friend of Rosa Luxemburg. Mayor of Berlin for the USPD from 1918. She published a book in memory of Rosa Luxemburg in 1929. Married to Karl Kautsky.

Landsberg, Otto (1869-1957): Lawyer and one of the leaders of the SPD. Member of the Council of People's Commissars after November 1918. Minister of Justice under Scheidemann from 1919 to 1920.

Lasalle, Ferdinand (1825-1864): One of the founders of the SPD.

Ledebour, Georg (1850-1947): SPD member of the Reichstag from 1900-18. One of the leaders of the USPD following the party's foundation. A member of the revolutionary committee during the 'Spartacist Uprising'.

Legien, Carl (1861-1920): SPD member of the Reichstag from the right wing of the party. The first chairman of the trade union federation, the ADGB.

Levi, Paul (1883-1930): A member of the SPD from 1906. As a revolutionary, he was opposed to the war and worked with Lenin in Switzerland for its duration. He later joined the Spartacus League and became a member of the Central Committee of the KPD and was a central leader of the party following the murder of Leo Jogiches in 1919. He opposed the ultra-left turn in 1919 and became chairman of the United Communist Party in 1920. However, he stepped back in 1921 and was expelled from the party for publicly denouncing the 'March Action' of that same year. He published Rosa Luxemburg's article 'The Russian Revolution' in 1922 after breaking with the KPD. In the same year, he joined the USPD and later the SPD, in which he organised a left opposition until his death in 1930.

Liebknecht, Karl (1871-1919): Son of one of the SPD's founders, Wilhelm Liebknecht, he joined the party in 1900. He established the Socialist Youth

International in 1907 and was imprisoned the same year for writing the pamphlet 'Militarism and Anti-Militarism'. He was an alternate member of the Reichstag from 1912 and became the first member of the Reichstag to vote against war credits in December 1914. He was a founding member of the Spartacus League. Imprisoned in 1916 for agitation against the war, he was amnestied in 1918. Leader of the KPD. He led the revolutionary committee during the 'Spartacist Uprising' in Berlin in January 1919. He was murdered by the Freikorps in January 1919, together with Rosa Luxemburg.

Liebknecht, Sophie (1884-1964): Member of the SPD and later of the KPD. A close friend of Rosa Luxemburg. Married to Karl Liebknecht.

Ludendorff, Erich (1865-1937): German general. Practically led Germany, along with Hindenburg, in the closing period of the First World War. He represented the far-right German Völkisch Freedom Party (*Deutschvölkische Freiheitspartei*) and supported the Kapp Putsch.

Marchlewski, Julian (1866-1925): Known by the alias Karski. Co-founder of the SDKPiL, he joined the Bolsheviks in 1906. Moved to Germany in 1907 and was active on the left wing of the SPD. A close collaborator with Rosa Luxemburg.

Martov, Julius (1873-1923): Participated in the publication of *Iskra* in 1900. Became a leading figure in the minority ('Menshevik') faction of the Russian Social Democratic Labour Party after its second congress in 1903. A leader of the 'Menshevik Internationalists'. He opposed the seizure of power by the soviets in 1917.

Mehring, Franz (1846-1919): Leading member of the SPD. During the war he collaborated with Rosa Luxemburg in the Spartacus League. He was very ill when he learned of the murders of Rosa Luxemburg and Karl Liebknecht in January 1919, and died less than two weeks later in Berlin.

Millerand, Alexandre (1859-1943): French socialist. First socialist to take a ministerial position in a bourgeois government, sparking a polemic in the Second International. President of France from 1920-4.

Müller, Richard (1880-1943): Chairman of the metalworkers' trade union in Berlin. Leader of the Revolutionary Stewards. Initially a member of the SPD then the USPD, until he joined the Communist Party in 1920.

Noske, Gustav (1868-1946): Leader of the SPD and member of the right wing of the party. He was a member of the Council of People's Commissars from 1918-9. Minister of war from December 1918 until March 1920. He organised the suppression of the revolutionary movement in January 1919 and stepped down from office following the Kapp Putsch, after which he became president of the Hannover province until he was dismissed by the Nazis. He was imprisoned twice by the Nazis.

Parvus (1867-1924): A Russian–German social democrat, born Israel Lazarevich Gelfand in a Jewish-Lithuanian family. During the Russian Revolution of 1905 he was active on the left wing of the Russian movement. He then fled to Germany where he settled. His credentials as a revolutionary were tainted by numerous scandals and business ventures that made him a wealthy war profiteer and his allegiances questionable.

Plekhanov, Georgi (1856-1918): Known as the 'father of Russian Marxism' and the founder of the Russian social democracy. He went over to the Mensheviks shortly after the second congress of the Russian Social Democratic Labour Party in 1903. He became a social patriot during the war and fiercely opposed the seizure of power by the soviets in October 1917.

Potresov, Alexander (1869-1934): One of the early members of the Russian social-democratic movement. He joined the Mensheviks after failing to be elected to the editorial board of *Iskra* at the second congress of the Russian Social Democratic Labour Party, and he remained on the right wing of the party. He maintained good connections with the SPD.

Radek, Karl (1885-1939): Active in the Polish revolutionary movement from the age of eighteen. He was involved in the Polish Revolution of 1905 and supported the left wing of the SPD in Germany in 1908. Along with Lenin, he was a part of the 'Zimmerwald Left' in 1915. He joined the Bolsheviks in 1917 and was secretly sent to Germany in 1918. He was arrested in February 1919 and released again in January 1920. Played a leading role in the Executive Committee of the Communist International and later joined Trotsky's opposition to Stalin. He was expelled from the Communist Party in 1927 and deported to Alma Ata but capitulated in 1929 and became an apologist for Stalin. He was arrested in 1937 during the Moscow show trials and died in prison.

Roland-Holst, Henriette (1869-1952): Dutch writer and socialist. Member of the Dutch Communist Party from 1918.

Rühle, Otto (1874-1943): Opposed to the First World War. Joined the Spartacus League and the KPD but was later expelled. He joined the SPD in 1923 but left Germany in 1933 and went to Mexico.

Scheidemann, Phillip (1865-1939): Right-wing member of the SPD's Reichstag group, Scheidemann became one of the central leaders of the party after Bebel's death in 1913. He led the SPD's support for the war from 1914 and became the party's co-chairman in 1917. He was proclaimed minister without portfolio by the emperor in October 1918 and proclaimed the republic in November of the same year. A member of Ebert's Council of People's Commissars, he led the suppression of the revolution from 1918 to 1919 and was made chancellor in 1919. In 1933 he was forced into exile when the Nazi Party rose to power.

Thalheimer, August (1884-1948): Involved with the Spartacists during the war years, he later played a key role in the KPD. He was critical of the party's ultra-left turns, and was made a scapegoat for the defeat in the 1923 Revolution. He was expelled from the KPD in 1929. Helped form the Right Opposition in Germany. After being detained in France he was sent to exile in Cuba.

Waldeck-Rousseau, Pierre (1846-1904): French republican politician.

Warszawski, Jerzy Adolf (1868-1937): Known by the alias 'Warski', he co-founded the SDKPiL and was a member of the Executive Committee of the party. He was a member of the Central Committee of the Polish Communist Party from 1919 to 1929.

Wels, Otto (1879-1939): Right-wing member of the SPD. Chief commander of Berlin and responsible for crushing the left from January to March 1919. He led the opposition against Hitler in the Reichstag in 1933 and advocated "legal, non-violent resistance". He was exiled to Paris from 1933.

Wilhelm II, Friedrich (1859-1941): German emperor from 1888 until his abdication in 1918.

Wurm, Emanuel (1857-1920): Member of the SPD and later of the USPD. Married to Mathilde Wurm.

Wurm, Mathilde (1874-1939): Initially a member of the Reichstag for the SPD and then the USPD in the period 1920-1933. Married to Emanuel Wurm.

Zasulich, Vera (1849-1919): Along with Plekhanov, she co-founded the Emancipation of Labour Group – the predecessor of *Iskra* and of Russian social democracy.

Zetkin, Clara (1857-1933): Played a leading role in the SPD. Editor of the SPD's women's magazine, *Die Gleicheit*, from 1891 to 1917. Joined the Spartacus League and later the KPD, for which she was a member of the Central Committee from 1927-1929. Zetkin was a member of the Executive Committee of the Communist International from 1921 to 1933, and a KPD Reichstag deputy from 1923 until 1933. Close friend of Rosa Luxemburg.

Zetkin, Konstantin (1885-1980): Clara Zetkin's son and, for a period, Rosa Luxemburg's lover.

Zinoviev, Grigory (1883-1936): A leading Bolshevik in 1917. He became a leading figure in the Communist International and was later made responsible for Germany. He was removed from all leading positions by Stalin in 1926 and executed during the show trials of 1936.

Bibliography

Broué, Pierre, *The German Revolution, 1917-1923*, Brill Academic Publishers, 2005.

Comenetz, Jacob, 'Mysterious Berlin corpse probably Rosa Luxemburg', 29 May 2009, *Reuters,* https://www.reuters.com/article/idUSLT1020262 (accessed 18 January 2022).

Engels, Friedrich, *Anti-Dühring*, Wellred Books, 2017.

Ettinger, Elzbieta, *Comrade and Lover: Rosa Luxemburg's Letters to Leo Jogiches*, Pluto Press, 1981.

Foldager, Jonas and Frederiksen, Marie, *Den Russiske Revolution og borgerkrig - da arbejderne tog magten*, Forlaget Marx, 2017.

Frölich, Paul, *Rosa Luxemburg*, Haymarket, 2010.

Le Blanc, Paul, *Lenin and the Revolutionary Party*, Haymarket Books, 2015.

Lenin, V. I. *Collected Works*, Lawrence and Wishart, 1960.
— *State and Revolution*, Wellred Books, 2019.

Luxemburg, Rosa, *The Essential Rosa Luxemburg*, Haymarket Books, 2008.
— *Rosa Luxemburg Speaks*, Pathfinder Press, 1970.
— *Selected Political Writings of Rosa Luxemburg*, Monthly Review Press, 1971.
— *Letters to Karl and Luise Kautsky from 1896 to 1918*, Robert M. McBride and Co., 1925.
— *The Letters of Rosa Luxemburg*, Westview Press, 1978.
— *The Letters of Rosa Luxemburg*, Verso Books, 2013.
— 'The Dreyfus Affair and the Millerand Case', *Marxist Internet Archive,* https://www.marxists.org/archive/luxemburg/1899/11/dreyfus-affair.htm (accessed 18 January 2022).
— 'The Socialist Crisis in France', Part 3, *Marxist Internet Archive,* https://www.

marxists.org/archive/luxemburg/1901/socialist-crisis-france/ch03.htm (accessed 18 January 2022).

— *The National Question*, 'Chapter 1. The Right of Nations to Self-Determination', *Marxist Internet Archive,* https://www.marxists.org/archive/luxemburg/1909/national-question/ch01.htm (accessed 18 January 2022).

— 'Blanquism and Social Democracy', June 1906, *Marxist Internet Archive,* https://www.marxists.org/archive/luxemburg/1906/06/blanquism.html (accessed 18 January 2022).

— 'The Revolution in Russia (1905)', *Marxist Internet Archive,* https://www.marxists.org/archive/luxemburg/1905/02/08.htm (accessed 18 January 2022).

— 'The Next Step', March 1910, *Marxist Internet Archive,* https://www.marxists.org/archive/luxemburg/1910/03/15.htm (accessed 18 January 2022).

— 'Concerning Morocco', July 1911, *Marxist Internet Archive,* https://www.marxists.org/archive/luxemburg/1911/07/24.htm (accessed 18 January 2022).

— 'The Beginning', November 1918, *Marxist Internet Archive,* https://www.marxists.org/archive/luxemburg/1918/11/18b.htm (accessed 18 January 2022).

— 'The National Assembly', November 1918, *Marxist Internet Archive,* https://www.marxists.org/archive/luxemburg/1918/11/20.htm (accessed 18 January 2022).

— *Zur russischen Revolution*, Chapter 3, *Marxist Internet Archive*, our translation, https://www.marxists.org/deutsch/archiv/luxemburg/1918/russrev/index.htm, (accessed 18 January 2022).

— *The Accumulation of Capital – An Anti-Critique*, Kenneth J. Tarbuck (ed.), Monthly Review Press.

— *Politiske skrifter*, Tiderne Skifter, 1976.

— *Sozialreform oder Revolution*, Verlagsanstalt der Leipziger Volkszeitung, 1899.

— *Witnesses to Permanent Revolution: The Documentary Record*, Richard. B. Day and Daniel Gaido (eds.), Brill Academic Publishers, 2009.

Marx, Karl and Engels, Friedrich, Lenin, V. I., Trotsky, L., *The Classics of Marxism: Volume One*, Wellred Books, 2013.

— *The Classics of Marxism: Volume Two*, Wellred Books, 2015.

Marx, Karl and Engels, Friedrich, *Marx and Engels Collected Works*, Lawrence & Wishart, 1975.

— *Marx and Engels Selected Correspondence*, Foreign Languages Publishing House, 1955.

Nettl, John Peter, *Rosa Luxemburg*, Oxford University Press, 1966.

Schorske, Carl Emil, *German Social Democracy, 1905-1917: The Development of the Great Schism*, Harvard University Press, 1983.

Sewell, Rob, *Germany 1918-1933: Socialism or Barbarism*, Wellred Books, 2018.

Trotsky, Leon, *Writings of Leon Trotsky*, Pathfinder Press, 1969.

— *My Life*, Wellred Books, 2017.

— *Lessons of October*, New Park Publications, 1971.

—— *The History of Russian Revolution*, Wellred Books, 2007.

—— *Stalin*, Wellred Books, 2016.

Woods, Alan, *Bolshevism: The Road to Revolution*, Wellred Books, 2017.

Woods, Alan and Albin Svensson, Niklas, 'Rosa Luxemburg – Reform or Revolution', 15 January 2018, *In Defence of Marxism,* https://www.marxist.com/prologue-to-rosa-luxemburgs-reform-or-revolution.htm (accessed 18 January 2022).

Index

List of Titles by Wellred Books

Wellred Books is a UK-based international publishing house and bookshop, specialising in works of Marxist theory. A sister publisher and bookseller is based in the USA.

Among the titles published by Wellred Books are:

Anti-Dühring, Friedrich Engels

Bolshevism: The Road to Revolution, Alan Woods

Chartist Revolution, Rob Sewell

China: From Permanent Revolution to Counter-Revolution, John Roberts

The Civil War in France, Karl Marx

The Class Struggles in France, 1848-1850, Karl Marx

The Classics of Marxism: Volume One and Two, Various authors

Dialectics of Nature, Friedrich Engels

The Eighteenth Brumaire of Louis Bonaparte, Karl Marx

The First Five Years of the Communist International, Leon Trotsky

The First World War: A Marxist Analysis of the Great Slaughter, Alan Woods

Germany: From Revolution to Counter-Revolution, Rob Sewell

Germany 1918-1933: Socialism or Barbarism, Rob Sewell

History of British Trotskyism, Ted Grant

The History of Philosophy, Alan Woods

The History of the Russian Revolution: Volumes One to Three, Leon Trotsky

The History of the Russian Revolution to Brest-Litovsk, Leon Trotsky

The Ideas of Karl Marx, Alan Woods

Imperialism: The Highest Stage of Capitalism, V. I. Lenin

In Defence of Marxism, Leon Trotsky

In the Cause of Labour, Rob Sewell

Lenin and Trotsky: What They Really Stood For, Alan Woods and Ted Grant

Lenin, Trotsky and the Theory of the Permanent Revolution, John Roberts

Marxism and Anarchism, Various authors

Marxism and the USA, Alan Woods

Materialism and Empirio-criticism, V. I. Lenin

My Life, Leon Trotsky

Not Guilty, Dewey Commission Report

The Origin of the Family, Private Property and the State, Friedrich Engels

The Permanent Revolution and Results & Prospects, Leon Trotsky

Permanent Revolution in Latin America, John Roberts and Jorge Martin

Reason in Revolt, Alan Woods and Ted Grant

Reformism or Revolution, Alan Woods

Revolution and Counter-Revolution in Spain, Felix Morrow

The Revolution Betrayed, Leon Trotsky

The Revolutionary Legacy of Rosa Luxemburg, Marie Frederiksen

The Revolutionary Philosophy of Marxism, John Peterson [Ed.]

Russia: From Revolution to Counter-Revolution, Ted Grant

Spain's Revolution Against Franco, Alan Woods

Stalin, Leon Trotsky

The State and Revolution, V. I. Lenin

Ted Grant: The Permanent Revolutionary, Alan Woods

Ted Grant Writings: Volumes One and Two, Ted Grant

Thawra hatta'l nasr! - Revolution until Victory!, Alan Woods and others

What Is Marxism?, Rob Sewell and Alan Woods

What Is to Be Done?, V. I. Lenin

To order any of these titles or for more information about Wellred Books, visit wellred-books.com, email books@wellredbooks.net or write to Wellred Books, 152-160 Kemp House, City Road, London, EC1V 2NX, United Kingdom.